Federalism and Internal Conflicts

Series Editors
Soeren Keil
School of Psychology, Politics and Sociology
Canterbury Christ Church University
Canterbury, UK

Eva Maria Belser
University of Freiburg
Freiburg, Switzerland

This series engages in the discussions on federalism as a tool of internal conflict resolution. Building on a growing body of literature on the use of federalism and territorial autonomy to solve ethnic, cultural, linguistic and identity conflicts, both in the West and in non-Western countries, this global series assesses to what extent different forms of federalism and territorial autonomy are being used as tools of conflict resolution and how successful these approaches are.

We welcome proposals on theoretical debates, single case studies and short comparative pieces covering topics such as:

- Federalism and peace-making in contemporary intra-state conflicts
- The link between federalism and democratization in countries facing intra-state conflict
- Secessionism, separatism, self-determination and power-sharing
- Inter-group violence and the potential of federalism to transform conflicts
- Successes and failures of federalism and other forms of territorial autonomy in post-conflict countries
- Federalism, decentralisation and resource conflicts
- Peace treaties, interim constitutions and permanent power sharing arrangements
- The role of international actors in the promotion of federalism (and other forms of territorial autonomy) as tools of internal conflict resolution
- Federalism and state-building
- Federalism, democracy and minority protection

For further information on the series and to submit a proposal for consideration, please get in touch with Ambra Finotello ambra.finotello@palgrave.com, or series editors Soeren Keil soeren.keil@canterbury.ac.uk and Eva Maria Belser evamaria.belser@unifr.ch

More information about this series at
http://www.palgrave.com/gp/series/15730

Hanna Shelest • Maryna Rabinovych
Editors

Decentralization, Regional Diversity, and Conflict

The Case of Ukraine

Editors
Hanna Shelest
Security Studies Programme
Foreign Policy Council
"Ukrainian Prism"
Odesa / Kyiv, Ukraine

Maryna Rabinovych
Faculty of Law
University of Hamburg
Hamburg, Germany

Federalism and Internal Conflicts
ISBN 978-3-030-41767-3   ISBN 978-3-030-41765-9   (eBook)
https://doi.org/10.1007/978-3-030-41765-9

© The Editor(s) (if applicable) and The Author(s), under exclusive licence to Springer Nature Switzerland AG 2020
This work is subject to copyright. All rights are solely and exclusively licensed by the Publisher, whether the whole or part of the material is concerned, specifically the rights of translation, reprinting, reuse of illustrations, recitation, broadcasting, reproduction on microfilms or in any other physical way, and transmission or information storage and retrieval, electronic adaptation, computer software, or by similar or dissimilar methodology now known or hereafter developed.
The use of general descriptive names, registered names, trademarks, service marks, etc. in this publication does not imply, even in the absence of a specific statement, that such names are exempt from the relevant protective laws and regulations and therefore free for general use.
The publisher, the authors and the editors are safe to assume that the advice and information in this book are believed to be true and accurate at the date of publication. Neither the publisher nor the authors or the editors give a warranty, expressed or implied, with respect to the material contained herein or for any errors or omissions that may have been made. The publisher remains neutral with regard to jurisdictional claims in published maps and institutional affiliations.

Cover credit: Westend61 / Getty Images

This Palgrave Macmillan imprint is published by the registered company Springer Nature Switzerland AG.
The registered company address is: Gewerbestrasse 11, 6330 Cham, Switzerland

PREFACE

There has been an increase in the number of ethnic, cultural, linguistic, and identity conflicts within states around the globe, often marked by extensive foreign support for one of the conflicting parties. Eventually, such conflicts tend to result in establishment of quasi- or *de facto* states, experiencing the challenges of non-recognition, isolationism, economic downturn, and emigration. Territorial self-government arrangements (TSGs) represent a frequently used tool in the management of different types of conflict, yet, little evidence exists about TSGs' application in the context of extensive foreign support for one or several conflicting parties.

The ongoing "crisis in and around Ukraine", encompassing the Russian Federation's illegal annexation of Crimea in 2014 and the armed conflict in the east of the country, makes Ukraine an insightful case to unpack the complex business of the use of decentralization as a conflict-management tool. Hence, this book revolves around four themes: first, exploring the substance of the regional diversity in Ukraine and government policies thereto; second, critically examining legal definitions of the conflict and regarding government-uncontrolled territories; thirdly, assessing Ukraine's experience of using decentralization as a conflict-resolution tool, and, finally, considering the nexus between decentralization reform and the processes of democratization, modernization, and European integration in Ukraine. Based on the experience of Ukraine, the study reveals a handful of risks that top–bottom or internationally imposed TSG arrangements may bring under the circumstances of extensive foreign support for one of the sides to the conflict.

v

This publication will be of key interest to scholars and students of conflict studies, federalism and Eastern European Studies, and, more broadly, political science, sociology, law and international relations.

Canterbury, UK
Freiburg, Switzerland

Soeren Keil
Eva Maria Belser

CONTENTS

1 Introduction: Regional Diversity, Decentralization, and Conflict in and around Ukraine   1
Maryna Rabinovych and Hanna Shelest

Part I   Regional Diversity in Ukraine and Its Accommodation in Government Policies   15

2 Regionalism in Ukraine: Historic Evolution, Regional Claim-Making, and Centre–Periphery Conflict Resolution   17
Oksana Myshlovska

3 Navigating Ethnopolitical Disputes: Ukraine's Constitutional Court in the Tug-of-War over Language   49
Andrii Nekoliak and Vello Pettai

4 Crimean Tatars and the Question of National and Ethnic Belonging in Ukraine   81
Alina Zubkovych

Part II   The "Crisis In and Around Ukraine", Occupied Territories and their Reintegration: The Legal Dimension   105

vii

viii CONTENTS

5 The Domestic Dimension of Defining Uncontrolled
Territories and Its Value for Conflict Transformation in
Moldova, Georgia, and Ukraine   107
Maryna Rabinovych

6 The Reintegration of Donbas Through Reconstruction
and Accountability. An International Law Perspective   145
Tomasz Lachowski

Part III   Federalization / Decentralization as a Tool
of Conflict Resolution: Discursive and Foreign
Policy Perspectives   185

7 Three Faces of Federalism in the Foreign Policy: Russian
and German Approaches to the "Ukraine Crisis"   187
Nadiia Koval

8 The Dark Side of Decentralization Reform in Ukraine:
Deterring or Facilitating Russia-Sponsored Separatism?   211
Jaroslava Barbieri

Part IV   Decentralization, Its Perceptions and Linkage to
Democratization, Modernization, and European
Integration of Ukraine   257

9 Decentralization and a Risk of Local Elite
Capture in Ukraine   259
Max Bader

10 Signs of Progress: Local Democracy Developments in
Ukrainian Cities   283
Aadne Aasland and Oleksii Lyska

11 Decentralization Reform: An Effective Vehicle for
Modernization and Democratization in Ukraine?   311
Olga Oleinikova

CONTENTS ix

12 Decentralization in Ukraine and Bottom-Up European Integration 339
Anne Pintsch

13 Conclusions and Directions for Further Research 365
Maryna Rabinovych and Hanna Shelest

Index 371

Notes on Contributors

Aadne Aasland is a Senior Researcher at the Norwegian Institute for Urban and Regional Research (NIBR) at Oslo Metropolitan University. His research interests include social inclusion and exclusion, ethnicity issues, migration, and local governance. He has been in charge of several large-scale international projects, for example in Russia, the Baltic States, and Ukraine. Since 2008 he has been leading a research part of the project on local government reform and local democracy in Ukraine in collaboration with the Association of Ukrainian Cities and the Norwegian Association of Local and Regional Authorities. He currently leads the ARDU project studying the accommodation of ethnocultural diversity in Ukrainian border regions.

Max Bader is an Assistant Professor at the Department of Russian and Eurasian Studies at Leiden University, the Netherlands. His research interests include elections, corruption, authoritarian politics, and democratization, with a regional focus on post-Soviet Eurasia. He has published widely in the area of comparative politics in journals such as *Post-Soviet Affairs*, *Democratization*, *Europe–Asia Studies*, *East European Politics*, and *Russian Politics*.

Jaroslava Barbieri is a PhD candidate in Russian and Eastern European Studies at the Department of Political Science and International Studies, University of Birmingham, the United Kingdom. Her research interests include Russian foreign and security policy, Russian disinformation tactics, and influence networks in the EU and its neighborhood, Ukraine's foreign and security policy, EU relations with Eastern Partnership (EaP) countries, and the politics of memory in the post-Soviet region. She has collaborated in a research assistant capacity with the Russia and Eurasia Programme at Chatham House, the Conflict Studies Research Centre, the Arena Project at the LSE's Institute of Global Affairs, and One Philosophy Group. She was also a research associate for EU-STRAT, an EU-funded project on the links between the EU and EaP countries.

Nadiia Koval leads Central Europe Studies at the Foreign Policy Council "Ukrainian Prism" and lectures on European integration at the Kyiv School of Economics. She has previously served as a Head of the Centre for International Studies at the Diplomatic Academy of Ukraine and worked as an analyst in foreign policy and security issues at the National Institute for Strategic Studies and the Ukrainian Institute for the Future. Her research interests include post-conflict settlement and reconciliation policies and Ukraine's foreign policy towards Central and Western European states.

Tomasz Lachowski is a researcher in the Faculty of Law and Administration, University of Łódź, Poland. His PhD dissertation was devoted to the issue of "Transitional Justice in International Law: With Special Reference to Victims' Justice (Right to Justice, Right to Truth and Right to Reparation)". Due to the interdisciplinary character of the research, in addition to the basic legal methodology, he conducted his field research in numerous post-violence states coming to terms with historical injustices, such as Bangladesh, Bosnia and Herzegovina, the Caucasus region (Georgia, Armenia), Egypt, Moldova, Mozambique, and Ukraine. His current research focuses on the application of transitional justice in ongoing conflicts and post-conflict reconstruction, with special emphasis on post-Maidan Ukraine and the question of reintegration of Donbas.

Oleksii Lyska is a regional coordinator at the German Corporation for International Cooperation (GIZ). As a researcher, he was affiliated with the Association of Ukrainian Cities within the framework of the Ukrainian–Norwegian project "Evidence-Based Local Government Policy Development in Ukraine." Previously, he worked as a Business Analyst for USAID / Chemonics International Inc. in the Ukraine Confidence Building Initiative. And prior to this, he was a Head of Analytics and Presentation Division in the Department for Improvement of Regional Competitiveness of Kharkiv Regional State Administration and an Associate

Professor at the Simon Kuznets Kharkiv National University of Economics. His research interests include public participation in government, involvement of local communities in decision-making, administrative services, and decentralization in Ukraine.

Oksana Myshlovska is a researcher at the University of Bern and the Graduate Institute in Geneva, Switzerland. She contributes to a project that focuses on a role of civil society in conflict transformation and reconciliation in relation to the history and memory in Ukraine, Chechnya, and Georgia. In 2017–2018, she was a principal investigator for the Institute of Development Studies (Sussex University) and the Swiss Development Agency contributing to "A Learning Journey on Governance in Fragile and Conflict-Affected Contexts." Previously, she was a researcher at the University of St. Gallen and the Global Studies Institute in Geneva. Her research is at the intersection of memory studies, history, transitional justice, and conflict transformation in Eastern Europe, with a focus on Ukraine.

Andrii Nekoliak is a PhD candidate at the Skytte Institute of Political Studies, University of Tartu, Estonia, focusing on memory politics and law in Poland, Ukraine, and Estonia. He holds master's degrees in law (2014) and in democracy and governance (2017) from Yaroslav Mudryi National Law University in Ukraine and the University of Tartu, respectively.

Olga Oleinikova is a Lecturer and Director of the Ukraine Democracy Initiative in the School of Communication, University of Technology Sydney, Australia. She is a winner of the "Forbes 30 Under 30" award and a finalist for the Australia's Council of Humanities, Arts, and Social Sciences Future Leader Award. She is an author of *Achiever or Survivor? Life Strategies of Migrants from Crisis Regimes* (2020) and an editor of *Democracy, Diaspora, Territory: Europe and Cross-Border Politics* (2019). She has published articles and media commentaries on democracy in Ukraine, migration from Europe to Asia-Pacific, the problems of transition in Eastern Europe, transnationalism, and globalization.

Vello Pettai is a Director of the European Centre for Minority Issues in Flensburg, Germany. He holds an additional appointment as a Professor of Comparative Politics at the University of Tartu, Estonia. For more than twenty years he has been publishing on ethnic politics in the Baltic states, including the effect of constitutional court decisions on minority issues in

Estonia and Latvia in the *East European Constitutional Review*. He is an author of *Varieties of Democracy in Post-Communist Europe* (forthcoming in the BASEES/Routledge Series on Russian and East European Politics).

Anne Pintsch is an Associate Professor at the Department of Political Science and Management at the University of Agder, Norway. Her previous positions include an Interim Professor for Empirical Democracy Research at the University of Mannheim, a Project Director at the Mannheim Centre for European Social Research (MZES), Germany, and a post-doctoral fellow at Gent University, Belgium. Her research focuses on external democracy promotion, international organizations with a focus on the European Union, and political transformation in Central and Eastern Europe. She has published extensively on political developments in Ukraine, including the book *Democracy Promotion by Functional Cooperation: The European Union and its Neighbourhood* (with T. Freyburg, S. Lavenex, F. Schimmelfennig, T. Skripka, 2015) and articles in the *Journal of European Public Policy, Democratization* and *Eurasian Geography and Economics*.

Maryna Rabinovych holds a PhD in Legal Studies from the University of Hamburg, Germany. During her PhD studies, she held visiting positions at the Aristotle University of Thessaloniki, the University of Vienna, and the National Autonomous University of Mexico. Prior to this, she was an expert on regional development with the German Corporation for International Development (GIZ) in Ukraine. Her research interests include EU external relations and their legal regulation, the EU Neighbourhood Policy, EU–Ukraine relations, as well as political and legal dynamics in Eastern Europe and Ukraine.

Hanna Shelest is a Director of Security Programmes at the Foreign Policy Council "Ukrainian Prism" and an Editor-in-chief at *UA: Ukraine Analytica*. Prior to this, she had served for more than 10 years as a Senior Researcher at the National Institute for Strategic Studies under the President of Ukraine. In 2014, she served as a Visiting Research Fellow at the NATO Defense College in Rome. She was also an adviser of the working group preparing the Ukrainian Navy Strategy 2035. Her research interests include conflict resolution, security and cooperation in the wider Black Sea Region and the Middle East, and the foreign policy of Ukraine.

Alina Zubkovych is currently a Deputy Director of the Ukrainian Institute of Sweden. She was a post-doctoral research fellow at the Centre for Baltic and East European Studies (CBEES) at Södertorn University. She is an author of *Dealing with the Yugoslav Past: Exhibition Reflections in the Successor States* (2017). Her current research focuses on the identification processes in post-Maidan Ukraine. She conducted interviews with Crimean Tatars who moved to mainland Ukraine after the annexation of Crimea, and also studies how the image of Crimea is changing today.

CHAPTER 1

Introduction: Regional Diversity, Decentralization, and Conflict in and around Ukraine

Maryna Rabinovych and Hanna Shelest

INTRODUCTION

A decrease in interstate wars (Holsti 2016, 43) is one of the trends shaping the post-World War II global security environment. There has, however, been an increase in ethnic, cultural, linguistic, and identity conflicts within states, often involving an establishment of the "breakaway" or "de-facto" states, and external (foreign) "support" to the parties of such conflicts, reinforcing polarization (Dupuy and Rustad 2018). Hence, third-state ideational, political, financial, and military "support" to the parties to intrastate conflicts, including the administration of de-facto states, gives rise to the emergence of complex conflict constellations, embracing the intra- and interstate aspects.

M. Rabinovych (✉)
University of Hamburg, Hamburg, Germany

H. Shelest
Foreign Policy Council "Ukrainian Prism", Odesa/Kyiv, Ukraine

© The Author(s) 2020
H. Shelest, M. Rabinovych (eds.), *Decentralization, Regional Diversity, and Conflict*, Federalism and Internal Conflicts,
https://doi.org/10.1007/978-3-030-41765-9_1

Territorial self-governance arrangements (TSG) (federalization and different forms of decentralization) have been widely applied as a tool of managing intrastate conflicts rooted in interethnic, cultural, linguistic, and identity-related cleavages (e.g. federalization of Bosnia and Herzegovina, re-federalization in Nigeria, decentralization in Uganda and Sri Lanka) (Wolff 2013). Despite the fact that the vast majority of proposed conflict settlements for societies, experiencing such conflicts, involve some form of TSG, there is no consensus in scholarship whether the application of TSG, in general, or of particular governance arrangements under this umbrella term, allow for successful conflict resolution and promote stability (Martínez-Herrera 2010; Wolff 2011, 2013; Keil 2012; Breen 2018; Walsch 2018). The variation in the results of TSG application in different conflict settings is determined by numerous factors, including peculiarities of a particular conflict, involvement of third parties and the design of conflict settlement (Wolff 2010). Similar arguments can be made about decentralization, which may both decrease an intrastate conflict through bringing governments closer to the people, and indirectly encourage it through supporting the growth of regional parties (Brancatti 2006). Notably, while there are studies systematically examining the relationship between the duration of intrastate conflicts and third-party involvement, virtually no attention has been paid to the functioning of TSG, in general, and decentralization, in particular, under the circumstances of conflict constellations, involving both the intra- and interstate dimensions. Subsequently, unpacking the complexity pertaining to the intrastate divides and third-party involvement, as well as the potential of TSG and decentralization as conflict resolution tools, requires an in-detail insight into the historical roots of divides of a particular society, existing power-sharing arrangements, and a discursive and legal framing of the third-party involvement.

The case of Ukraine is highly illustrative for research into the scope of the problem outlined above: it features a historical constitution of ethnically, linguistically, and culturally diverse societies; power-sharing and an accommodation of diversity in state policies; a complexity of conflict, involving the intra- and interstate dimensions; foreign support for de-facto states' administrations; and, finally, an application of decentralization as a tool to settle the conflict with extensive third-party participation. As underlined by Oksana Myshlovska, an author of "Regionalism in Ukraine: Historic Evolution, Regional Claim-Making and Centre-Periphery Conflict Resolution", Chap. 2 in this volume, "throughout history the

1 INTRODUCTION: REGIONAL DIVERSITY, DECENTRALIZATION... 3

present territory of Ukraine has been an arena of competing influences of global, regional and local powers. In particular, different territories comprising contemporary Ukraine, used to belong to, among others, the Kyivan Rus (ninth to thirteenth century), the kingdom of Galicia-Volhynia (twelfth to fourteenth century), the Grand Duchy (Principality) of Lithuania (fourteenth to the end of the eighteenth century), the Polish-Lithuanian Commonwealth (sixteenth to eighteenth century), the Russian Empire (end of the eighteenth to early twentieth century), the Austro-Hungarian Empire (nineteenth to early twentieth century) and the Soviet Union (twentieth century). Consequently, Ukrainian regions differ in terms of ethnic composition, national and regional identities, language identities and practices, religious affiliation, beliefs and practices, and foreign policy attitudes. Until the highly controversial presidential campaign of 2004, the problem of diversity received relatively modest attention from policy makers and scholars, despite differences that led a notable observer of Ukraine to refer to a "deeply divided society with a pronounced pattern of regional diversity" (Wilson 1997, 1). Moreover, until the launch of the decentralization reform in 2014, Ukraine had been a centralized state with few competencies ceded to local territorial self-government units. An important feature, characterizing the power-sharing arrangements in post-independence Ukraine, has been the legacy of neopatrimonialism, combining strong presidential power, clientelism (the exchange of goods and services for political support) and regime corruption (the use of public resources for private purposes or political support) (Bratton and van den Walle 1997). Under such circumstances, the development of local self-government with an account of multi-aspect diversity had been impeded by an array of factors, such as the lack of public debate on diversity and its reflection in state policies; the proliferation of simplified constructs of diversity, such as the "Two Ukraines" concept of Riabchuk (2002), explaining Ukraine's macro-level division into the pro-European Ukrainian-speaking west and center and the pro-Russian southeast; centralized management of resources, reflected in the limited competencies exercised by bodies of local self-government; and the absence of transparency of resource distribution among local territorial self-government units (*hromadas*).

The annexation of Crimea by the Russian Federation in March 2014, allegedly supported by more than 80 percent of voters, and the outbreak of violent conflict in eastern Ukraine, gave new impetus to the debate on regional diversity. In particular, a considerable number of surveys and academic contributions have aimed at offering a detailed analysis of the substance of ethnic, religious, linguistic, and cultural diversity in Ukraine, Ukrainians' geopolitical and foreign policy preferences, and their dynamics over the period since the 2013 Euromaidan[1] Revolution (the "Revolution of Dignity") to the present era. Furthermore, given the Russian Federation's explicitly unlawful annexation of Crimea and its extensive support to "rebels" in eastern Ukraine and, later on, its leadership of the self-proclaimed so-called Donetsk and Luhansk People's Republics ("DPR" and "LPR"), the "crisis in and around Ukraine" has provoked intense discussion on the interplay of the intra- and interstate factors triggering the conflict, and its qualification under international law. Whilst the "reunification of Crimea with Russia" is widely acknowledged to violate the foundations of public international law, qualifying the situation in eastern Ukraine under international law is a more complex task. In this vein, it is challenging to develop an objective and in-depth understanding of the "distribution of roles" between diversity and its mismanagement by Ukrainian authorities and Russia's extensive involvement in the proliferation of secessionist beliefs, actions and movements in eastern Ukraine that eventually led to the establishment of the DPR and the LPR.

Reaffirming its "full support for the sovereignty, independence, and territorial integrity of Ukraine", the UN Security Council has been very cautious about either mentioning the parties to the conflict or qualifying it (UN Security Council 2014, 2015, 2018). Similarly, the definition put forward by the Organization for Security and Cooperation in Europe (OSCE) of the "crisis in and around Ukraine" only implies third-party involvement by incorporating the "around" dimension (OSCE 2015). So far, only the International Criminal Court has pointed to the parallel existence of "direct military engagement between the respective armed forces of the Russian Federation and Ukraine" and "the non-international armed conflict" in eastern Ukraine (International Criminal Court 2018, paras. 72–73). Looking ahead, it should be mentioned that modern scholarship offers different conceptualizations of the conflict in Ukraine, ranging from a "separatist war"/ civil conflict/ civil war (Katchanovski 2016; Wilson 2016) to the Ukraine–Russia "hybrid" conflict (Kofman and Rojanski

---

[1] Euromaidan was a wave of demonstrations sparked by the Ukrainian government's decision to suspend the signing of an association agreement with the European Union. They started on November 21, 2013 in Maidan Nezalezhnosti (Independence Square) in Kiev and eventually led to the 2014 Ukrainian revolution.

1 INTRODUCTION: REGIONAL DIVERSITY, DECENTRALIZATION... 5

2015; Lanoszka 2016), challenging the post-Cold War world order (Allison 2014). Notwithstanding the above, Russia's support for separatist forces in Donbas is a factor, seldom contested even by the proponents of the so-called "civil war" approach. Thus, the challenge of establishing causal links between the intrastate and interstate dimensions of the conflict makes Ukraine an appealing case for those interested in researching and qualifying conflicts marked by strong external support for one of the parties.

In view of the above mentioned complexity, Ukraine's crisis response strategy has been comprised of three key axes: security operations, such as the Anti-Terrorist Operation (ATO) (2014–2018), led by the Security Services of Ukraine (SBU), and, later on the Joint Forces Operation under the leadership of the military (2018–ongoing) (Verkhovna Rada 2018); diplomatic efforts, on both building international coalition against the Russian Aggression and pertaining to the Minsk Agreements and their implementation; and domestic reforms, including *inter alia* the decentralization reform.

Launched in April 2014, shortly after the illegal annexation of Crimea by the Russian Federation and the outbreak of violence in eastern Ukraine, the reform of decentralization primarily aims at transferring a significant share of authority, resources, and responsibility to local self-government bodies. The effective fulfilment of this umbrella goal has inter alia encompassed the amalgamation of hromadas, aimed at strengthening their capacity, an advancement of direct democracy at the local level, and a reform of regional policies (e.g. state financing for infrastructure projects at regional level) (Decentralization 2019). While the reform was much appreciated by both Ukrainian stakeholders at different levels and foreign donors, little research has been done on its possible role in conflict resolution and actual effectiveness for conflict management. Hence exploring the role of ongoing decentralization reform in conflict resolution is of high value for the implementation of the Minsk II Agreements and the package of measures for its implementation that stress decentralization as a core component of the political settlement. Thus, the application of decentralization as a form of territorial self-governance arrangement in Ukraine under extensive external involvement and the, so far, limited insights into its role in conflict resolution is the last, but not least, reason to focus on the case of Ukraine in terms of the "Federalism and Internal Conflict" series.

OBJECTIVES AND STRUCTURE

In view of the above, this volume focuses on four themes. Firstly, it explores the matter of regional diversity in Ukraine and government policies thereto prior to the outbreak of the "crisis in and around Ukraine"[2] and soon thereafter. The second part of the volume zooms in on the legal perspectives pertaining to the conflict and government-controlled territories, stressing the securitization of regional diversity issues. Thirdly, the volume assesses an application of the decentralization reform as a means of conflict resolution. Finally, yet importantly, it considers decentralization's broader effects with respect to Ukraine's modernization, democratization, and European integration. Consequently, the book is divided into four parts.

Part I: Regional Diversity in Ukraine and its Accommodation in Government Policies

The three chapters in Part I revolve around the problem of regional diversity in Ukraine and how it had reflected in governmental policies prior to the outbreak of the "crisis in and around Ukraine" and shortly thereafter. In sum, the historical, sociological, and legal perspectives, embraced by Part I, reveal that, notwithstanding the multi-aspect nature of diversity in Ukraine, there had been no unified strategy to accommodate it until the launch of decentralization reform in 2014. Prior to this there had been attempts to apply asymmetric state structures, subsidies and budget disbursements, and special economic zones, which were functioning differently in different areas of the country. Moreover, an overview of surveys and academic contributions, commissioned prior to the Revolution of Dignity, demonstrated that this diversity was hardly conceptualized as an actual or potential source of a conflict. The Revolution of Dignity, followed by the Russian Federation's illegal annexation of Crimea and the outbreak of the conflict in eastern Ukraine seem to have played a threefold role with regard to the regional diversity and its accommodation. First of all, these events exerted considerable impact on the politics of belonging in Ukraine, with a category of "being Ukrainian" defined beyond strictly ethnonational terms. Secondly, they fueled the debate on regional diversity, and national,

---

[2] Here and after we use official terminology recognized and used by international organizations, such as the Organization for Security and Cooperation in Europe. See for example: https://www.osce.org/ukrainecrisis.

1 INTRODUCTION: REGIONAL DIVERSITY, DECENTRALIZATION... 7

language, and civic identity in Ukraine. In this light, the ongoing reforms have already addressed some of the obstacles to the accommodation of regional diversity, such as the non-transparent distribution of state funds, through establishing new budgetary and fiscal rules.

In Chap. 2, Oksana Myshlovska presents an overview of the historical constitution of Ukraine's territory, focusing on roots and the substance of regional cleavages and differences. She also offers a crucial analysis of the nature of Ukraine's political regime, center–periphery relations, and regional politics as factors that may contribute to the emergence of a violent conflict, but also can be consonant with objectives of conflict resolution and peace-building. Notably, in the first part of her analysis, Myshlovska does not only shed light on the historical processes that determined the regional diversity of contemporary Ukraine, but delves into interpretations of such a diversity, thus, enabling a reader to follow landmark turns in the diversity discourse in Ukraine. The chapter points to the excessive concentration of competencies at the central level and the non-transparent distribution of funds among regions and local communities as crucial failings of pre-Euromaidan center-periphery relations. The author finds these structural deficiencies to have been effectively addressed by ongoing decentralization reform. Notwithstanding the post-Euromaidan increase in self-identification with Ukrainian citizenship and a high level of popular support for decentralization, Myshlovska identifies regional differences in terms of historical memories and attitudes to Euromaidan as "a source of vulnerability to future regional mobilizations."

In Chap. 3, Andrii Nekoliak and Vello Pettai contribute to our understanding of the regional diversity of Ukraine by exploring a language issue and language policy in Ukraine, with a particular focus on the practice of the Constitutional Court of Ukraine in cases involving the state language policy and legislation before 2014. The added value of this contribution lies in its insight into the status and institutionalization of Ukrainian and Russian languages in Ukraine, being one of few contributions that deal with a judicial dimension of language politics in Ukraine. The chapter demonstrates that, even though the Constitutional Court of Ukraine is fairly accessible across a number of eligible appellants, it has been predominantly used by members of parliament in order to strengthen the position of Ukrainian as a state language, *inter alia,* by calling for thwarting alternative legislation that would favor the rights of Russian-language users. A close look into the court's reasoning in language-related cases enables Nekoliak and Pettai to highlight the contentious nature of the language issue in Ukraine, as well as to label the court as a "minimalist" institution, aspiring to uphold parliament's prerogative to regulate the use of language in the state.

In Chap. 4, Alina Zubkovych highlights the dynamics of national and ethnic identifications of Crimean Tatars in the mainland, with an emphasis on changes that occurred as a consequence of the illegal annexation of Crimea. Zubkovych stresses the novelty of the Crimean Tatars' forced extensive exodus from Crimea to mainland Ukraine and seeks to distinguish its implications for their national belonging. Based on in-depth interviews with Crimean Tatars in Kyiv and Lviv, the chapter stresses a broadening of the category of "being Ukrainian" from the solely ethnonationalist to one incorporating citizenship and a language as factors constitutive of one's understanding of belonging. Agreeing with Myshlovska, Zubkovych affirms an increase in her researched group's self-identification as Ukrainians, despite a frequency of the multiplication of performed identities through language use. Last but not least, Zubkovych stresses terminological ambiguities, shaping the studies of the identity in contemporary Ukraine.

Part II: The "Crisis In and Around Ukraine", Occupied Territories and their Reintegration: The Legal Dimension

This part of the volume explores the legal perspectives pertaining to the ongoing "crisis in and around Ukraine," occupied territories and their potential reintegration, drawing parallels to the cases of Transnistria, South Ossetia, and Abkhazia. Striving to analyze the legislation, relevant for understanding a nature of the conflict and peculiarities of the securitization of regional diversity in the Ukrainian context, we opted to utilize the OSCE's term "crisis in and around Ukraine" for two reasons. Firstly, it allows us to promote the consistency of our collaborative work. Secondly, even though there is a broad consensus on the Russian Federation's involvement in the conflict, we see the phrase "crisis in and around Ukraine" as the term accepted by the international community, thus eradicating a bias factor, and also allowing one to analyze the situation in *all* regions of Ukraine within its internationally recognized borders. At the same time, subject to relevant substantiation, we did not limit the authors' freedom to apply other terms, such as a "hybrid war" or the Russian aggression, especially in the context of further discussion on the effects of decentralization and its implications for conflict resolution.

Chapter 5, by Maryna Rabinovych, offers a comparative analysis of the domestic regulations concerning uncontrolled territories in Moldova, Georgia, and Ukraine. The chapter demonstrates striking differences in approaches in Moldovan and Georgian legislation in determining the legal status of the uncontrolled territories, largely consonant with the dynamics of international efforts to settle respective conflicts. Subsequently, Rabinovych characterizes Ukrainian domestic legislation concerning the uncontrolled territories as "hybrid" one, applying "soft", conflict-transformation-directed and "hard," reintegration-oriented legislation simultaneously. Based on her analysis of the negotiation of the notorious "Steinmeier Formula,"[3] the author points to a significant role of Ukrainian domestic legislation in international conflict resolution efforts. Overall, underlining the multiplicity of nexuses between the domestic dimension of defining uncontrolled territories and international conflict resolution efforts, Rabinovych suggests focusing researchers' attention on the domestic legislation of states that are deprived of effective control over some of their territories.

In Chap. 6, Tomasz Lachowski substantiates a definition of Russia's involvement in the conflict in eastern Ukraine as a crime of aggression under international law, and explores the international law pathways the government of Ukraine can utilize to promote the reintegration of occupied territories. Whilst Russia's support for separatists and administrations of the so-called Donetsk People's Republic (DPR) and Luhansk People's Republic (LPR) has already been examined by scholars from the critical international law perspective, the added value of Lachowski's contribution lies in its application of reintegration-oriented peace-building and transitional justice perspectives. In this vein, Lachowski emphasizes the importance of regional positions in the reintegration process, given the securitization of regional differences in the DPR/LPR narratives.

Part III: Federalization/Decentralization as a Tool of Conflict Resolution. Discursive and Foreign Policy Perspectives

The chapters in this part engage with the core concerns of the "Federalism and Internal Conflict" series, namely, the extent to which and the circumstances under which different forms of TSG can serve the objectives of

---

[3] The Steinmeier Formula calls for elections in the separatist-held territories under Ukrainian legislation and the supervision of the OSCE. If the OSCE accepts that balloting was free and fair, then self-governing status for the territories will be introduced. Representatives of Ukraine, Russia, DPR, LPR, and the OSCE signed it on October 1, 2016.

conflict resolution. Here, authors substantiate two arguments to make in the broader debate on TSGs as a conflict resolution tool. Firstly, It is argued that, in the case of Ukraine, Russia-sponsored scenarios of federalization, and even Ukrainian-led decentralization reform (if misinterpreted) bear considerable security risks for Ukraine. Secondly, it is argued that through implementing part of the Minsk Agreements the reform of decentralization in Ukraine has not (so far) proven to be an effective tool of conflict resolution or conflict management. In the future, the validity of this statement will, however, depend on outcomes of current peace-oriented policies conducted by President Volodymyr Zelenskyy—*inter alia*, new rounds of "Normandy format" negotiations or adoption of new "special status" legislation.

In Chap. 7, Nadiia Koval considers a discursive use of federalism as applied to the conflict in eastern Ukraine in the official discourses of Russia and Germany, with the former extensively supporting pro-Russian forces in Eastern Ukraine, and both countries being involved into the peace process. Koval shows that, for the Russian Federation, federalization represents "the long-term primary strategic goal, regarded as a means to regain lost influence in the post-Soviet states and at minimum to limit their integration into Western political and security institutions", thus bearing an existential threat for Russia's neighbors. By contrast, given its commitment to the resolution of the crisis in and around Ukraine by diplomatic means, and its historical legacy of federalism, Germany tends to refer to the potential federalization of Ukraine as both a conflict-resolution and a good-governance tool. The difference in discursive use of federalism by key engaged international players testifies to the problematic nature of internationally imposed (promoted) federalism.

In Chap. 8, Jaroslava Barbieri challenges the prevailing argument according to which "ongoing decentralization reform in Ukraine can act as a powerful deterrent against Russia-sponsored separatism". According to Barbieri, key concerns to be taken into account include a continued non-establishment of the institution of prefects as a form of state oversight of the implementation of decentralization; local elites' long-lasting links with pro-Russian forces (members of the former Anti-Maidan movement) and the nexus between the reform of decentralization and Donbas's "special status." Largely in line with the findings by Rabinovych and Koval, Barbieri shows how President Zelenskyy's commitment to reach significant progress in peace talks "opened a window of opportunity for the Russian leadership to reboot the Minsk process to its own advantage".

Thus, in contrast to many scholars, Barbieri analyzes the "dark side" of Ukraine's decentralization as a conflict-resolution tool—an exercise, very much needed, when considering TSGs as a means of conflict resolution.

Part IV: Decentralization, its Perceptions and Linkage to Democratization, Modernization, and European Integration of Ukraine

The last part of the book goes beyond the decentralization–conflict resolution nexus, and seeks to examine decentralization's implications for the processes of democratization, modernization, and the European integration of Ukraine. We argue that, although it does not immediately represent a viable conflict-resolution tool, and although it bears security risks, decentralization reform is consonant with Ukraine's long-term policy objectives of democratization, modernization, and European integration.

In this vein, in Chap. 9 Max Bader examines the promises and flaws of decentralization with an emphasis on the risk of capture by a local elite that may further reduce citizens' trust in decentralization and consequently, adversely affect the reform's democratization potential. Like Barbieri in Chap. 8, Bader expresses concern about the Ukrainian government's failure to introduce prefects, an innovation that was intended to act as a counterbalance to empowered communities.

Furthermore, as is established by Aadne Aasland and Oleksii Lyska in Chap. 10 with respect to Ukrainian cities, popular support for decentralization can indirectly promote consensus-building and, consequently, the mitigation of intrasocietal cleavages. However, an increase in local elites' role in communities' amalgamation (a local elite capture) may gradually destroy citizens' support for decentralization, thus, diminishing decentralization's positive implications for democratization and modernization.

The contribution by Aadne Aasland and Oleksii Lyska examines citizens' perceptions of and interaction with local authorities, based on two democracy surveys conducted in early 2014 (prior to the launch of the reform) and at the end of 2017 in 20 Ukrainian cities. The surveys show the signs of progress in terms of both citizens' perceptions of the responsiveness of local authorities and the opportunities for civic participation at the local level in many cities. Nevertheless, Aasland and Lyska record Ukrainian citizens' extremely low level of trust in public institutions at national level as a hindrance to the speedy progress of top–bottom decentralization reform.

In Chap. 11, Olga Oleinikova continues the examination of the nexus between decentralization and modernization, also touching upon the democratization processes. Her research offers an extensive meta-analysis of the interplay between decentralization, modernization, and democratization processes from Western and Eastern European perspectives. Based on this, she argues that decentralization can serve as a "vehicle for modernization" under a number of conditions, such as a secure existence and financing of local governments, clear definition of priorities for industrial development, and a possibility of autonomy in the use of resources for the implementation of socioeconomic initiatives.

In Chap. 12, Anne Pintsch examines the linkage between the decentralization reform and Ukraine's strategic foreign policy goal of European integration. More specifically, the chapter considers the transnational relations of the amalgamated territorial communities, in particular, an operation of community twinning partnerships with counterparts abroad and membership of transnational European networks. Based on the sociological perspective of the European integration and results of an ambitious survey, conducted among the communities, Pintsch highlights the value of decentralization reform for bottom-top Ukrainian European integration.

The book concludes with Chap. 13 reflecting on the lessons that the case of Ukraine supplies to the study of the interconnection and correlation between regional diversity, decentralization, and conflicts, especially those with foreign involvement, and proposes directions for further research.

References

Allison, Roy. 2014. Russian 'Deniable' Intervention in Ukraine: How and Why Russia Broke the Rules. *International Affairs 90* (6): 1255–1297.

Brancatti, Dawn. 2006. Decentralization: Fueling the Fire or Dampening the Flames of Ethnic Conflict and Secession. *International Organization 60* (3): 651–685.

Bratton, Michael, and Nicolas van den Walle. 1997. *Democratic Experiments in Africa. Regime Transitions in Comparative Perspective.* Cambridge: Cambridge University Press.

Breen, Michael G. 2018. *The Road to Federalism in Nepal, Myanmar and Sri Lanka.* London and New York: Routledge.

Decentralization. 2019. About the Reform. https://decentralization.gov.ua/en/about

Dupuy, Kendra, and Siri Aas Rustad. 2018. Trends in Armed Conflict, 1946–2017. *PRIO Conflict Trends*. https://reliefweb.int/sites/reliefweb.int/files/resources/Dupuy%2C%20Rustad-%20Trends%20in%20Armed%20Conflict%2C%201945%E2%80%932017%2C%20Conflict%20Trends%205-2018.pdf

Holsti, Kalevi. 2016. *Major Texts on War, the State, Peace, and International Order*. Berlin: Springer.

International Criminal Court. 2018. Report on Preliminary Examination Activities. https://www.icc-cpi.int/itemsDocuments/181205-rep-otp-PE-ENG.pdf

Katchanovski, Ivan. 2016. The Separatist War in Donbas: A Violent Break-Up of Ukraine? *European Politics and Society* 17: 473–489.

Keil, Soeren. 2012. Federalism as a Tool of Conflict Resolution. *L'Europeen Formation*, no. 1: 205–218.

Kofman, Michael, and Matthew Rojanski. 2015. A Closer Look at Russia's "Hybrid War". *Kennan Cable*, no. 7 (April).

Lanoszka, Alexander. 2016. Russian Hybrid Warfare and Extended Deterrence in Eastern Europe. *International Affairs* 92 (1): 175–195.

Martínez-Herrera, Enric. 2010. Federalism and Ethnic Conflict Management: Rival Hypotheses, the Attitudinal Missing Link and Comparative Evidence. In *New Directions in Federalism Studies*, ed. Jan Erk and Wilfried Swenden, 173–192. London: Routledge.

OSCE. 2015. OSCE Response to the Crisis in and Around Ukraine. https://www.osce.org/home/125575?download=true

Riabchuk, Mykola. 2002. Ukraine: One State, Two Countries? *Eurozine*. September 16, 2002. https://www.eurozine.com/ukraine-one-state-two-countries/?pdf

United Nations Security Council. 2014. Resolution 2166, adopted by the Security Council at its 7221st meeting, on 21 July 2014. S/RES/2166(2014). https://www.securitycouncilreport.org/atf/cf/%7B65BFCF9B-6D27-4E9C-8CD3-CF6E4FF96FF9%7D/s_res_2166.pdf

———. 2015. Resolution 2202, adopted by the Security Council at its 7384th meeting, on 17 February 2015. S/RES/2202(2015). https://www.securitycouncilreport.org/atf/cf/%7B65BFCF9B-6D27-4E9C-8CD3-CF6E4FF96FF9%7D/s_res_2202.pdf

———. 2018. Statement by the President of the Security Council. S/PRST/2018/12, June 6. https://undocs.org/S/PRST/2018/11

Verkhovna Rada. 2018. Pro Osoblyvosti Derzhavnoyi Polityky iz Zabezpechennya Derzhavnogo Suverenitetu Ukrayini na Timchasovo Okupovanyh Teritoriyah u Doneckij ta Luhanskij Oblastyah [On the Peculiarities of State Policy on Guaranteeing State Sovereignty of Ukraine on the Temporarily Occupied Territories in Donetsk and Luhansk Oblasts]. January 18, 2018. https://zakon.rada.gov.ua/laws/show/2268-19.

Walsch, Dawn. 2018. *Territorial Self-Government as a Conflict-Management Tool*. Basingstoke: Palgrave Macmillan.

Wilson, Andrew. 1997. *Ukrainian Nationalism in the 1990s: A Minority Faith*. Cambridge: Cambridge University Press.

———. 2016. The Donbas in 2014: Explaining Civil Conflict, Perhaps, but Not Civil War. *Europe-Asia Studies* 68 (4): 631–652. https://doi.org/10.108 0/09668136.2016.1176994.

Wolff, Stefan. 2010. Approaches to Conflict Resolution in Divided Societies: The Many Uses of Territorial Self-Governance. *Ethnopolitics Papers*, 5. https://www.psa.ac.uk/sites/default/files/page-files/EPP005_0.pdf.

———. 2011. Territorial Approaches to Conflict Resolution in Divided Societies. In *Conflict Resolution: Theories and Practice*, ed. Stefan Wolff and Christalla Yakinthou, 1–25. London: Routledge.

———. 2013. Conflict Management in Divided Societies: The Many Uses of Territorial Self-Governance. *International Journal on Minority and Group Rights* 20 (1): 27–50. https://doi.org/10.1163/15718115-02001003.

PART I

Regional Diversity in Ukraine and Its Accommodation in Government Policies

CHAPTER 2

Regionalism in Ukraine: Historic Evolution, Regional Claim-Making, and Centre–Periphery Conflict Resolution

Oksana Myshlovska

INTRODUCTION

Recently, scholars have been occupied with explaining why the previous phases of contention in Ukraine had unfolded in a non-violent manner, while the 2013–2014 contention cycle turned into a violent conflict. One of the most contested issues in the scholarly debate has been the nature and meaning of the conflict that started in early 2014, some interpreting it as a "civil war," others as "Russian aggression against Ukraine," and the recognition of an internal dimension to the conflict (Kudelia 2014; Kuzio 2017; Matveeva 2017). Wilson (2016) holds that while historical and identity factors, economic fears and alienation from the new government that had come to power in 2014 played a role in the outbreak of the violent conflict, it was the

O. Myshlovska (✉)
University of Bern, Bern, Switzerland
e-mail: oksana.myshlovska@hist.unibe.ch

© The Author(s) 2020
H. Shelest, M. Rabinovych (eds.), *Decentralization, Regional Diversity, and Conflict*, Federalism and Internal Conflicts,
https://doi.org/10.1007/978-3-030-41765-9_2

17

intervention of Russia and the role of local elites in Donbas[1] that were the key triggers. Other studies analyze the economic drivers of the conflict (Zhukov 2016; Giuliano 2018) and mobilizations on both sides of the conflict (Matveeva 2017; Kudelia 2019; Umland 2019).

The chapter aims to make several contributions. First, it analyzes identity and regional cleavages in Ukraine and the evolution and dynamics of claim-making and center-periphery contention related to them in different regions. The findings are in line with grievances-based explanations of civil war onset that find strong association between political exclusion of groups and competition along ethnic lines and internal conflict (Cederman et al. 2010; Cederman et al. 2013; Wucherpfennig et al. 2016). Second, it studies the non-violent forms of contention in Ukraine from the late 1980s until the eruption of violent conflict in 2014. The findings are consistent with theories of conflict that posit that non-violent forms of conflict precede escalation into violent conflict. Drawing on the contentious politics literature that holds that it cannot be assumed that the causes of non-violent and violent conflict are different (McAdam et al. 2001), Germann and Sambanis (forthcoming) find that grievances such as political exclusion and lost autonomy are associated with the emergence of nonviolent separatist claims and the escalation of nonviolent separatist claims to violent conflict. By examining a long period of contention preceding the eruption of violent conflict, the chapter's findings challenge the prevalent conflict analysis that puts the Euromaidan as the starting point of the conflict. Third, the chapter examines contention around issues of history and memory that receives less attention in the social science analysis of civil war onset and conflict dynamics. Finally, it also examines the persisting internal cleavages in the government-controlled areas that have been overshadowed by the focus on violent conflict in and around Ukraine.

The chapter starts with a review of the historical constitution of the present territory of Ukraine and its administrative–territorial system. Then it examines regional cleavages and differences and their dynamics, focusing on the different dimensions of regionalism outlined below. Next, it studies the regions with substantial ethnic diversity and with territorial units where some ethnic minority groups constitute a majority, namely the

---

[1] Donbas is a shortening from "Donetsk Coal Basin," which encompasses parts of eastern Ukraine (partially Donetsk, Luhansk, Dnipropetrovsk, and Zaporizhzhia oblasts) and of the Rostov region in Russia. In this chapter, it is used to define Donetsk and Luhansk regions.

Autonomous Republic of Crimea (ARC), Transcarpathia, and Donbas,[2] which have witnessed regional mobilizations around the issues of language, ethnicity, and political or economic autonomy passing through several stages of regional and center–periphery contention since the late 1980s. Finally, the chapter examines different forms of accommodation of claims such as an asymmetric state structure in the case of Crimean autonomy, power devolution, free economic zones, subsidies and budget disbursements, power-sharing at the national level, and local and regional legislation on historical memory and languages.

Looking at the drivers in the "making of regions" in post-socialist Europe, Melanie Tatur (2004, 15) argues that among factors that led to the rise of regionalism were the dismantling of mechanisms of central redistribution and of regional equalization, the rebalancing of economic regions in view of changing positions in the global markets, and the opening of opportunities for regional diversity, competition, and identity redefinition due to political liberalization and democratization. In the last few decades, dozens of projects, surveys, and studies have been conducted to investigate the phenomenon of regionalism in Ukraine. Indeed, it has become an important factor in modern Ukraine. Multiple studies have examined the configuration of regions and their number, the nature and importance of regional cleavages, the "regional effect" and its meaning (Birch 2000; O'Loughlin 2001; Sasse 2001, 2010; Kubicek 2002; Barrington and Herron 2004; Shulman 2004; Malanchuk 2005; Katchanovski 2006; Hrytsak et al. 2007; Rogers 2007; Kulyk 2011; Lewicka and Iwańczak 2019).

One of prominent approaches to the study of regionalism in Ukraine is a mapping of regions based on declared attitudes and identifications using the results of surveys or comparing pre-defined regions using the selected criteria. Lewicka and Iwańczak (2019, 30) define a region as "a homogenous topographical area, different from neighbouring areas" which is "related people's identities and the feelings that people have for their place of living." Surveys have captured territorial identification targets, regional, national, and transnational identities (for example, eastern Slav or European), various non-territorial identification targets, historical consciousness and mnemonic practices, language identity and practices,

---

[2] Another relevant region where similar processes of regional contestation and mobilization took place is Bukovyna (Kruglashov 2010–2011), however, it is not studied in the present chapter.

attitudes to bilingualism, and the use of languages in different spheres. Moreover, they inquired about religious affiliation, religious beliefs and practices, geopolitical and foreign policy orientations, attitudes to material belongings, to corruption, risk, and trust.

Another approach has been to look at the "regional effect"—a salience of regions as factors in themselves due to different historical experiences rather than "compositional" effects of individual sociodemographic attributes such as ethnicity or language. Some studies defined regions looking at a variety of criteria such as historical legacies (belonging to different states), industrialization, urbanization, demographics, ethnic composition and languages (Barrington and Herron 2004). Other studies have used the method of historical contextualization, and have investigated the role of a variety of factors such as patterns of settlement, violence and migration, socio-economic processes, state language, nationality and population management policies, state-society and center–periphery relations on the constitution of the present institutions, social capital, identifications, values and preferences (examples of such studies are Kuromiya 1998, 2016 for Donbas; Šabić 2004; Zimmer 2004, 2007; Hrytsak 2007 for Galicia; Sasse 2002, 2007 for Crimea).

Furthermore, regions have also been defined as mental constructs involving myths, symbols and social imagining at a sub-national level. Keating (1998, 84) holds that similar to national imagining, regional identity-building requires "the search for a 'usable past', a set of historical referents which can guide a regional society on its distinct road to modernization, bridging the past, via the present, with the future." Zimmer (2007, 98) also highlights the socially constructed nature of a region and defines it as "a multi-layered and contradictory space that is not to be understood in territorial terms, but as socially constructed by actors' discourse as well as their action and interaction." In terms of the study of symbolic politics and the production of a "usable past" at a regional level by regional elites and other actors the best-studied regions in Ukraine are Donbas (Wilson 1995; Sereda 2007; Studenna-Skrukva 2014), Slobozhanshchyna (Zhurzhenko 2004a, b), Galicia (Šabić 2004; Sereda 2007), Crimea (Plokhy 2000; Charron 2016) and Bukovyna (Kruglashov 2010–2011). More recently, other regions (Dnipro, Zaporizhzhya, and Kharkiv) started to be studied in terms the politics of memory, myth-making and symbolic politics (Kasianov 2018). Scholars also note the competition of different memories and competing narratives of the past held by different mnemonic communities at a regional level (for example, for the case of Crimea Plokhy 2000 and Charron 2016).

Finally, Zimmer (2007, 98) notes that "[d]iscourses... cannot be separated from the political, social and economic powers that create them; and it is constellations of actors that condition the use of the available cultural resources." Historical uniqueness and particularities of regions can be used by different actors to make a variety of claims such as demands for fiscal, political or cultural autonomy and more powers at the regional and local levels. Scholars note that flexibility, openness to negotiation and compromise between the center and regions, and the role of external powers in relation to their ethnic kin are important factors for the accommodation of claims and management of center–periphery conflicts (Sasse 2002).

I. HISTORICAL CONSTITUTION OF THE UKRAINIAN TERRITORY

Throughout history, the present territory of Ukraine has been an arena of competing influences of global, regional and local powers. Parts of the territory were integrated into competing or co-existing state formations. The medieval Kyivan Rus and then the kingdom of Galicia–Volhynia, considered as indigenous entities in national historiography, fell under the rule of the Golden Horde, the Grand Principality of Lithuania, Poland and then the Polish-Lithuanian Commonwealth. The Crimean Khanate existed from the fifteenth century until 1783, first as an independent state, then Ottoman-ruled. Transcarpathia was part of the medieval kingdom of Hungary from the eleventh century until 1699 when it was integrated into the Habsburg Empire. During the seventeenth to nineteenth centuries, the Russian state expanded westwards and absorbed left-bank and then right-bank Ukraine,[3] abolishing the autonomy of the Cossack Hetmanate. In the eighteenth to nineteenth centuries, the theatres of conflict concerned the territories of the declining Ottoman Empire. Following a series of Russian–Turkish wars, Russia had incorporated southern Ukraine and Crimea by 1783. After the division of the Polish–Lithuanian Commonwealth between the Russian empire, the Kingdom of Prussia, and Habsburg Austria at the end of the eighteenth century, the

---

[3] Left and right banks of the Dnieper, which runs roughly north–south through present-day Ukraine.

borderland between the three states remained peaceful until the outbreak of World War I in 1914 (Prusin 2010).

In the Austro-Hungarian Empire, the crown lands of Galicia and Bukovyna were home to a sizable Ukrainian population; Transcarpathia was in the Hungarian-administered part of the empire as of 1867. These territories were characterized by substantial ethnic, religious, and linguistic diversity. In 1910, the Ukrainian share of the population was 64 percent in eastern Galicia, 56.3 percent in Transcarpathia and 37.1 percent in Northern Bukovyna (Prusin 2010, 15). In the Russian empire, an administrative-territorial organization comprising three levels (*gubernia*, *povit*, and *volost*) was introduced at the end of the eighteenth century. There was a majority Ukrainian-speaking population in nine gubernias of the Russian empire: Kyivska, Kharkivska, Chernihivska, Poltavska, Volynska, Podilska, Katerynoslavska, Khersonska, and Tavriiska.

Until the early 1900s, the Ukrainian population was overwhelmingly illiterate. Ukrainian political and civil society institutions, language planning, literature, and education emerged and developed at different paces and dynamics in the different states to which the territories with a sizable Ukrainian population belonged. The Ukrainians claimed common ancestry but lacked a common standardized language and other common national institutions. The development of national movements and national awakening took place in the framework of multinational empires that differed in their management of ethnic, linguistic, and religious diversity (Berger and Miller 2014). With the coming of the national awakening era in the nineteenth century Poles and Ukrainians started to develop their national consciousness and national territorial claims, with different hopes and expectations about relations with imperial centers. As a rule, other socio-cultural groups, most importantly Jews, were excluded from these group national imagining processes (Bartov 2018).

During the first half of the twentieth century, the territory of Ukraine became a major theater of geopolitical and local conflict, ethnic cleansing, forced population exchanges, and other types of violence, resulting in immense population losses and migrations (Prusin 2010; Levene 2015). During World War I and the frontier wars of 1918–1920, rule over the contested territories between the Russian, Austro-Hungarian and German empires changed several times; then, after imperial collapse, rule over the territories was contested by a growing number of political entities and groups. Several new states—Poland, Finland, Estonia, Latvia, Lithuania, and the Soviet Union—emerged out of the frontier and civil wars while other short-lived states, including the Ukrainian People's Republic (UNR) and the Western Ukrainian People's Republic (ZUNR), were unable to survive. During the period of the Ukrainian Central Council [*Ukrayinska Tsentralna Rada*], the UNR and the Ukrainian State (under the leadership of Hetman Pavlo Skoropadskyi in 1918), new proposals for the administrative–territorial organization and delineation of a Ukrainian "ethnic" territory were debated, but were never fully implemented. The UNR guaranteed broad political and national rights to ethnic minorities, including representation in state governance bodies. During the period of revolution, various Ukrainian authorities initiated the standardization of the Ukrainian language, the establishment of Ukrainian-language education, and other institutions of modern statehood. However, the processes of modernization and the establishment of the core institutions of modern statehood were only completed as part of a Soviet nation-building project. The initial primary motivation of the Soviet nationality policy was to show that the Soviet state was different to the Russian empire dubbed "the prison of the peoples." Soviet rule was established with the promise of self-determination, though it was to be self-determination in the framework of Soviet statehood and governance opposed to forms labeled "bourgeois." In the Soviet Union, various forms of administrative–territorial arrangements, most importantly national homes for "titular nations," were introduced (Martin 2001).

The 1919 Paris Peace Conference did not support the demands of the UNR delegation for the independence of Ukraine. The Polish state came into existence as a result of its military victories and with the support of the Entente powers. Poland took eastern Galicia, Vilnius, western Byelorussia, and Volhynia; the incorporation of these territories into Poland was confirmed in the Polish–Soviet Treaty of Riga in 1921. Romania, which had been on the Entente side, gained Bessarabia and Bukovyna, and Czechoslovakia seized Transcarpathia, thanks in large part to the lobbying of Rusyn groups in the United States. International minorities' treaties were devised to deal with the issue of the substantial number of minorities who found themselves in the young states of the interwar period. The administrative borders between the Ukrainian Soviet Socialist Republic (SSR) and the Russian Soviet Federative Socialist Republic (SFSR) were established in the 1920s, though they were adjusted several times during the early Soviet period (Yefimenko 2016).

In 1922–1923, a new three-level administrative system consisting of *okruhs*, *rayons*, and villages was adopted by the Ukrainian SSR, and 102 *povity* and 1989 *volosti* were transformed into 53 okrhuhs and 706 rayons. The number of village councils was decreased through a process of amalgamation. In 1930–1932, a two-level system was introduced, which was replaced again in 1932 by a three-level system of oblasts, rayons and village councils. In 1932, Kharkiv, Kyiv, Vinnytsia, Dnipropetrovsk, Odesa, Donetsk, and Chernihiv oblasts were created; in 1937, Zhytomyr, Mykolayiv, Poltava, and Kamyanets-Podilsk (renamed Khmelnytsk oblast in 1954); and in 1939, Zaporizhzhya, Kirovohrad and Sumy oblasts. In 1938, Donetsk oblast was divided into Stalinska (renamed Donetsk oblast in 1961) and Voroshylovhradska (renamed Luhansk in 1961) (Bazhan et al. 1965, 639–640).

During and immediately after World War II, Transcarpathia was annexed by Hungary, then again by Czechoslovakia before being integrated into the Ukrainian SSR. Northern Bukovyna was annexed to the Ukrainian SSR in 1939. During the war, Romania reoccupied Bukovyna and parts of Odeska, Mykolayivska, and Vinnytska oblasts. During the Nazi occupation, 1.43 million Jews were annihilated on the territory of Ukraine (Altman 2002, 303), and a number of conflicts involving underground groups (the Ukrainian nationalist underground, the Polish underground (AK), Jewish groups, Soviet partisans, and other armed groups) erupted in the contested territories in eastern Galicia and Volhynia (Prusin 2010). These regions became the site of mass ethnic cleansing. The conflicts in the western borderlands between the nationalist underground and the Soviet military and security forces continued for a few years after the end of the World War II, even while the final territorial and forced population-exchange settlements in Eastern Europe were being arranged between the allied powers at the end of World War II.

After the annexation of western Ukraine, Northern Bukovyna and parts of Bessarabia, Volynska, Drohobytska, Lvivska, Rovenska, Stanislavska, Ternopilska, Izmailska and Chernivetska oblasts were created in 1939–1940. Between 1924 and 1940, the Moldavian Autonomous Soviet Republic was included in the administrative system of the Ukrainian SSR. Khersonska oblast was created in 1944, Zakarpatska in 1946, and Cherkaska in 1954. In 1954, responsibility for Krymska oblast (which had the status of an autonomous soviet republic from 1922 to 1945) was transferred to the Ukrainian SSR from the Russian SFSR. Finally, Izmailska oblast was united with Odeska oblast, and Drohobytska with Lvivska oblast in 1959–1963 and a substantial amalgamation at the rayon level took place at the same time (Bazhan et al. 1965, 639–640). This administrative–territorial system was inherited by independent Ukraine.

So, as can be seen, the different parts of the current territory of Ukraine changed hands many times in the twentieth century. Multiple layers of the historical past provide a rich symbolic capital for national and regional actors to draw upon for the construction of regional frameworks of meaning; equally, they provide space for multiple contested claims by international, national, and local actors and for the political mobilization of regional cleavages in terms of historical memories and identifications.

II. Regional Cleavages and Differences

One of the divisions that has recurred in discussions of regionalism in Ukraine has been the split generated by centuries of "western (Polish-Lithuanian and Austro-Hungarian) and eastern (Russian) influences" (Lewicka and Iwańczak 2019, 25), reflected most importantly in regional differences in attitudes toward Russia and the Russian language, nationalism, and the independence of Ukraine. With his publications "One Nation, Two Languages, Three Cultures" in 1999 and *Two Ukraines* in 2003, Mykola Riabchuk (1999, 2003) initiated a protracted debate about the macro-level division of Ukraine into a pro-Western, democratic west and center, and a pro-communist, pro-Russian south and east. He further developed his theses in 2015:

> the main—and indeed the only important—divide is not between ethnic Russians and Ukrainians, or Russophones and Ukrainophones, or the "East" and the "West." The main fault line is ideological—between two different types of Ukrainian identity: non/anti-Soviet and post/neo-Soviet, "European" and "East Slavonic." All other factors, such as ethnicity, language, region, income, education, or age, correlate to a different degree with the main one. (Riabchuk 2015, 138)

Other studies draw a dividing line between the regions with developed national identity and regions characterized by non-national forms of attachment—fluid, ambiguous, and mixed identifications. For example, Shulman (2004) sees the dominance of two identifications: ethnic Ukrainian in the west of Ukraine and Slavic in the east. Some studies explained the split in the attitude to Ukrainian independence reflected in differences in regional electoral behavior by reference to historical legacies of belonging to different states. Katchanovski (2006) examined persistent regional political cleavages in Ukraine between 1991 and 2006. He found that regions that had been under the Austro-Hungarian, Polish, Romanian, and Czechoslovak rule generally voted for political parties that supported the independence of Ukraine, whereas many in eastern regions supported pro-communist and pro-Russian parties in favor of the preservation of the Soviet Union.

Some studies focused on defining a configuration of the regions and their number by integrating a variety of factors. Birch (2000) uses historical experiences combined with economic development to propose a division of Ukraine into five regions—the former Habsburg regions, western Volhynia, the right bank of the Dnieper, the left bank of the Dnieper, and the former Ottoman lands of the Black Sea littoral. Birch (2000, 1017) holds that "careful analyses of individual-level data reveal that even when socio-demographic attributes are controlled for, region still exerts an independent influence." Barrington and Herron (2004) divide Ukraine into eight regions, identifying such factors as historical legacy (having belonged to different states), industrialization, urbanization, demographics, a national profile, and language use as important factors in the constitution of regions. Like Birch (2000), they underline the importance of historical experience rather than personal attributes such as language, nationality, religion, or education in explaining differences in regions' attitudes. Other scholars have refined the configuration of regions, arguing that there are further sub-divisions in the Barrington and Herron eight-region model. Rogers (2007) and Hrytsak (2019) show differences between regions in the southeast, and between Luhansk, on the one hand, and Kharkiv and Sumy oblasts, on the other, that mainly consist in the different levels of support for Ukrainianization policies. Rogers (2007) also highlights differentiations within the western Ukrainian region, where eastern Galicia stands out in stark contrast to its neighbors. Riabchuk's stance has been criticized for the simplification of complex and overlapping regional divisions and for taking a normative approach to the definition of regions based on stages of national development (Hrytsak et al. 2007; Rogers 2007; Hrytsak 2019; Schmid and Myshlovska 2019).

Since the early 1990s, the central government in Kyiv has faced several cases of claim-making from regions and groups demanding additional fiscal, political, or cultural autonomy or protection of linguistic–cultural rights in comparison with other territorial units. The most prominent cases have been Donbas, Crimea, Transcarpathia, and Bukovyna. What these regions have in common is the diversity in their ethnic composition. According to the national census of 2001, ethnic Ukrainians constituted a majority in all oblasts of Ukraine except for the Autonomous Republic of Crimea (ARC) and the city of Sevastopol. Russians constituted a majority in the ARC (58.3 percent) and in all of its urban centers, and in Sevastopol (71.7 percent). At the rayon and city levels, ethnic Russians were a slight majority in smaller towns, such as Ternivka of Dnipropetrovsk oblast (52.9 percent), Makiyivka of Donetsk oblast (50.8 percent), Krasnodon (63.3 percent), Stakhanov (50.1 percent), Krasnodonskyi rayon (51.7 percent) and Stanychno-Luhanskyi rayon (61.1 percent) of Luhansk oblast, and in Putyvlskyi rayon of Sumy oblast (51.6 percent). Hungarians comprised a majority in Berehovo rayon of Zakarpatska oblast (76.1 percent), Bulgarians in Bolhradskyi rayon of Odesa oblast (60.8 percent), Romanians in Vyzhnytskyi rayon of Chernivtsi oblast (91.5 percent), and Moldovans in Novoselytskyi rayon of Chernivtsi oblast (57.5 percent) (all data from Dnistryanskyi 2006).

The most multicultural regions with several important national groups were Crimea (58.3 percent Russians, 24.3 percent Ukrainians, and 12 percent Crimean Tatars), Transcarpathia (80.5 percent Ukrainians, 12.1 percent ethnic Hungarians, 2.6 percent Romanians, and 2.5 percent Russians), Odesa oblast (62.8 percent Ukrainians, 20.7 percent Russians, 6.1 percent Bulgarians, and 5 percent Moldovans) and Chernivtsi oblast (75 percent Ukrainians, 12.5 percent Romanians, 7.3 percent Moldovans, and 4.1 percent Russians). At the rayon level, Prymorskyi rayon of Zaporizhzhia oblast consisted of 52.5 percent Ukrainians, 23.4 percent Bulgarians, and 22.2 percent Russians. The two binational regions were Donetsk (56.9 percent Ukrainians and 38.2 percent Russians) and Luhansk (58 percent Ukrainians and 39 percent Russians) oblasts (all data from Dnistryanskyi 2006).

This section will proceed with a review of the studies on the particulars and dynamics of identifications, attitudes, and historical memories in Galicia, Donbas, and Crimea, and Section 3 will focus on the processes of claim-making and accommodation of claims in the regions of Transcarpathia, Crimea, and Donbas. Kruglashov (2010–2011) explores the particularities of regional identifications and loyalties in the region of Bukovyna and Zhurzhenko (2004a, b) of Sloboshchanshyna; however, these cases are not studied in the present chapter.

With western and eastern Ukrainian regions seen as opposite poles in regional differentiation, there have been a number of comparative studies of identities and identifications in these regions (Tatur 2004; Hrytsak et al. 2007). Surveys of a hierarchy of identities was conducted by a group of scholars in Lviv and Donetsk in 1994, 1999 and 2004 (Hrytsak et al. 2007). The surveys proposed 28 identification targets. Both Lviv and Donetsk showed stability in the top identifications. National identification was dominant in Lviv and selected as top identity by 73.1 percent in 1994, 74.8 percent in 1999, and 72.1 percent in 2004. It was closely followed by regional Lvivite identification. Regional identification was dominant in Donetsk: 55.6 percent selected it as a dominant identification in 1994, 56.4 percent in 1999 and 68.4 percent in 2004 (Hrytsak 2007, 49–50). At the same time, while the hierarchy of identification targets was stable in Lviv (the top five being Ukrainian, Lvivite, woman, Greek Orthodox, and Zakhidniyak (chka)), there were substantial changes in the hierarchy of identifications beyond the top two (regional and woman) in Donetsk. A prominent dynamic in Donetsk was the decreasing salience of the Soviet (from 40.1 percent to 9.9 percent) and the slight increase in the importance of Ukrainian (from 39.4 percent to 42.7 percent) identification between 1994 and 2004.

Another region that has stood out in terms of regional identity has been Crimea. Sasse (2002, 23, fn 4) cites a survey undertaken in Crimea and published in a local newspaper in January 1996 that showed that 32 percent identified the USSR as their homeland, 28 percent Crimea, 16 percent Russia and only 11 percent Ukraine. Charron (2016) analyzed identities and political preferences of the Crimean population on the basis of a survey he conducted in Crimea in 2011. His research shows that living in Crimea was the strongest territorial factor of identity among all groups (69.9 percent) (Russians, Ukrainians, Crimean Tatars, and others), and it was the highest for the Crimean Tatars. In comparison, living in Ukraine was supported by 33.1 percent of respondents. The three cultural aspects of identity (nationality, native language, and religious beliefs) are also salient. In terms of defining their homeland [*rodina*], Charron concludes (2016, 246) that "Crimeans by and large did not equate homeland with either Russia or Ukraine, but rather with Crimea itself." A sense of belonging to Ukraine was higher than belonging to Russia or the Soviet Union. Only 1.6 percent of ethnic Russians and less than 1 percent of other groups indicated Russia as their homeland, and only 8.3 percent of Russians, 3.8 percent of Ukrainians, 3.1 percent of Crimean Tatars and 4.1 percent of Other considered the Soviet Union as their homeland (Charron 2016, 250).

Furthermore, some studies explored strength, complexity (number of identification targets), and internal consistency of identifications using both territorial and non-territorial identification targets (Lewicka and Iwańczak 2019). Analyzing the results of a survey undertaken in 2013, Lewicka and Iwańczak (2019) established that there are regional differences not only in the content of identifications but also in their strength. Place and national identifications were significantly weaker in the east, particularly in the Donbas region, than in western regions. Eastern regions were characterized by having overall the weakest emotional attitudes toward places of living (cities and regions), weaker overall local identity, and more neutral responses to all national issues. Lewicka and Iwańczak (2019) also find that Galicia and central Ukraine is the most homogenous region in Ukraine and has the strongest identity profile focused on Ukrainian identification.

Following the Russian annexation of Crimea and the beginning of a conflict in eastern Ukraine in early 2014, debates about the role of regional cleavages in Ukraine have taken on a new prominence. Many new surveys have been commissioned to understand the dynamics of identifications and attitudes, especially in eastern Ukraine and in the non-government controlled areas of Donbas (examples include Tsentr Razumkova 2016; Haran and Yakovlyev 2017; Arel 2018; Kulyk 2018, 2019; Onuch et al. 2018; and Sasse and Lackner 2018). Surveys undertaken by the Institute of Sociology of the National Academy of Sciences of Ukraine in 2013, 2014, 2015 and 2017 in the Donbas region (Zolkina 2017)[4] reflected the same general trends—the prominence of both local and national identifications as the most important in the region and the changing nature of identifications. However, these surveys were carried out using a somewhat different methodology than the Lviv–Donetsk study. They measured one ("first and foremost") identification, divided a sub-national identification into an identification with a locality where a respondent lived and a region, and finally added an identification as a citizen of Ukraine (instead of the ambiguous category "Ukrainian" as in the Lviv–Donetsk study). Surveys showed that in 2013, local and regional identity (together 43.4 percent) was of almost the same prominence as citizen of Ukraine identity (41.7 percent) in Luhansk and Donetsk oblasts. The identification as a citizen of Ukraine reached the lowest level in 2014 (34.3 percent) with a concomitant increase in identification as citizens of the former Soviet Union and citizens of the world; the proportions of local and regional identifications were stable, however, with substantial fluctuations between the local and

---

[4] The 2014, 2015 and 2017 surveys covered only the government-controlled areas.

regional levels. After the increase in 2014, identification as a citizen of the former Soviet Union fell sharply, from 13.9 percent to 5.4 percent in 2015 (Zolkina 2017, 160). Regional surveys carried out by the Democratic Initiatives Foundation (DIF) and the Ukrainian Sociology Service in 2015 and 2017 showed important differences between Donetsk and Luhansk oblasts, with identification as a citizen of Ukraine being more pronounced in the latter than in the former (Zolkina 2017, 162).

Furthermore, surveys have also shown regional differences in terms of attitudes to Ukrainian independence, a vision of the administrative–territorial structure of Ukraine, and the political status of regions. Western Ukraine has differed not only in the stability of its hierarchy of identities (Hrytsak et al. 2007), but also in its support for independence in a hypothetical referendum (between 93 percent and 96 percent in 1991, 2006, 2011 and 2016) (Bekeshkina 2017, 11). According to the DIF surveys, the proportion of those who would vote against the act of independence increased from 11.3 percent in 1991 to 29.8 percent in 2006 and 32.9 percent in 2011. The highest proportion of those who would vote against was in the south (including the ARC) and the east—42.8 percent and 51 percent in 2006 respectively and 52.9 percent and 47 percent in 2011. Support for independence in these regions dramatically increased in 2016 (Bekeshkina 2017, 11).

Both Donbas and Crimea stood out in the way respondents saw the administrative–territorial structure of Ukraine and the political future of the regions. Support for federalization of Ukraine was the highest in the two regions. In 1991, 67 percent of the population in Luhansk and Donetsk oblasts were in favor of a unitary centralized state with all power based in the center and 29 percent were in favor of a federal Ukraine with autonomous regions (Adamovych 2006, 39). The survey conducted by Charron (2016, 254) showed that, in 2011, 45.5 percent of the population of Crimea preferred joining Russia, 39.1 percent preferred remaining in Ukraine regardless of whether or not Crimea was autonomous, and 15.4 percent preferred independence or some other status. According to a sociological survey carried out by the Kyiv International Institute of Sociology (KIIS) in eight oblasts of southern and eastern Ukraine between 10 and 15 April 2014, 15.4 percent of the population in the regions supported separation from Ukraine and unification with Russia, 24.8 percent a federal state system and 45.2 percent a unitary decentralized state. The highest support for separation from Ukraine and unification with Russia and for federalization among the eight oblasts surveyed was in Luhansk oblast (30.3 percent and 41.9 percent respectively) and in Donetsk oblast

2 REGIONALISM IN UKRAINE: HISTORIC EVOLUTION, REGIONAL... 31

(27.5 percent and 38.4 percent respectively). Support for a unitary decentralized state was 34.2 percent in Luhansk oblast and 41.1 percent in Donetsk oblast, while support for a state with its current rights intact stood at 12.4 percent for Luhansk oblast and 10.6 percent for Donetsk oblast (KIIS 2014).

The attitude of the population of Donbas dramatically changed between two nationwide surveys conducted by the DIF in January and July 2015. The federalization option dropped from 30.4 percent to 12 percent, creation of an independent state from 19.8 percent to 0 percent and separation from Ukraine and joining another state from 14.8 percent to 4.8 percent. There was an increase in support for a unitary Ukraine with existing rights from 2.5 percent to 22.9 percent and a unitary state with expanded rights from 26.9 percent to 44 percent (Bekeshkina 2017, 26). According to a survey carried out by the Razumkov Center, in 2016, only 5 percent in Luhansk oblast and 8 percent in Donetsk oblast supported separation from Ukraine and joining another state, and 8 percent in Luhansk oblast and 15 percent in Donetsk oblast supported an autonomous status in a federalized Ukraine. At the same time, the share of those supporting a unitary state with expanded rights increased to 49 percent in Donetsk and 57 percent in Luhansk oblasts (Tsentr Razumkova 2016, 65).

In comparison to other oblasts of the northeast, Donetsk and Luhansk oblasts stood out in their attitudes to the protests of 2013–2014, the change of government in 2014, and on the nature of the armed conflict in the east (KIIS 2014). According to the KIIS survey of April 2014, 70.5 percent in Donetsk oblast and 61.3 percent in Luhansk oblast considered the Euromaidan as a coup d'état organized by the opposition with support from the west (KIIS 2014).[5] The two oblasts also had the highest share of those who considered the new authorities that came to power following the Euromaidan to be illegitimate. The 2015 Region, Nation and Beyond survey showed that the regional divisions over the Euromaidan persisted, with 71.5 percent supporting the Euromaidan in the west and only 8.4 percent supporting it in the government-controlled part of Donetsk oblast (Chebotarova 2019, 418–419). Furthermore, Ukrainian society seemed divided about the nature of the conflict. In December 2015, 49.3 percent considered that it was a war of aggression against Ukraine (75.2 percent in the west and 23.6 percent in Donbas), 20.2 percent a civil conflict between pro-Ukrainian and pro-Russian residents of Ukraine (6.4 percent in the west and 24.6 percent in Donbas), and

---

[5] Euromaidan—see Chap. 1, fn 1.

15.2 percent a conflict between Russia and the United States for spheres of influence (8.8 percent in the west and 31.8 percent in Donbas) (Tsentr Razumkova 2016, 50).

The Lviv–Donetsk study also initiated research into regional divisions related to historical memories and identities. This study was further developed in the Nation, Region and Beyond surveys conducted in 2013, 2015 and 2017. In her study of historical identities and memories of Lviv and Donetsk residents through surveys in 1994, 1999 and 2004, and incorporating a review of local press, a Ukrainian sociologist, Viktoria Sereda (2007), found substantial differences between Lviv and Donetsk in their celebration of holidays and in their identifications of the most important historical periods, figures, and events. The 2013 Nation, Region and Beyond survey reconfirmed the main findings of the previous study on historical memories: Soviet-period holidays (Defenders of the Motherland Day, Women's Day, and Victory Day) were much more rooted in popular practices than the holidays instituted after Ukraine became an independent state; however, Ukrainian holidays were gradually gaining in importance. Ukrainian holidays were mostly celebrated in Galicia, Volhynia, and central Ukraine, while Soviet holidays dominated all over Ukraine except for Galicia. Stepan Bandera and Lenin were the most regionally divisive historical figures, while the wartime and postwar activities of OUN and UPA, Holodomor, and World War II were the most polarizing historical events (Survey 2013).

The studies discussed above provide a view of regional differences of identifications, attitudes and historical memories. Quantitative studies based on censuses and survey data are complemented by qualitative studies using methodologies such as historical contextualization and oral histories that allow to understand the historical constitution of identities, attitudes, and memories and their meaning. For example, Šabić (2004, 140) explains the prominence of ethnic nationalism in eastern Galicia by the destruction of the pre-war Polish, Jewish, and Ukrainian elites and their replacement by "a peasant one socialized and educated in the Soviet system." Based on semi-structured interviews, Tatur (2004, 380) describes Donbas as a region "without history" due to symbolic poverty resulting from a history in which industrialization amid the steppe occupies a central place. Respondents "expressed strong feelings of belonging … directed towards the place, the community, the here and now without reference to a narrative of 'historic identity'." Local elites described the region as an "old industrial region" that prides itself in physical work and technical competence, and referred to a region's "borderland position, openness, multi-ethnic composition and tolerance as an industrial melting pot of people" (Tatur 2004, 380). Another important characteristic noted by the authors is the lack of civil social capital due to the dependence of workers on large companies that dominate the region and their patrons. Similarly, for Kuromiya (1998, 2016), the Donbas region, colonized late, sparsely populated and "dyke pole"[6] located at the periphery of the main centers of power, always provided a refuge for freedom-seekers defying all authorities. According to Kuromiya (1998, 2016), the region was a perpetual headache for all regimes, including the Soviet. With a high turnover of workforce from different parts of the Soviet Union, Donbas became the melting pot of cultures, with its own industry-related social imaginary.

The above longitudinal analysis of various dimensions of regionalism in Ukraine enables us to define several obstinate tendencies. Regional and local attachments have persistently been selected over national-level attachments in Crimea and Donbas. Another feature of regionalism has been the stability of identities, loyalties, and beliefs in western Ukraine in contrast to their fluctuations in the rest of Ukraine. The overall weaker identification profiles outwith western Ukraine identified in the study by Lewicka and Iwańczak (2019) help explain these considerable fluctuations. The above analysis also seems to establish that while there has been an increasing identification with Ukrainian citizenship and support for decentralization, important regional differences persist in terms of historical memories, and attitudes to the Euromaidan and the nature of the ongoing conflict. Also, one has to consider that the pervasive use of propaganda by Russia (Kyiv International Institute of Sociology and Detector Media 2017) and the manipulation of identifications, views, and attitudes by local elites have become a factor in regionalist politics.

III. Contentious Center–Periphery and Regional Politics, and the Accommodation of Claims

This section studies the claims that have been advanced in the regions or on behalf of the regions with regional particularities studied in Section 2, namely Transcarpathia, Crimea, and Donbas. It also investigates the role of the political system, institutions, and center–periphery relations in accommodating

---

[6] "Dyke pole"—romanized version of the Ukrainian for "Wild Fields," a historical term used in Polish–Lithuanian documents of the sixteenth to eighteenth centuries.

the claims. Sasse (2002, 1) asserts that one of the main drivers of conflict in the post-Soviet space is the centralization of power and institutional rigidity, "both of which are not conducive to the flexible management of ethnic and regional diversity." Until the launch of decentralization in 2014, Ukraine was a highly centralized state with few competences at the local level. Almost all taxes collected at the local level were transmitted to the regional and national levels and then redistributed back from the center to regions that in their turn distributed to the local level. The distribution of funds from the state budget to a sub-national level was non-transparent and served as a way of rewarding the loyalty of regional elites. Resources were redistributed from more-developed to less-developed oblasts through a centralized system that promoted corruption, neo-patrimonial relations and reinforced inter-regional tensions, biases, and grievances. Furthermore, there was no efficient mechanism of oversight of the legality of decisions at the local level or rectification of violations of national legislation. Regions also had different levels of economic diversification and export orientation, with eastern Ukraine's subsidized heavy industry primarily oriented toward the Russian market, a factor that created many fears at the local level about the implications for the local economy of the proposed Association Agreement with the EU (Giuliano 2018).

Furthermore, as there were no established and transparent rules concerning the distribution of budgetary funds, leading to a proliferation of patron–client relations between the center and lower levels of governance, a change of the government at the national level, and hence of ruling clans, provoked uncertainty and fears about the inflow of budgetary resources. Stroschein (2012, 202) argues that "the uncertainty that reigns during periods of severe institutional change is particularly ripe for tension and mobilization, as groups fear that even the smallest gains by their opponents might grant them wide-ranging and permanent advantages." The periods of transition and turmoil such as perestroika and the dissolution of the Soviet Union, the miners' strikes of the early 1990s, "Ukraine without Kuchma" protests, the Orange Revolution, and the Euromaidan became periods of uncertainty, resulting in claim-making and renegotiation of power-sharing and institutional arrangements.

The period of perestroika and glasnost in the 1980s opened opportunities for multiple public claim-making processes. One level of contention was between the republic (Kyiv) and central (Moscow) levels of governance. Claims advanced by dissidents and human rights movements that emerged in Soviet Ukraine following the de-Stalinization period in the mid-1950s about the violation of civic, national, and linguistic rights of groups in the Soviet Union, the rectification of past injustices, and the need to provide more autonomy and "real" rights to the Soviet republics resulted in the adoption of legislation at the republic level on languages and the rehabilitation of victims of political repressions, as well as the preparation of a more democratic version of the Union Treaty. In 1988, the Secretary General of the union Communist Party, Mikhail Gorbachev, initiated a partial transfer of responsibilities from party organs to the soviets (councils) in the framework of a future constitutional reform. A series of laws adopted by the Verkhovna Rada of the Ukrainian SSR on military service on the territory of the Ukrainian SSR and economic sovereignty, accompanied by a declaration of sovereignty, laid the ground for the proclamation of independence in 1991. The overall peaceful dissolution of the Soviet Union (with the exception of Transnistria and the Caucasus) has been largely attributed to the lack of revisionist intentions from neighboring countries such as Poland and Germany and a decision by the Soviet and then Russian leadership not to use force against national movements in the Soviet republics (Prusin 2010).

In western Ukraine, the vote for independence in 1991 was seen as a culmination of the struggle of the Ukrainian people for independence, while in the rest of Ukraine, especially in the east and in Crimea, the predominant motivation was an economic one. In the latter two regions, it was believed that national sovereignty would mean that taxes would be kept in the republic to improve the economic situation and wellbeing of the population. Striking Donbas miners concluded a situation alliance with the Ukrainian anti-communist and pro-independence intelligentsia in supporting the independence of Ukraine in 1991 (Mykhnenko 2003). The period from the late 1980s to the early 1990s was the only period when the local elites lost control of the workers' protests in Donbas (Kovaleva 2007, 66). The economic collapse in the early 1990s, meant the central government started to lose hope and trust related to national independence.

In the early 1990s, central government faced cases of claim-making in several regions. In Transcarpathia, a referendum on seeking to become an "autonomous status within independent Ukraine" was held at the same time as the referendum for independence; it was approved by 78 percent of voters. Another vote was held in Berehove rayon, which has a majority Hungarian population, on setting up a Hungarian autonomous district within Transcarpathia; that proposition was approved by 81.4 percent of voters (Stroschein 2012, 194). The autonomy of Transcarpathia was envisioned as multi-ethnic in character, justified by the historic uniqueness of the region, while that of the Berehove rayon was envisioned as an ethnic one (Stroschein 2012, 195). Claims for regional sovereignty were also advanced by the Society of Carpathian Ruthenians. These votes were all preceded by mobilization of different ethnic groups and debates in local councils where compromises and decisions, seen as outcomes of a legitimate process, were achieved. After the initial demands for local autonomy had been rejected by the central government, the region of Transcarpathia settled on a compromise solution of a free economic zone (Stroschein 2012). Finally, Stroschein (2012, 231) highlights the role of the devolution of power and elections in the moderation of demands: "The codification of local government structures in the form of Law #64 of 1994, and the holding of elections that year, alleviated contention and claims over autonomy for the region."

Mobilization around Crimean autonomy and separatism also started in the early 1990s. A referendum on the establishment of the Crimean ASSR within the USSR was held on 20 January 1991, and was supported by 93.26 percent of votes. Before the proclamation of Ukrainian independence, agreement was reached to retain Crimea's autonomous status within the Ukrainian SSR (Sasse 2002, 14). A Russian national and separatist movement spearheaded a vote by the local Supreme Soviet for the independence of Crimea in 1992 and passed a Crimean Constitution. Internal disagreements within the movement and failure to deliver stability and economic growth opened opportunities for a dialogue with Kyiv. Sasse (2002) regards the asymmetric autonomy arrangement, albeit constitutionally ambiguous and weakly implemented, that was achieved in Ukraine in the 1990s through a lengthy process of political negotiation as a factor in preventing conflict until 2014. Her core argument is that "the political *process* of negotiation and central and regional elite bargaining rather than the institutional *outcome* per se was important for conflict prevention" (emphasis in original). Among factors that contributed to the prevention of conflict Sasse (2002) gives particular weight to weak ethnopolitical mobilization and polarization due to regional diversity, Kyiv's readiness for compromise on language and ethnicity issues, and the cautious approach of Russia and Turkey in their dealings with their ethnic kin groups. At the same time, while the autonomy solution helped to regulate center–periphery relations, it did not accommodate claim-making by non-dominant groups in Crimea such as Crimean Tatars, Ukrainians, and other minorities.

History and symbolic politics have been an important part of claim-making by different groups (Plokhy 2000). Charron (2016) describes the historical mythologies and narratives that were mobilized by Russia and Ukraine in constructing their claims to Crimea. For instance, the Russian claim to Crimea was justified by the importance of the region for the adoption of Christianity following the baptism of Prince Volodymyr of Kyivan Rus in 988, by the Sevastopol myth as a city of Russian military glory, a legend that arose in the aftermath of the Crimean War of 1853–1856, the battles of the Great Patriotic War, and nostalgia for the Soviet past (Charron 2016). The deportations of Crimean Tatars in 1944 to Central Asia and Siberia became a central event in their memory and national identity as well as a concrete illustration of Crimea as their home and.

In Donbas, the local elites took advantage of the growing popular dissatisfaction with the economic failings and the Ukrainization policies of central government in the early 1990s. The national and local elections in the 1990s saw the return of a party nomenclatura and Soviet regional economic leaders (Zimmer 2004). Another wave of miners' strikes started in the 1990s in support of regional autonomy for Donbas, calling for the right of local law-making, policing, budgeting, economic activity, and cultural autonomy, and the resignation of the president and central government (Mykhnenko 2003; Adamovych 2006, 35–38). Donetsk oblast held a local referendum together with the parliamentary elections in March 1994, 80 percent voted for a federal Ukraine, 87 percent voted for Russian to be given the status of the second state language, 89 percent agreed with the proposition that Russian should be a language of education, science, and administration in Donetsk oblast, and 89 percent that Ukraine should become a full member of the CIS Economic Union and Parliamentary Assembly (Kovaleva 2007, 68).

While local councils in Transcarpathia became the platforms for claim-making, debate and consensus-seeking between different ethnic groups and organizations representing them, in Donbas regional elites co-opted the workers' movement, which failed to become inclusive and build connections with other civil society organizations (Mykhnenko 2003; Kovaleva 2007). Local elites established control over local government, media, and civil society at the regional level with little contention at the sub-regional level (Zimmer 2004; Adamovych 2006). Zimmer (2007, 100) calls the regional regime that was established a "captured region" and argues that "the capture includes not only the control of the political arena and the economic realm, but also the determination and imposition of public discourse by that regional elite." The main line of contention was between the center and regional elites. The conflict between Kyiv and Donbas was resolved by partial power-sharing at the national level when local political and economic leaders, for example, Yuhym Zvyahilskyi and Viktor Yanukovych, were offered positions in the center. Furthermore, the regional elites were awarded other privileges by the center such as subsidies for the region's mining industry and heavy industry, and the status of a special economic zone blessed with a favorable tax regime and exemption from import duties (Kovaleva 2007).

In terms of history and symbolic politics, the main line of contestation was not between different local mnemonic communities, as in Crimea, but rather between Kyiv and Donbas. Wilson (1995) studied the divergence between national and local history narratives about the region in the early 1990s. Local historians and publicists sustained a regional interpretation of the past that established an indigeneity of the presence of ethnic Russians in the region and ignored or delegitimized claims of Ukrainian historiography to the presence of Ukrainians or proto-Ukrainians and Ukrainian state structures in the region. Wilson (1995) claims that the development of such alternative historical mythologies has been one of the underlying causes of claims of separatism and autonomy in the region: "Russophile historiography … has created the ideological basis for a movement for regional autonomy or even separatism in the Donbas. The key point in Russophile historiography is that Russians are not 'immigrants' in the Donbas, but a 'rooted [or indigenous] people'." Identities and symbolic politics are dynamic and influenced by the changing international, national, regional and local circumstances. Zimmer (2004, 320–321) holds that difficulties in competing in international markets and failure to attract foreign investment by industries in Donbas led to local industries' increasing self-reliance and dependence on eastern, above all Russian, markets, which in turn led to changes in discourse and symbolic politics.

Another round of regional mobilization and contention started in 2004. Following the second round of presidential elections on 21 November 2004 and the beginning of the Maidan protests, the Luhansk Oblast Council declared a creation of the Autonomous South-Eastern Ukrainian Republic on the territory of nine oblasts of eastern and southern Ukraine, and the ARC with a capital in Kharkiv, sent a request to the Russian Federation to officially recognize the republic. Calls for separation from Ukraine were articulated at the rallies organized by the local authorities in eastern Ukraine in support of Viktor Yanukovych in 2004

(Adamovych 2006, 93). After the parliament of Ukraine annulled the results of the second round of the presidential elections, an All-Ukrainian Assembly of members of the parliament and members of local councils took place on 28 November 2004 in Severodonetsk (in Luhansk oblast), recognizing the legitimacy of the election of Viktor Yanukovych as a president and claiming the right to organize a referendum on the status of territories in response to what it claimed was an unconstitutional seizure of power. Russia remained cautious during the 2004 events. While it officially endorsed Yanukovych, as a presidential candidate, and sent a representative to the Severedonetsk assembly, it refrained from openly supporting separatist movements in eastern and southern Ukraine. Decisions to grant Russian the status of the regional language were taken by Donetsk, Luhansk, and some other local authorities in eastern and southern Ukraine during Yushchenko's presidency. The 2004 crisis was defused by a power-sharing agreement between Yushchenko and Yanukovych in 2006.

The contestation took new forms in 2013–2014. By January 2014, the supporters of the Euromaidan had occupied administrative buildings and declared the creation of "people's councils" [*narodna rada*] in many locations in western and central Ukraine. Some local councils in the regions also adopted resolutions in support of the Euromaidan and the European integration of Ukraine, acts which exceeded the responsibilities of local authorities. On 22 February 2014, the day the parliament of Ukraine officially declared for the self-removal of Yanukovych from his responsibilities, the leaders of the Party of Regions, Mykhaylo Dobkin, the governor of the Kharkiv Council, and members of parliament Vadym Kolesnichenko and Oleh Tsarev, called a second assembly of deputies of all levels of the southeastern oblasts, the city of Sevastopol, and the ARC in Kharkiv. The organizers claimed that more than 3,000 participants participated in the assembly. There, Tsarev declared that an armed coup d'état had taken place in Ukraine. The assembly adopted a resolution that stated that in view of the disruption in the constitutional order, the organs of local governance, the Verkhovna Rada of the ARC, and the city council of Sevastopol were to take responsibility for the preservation of constitutional order, respect for law and human rights and the safety of citizens in the territories. In contrast to the events of 2004, a delegation from Russia, including Aleksei Pushkov, the head of the State Duma committee on international relations, participated in the assembly and officially supported the gathering (Mediaport 2014). In an interview he gave to a researcher Anna

Matveeva in 2017, Oleh Tsarev recognized that the expectation was that the role of anti-Maidan protests and the setting up of a Coordination Council of the Southeast in spring 2014 would be similar to the 2004 congress in Severodonesk in opposition to the Maidan protests. However, the regional elites lost control of the events (Matveeva 2017, 81–82). Tsarev also states that the regional elites were afraid of losing their jobs in the event of Maidan's victory (ibid.).

In comparison with the earlier stages of contention, the situation in 2014 became more complex with the opening of new lines in the conflicts. While the internal dimension in center–periphery contestation and inter-regional differences in identifications, attitudes, and memories remained, there was a fragmentation of actors at the regional level, participation of external actors opening new dimensions in the conflict, and loss of control by the regional elites. An important research question that remains is the role of decentralization and democratic governance reforms that began to be implemented by the government that came to power following the Euromaidan on the management of persisting internal cleavages and the claims of regional and local elites.

Ongoing reforms have already addressed one of the underlying structural causes of the conflicts—the non-transparent and corrupt distribution of state funds—by establishing rules for defining the amount of funding for regional development on the basis of a formula and direct budget relations between communities and the state budget. By making the collection of taxes and financial flows from the center more predictable and transparent, decentralization removed, to a degree, the opportunities for national and elites to engage in patron–client dealings. None the less, somes of the funds from the state budget are still distributed in a non-transparent manner. Also, there has been a decrease in support for federalization and an increase in support for decentralization in eastern Ukraine (Fond Demokratizatsiya 2017), which is another factor indicating a potentially positive role of decentralization in conflict resolution and peace-building.

Conclusions

The chapter has shown that regional differences in terms of identity and historical legacies have been used to make a variety of claims, including separatist and autonomy claims, and have been reshaped in the process of center-periphery contention since the late 1980s. Beyond the widely acknowledged role of external intervention in the escalation of conflict in eastern Ukraine in 2014, the chapter has examined the long-term non-violent contention related to regional cleavages prior to the escalation of the conflict and political exclusion. It has shown the differences in the claim-making and accommodation of claims between the three regions studied: Transcarpathia, Crimea, and Donbas. While in the case of Transcarpathia and Crimea, local councils and parliaments and elections played an important role as sites of contestation, deliberation, and consensus-seeking that were recognized as legitimate by all parties, in the case of Donbas, characterized as a "captured region," control of local government, media, and civil society by regional elites prevented similar processes, and center–periphery conflicts were resolved not through the use of institutions but rather through elite pacts. This chapter has examined a variety of means for the accommodation of claims at the regional and local levels such as an asymmetric state structure, power devolution, free economic zones, subsidies and budget disbursements, power-sharing at the national level, and local and regional legislation on historical memory and languages. Because of Ukraine's regional particularities, different forms of accommodation have worked in different regions, which means that decentralization could work differently in different regions. This requires further research.

While the blurred nature of ethnic, linguistic, and regional divisions, and an absence of stable regions in Ukraine, are widely acknowledged (Schmid and Myshlovska 2019), this chapter has identified several important features of regionalism since 2014: a persistence of regional and local attachments in Donbas (in the government-controlled areas); changing attitudes to the independence of Ukraine and to the nature of the administrative–territorial structure beyond western Ukraine; and so important inter-regional differences in terms of historical memories, attitudes to the Euromaidan and the nature of the ongoing conflict.

While the core focus of conflict-resolution efforts has been on the violent conflict in eastern Ukraine, the persisting internal dimensions of the conflict have received less attention. In the last few years there has been an increasing identification with Ukrainian citizenship and support for decentralization, so important regional differences in terms of historical memories, attitudes to the Euromaidan, and the nature of the ongoing conflict remain and may be a source of vulnerability to future regional mobilizations. The effect of the ongoing reforms in decentralization and democratic governance on the resolution of center–periphery conflicts and the accommodation of regional claims remains to be seen.

42   O. MYSHLOVSKA

REFERENCES

Adamovych, Serhiy. 2006. *Donbas u Suspilno-Politychnomu Zhytti Ukrayiny (1991–2005 rr)* [Donbas in the Social and Political Life of Ukraine (1991–2005)]. Ivano-Frankivsk: Horytsvit.

Altman, Ilya. 2002. *Zhertvy Nenavisti. Kholokost v SSSR, 1941–1945 gg.* [Hatred Victims. Holocaust in the USSR, 1941–1945]. Foundation "Kovcheg".

Arel, Dominique. 2018. How Ukraine has Become More Ukrainian. *Post-Soviet Affairs* 34 (2–3): 186–189.

Barrington, Lowell W., and Erik S. Herron. 2004. One Ukraine or Many? Regionalism in Ukraine and Its Political Consequences. *Nationalities Papers* 32 (1): 53–86.

Bartov, Omer. 2018. *Anatomy of a Genocide: The Life and Death of a Town Called Buczacz*. New York: Simon & Schuster.

Bazhan, Mykola, et al. 1965. *Ukrayinska Radyanska Entsyklopediya. Ukrayinska Radyanska Sotsialistychna Respublika*. Kyiv: Akademiya Nauk USSR.

Bekeshkina, Iryna. 2017. Decisive 2014: Did it Divide or Unite Ukraine? In *The Attitudes of Ukrainians during the War in the Donbas*, 1–33. Kyiv: Stylos Publishing.

Berger, Stefan, and Aleksei Miller. 2014. *Nationalizing Empires*. Historical Studies in Eastern Europe and Eurasia 3. Budapest: Central European University Press.

Birch, Sarah. 2000. Interpreting the Regional Effect in Ukrainian Politics. *Europe-Asia Studies* 52 (6): 1017–1041.

Cederman, Lars-Erik, Andreas Wimmer, and Brian Min. 2010. Why Do Ethnic Groups Rebel? New Data and Analysis. *World Politics* 62 (1): 87–119.

Cederman, Lars-Erik, Kristian Skrede Gleditsch, and Halvard Buhaug. 2013. *Inequality, Grievances, and Civil War*. Cambridge: Cambridge University Press.

Charron, Austin. 2016. Whose Is Crimea?: Contested Sovereignty and Regional Identity. *Region: Regional Studies of Russia, Eastern Europe, and Central Asia* 5 (2): 225–256.

Chebotarova, Anna. 2019. Renegotiating Ukrainian Identity at the Euromaidan. In *Regionalism without Regions: Reconceptualizing Ukraine's Heterogeneity*, ed. Ulrich Schmid and Oksana Myshlovska, 393–426. Budapest: Central European University Press.

Detector Media. 2017. Riven Doviry do Ukrayinskykh Telekanaliv Znyzyvsya—Doslidzhennya KMIS na Zamovlennya «Detektora media» [Confidence in Ukrainian TV Channels has Dropped—KIIS Commissioned by 'Detector Media']. February 13, 2017. http://detector.media/info-space/article/123095/2017-02-13-riven-doviri-do-ukrainskikh-tele-kanaliv-znizivsya-doslidzhennya-kmis-na-zamovlennya-detektora-media/.

Dnistryanskyi, Myroslav. 2006. *Etnopolitychna Heohrafiya Ukrayiny* [Ethno-political Geography of Ukraine]. Lviv: Litopys.

2 REGIONALISM IN UKRAINE: HISTORIC EVOLUTION, REGIONAL... 43

Fond Demokratizatsiya. 2017. Hromadska Dumka Naselennya Shchodo Reformy Detsentralizatsiyi [Public Opinion on Decentralization Reform], July 24, 2017. http://dif.org.ua/article/gromadska-dumka-naselennya-shchodo-reformi-detsentralizatsii.

Germann, Micha, and Nicholas Sambanis. (forthcoming). Political Exclusion, Lost Autonomy, and Escalating Conflict Over Self-Determination. *International Organization*.

Giuliano, Elise. 2018. Who Supported Separatism in Donbas?: Ethnicity and Popular Opinion at the Start of the Ukraine Crisis. *Post-Soviet Affairs* 34 (2–3): 158–178.

Haran, Olexiy, and Maksym Yakovlyev, eds. 2017. *Constructing a Political Nation: Changes in the Attitudes of Ukrainians during the War in the Donbas*. Kyiv: Styl.us Publishing.

Hrytsak, Yaroslav. 2007. Istoriya Dvokh Mist: Lviv i Donetsk u Porivnyalniy Perspektyvi [Two Cities History: Lviv and Donetsk in Comparative Perspective]. In *Lviv–Donetsk: Sotsialni Identychnosti v Suchasniy Ukrayini* [Lviv—Donetsk: Social Identities in Contemporary Ukraine] (special issue of *Ukrayina Moderna*), ed. Yaroslav Hrytsak, Andriy Portnov, and Viktor Susak, 27–60. Kyiv and Lviv: Krytyka.

———. 2019. Ukraine in 2013–2014: A New Political Geography. In *Regionalism Without Regions: Reconceptualizing Ukraine's Heterogeneity*, ed. Ulrich Schmid and Oksana Myshlovska, 367–392. Budapest: Central European University Press.

Hrytsak, Yaroslav, Andriy Portnov, and Viktor Susak, eds. 2007. *Lviv—Donetsk: Sotsialnii Identychnosti v Suchasniy Ukrayini* [Lviv—Donetsk: Social Identities in Contemporary Ukraine] (special issue of *Ukrayina Moderna*). Kyiv and Lviv: Krytyka.

Kasianov. Georgii, ed. 2018. *Polityka i Pamiat. Dnipro—Zaporizhzhia—Odesa—Kharkiv vid 1990-kh do Syohodni* [Politics and Memory. Dnipro—Zaporizhzhia—Odesa—Kharkiv from the 1990s Until Today]. Lviv: FOP Shumylovych.

Katchanovski, Ivan. 2006. Regional Political Divisions in Ukraine in 1991–2006. *Nationalities Papers* 34 (5): 507–532.

Keating, Michael. 1998. *The New Regionalism in Western Europe. Territorial Restructuring and Political Change*. Cheltenham: Edward Elgar.

Kovaleva, Elena. 2007. Regional Politics in Ukraine's Transition. In *Re-Constructing the Post-Soviet Industrial Region. The Donbas in Transition*, ed. Adam Swain. London and New York: Routledge.

Kruglashov, Anatoliy. 2010–2011. Bukovyna: A Border Region with a Fluctuating Identity. *Journal of Ukrainian Studies* 35–36: 121–140.

Kubicek, Paul. 2002. Regional Polarisation in Ukraine: Public Opinion, Voting, and Legislative Behaviour. *Europe-Asia Studies* 52 (2): 273–294.

Kudelia, Serhiy. 2014. Domestic Sources of the Donbas Insurgency. *PONARS Eurasia Policy Memo*, 351, September. http://www.ponarseurasia.org/memo/domestic-sources-donbas-insurgency.

———. 2019. How They Joined? Militants and Informers in the Armed Conflict in Donbas. *Small Wars & Insurgencies* 30 (2): 279–306.

Kulyk, Volodymyr. 2011. Language Identity, Linguistic Diversity and Political Cleavages: Evidence from Ukraine. *Nations and Nationalism* 17 (3): 627–648.

———. 2018. Shedding Russianness, Recasting Ukrainianness: The Post-Euromaidan Dynamics of Ethnonational Identifications in Ukraine. *Post-Soviet Affairs* 34 (2–3): 119–138.

———. 2019. Identity in Transformation: Russian-Speakers in Post-Soviet Ukraine. *Europe-Asia Studies* 71 (1): 156–178.

Kuromiya, Hiroaki. 1998. *Freedom and Terror in the Donbas—A Ukrainian-Russian Borderland, 1870s–1990s*. Cambridge: Cambridge University Press.

———. 2016. *Zrozumity Donbas [Understand Donbass]*. Kyiv: Dukhi Litera.

Kuzio, Taras. 2017. *Putin's War Against Ukraine: Revolution, Nationalism, Crime*. Toronto: CreateSpace.

KIIS (Kyiv International Institute of Sociology). 2014. Dumky ta Pohlyady Zhyteliv Pivnichno-Skhidnykh Oblastei Ukrayiny [Opinions and Attitudes of the Residents of the South-East of Ukraine]. April 2014. http://kiis.com.ua/?lang=rus&cat=reports&id=302&page=1.

Kyiv International Institute of Sociology and Detector Media. 2017. Russian Propaganda Influence on Public Opinion in Ukraine. February 13, 2017. http://osvita.mediasapiens.ua/detector_media_en/reports_eng/survey_of_russian_propaganda_influence_on_public_opinion_in_ukraine_findings/.

Levene, Mark. 2015. *Crisis of Genocide: The European Rimlands 1912–1938*. Oxford: Oxford University Press.

Lewicka, Maria, and Bartłomiej Iwańczak. 2019. The Regional Differentiation of Identities in Ukraine: How Many Regions? In *Regionalism Without Regions: Reconceptualizing Ukraine's Heterogeneity*, ed. Ulrich Schmid and Oksana Myshlovska, 25–65. Budapest: Central European University Press.

Malanchuk, Oksana. 2005. Social Identification versus Regionalism in Contemporary Ukraine. *Nationalities Papers* 33 (3): 345–368.

Martin, Terry. 2001. *The Affirmative Action Empire: Nations and Nationalism in the Soviet Union, 1923–1939*. Ithaca, NY: Cornell University Press.

Matveeva, Anna. 2017. *Through Times of Trouble: Conflict in Southeastern Ukraine Explained from Within*. Russian, Eurasian, and Eastern European Politics. Lanham, MD: Lexington Books.

McAdam, Doug, Sidney G. Tarrow, and Charles Tilly. 2001. *Dynamics of Contention*. Cambridge: Cambridge University Press.

Mediaport. 2014. Siezd Deputatov Vsekh Urovney v Kharkove. Tekstovaya Translyatsiya [Congress of Deputies of All Levels in Kharkov. Text Broadcast].

February 22, 2014. https://www.mediaport.ua/sezd-deputatov-vseh-urovney-v-harkove-tekstovaya-translyaciya.

Mykhnenko, Vlad. 2003. State, Society and Protest under Post-Communism: Ukrainian Miners and Their Defeat. In *Uncivil Society? Contentious Politics in Post-Communist Europe*, Series: Routledge Studies in Extremism & Democracy, ed. Mudde Cas and Petr Kopecký, 93–113. London: Routledge.

O'Loughlin, John O. 2001. The Regional Factor in Contemporary Ukrainian Politics: Scale, Place, Space, or Bogus Effect? *Post-Soviet Geography and Economics* 42 (1): 1–33.

Onuch, Olga, Henry E. Hale, and Gwendolyn Sasse. 2018. Studying Identity in Ukraine. *Post-Soviet Affairs* 34 (2–3): 79–83.

Plokhy, Serhii. 2000. The City of Glory: Sevastopol in Russian Historical Mythology. *Journal of Contemporary History* 35 (3): 369–383.

Prusin, Alexander V. 2010. *The Lands Between: Conflict in the East European Borderlands, 1870–1992*. Oxford: Oxford University Press.

Riabchuk, Mykola. 1999. A Future Ukraine: One Nation, Two Languages, Three Cultures? *Ukrainian Weekly* 67 (23): 8–9.

———. 2003. *Dvi Ukrayiny: Realni Mezhi, Virtualni Viiny* [Ukraine: Real Borders, Virtual Wars]. Kyiv: Krytyka.

———. 2015. The 'Two Ukraines' Reconsidered: The End of Ukrainian Ambivalence? *Studies in Ethnicity and Nationalism* 15 (1): 138–156.

Rogers, Peter. 2007. Division, Difference and Diversity: Regionalism in Ukraine. In *Lviv–Donetsk: Sotsialni Identychnosti v Suchasniy Ukrayini* [Lviv—Donetsk: Social Identities in Contemporary Ukraine] (special issue of *Ukrayina Moderna*), ed. Yaroslav Hrytsak, Andriy Portnov, and Viktor Susak, 210–236. Kyiv and Lviv: Krytyka.

Šabić, Claudia. 2004. The Ukrainian Piedmont: Institutionalisation at the Borders of East Central Europe. In *The Making of Regions in Post-socialist Europe—The Impact of Culture, Economic Structure and Institutions*, ed. Melanie Tatur, vol. 2, 135–229. Wiesbaden: Springer VS.

Sasse, Gwendolyn. 2001. The 'New' Ukraine: A State of Regions. *Regional and Federal Studies* 11 (3): 69–100.

———. 2002. Conflict-Prevention in a Transition State: The Crimean Issue in Post-Soviet Ukraine. *Nationalism and Ethnic Politics* 8 (2): 1–26.

———. 2007. *The Crimea Question: Identity, Transition, and Conflict*. Cambridge, MA: Harvard University Press.

———. 2010. The Role of Regionalism. *Journal of Democracy* 21 (3): 99–106.

Sasse, Gwendolyn, and Alice Lackner. 2018. War and Identity: The Case of the Donbas in Ukraine. *Post-Soviet Affairs* 34 (2–3): 139–157.

Schmid, Ulrich, and Oksana Myshlovska, eds. 2019. *Regionalism Without Regions: Reconceptualizing Ukraine's Heterogeneity*. Budapest: Central European University Press.

Sereda, Viktoria. 2007. Regional Historical Identities and Memory. In *Lviv—Donetsk: Sotsialni Identychnosti v Suchasniy Ukrayini* [Lviv—Donetsk: Social Identities in Contemporary Ukraine] (special issue of *Ukrayina Moderna*), ed. Yaroslav Hrytsak, Andriy Portnov, and Viktor Susak, 160–209. Kyiv and Lviv: Krytyka.

Shulman, Stephen. 2004. The Contours of Civic and Ethnic National Identification in Ukraine. *Europe-Asia Studies* 56 (1): 35–56.

Stroschein, Sherrill. 2012. *Ethnic Struggle, Coexistence, and Democratization in Eastern Europe*. Cambridge Studies in Contentious Politics. Cambridge: Cambridge University Press.

Studenna-Skrukva, Marta. 2014. *Ukrayinskyi Donbas: Oblychchya Rehionalnoyi Identychnosti* [Donbas: the Face of Regional Identity]. Kyiv: Laboratory of Legislative Initiatives.

Survey. 2013. Region, Nation and Beyond. A Transcultural and Interdisciplinary Reconceptualization of Ukraine. DACH project sponsored by the Swiss National Fund Grant CR1I1I1L_135348.

Tatur, Melanie. 2004. Introduction: Conceptualising the Analysis of "Making Regions" in Post-socialist Europe. In *Making Regions in Post-Socialist Europe: The Impact of Culture, Economic Structure, and Institutions. Case Studies from Poland, Hungary, Romania and Ukraine*, ed. Melanie Tatur, vol. 1, 15–48. Wiesbaden: Springer VS.

Tsentr Razumkova. 2016. Identychnist Hromadyan Ukrayiny v Novykh Umovakh: Stan, Tendentsiyi, Rehionalni Osoblyvosti. Informatsiyno-analitychni Materialy do Fakhovoyi Dyskusiyi "Formuvannya Spilnoyi Identychnosti Hromadyan Ukrayiny: Perspektyvy ta vyklyky" [Shaping the Common Identity of Ukrainian Citizens: Perspectives and Challenges]. June 7, 2016. http://razumkov.org.ua/uploads/journal/eng/NSD161-162_2016_eng.pdf.

Umland, Andreas. 2019. Irregular Militias and Radical Nationalism in Post-Euromaydan Ukraine: The Prehistory and Emergence of the "Azov" Battalion in 2014. *Terrorism and Political Violence* 31 (1): 105–131.

Wilson, Andrew. 1995. The Donbas between Ukraine and Russia: The Use of History in Political Disputes. *Journal of Contemporary History* 30 (2): 265–289.

———. 2016. The Donbas in 2014: Explaining Civil Conflict Perhaps, but not Civil War. *Europe-Asia Studies* 68 (4): 631–652.

Wucherpfennig, Julian, Philipp Hunziker, and Lars-Erik Cederman. 2016. Who Inherits the State? Colonial Rule and Postcolonial Conflict. *American Journal of Political Science* 60 (4): 882–898.

Yefimenko, Hennadiy. 2016. Skhidnyi Kordon [Eastern Frontier]. In *Narodzhennya Krayiny* [Birth of the Country], ed. Kyrylo Halushko, 205–256. Kharkiv: Klub simeinoho dozvillya.

Zhukov, Yuri. 2016. Trading Hard Hats for Combat Helmets: The Economics of Rebellion in Eastern Ukraine. *Journal of Comparative Economics* 44: 1–15.

Zhurzhenko, Tatiana. 2004a. Cross-border Cooperation and Transformation of Regional Identities in the Ukrainian-Russian Borderlands: Towards a Euroregion "Slobozhanshchyna"? Part 1. *Nationalities Papers* 32: 207–232.

———. 2004b. Cross-border Cooperation and Transformation of Regional Identities in the Ukrainian-Russian Borderlands: Towards a Euroregion "Slobozhanshchyna"? Part 2. *Nationalities Papers* 32: 497–514.

Zimmer, Kerstin. 2004. The Captured Region: Actors and Institutions in the Ukrainian Donbas. In *The Making of Regions in Post-socialist Europe—The Impact of Culture, Economic Structure and Institutions*, ed. Melanie Tatur, vol. 2, 231–348. Wiesbaden: Springer VS.

———. 2007. Trapped in a Past Glory: Self-identification and Self-symbolization in the Donbas. In *Re-constructing the Post-Soviet Industrial Region. The Donbas in Transition*, ed. Adam Swain, 97–121. London and New York: Routledge.

Zolkina, Maria. 2017. The Donbas. New Trends in Public Opinion. In *Constructing a Political Nation: Changes in the Attitudes of Ukrainians during the War in the Donbas*, ed. Olexiy Haran and Maksym Yakovlyev, 159–182. Kyiv: Stylus Publishing.

CHAPTER 3

Navigating Ethnopolitical Disputes: Ukraine's Constitutional Court in the Tug-of-War over Language

Andrii Nekoliak and Vello Pettai

INTRODUCTION

Ethnopolitical controversies are often seen as zero-sum and difficult to resolve by negotiation between conflicting sides. Mediation and even arbitration sometimes seem like the only ways out, especially when a dispute has reached boiling point. Needless to say, the most extreme version of such intervention comes in the form of international involvement. However, before such a drastic situation can arise, democratic institutions within countries themselves should provide mechanisms for resolving ethnopolitical disagreements by fostering dialogue and establishing legitimate decision-making mechanisms. Parliaments are meant, of course, to

---

A. Nekoliak (✉) • V. Pettai
Johan Skytte Institute of Political Studies, University of Tartu, Tartu, Estonia
e-mail: vello.pettai@ut.ee

© The Author(s) 2020
H. Shelest, M. Rabinovych (eds.), *Decentralization, Regional Diversity, and Conflict*, Federalism and Internal Conflicts,
https://doi.org/10.1007/978-3-030-41765-9_3

49

nurture such conflict resolution in the first instance by ensuring representation for all groups in a society as well as acting as a site for interest aggregation, exchange, and negotiation. Further, liberal constitutionalism is intended to provide additional, counter-majoritarian protections through non-elected institutions such as ombudsman and, above all, courts of law. It is this dimension of ethnopolitics that this chapter addresses: how has Ukraine's Constitutional Court navigated appeals brought to it by competing plaintiffs in cases involving the country's language policy and language legislation?

For three decades, the language issue (together with issues of historical memory and identity) has loomed large in public and academic debates in and about Ukraine. Among others, the discourse of "two Ukraines" (*dvi Ukrainy*) has emerged in public intellectuals' understanding of the country's regional diversity (Riabchuk 2003). Although it is speculative to believe that this diversity might undermine the idea of establishing an enduring and workable Ukrainian nation-state, it is clear that ethnopolitics are at play throughout Ukrainian society and therefore warrant scholarly attention.

The contribution made by this chapter comes from its focus on language issues and how the law plays into the status and institutionalization of the two major languages of the country: Ukrainian and Russian. Current studies usually provide an overview of the evolution of governmental language policy and of how various language legislation initiatives were introduced in post-Soviet Ukraine (Arel 1995; Besters-Dilger 2009; Kulyk 2009, 2013; Moser 2013).To date, only a handful of studies have focused more extensively on legal or judicial dimensions of language policy. Bowring (2009) analyzed Ukraine's obligations according to international law in the domain of language use and minority protection. Trach (2009) focused on language legislation and the usage of Ukrainian and Russian in the judicial sphere. However, the latter contribution surveyed the developments in the area of legislation on language in the courts and did not pay attention to the role of constitutional review and judicial politics in managing language policy in Ukraine, as this chapter will do.

We argue that the narrative of Ukraine's Constitutional Court over language matters and legislation can be expressed as follows. The court argues and upholds prerogative of the parliament to regulate social relations and language use in the country. This means that, on the one hand, it refrains from introducing policy tools for language management and usually waives appellants' arguments to deal with content of language legislation;

3 NAVIGATING ETHNOPOLITICAL DISPUTES: UKRAINE'S CONSTITUTIONAL... 51

on the other hand, when it does exercise constitutional review and makes a decision to invalidate a certain piece of language legislation, the court checks if parliament abided by constitutional procedure for adopting a piece of legislation. In other words, when language legislation matters are under its review, the Constitutional Court considers the prerogative of constitutional review in a "narrower" sense as conformity of legislation to constitutional procedure of adoption. As the analysis below demonstrates, the court is more vocal on the ethnopolitics of language matters when it is not being asked to issue a direct policy-outcome decision or when it adjudicates in a separate policy domain, where the court will not alter the legal framework on languages formally. This allows one to conceptualize the Constitutional Court as a "minimalist" institution that treats law as something that is created first and foremost according to, and enshrined in, a proper procedure. Therefore, this chapter echoes the conclusion published previously by Wolczuk (2002b) that the Constitutional Court is an adherent of positivism in legal doctrinal sense.

The chapter is structured as follows. The first section elaborates briefly on the phases of language policy in Ukraine, including the new language law of April 2019. The second section elaborates the framework of Ukraine's Constitutional Court, its evolution and main parameters. Thereafter, the next three sections present emblematic cases from the Ukraine's Constitutional Court on language-related matters. The sections showcase how different Ukrainian-minded and Russian-minded appellants have engaged the court in order to foster competing views and agendas over the status of Ukrainian and Russian in the country. The implication of the chapter is to illustrate the challenge for any constitutional or high court to remain a credible institution in light of growing "judicialization" of politics. Ultimately, the magnitude of the task is even greater for constitutional courts dealing with sensitive and divisive ethnopolitical issues.

I. THE LANGUAGE ISSUE AND PHASES OF LANGUAGE POLICY IN UKRAINE

As with many republics of the former Soviet Union, Ukraine has had to struggle since the late 1980s with a process of re-equilibration of its language landscape and language policy away from the preponderant role previously played by Russian. Not only was Russian the privileged language of communication across the disparate parts of the USSR, it also seeped its way deep into the individual national republics, often becoming a prevalent language in local state administration, written regulation, and day-to-day operation. Part of this process was, of course, driven by the proportion of ethnic Russians in a given republic or even region of a republic: where Russians constituted large majorities of the regional population, the Russian language ended up dominating the linguistic landscape. However, with the advent of national independence for all of the former Soviet republics, the question of how much titular language should now become the mainstay of state administration and public communication across these territories quickly came to constitute the essence of ethnopolitics around language policy. How would different political forces take steps to defend or alter such linguistic balances and language regimes? What specific changes would be enacted by language laws and their amendments when they succeeded in being adopted? Would there also be reversals in this process? Before looking, therefore, at how the Ukrainian Constitutional Court would be pulled into these different struggles, a brief overview of the actual course of language policy in Ukraine is in order.

Ukraine's history of language policy begins (as it did in many ex-Soviet republics) during the heyday of Mikhail Gorbachev's perestroika reforms, when, in 1989, the Supreme Soviet of the Ukrainian Soviet Socialist Republic adopted a law "On Languages in the Ukrainian SSR."[1] Akin to many other Soviet republics, the Ukrainian parliament declared the Ukrainian language as the official state language, while at the same time acknowledging the special status of Russian in certain domains. While this was an important first symbolic step toward determining the new language regime, in practice Russian continued to dominate across many areas of societal life (Kulyk 2006). Moreover, as Wolczuk (2002a, 88–89) notes, the law remained vague on how to enforce or upgrade the status of the Ukrainian language in practice.

This becomes an important parameter of the language issue in Ukraine, since for the next two decades this relatively ambiguous law would remain on the books, despite attempts to amend or even repeal its provisions. In other words, stalemate around a dysfunctional legislative framework meant that different political forces would end up seeking recourse through other institutions, including the Constitutional Court. In the meantime,

---

[1] The official Ukrainian-language titles of national laws discussed in this chapter are listed at the end of the chapter under "Laws of Ukraine [Verkhovna Rada Ukrainy]".

however, a second nominal development occurred in 1996—the adoption of a new Constitution. In addition to revamping all of Ukraine's political institutions, the Constitution reaffirmed in its Article 10 Ukrainian's pre-eminent linguistic status. Moreover, it decreed, "The State shall ensure comprehensive development and functioning of the Ukrainian language in all spheres of social life throughout the entire territory of Ukraine." While the new document singled out the "free development, use and protection of Russian" as guaranteed in the country, it did not accord it any special rights in state administration or other official domains.

In this respect, Ukraine continued with two oftentimes largely declarative, and yet still highly significant, affirmations of the new language regime in the country. Moreover, because of this flux and ambiguity, language struggles would continue throughout the 1990s and 2000s, with different sides trying to tilt the balance in one way or another. These pitched battles would flare up around different lower-level regulatory changes, during the ratification of the European Charter for Regional and Minority Languages and during efforts to regulate cinematography and language usage in courts. As we will see below, this is where the Constitutional Court would frequently be brought into the ethnopolitical fray.

A game-changer of sorts took place, however, in 2012 with the adoption of a new law "On Principles of the State Language Policy" promoted by President Viktor Yanukovych and the language warriors in his camp.[2] The law was aimed at turning around the previous institutionalization and strengthening of Ukrainian language in favor of a leveling up of regional—mostly Russian—languages in the country. As is known, this move came to be one of the broader reasons for Yanukovych's downfall during the Maidan Revolution in 2014. However, before this demise, the Kivalov–Kolisnichenko law had become an object of dispute before the Constitutional Court.

Unsurprisingly, the victory of the pro-Ukrainian forces during the 2014 Revolution led to a renewed push to strengthen the position of Ukrainian language in society, including legislation that imposed obligatory quotas of Ukrainian on radio (Zakon Ukrainy 2016), on TV (Zakon Ukrainy 2017a), and limited the scope of minority language education

---

[2] In Ukraine, the law is usually referred to as the Kivalov–Kolisnichenko Law after the influential "Party of Regions" MPs, Serhiy Kivalov and Vadym Kolisnichenko, who pushed the law through in 2012.

(Zakon Ukrainy 2017c; Kulyk 2018, 2019). Most prominently, in 2018, the Constitutional Court annulled the 2012 law, paving the way for the adoption in 2019 of an entirely new law "On Provision of Functioning of Ukrainian Language as the Official Language." This law would further bolster Ukrainization by, among other things, consolidating the use of Ukrainian in the entertainment industry, customer service, television broadcasting, advertising, print media, and other spheres; establishing a position of the language "ombudsman" to deal with the protection of the state language; and establishing liability (fines) for failure to comply with the law's comprehensive requirements (Zakon Ukrainy 2019).

In the broad scheme of things, therefore, political struggles over language in Ukraine have ebbed and flowed, with the last decade, of course, witnessing a number of dramatic shifts and tensions. Closer analysis of how the country's Constitutional Court has attempted to adjudicate complaints within this struggle will show that courts cannot necessarily take on a full-scale role of arbiter or promulgator of final justice, especially on sensitive ethnopolitical matters. It is more likely that it will stick to procedural questions where possible, and where not, it will concur with legislatures' rights to enact policy, but will not pronounce on whether a policy is ethnopolitically fair or not.

II. The Constitutional Court of Ukraine

Ukraine's Constitutional Court (KSU) was created in 1996 following the adoption of the new constitution that revamped the country's institutions after the period of flux of the first independent years. An initial attempt at creating a constitutional review structure had begun in 1992, but this institution never got off the ground (see Wolczuk 2002b, 329–330). Currently, the KSU consists of 18 justices, six appointed by the President, six by parliament, and six by the Congress of Judges, all for 9-year terms. First and foremost, the Court is empowered to review the conformity of parliamentary legislation with the Constitution. In addition, it may rule on the constitutional conformity of other parliamentary acts, decrees of the President, decisions of the Cabinet of Ministers, and legislative acts of the Crimean Parliament. Additionally, it may provide official interpretations of the Constitution, and during the 1996–2016 period, it was tasked explicitly with interpreting national legislation when called upon to do so. Such interpretations were seen as a type of adjudication in that they constituted a binding legal opinion concerning the understanding and application of pieces of legislation in practice. Finally, in a number of situations, the KSU has been further asked to provide official inferences (*vysnovky*) on a number of defined matters such as the constitutionality of international agreements or questions put to a national referendum by popular initiative.[3]

Although the original law governing the Constitutional Court's work was changed several times during its first 20 years, none of these changes significantly altered its main framework, with the amendments usually having a merely technical character.[4] At the same time, the court also developed a major credibility crisis, since the appointment of justices by the three constitutionally designated institutions often became politicized, especially by the presidency. These twists and turns echoed the overarching political struggles across the presidencies of Viktor Yushchenko, Viktor Yanukovych and finally Petro Poroshenko. Presidents sought to use the Constitutional Court in their separate struggles with the legislature.

An important shift took place in 2016, when the range of eligible appellants to the court regarding matters of constitutionality was expanded to include single individuals. Prior to that, individuals had only been able to ask for an official interpretation of legislation. Secondly, the new amendments limited the prerogative of the court to issue official interpretations only in relation to the Constitution and not to ordinary legislation. Thirdly, the professional requirements for being a constitutional court justice were raised to having at least 15 years of experience in the legal profession (up from 10 years), as well as a need to have demonstrated "high moral traits" during their prior career. A second wave of changes took place in 2017, when a series of amendments to the Constitution prompted the adoption of an entirely new law on the Constitutional Court and its

---

[3] See Article 7 of the 2017 Law on the Constitutional Court for a full list of these domains.

[4] To illustrate this point further, in 2006, the new amendment reiterated the provision of the Law of 1996 that a constitutional judge takes the oath during the session of the parliament with the President, the Head of the Supreme Court, and the Prime Minister being present in the session (Zakon Ukrainy 2006). Simultaneously, the amendment removed a caveat that the oath should be taken a month after a judge's appointment to the Constitutional Court (ibid.). Furthermore, a more important provision of the Law of 1996 was annulled in 2009. The provision of Article 6 of the original Law on the Constitutional Court from 1996 established that the president was to hold consultations with the prime minister and the minister of justice regarding new appointees to the Court. According to the provision, the prime minister and minister of justice had to co-sign presidential degrees on new appointees. This provision was proclaimed unconstitutional by the Constitutional Court in a decision in 2009 as infringing on constitutional prerogatives of the president (KSU 2009).

proceedings. In particular, the 2017 law restructured the work of the court into six chambers or collegiums, two senates and one Great Chamber. This change was meant in part to give the court a better division of labor so that it could deal more efficiently with the new reality of individual constitutional complaints. Hence, the new senates were tasked with adjudicating individual constitutional complaints, the collegiums would decide on opening or refusing constitutional appeals, while the Chamber would constitute the Constitutional Court's sitting *en banc* to decide on matters of ultimate constitutionality (Zakon Ukrainy 2017b). While these changes helped to alleviate some of the paralysis of the court (for example, in 2017 the court issued barely any rulings because of this period of flux), questions remained about how it would deal with the new heavy inflow of individual complaints, numbering already in the hundreds (Lovin and Vovk 2018; Slidenko 2018).

III. Constitutional Court Cases on Language Matters

Political science scholarship on constitutional adjudication in Ukraine has been thin, with most studies focusing on the Constitutional Court's role in mediating overall power politics in the country (D'Anieri 2003, 2006, 91, 179, 205).A few scholars have aimed to profile the court's jurisprudence in a more thorough manner (Wolczuk 2002b; Brown and Wise 2004; Protsyk 2005). In this research, the court emerges as a "navigating" institution in Ukraine's power politics, often seen as succumbing to the demands of the presidency. In terms of defending rights or taking clearer stances on normative issues, Wolczuk (2002a, b) found the court's jurisprudence to be enshrined in legal positivism and that it "has generally exercised restraint and largely avoided rulings concerned with rights, which would take it beyond the remits of the Constitution into the wider terrain populated by such concepts as 'the rule of law', 'social justice', 'social state', or 'fundamental rights'" (Wolczuk 2002b, 327). Likewise, Wolczuk concluded that the court was often prone to "political expediency" in how it resolved political power conflicts between the president and parliament in the late 1990s (Wolczuk 2002a, 240, 259–280). In our analysis of language issues, we will find similar reticence and careful decision-making on the part of the court.

3 NAVIGATING ETHNOPOLITICAL DISPUTES: UKRAINE'S CONSTITUTIONAL... 57

Table 3.1 Eligible appellants and appeal types to the Ukrainian Constitutional Court, and the number of appeals concerning language politics by each category, 1996–2019

Appellants	Constitutionality	Official interpretation of the Constitution	Official interpretation of ordinary legislation
President of Ukraine			
Parliamentary deputies	11*	1	2
Supreme Court of Ukraine			
Ombudsman			
Crimean Parliament	1		
Cabinet of Ministers			
Territorial self-government			3
Individuals			

Note: Shaded boxes denote appellants who lost respective standing before the Court after 2016

*As of August 2019, one appeal was still pending before the Court. It was from the Opposition Bloc (*Oposyciynyt Blok*, i.e. former members of President Yanukovych's Party of Regions) to review the constitutionality of the new law "On Provision of Functioning of Ukrainian Language as the Official Language" (KSU 2019a).

In Table 3.1, we provide an overview of appellants and appeals on language legislation and issues brought before the Constitutional Court since 1996. The table encompasses the respective provisions of the Constitution, and the two Laws on the Constitutional Court from 1996 and 2017. As noted earlier, there are two main modes of court decision-making: reviewing the constitutionality of ordinary legislation and other legal acts, and providing official interpretation of the Constitution and other legal acts. The shaded boxes indicate when a respective appellant does not have the right to request a corresponding mode of adjudication from the Constitutional Court.[5]

The range of institutions that have standing before the court as well as their rights to obtain certain rulings from the court changed as a result of

[5] For a chronological outline of the cases covered in this chapter, see Table 3.2 in the appendix

the constitutional amendments in 2016 and the adoption of the 2017 Constitutional Court law. On the one hand, the rights of individual appellants were strengthened thanks to the ability to lodge formal constitutional complaints as a way to appeal final decisions of ordinary courts granted in the new law. On the other hand, they lost the right to request official interpretations, which in some ways were more effective. In addition, the Cabinet of Ministers was and remains able to request a constitutional review, but only regarding the question of Ukraine joining international agreements. Lastly, other governmental offices and bodies of territorial self-government have never had the capacity to request constitutional review, and the avenue of requesting official interpretations of legislation was closed for them in 2017. Although none of these pathways to the court has so far played a role in judicial politics concerning language issues, it is important keep this range in mind in seeking to understand the options that political forces might have in pursuing their ethnopolitical aims.

As Table 3.1 shows, judicial struggles over language legislation have mostly taken place via parliamentary politics, with different MPs seeking to transfer recurring battles over language legislation to the Constitutional Court for further contestation. Moreover, MPs have generally aimed to obtain "harder" and more impactful rulings on actual constitutionality rather than the "softer" avenue of mere official interpretation. Because the struggle over language legislation has generally involved attempts to pitch the regime toward either increased Ukrainian predominance or a protection of Russian language spheres, the various cases brought before the Constitutional Court can also be seen as serving to further one or the other faction. Moreover, within the context of parliamentary politics, one can see many of the well-known political forces on both sides of this aforementioned struggle over language legislation using the Constitutional Court as part of their ethnopolitical campaigns. Hence, during the early years of the court in the second half of the 1990s, it was the People's Movement of Ukraine (*Narodnyi Rukh*) or national-democratic opposition party in the parliament that campaigned for a more solid standing for Ukrainian in Ukrainian public life. Rukh originated in the late 1980s as an equivalent of the popular front movements in the Baltic states. It gathered within its ranks former dissidents and Ukrainian-minded intellectuals and activists and had its electoral base mostly in western Ukraine. It was also the first political force to take up the avenue of constitutional appeal when trying to draw attention to what, in their mind, was the toothless nature of 1990s language legislation. Moreover, as will be described below, Rukh would pursue these aims not only in terms of national constitutional law, but also via international law, drawing on the European Charter for Regional and Minority languages.

After Rukh declined in prominence, other national-democratic political parties such as Our Ukraine (*Nasha Ukraina*) and Fatherland (*Batkivschyna*) took the lead in making appeals to the Constitutional Court. These efforts reached a fever pitch after 2012, when President Yanukovych and his Party of Regions (*Partia Rehioniv*) pushed through approval of the Law "On Principles of the State Language Policy" that many saw as promoting the interests of the Russian language in the country by granting it a special regional status. It was at this point that the ethnopolitical contest broadened to include a number of western Ukrainian regional councils, who employed their right to request legal interpretations from the Constitutional Court as a way of further stemming the new shift in language regime.

At the same time, the judicial path of contestation was also employed by Russian-minded parliamentarians. These forces arose from among the Ukrainian Communist Party as well as at times from the Crimean Parliament. In the case of the former, the party attempted in 2002 to amend the Constitution to create a category of "official language" for Russian. In order to bolster these aims, the party turned to the Constitutional Court for a comment on the permissibility of such a change. Meanwhile, the Crimean Parliament (along with support from Communist deputies) sought relief from the court for what they claimed was a downgrading of the status and scope of Russian language on the peninsula and in the country as a whole. Their focus was on language rights in the administration of justice and the language provisions contained within different procedural codes. All of these instances are described in greater detail in the following sections on Constitutional Court jurisprudence.

The focus of post-independence language struggles on the Ukrainian/Russian cleavage delayed Constitutional Court consideration of individual constitutional complaints about the near-absence of effective legislation for other minority languages. As will be shown in the following sections, high-profile political actors in the parliament, concerned with institutionalizing Ukrainian vis-a-vis Russian, were the main drafters and the main presenters of language appeals. In some of the cases (most notably, addressing the post-Euromaidan education law of 2017), the usage of ethnic minority languages other than Russian was directly impacted by the court's decisions. However, even in such cases the focus of adjudication was still predicated on the main language cleavage in Ukraine, sidelining the attention to minority languages other than Russian (e.g. Hungarian and Romanian) in various domains of public life. This situation may change in the future as there is more space for individuals to appeal to the court following the judicial reform in 2016. The question, however, is whether such potential appeals will break the well-established patterns of the court's reasoning on language legislation matters.

IV. INSTITUTIONALIZING UKRAINIAN AND FAVORING THE PREROGATIVE OF THE PARLIAMENT IN LANGUAGE POLICY DEVELOPMENT

Amidst the ambiguity of Ukraine's language regime during the 1990s— operating under an arguably archaic language law from 1989, while having adopted merely declaratory assertion of Ukrainian as the sole state language per the new 1996 Constitution—it became the task of the Constitutional Court to breathe some life into this framework in 1999, after a group of mostly Rukh parliamentarians sought the court's interpretation of Article 10 of the Constitution, defining the role of languages in the country. It is at this point that we begin to see the nuanced role that is played in Ukrainian linguistic ethnopolitics by institutional provisions such as the interpretive acts issued by the Constitutional Court, since it is this constellation of procedures that allowed a kind of soft supremacy of Ukrainian to be legitimized, while not occasioning direct political confrontation via a harder ruling regarding constitutionality of a legal act per se.

In their appeal, the nationalist parliamentarians claimed that, despite the new Constitution's stipulations, the state language still did not enjoy the status it should in the actual operation of government. They maintained that Russian continued to be used widely in the management of public affairs and that this practice violated Article 10 of the Constitution by overlooking Ukrainian as the state language (KSU 1997). At the same time, the deputies' appeal was not about a single institution or defendant violating these norms. Rather, they sought an official interpretation from the Constitutional Court about how seriously Article 10 should be taken. This would engender a situation where the court would issue a pronouncement on how to understand the parameters of Ukraine's new language regime, but would leave it up to the legislature to determine the more precise details.

In its decision, the court began by reiterating the constitutional norm and role of Ukrainian language as an "obligatory tool of communication on the territory of Ukraine by bodies of public authority, territorial self-government (the language of official acts, workings, internal documentation flow etc.), and also in other public spheres of the life of society, which are specified by the law" (KSU 1999). At the same time, it reaffirmed sections of the Constitution (such as Article 11) declaring that the state shall promote "the linguistic identity of all indigenous peoples and national minorities of Ukraine." Turning to more specific societal domains, the court established that Ukrainian should be used as the main language of instruction in public and municipal educational establishments starting from the pre-primary level and up to higher education. At the same time, it acknowledged that other languages could be used alongside Ukrainian, but only as specified by law (KSU 1999). Further, the court enumerated a number of other arenas where Ukrainian language had already been legitimately promoted via legislation (such as within consumer affairs, the armed forces, and in public communications by state authorities). This implied that the state had a right to enforce the norms of Article 10 and impose "hard" policy tools as necessary. For its part, however, the court offered its "soft" affirmation of these trends.

The court's next two decisions demonstrated how it dealt with policy issues in the aftermath of proclaiming "soft" supremacy of Ukrainian language and continuing to favor parliamentary prerogative in the management of language policy. In 2003, another group of nationalist MPs sought to pin the court down more specifically on language policy areas they felt were still being neglected or violated. Specifically, they challenged the constitutionality of the practice of Ukrainian government officials issuing citizenship and other identity documents that continued to have inscriptions in both Ukrainian and Russian. The deputies argued that this was unconstitutional as per the Constitution's Article 10. The deputies called for Article 14 of the 1989 language law (which facilitated this bilingualism) to be declared unconstitutional in light of Article 10 of the 1996 Constitution. They did soon the basis of the court's own previous 1999 ruling establishing the primacy of Ukrainian. Yet, on this occasion, the court steered away from letting itself be pulled into a blanket application of Ukrainian language primacy in state affairs. It turned instead to point 5 of Article 10 of the Constitution, which states "The use of languages in

Ukraine is guaranteed by the Constitution of Ukraine and is determined by law." It used this as cover to enable it to rule that it was parliament's duty to enforce (or perhaps clean up) legislation on the use of Ukrainian, and if parliament had not done so, the court was not in a position to do it in its stead, since the letter of the Constitution allowed for other languages to be used (KSU 2003).

A different situation arose in 2006 when another group of parliamentarians (this time representing Nasha Ukraina—President Yushchenko's group in the parliament) asked the court to provide an official interpretation of Article 14 of the Law "On Cinematography". This provision of the law had been seen as an affirmative action measure to support the use of the Ukrainian language in the movie industry (KSU 2006). However, this time the deputies sought affirmation from the court that the law required that all movies produced abroad and screened in Ukraine had to be either dubbed or subtitled into Ukrainian. The question at stake, therefore, was whether the legal provision could be seen as having an obligatory effect. In its decision, the court reiterated that the state can legitimately regulate social relations in this sphere and it supported the view that "the legislator has obliged every subject of cinematography to dub or subtitle foreign movies in the Ukrainian language before their distribution in Ukraine" (KSU 2007). Moreover, on a practical level, this meant that the issuing of licenses for distributing and screening movies could also made contingent on companies fulfilling the requirements of dubbing and subtitling movies into Ukrainian.

These two decisions demonstrated that the more the Constitutional Court was asked to get involved in language issues as a policy maker, the less it was inclined to intervene. In both cases, the appellants had referred to the court's decision from 1999, seeking it to make good on the soft supremacy of Ukrainian. Moreover, both cases dealt with the application of Ukrainian in societal spheres, where the legal regulation of language usage was seen as admissible. However, what differentiates the two cases is the type of ruling requested by the applicants. In the case involving language inscriptions on passports and other identity documents, the court was asked to check the formal constitutionality of existing administrative practice; Ukrainian-minded deputies sought to get the court to rule the practice of issuing bilingual passports unconstitutional. Had it decided to open proceedings and rule in the case, the court would have assumed the role of a policy maker. In the cinematography law case, however, the appellants asked only for clarification of the existing legal provision, which was introduced by the parliament quite intentionally. In this sense, the MPs wanted the court to remove any possible misreading of the language provision. It is important to reiterate that the official interpretation mode cannot lead to an annulment of legal provisions but the constitutional conformity mode can. Thus, in the former case, the court favored the status quo regarding the existing policy tool, that is, the practice of issuing bilingual passports. In the latter case, the court, without altering existing policy formally clarified how it should be understood. In this respect, we can also see that the nationalist MPs used the official interpretation mode as a means to alleviate their language concerns quite effectively: they got their desired policy ruling.

An even more emblematic case of confirming the supremacy of Ukrainian in spheres of public life came in 2019. On the one hand, the events of the case speak about post-Euromaidan language regime realities, that is, the "nationalizing" move of Ukraine's political elites in the domain of education that heavily influenced instruction in minority languages in the country. On the other hand, the decision on education law again demonstrates the unlikelihood of the Constitutional Court annulling a law or its provisions based on constitutionality claims by asking it to be a policy maker. In such cases, the court would confirm the legitimacy of a law's aims by aligning with the measures that were introduced by the parliament most naturally.

In 2017, the Ukraine's parliament adopted the new Law "On Education" that curtailed the ability to be educated in an ethnic minority language (Zakon Ukrainy 2017c). Article 7 of the law confined such education to elementary schools and established a presumption of the teaching process to be conducted exclusively in Ukrainian at higher levels. One caveat of Article 7 allowed for limited instruction of "one or few disciplines" in other languages than Ukrainian at middle and high school levels. In practice, this meant that after finishing elementary school, education in a minority language was limited to having a separate language or literature class within the curriculum. The new law sparked an intense international controversy and a particular outcry by the Hungarian government (Kulyk 2018; Slidenko 2019).

Following the law's adoption, a group of Opposition Bloc MPs contested it before the Constitutional Court on the ground of violation the right to education (KSU 2017). The deputies argued that a right to be educated in one's native language constituted an individual natural right. By the logic of the deputies, the measures of the new law infringed on this right by narrowing the scope and availability of education in a minority language. More generally, the deputies tried to weigh in Article 11 of the Constitution, which guaranteed free development of the linguistic identities of national minorities, against Article 10, which proclaimed Ukrainian as the state language. They also pointed to parts of the 1999 Decision reiterating protection of Russian and other minority languages. To add weight to their argument in the appeal, the MPs quoted the Framework Convention for the Protection of National Minorities (FCNM), ratified by Ukraine in 1997. In general, the appeal reinvigorated the question of the accommodation of minority languages in the country's constitutional regime as it applied to languages and as it operated in practice.

Following the pattern of institutionalizing Ukrainian language in the spheres of public life, the court rejected the appeal and, overall, took an even more assertive stance over supremacy of Ukrainian than it did in 1999. According to the court, "the state *must* [italics added] contribute to development and functioning of the Ukrainian language" (KSU 2019b, 4). In view of the court, the need for more Ukrainian language in schools was predicated foremost upon the premise of Article 10 of the Constitution. In other words, having more Ukrainian in education was in line with "constitutional status of the state language" (ibid., 6). Finally, in the decision, the court defined that the benefit of greater and more comprehensive socialization of national minorities into Ukrainian society legitimized the aim of the law.

V. Language Rights in Judicial Proceedings

In the language disputes previously discussed, the heart of the matter involved establishing language primacy in certain administrative documents or audiovisual recordings. In other words, they were inanimate objects. A different kind of language domain involves rights during interactive communication and administrative procedure. The judiciary itself is one such arena. Here, the language regime pertains to not only the language(s) in which documents are processed (including the language of final rulings), but also the language(s) the participants are allowed to use during their interaction. In this respect, this arena pits the principle of regulating the use of official language(s) in the public sphere up against individuals' active (political) right to obtain justice in the language that is most comfortable for them. During the 2000s, the court was asked twice to deal with balancing these imperatives. The two cases dealing with the language of justice in national courts demonstrate how the court navigated between competing requests coming from different aisles of Ukrainian politics. In resolving the cases, the court tilted toward defending the right of all plaintiffs in civil and administrative procedures to use the language of their choice, while upholding the primacy of Ukrainian within the judicial institution itself.

The first case emerged in 2004, when the Crimean Parliament petitioned the court to review the constitutionality of Article 7 of the Civil Procedural Code, set to take effect in 2005. The regional parliament argued that by declaring the state (Ukrainian) language as the only language of courtroom hearings, the Code would seriously disadvantage other languages (Verkhovna Rada Autonomnoi Respubliky Krym 2004). This was not least an issue in Crimea, where over 80 percent of the population claimed Russian as their first language. Moreover, the previous Civil Procedural Code of the Ukrainian SSR (from 1963) had guaranteed the right to conduct courtroom hearings and procedure in the language of the majority of a given region alongside Ukrainian (ibid.).This would no longer be the case under the new code.

While the Crimean Parliament submitted its appeal with regard to Ukraine's civil courts, an additional appeal was lodged by parliamentarians from the Communist Party, who challenged analogous changes set to take effect in the administrative courts. In their petition, the deputies brought out a further argument in that Article 22 of the Constitution does not allow for narrowing the content and scope of existing individual rights and freedoms by introducing new legislation (KSU 2005). Therefore, in the view of the appellants, the new procedural codes would infringe on individuals' opportunity to request the use of Russian in legal procedures prescribed by previous legislation. Finally, both the Crimean Parliament and the Communist deputies argued that the new procedural codes would violate the Constitution of the Autonomous Republic of Crimea from 1998 in as far as the regional constitution proclaimed that Russian can be used in the administration of justice, notary activity, and legal aid, given the language's majority status on the peninsula (Verkhovna Rada Autonomnoi Respubliky Krym 2004; KSU 2005).

While acknowledging the weight of many of these minority-language claims, the Constitutional Court ultimately confirmed the constitutionality of the new procedural codes. It did so by maintaining that the new codes continued to "reproduce content characteristics of rights of persons in judicial proceedings" that had existed under the previous procedural legislation (KSU 2008). Thus, in its view there was no narrowing of content or scope of minority language rights. Likewise, the court maintained that the overall constitutional provisions protecting the free use of Russian and preventing discrimination based on language continued to be in force. Therefore, implicitly plaintiffs in court could continue to communicate in Russian if they desired. However, the court also pointed out that the Crimean courts belonged to a unitary system of national courts, meaning that no exemptions from national procedural codes (especially regarding the language of judicial documents) could be granted (ibid.).

With this ruling, the court took a step toward reaffirming the primacy of Ukrainian as the language in judicial administration, while defending the rights of citizens to use the language of their choice in actual proceedings. Two years later, in 2010, the court came under fire from the other aisle of Ukrainian politics, when a group of MPs from the Batkivschyna party group in parliament claimed that a new Yanukovych-era law ("On the Judicial System and the Status of Judges") would favor the Russian language over Ukrainian in the administration of justice. Article 12 of that law established that the usage of "regional languages" and of "languages of national minorities" would be allowed in courts alongside Ukrainian. Here, the parliamentary deputies insisted on the primacy of Ukrainian without any reservations or caveats. In their view, the new law was a step back from court's soft supremacy decision from 1999. While the deputies did not demand that Ukrainian be the sole language in the judicial realm, they did argue that using regional languages and the language of national minorities should be confined to certain judicial districts with particular regional language habitats and only with regard to the submission of documents and evidence before the courts (KSU 2010).

On this score, the Constitutional Court rejected the deputies' arguments and reaffirmed the rights of individuals to uninhibited judicial access. The court ruled that a person's right to justice and their right to defend themselves in court encompassed the possible or necessary usage of Russian and other national minority languages (KSU 2011). In the court's view, "under certain circumstances, realization of a right to justice relies on a guarantee to use Russian and other minority languages freely" (ibid.). This also meant that anyone would have a right to use minority languages in national courts across the entire territory of Ukraine without caveats or reservations. In other words, the usage of these languages could not be confined to separate judicial districts.

VI. Procedural Violations as a Basis for Court Rulings

As is often the case in judicial rulings, courts must assess not only the substance of legal disputes, but also the propriety of prior legislative or judicial procedures. In other words, rulings may be handed down that do not decide the real essence of a claim, but rather pre-empt such determinations because of the discovery of an earlier procedural failing. In a number of cases, Ukraine's Constitutional Court has invalidated laws on these grounds. Moreover, as we will see in this section, some of these outcomes have arisen in relation to the most controversial language disputes, prompting the question whether the court has not sometimes used such procedural arguments as a convenient escape-hatch during contentious appeals. In these kinds of decisions, the court has acknowledged and articulated an inclination to review the constitutionality of language laws in a narrow sense as conformity to the procedure for their adoption. In this sense, the court has viewed the checking of the propriety of constitutional procedure as its primary responsibility with respect to constitutional review. At the same time, the pieces of legislation that the court has invalidated based on such findings has involved several high-profile attempts to bring about the most drastic changes to the country's language regime. The response of the court has been to waive claims about the substance of such changes and not get involved in the development of or debate over a proposed frameworks and policies.

A case in point began in December 1999, when the Ukrainian parliament adopted a law ratifying the European Charter for Regional or Minority Languages. This key international framework for promoting language diversity in Europe (sponsored by the Council of Europe) had been controversial in many countries where language disputes exist. In Ukraine, MPs from the nationalist Rukh party were no exception to these sentiments, and proceeded to appeal ratification to the Constitutional Court. Their concerns continued to be motivated by the anxieties touched upon earlier: that Ukrainian was not enjoying majoritarian status in the country politically and socially, and that implementation of the charter would subvert the state language regime. The plaintiffs expressed the view that the legal regulation of languages should be made by the country's laws and not by ratifying international treaties (KSU 2000a). Thus, on the substantive side, the Rukh representatives argued that the law ratifying the charter was not a legitimate tool for regulating language usage since it introduced "a regime of applying national minority languages, which discriminates against the state language in Ukraine" (Ibid, 3).

At the same time, parliamentarians spent a greater part of their appeal elaborating on alleged procedural inconsistencies committed during passage of the law in parliament. In particular, the deputies alleged that the manner in which the law had been promulgated was unconstitutional, and therefore the law itself should be annulled. The dispute involved Article 94 of the Constitution, which establishes that a piece of legislation, after having been signed by the Speaker of Parliament, must be sent to the President for final signature, promulgation and entry into force. However, the law ratifying the charter had been passed based on Ukraine's 1993 law "On International Treaties", which stipulates that legislation involving international treaties is signed only by the Speaker and enters legal force immediately thereafter. The Rukh parliamentarians argued that this was unconstitutional, and they used this procedural incongruity to question the validity of the entire charter.

The court bowed to these technical arguments, noting that parliament should have adhered to the 1996 Constitution and not the 1993 international treaties law. The basic framework of Article 94 in the Constitution was both exhaustive and supreme in the way it envisaged the procedure for signing pieces of legislation, and laws ratifying international treaties were no exception in this regard (KSU 2000b). Therefore, the court struck down both the ratification law and the respective provisions of the international treaties law. At the same time, the court, commenting on the appellants' substantive arguments regarding the charter, noted bluntly "With the regard to the constitutional appeal's point regarding unconstitutionality of some provisions of the Charter in their substance, the court came to conclusion that the law in question did not hold to constitutional procedure requirements for signing and publishing of laws (Article 94 of the Constitution), and the raised questions of substance were not a subject of the Court's review" (ibid.).While the Ukrainian parliament eventually passed the European Charter again, in due conformity with the Constitution, this case does serve as an example of how language ethnopolitics in Ukraine has sometimes ridden the waves of procedural hiccups.

Even more emblematic of this phenomenon was an episode beginning in 2002, when 165 MPs introduced a legislative amendment to grant a new kind of "official language" status to Russian in Ukraine's Constitution. The amendment was first proposed by parliamentarians from the Communist Party group in the parliament, who were delivering on a long-standing promise dating back to the 1990s to grant separate status to Russian in the Constitution. The amendment proposed to supplement Article 38 of the Constitution with a "right to use Ukrainian as a state language and Russian as an official language in the process of managing public affairs and in the bodies of territorial self-government" (Grach et al. 2002). Thus, the amendment was meant to establish a new binary language regime, circumventing the core Article 10 on language statuses in the Constitution.

In the event, the Constitutional Court again used a procedural argument to refuse even to rule on the case. It asserted that under Article 156 of the Constitution all changes concerning the main foundations of the state and society must be introduced to the parliament by no less than two-thirds of the body's members, hence at least 300 MPs. Although the Communists' amendment seem to concern a more innocuous section of the Constitution concerning citizens' rights in public administration, the court still found that the creation of a new kind of "official language" status for Russian would alter the main contours of Ukrainian statehood and therefore declared the amendment subject to the higher threshold for consideration. Since the amendment did not meet this threshold, the court said it "does not have a right to open constitutional proceedings in this case and to provide a legal decision regarding the amendment" (KSU 2004).

A final example of a backdoor release for the court from involvement in language ethnopolitics arose in 2018, when the justices were called upon to formally strike down the highly controversial law on "On Principles of the State Language Policy" adopted in 2012. Because of the way in which the law was seen as promoting the rights of the Russian language in different regions of the country, it had already been contested in a series of appeals to the court in 2012. But none of these ended up engendering real constitutional proceedings or rulings because of repeated technical shortcomings in the appeal documents. Even in the midst of the 2014 Euromaidan revolution, the country was unable to fully abolish of the 2012 language law, since although the parliament did pass a formal act of annulment, the interim President of Ukraine, Oleksandr Turchynov, refused to sign the document due to the societal turmoil at the time (Korrespondent 2014). Because of this, the law lingered on.

In July 2014, the nationalist party *Svoboda* called on the court to review the constitutionality of the language law in order to release the legislation from limbo. In their appeal, the deputies drew on both substantive and procedural arguments. The appellants argued that the introduction of regional languages disadvantaged Ukrainian in the country's constitutional framework. In the view of Svoboda MPs, Ukrainian language was being downgraded by a number of provisions which would privilege regional languages in, above all, public administration, local self-government, and the administration of justice. All of this was seen as being in violation of Article 10 of the Constitution (KSU 2014). Yet, the centerpiece of the appeal revolved around the procedure. The deputies argued that the way the law had been voted in plenary violated Article 84 of the Constitution, according to which members of parliament must vote for legislation in person. The plaintiffs maintained that on that day it had been observed that many parliamentarians had cast votes on behalf of other members, thus throwing into doubt the validity of the final approval.

True to its accumulating practice of concentrating first on procedure and then substance, the court chose to discharge the substantive aspects of the appeal and focus instead on the integrity of procedure. The court pointed out that "voting in person means direct exercise of a people's deputy's will regarding the issues under consideration of the parliament" (KSU 2018). In the court's view, this was in line with the nature of a people's deputy mandate to represent the Ukrainian people. Personal voting could therefore not be delegated, and no MP could be legitimately inhibited in the exercise of his/her capacity to vote. Most importantly, the court established that voting in person constituted a part of the constitutional procedure for adopting a piece of legislation (ibid.).

In turn, the court assessed evidences regarding the way in which voting took place on July 3, 2012. It established that the law was passed by MPs from the parliamentary majority using voting cards belonging to other colleagues in their absence. The court also identified a number of technical violations during that day that taken together undermined the integrity of the constitutional procedure significantly. Therefore, in light of the constitutional principle of personal voting, the court abolished the law in full. Moreover, at the end of its decision, the court stated explicitly its preference for ruling on the basis of procedural, rather than substantive grounds. The justices wrote: "The subject of the constitutional review [the appellant] argues the unconstitutionality of the Law by referring to not only a violation of the integrity of the constitutional procedure, but also to the unconstitutionality of the substance of the law. However, adhering to a constitutional procedure for legislative adoption is an element of legitimacy of legislative process. This means that when the procedure is violated, it is not the content of the law that warrants constitutional control, but rather the constitutional procedure of its adoption and endorsement" (ibid.).

CONCLUSION

This chapter had multiple aims. On an empirical level, it has sought to provide a synthesized analysis of how Ukraine's struggles over language policy have evolved specifically within the realm of the country's Constitutional Court. While the court has been fairly accessible across a range of eligible appellants, and has had a fairly broad mandate to not only review the constitutionality of legal acts, but also provide interpretation of them, it emerges that within the sphere of language politics it has mostly been members of the parliament who have sought substantiation from the court for their attempts to influence Ukraine's language regime. In particular, one can see how some Ukrainian parliamentarians have tried to get the court to weigh in on ways in which Ukrainian language might be imposed more authoritatively as the state language, based on the main stipulations on language in the 1996 Constitution. Moreover, these forces have used the court to thwart alternative legislation, when it has aimed to strengthen the rights of Russian-language users, such as the Yanukovych-era law on bolstering Russian as a regional language. At the same time, the court has been a sanctuary for Russian-minded leaders, who have sought to make clear before the justices that in some areas of the country the rights of Russian-speakers need to be protected and that blanket imposition of the Ukrainian across the administrative or judicial realm would be discriminatory. On this score, the court has also provided some relief.

Where does this Ukrainian example, therefore, leave us in terms of understanding the role that constitutional courts might play in mediating ethnopolitical disputes? As with many political phenomena, there are two important constellations of issues that come together to influence this prospect. The first is the ethnopolitical situation of the country itself. Ukraine is a country immersed in the kind of triadic nexus famously described by Rogers Brubaker (1996, 2011). While the role of the Ukrainian government as a "nationalizing state" has been mixed (in contrast to, say, the Baltic states), there remains a core aspiration (that seems to only have grown over the last two decades) to tilt the ethnopolitical balance more toward an understanding of Ukraine being fundamentally a Ukrainian-language nation-state. A Ukrainian-focused language policy naturally forms a part of this goal. It should be added though that not every "nationalizing" move is inherently villainous or indented to ostracize ethnic minorities of the country. In fact, there are legitimate sociolinguistic concerns that a Ukrainian-focused language policy naturally seeks to address. In this respect, the court must walk a fine line, since it is not arbitrating between necessarily equal political forces (as might be the case in a more diversely pluralistic country like Nigeria or India). It must instead be ready and able to balance the very strong sentiments of titular Ukrainian nation-statehood with contemporary principles and practices of minority protection, whilst all the while not letting the fact that the minority is linked to an overbearing, neighboring kin-state influence its judicial decision making. In other words, justices are being asked to decide essential identity issues about which they themselves may have subjective feelings and opinions—even more so moving forward following the outbreak of armed conflict over Crimea and the Donbas region.

Added to this particularity is, of course, the second "constellation", namely, the court itself, its institutional prerogatives, actual practices and overall political standing. All of these elements equally determine the way in which a constitutional court can play a role in certain ethnopolitical situations. While the Ukrainian Constitutional Court has been endowed with what might be called proactive powers (especially concerning the right to interpret legislation), within the sphere of language issues it has generally used these powers sparingly. Moreover, it has at times staked out a very technical approach, deciding to place procedural issues center-stage and thereby explicitly demur on adjudicating substantively between competing ethnopolitical claims. Lastly, it is unquestionable that the court's authority (not least in the eyes of ethnopolitical actors seeking to decide whether to "go the judicial route" with their claims) has suffered over the years, when the appointment of justices became politicized or when major structural changes paralyzed the court's overall functioning.

Putting these two parts of the equation together, the Ukrainian Constitutional Court's legal positivism as well as other moments of reserve with regard to deciding language ethnopolitics may be understandable. After all, courts themselves are not actually makers of policy, who should have to, or even just be able to, determine whether Ukraine must become more Ukrainian-dominant or, oppositely, even go bi-national. In a situation where core nation-statehood is on the line, constitutional courts will be hard-pressed to make rulings that will entirely contradict such pressures. Key elements to ensure that decisions remain balanced include a professional and impartial appointment process for justices as well as strong awareness of principles and practices of minority rights deriving from international experience, so that decisions are not made in a national vacuum.

APPENDIX

Table 3.2 Cases on language matters discussed in the chapter

Case	Date	Appeal type (OI/C)[a]	Decision[b]
The case on application of the Ukrainian language	1999	OI	Ukrainian
The case on ratification of the Charter on Languages	2000	C	Ukrainian
The case on &3, Article 10, and Article 14 of the Law of Ukrain an SSR "On Languages in Ukrainian SSR" from 1989	2003	C	Russian
The case on Russian language as official language	2004	C	Ukrainian
The case on distribution of foreign movies	2006	OI	Ukrainian
The case on the language of justice	2008	C	Both
The case of the Law "On Judicial System and Status of the Judges" from 2010	2011	C	Both
The case of the Law "On Principles of the State Language Policy" from 2012	2018	C	Ukrainian
The case of the Law "On Education" from 2017	2019	C	Ukrainian

[a]OI = Official Interpretation; C = Constitutional ruling
[b]"Decision" column refers to increased Ukrainian-language or Russian-language predominance in public life as an outcome of Constitutional Court decisions. That is, if the decision institutionalized Ukrainian, we put "Ukrainian" in the column and vice versa for Russian

REFERENCES

Arel, Dominique. 1995. Language Politics in Independent Ukraine: Towards One or Two State Languages? *Nationalities Papers* 23 (3): 597–622.

Besters-Dilger, Juliane, ed. 2009. *Language Policy and Language Situation in Ukraine: Analysis and Recommendations*. Frankfurt am Main: Peter Lang.

Bowring, Bill. 2009. Language Policy in Ukraine. International Standards and Obligations, and Ukrainian Law and Legislation. In *Language Policy and Language Situation in Ukraine: Analysis and Recommendations*, ed. Juliane Besters-Dilger, 57–100. Frankfurt am Main: Peter Lang.

Brown, Trevor L., and Charles R. Wise. 2004. Constitutional Courts and Legislative-Executive Relations: The Case of Ukraine. *Political Science Quarterly* 119 (1): 143–169.

Brubaker, Rogers. 1996. *Nationalism Reframed: Nationhood and the National Question in the New Europe*. Cambridge: Cambridge University Press.

———. 2011. Nationalizing States Revisited: Projects and Processes of Nationalization in Post-Soviet States. *Ethnic and Racial Studies* 34 (11): 1785–1814.

D'Anieri, Paul. 2003. Leonid Kuchma and the Personalization of the Ukrainian Presidency. *Problems of Post-Communism* 50 (5): 58–65.

———. 2006. *Understanding Ukrainian Politics: Power, Politics, and Institutional Design.* Armonk: M.A. Sharpe.

Grach, Leonid, Zarema Katusheva, and Ivan Vernidubov. 2002. *Proekt Zakonu pro vneseniazmin do statti 38 KonstytucyiUkrainy* [Project of the Law "On Amending Article 38 of the Constitution of Ukraine"]. http://w1.c1.rada.gov.ua/pls/zweb2/webproc4_1?pf3511=13843

Korrespondent. 2014. Turchynov Vidmovyvsia Pidpysaty Rishennia Rady pro Skasuvannia Zakonu pro Movy. [Turchinov Refused To Sign Rada's Decision to Abolish the Law on Languages] March 3, 2014. https://ua.korrespondent.net/ukraine/politics/3314338-turchynov-vidmovyvsia-pidpysaty-rishennia-rady-pro-skasuvannia-zakonu-pro-movy

Kulyk, Volodymyr. 2006. Constructing Common Sense: Language and Ethnicity in Ukrainian Public Discourse. *Ethnic and Racial Studies* 29 (2): 281–314.

———. 2009. Language Policies and Language Attitudes in Post-Orange Ukraine. In *In Language Policy and Language Situation in Ukraine: Analysis and Recommendations*, ed. Juliane Besters-Dilger, 15–56. Frankfurt am Main: Peter Lang.

———. 2013. Language Policy in Ukraine: What People Want the State to Do. *East European Politics and Societies and Cultures* 27 (2): 280–307.

———. 2018. Ukraine's 2017 Education Law Incites International Controversy over Language Stipulation. *PONARS Eurasia* Policy Memo 525, April 2018. http://www.ponarseurasia.org/memo/ukraines-2017-education-law-incites-international-controversy-over-language-stipulation

———. 2019. Memory and Language: Different Dynamics in the Two Aspects of Identity Politics in Post-Euromaidan Ukraine. *Nationalities Papers*, 1–18. https://doi.org/10.1017/nps.2018.6

Lovin, Anton, and Ruslana Vovk. 2018. Taking Stock: First Steps of the Renewed Constitutional Court of Ukraine. Democracy Reporting International. https://democracy-reporting.org/ru/taking-stock-first-steps-of-the-renewed-constitutional-court-of-ukraine/

Moser, Michael. 2013. *Language Policy and the Discourse on Languages under President Viktor Yanukovych (25 February 2010–28 October 2012).* Stuttgart: Ibidem-Verlag.

Protsyk, Oleh. 2005. Constitutional Politics and Presidential Power in Ukraine. *Problems of Post-Communism* 52 (5): 23–31.

Riabchuk, Mykola. 2003. *"Dvi Ukrainy" realni mezi, virtualni viyny.* Krytyka: Kyiv.

Slidenko, Igor. 2018. "Movnyi Zakon Mih Buty Skasovanyi Sudom Scze u 2014 Roci." [The Language Law Could Have Been Overturned by a Court in 2014] Interview by AllaShershen. Ukrinform. March 6, 2018. https://www.ukrinform.ua/rubric-society/2416765-igor-slidenko-sudda-konstituci-jnogo-sudu.html

————. 2019. Pretenzii Uhorshchyny shchodo Ukrainskoi Movy Dyvnym Chynom Synkhronizuvalysia z Pozytsiieiu Rosii. [Hungary's Claims on the Ukrainian Language Awesome Way Synchronized with Russia's Position]. Interview by AllaShershen. Ukrinform, July 23, 2019. Accessed November 11, 2019. https://www.ukrinform.ua/rubric-polytics/2746332-igor-slidenko-sudda-konstitucijnogo-sudu.html.

Trach, Nadiya. 2009. Language Policy and Language Situation in the Sphere of Legal Proceedings and Office Administration in Ukraine. In *Language Policy and Language Situation in Ukraine: Analysis and Recommendations*, ed. Juliane Besters-Dilger, 287–326. Frankfurt am Main: Peter Lang.

Verkhovna Rada Autonomnoi Respubliky Krym. 2004. Konstytutsyine Podannia sczodo Konstytutsyinosti Statti 7 Cyvilnoho Procesual'noho Kodeksu Ukrainy [Appeal to the Constitutional Court of Ukraine Regarding Constitutionality Article 7 of the Civil Procedural Code of Ukraine]. http://www.ccu.gov.ua/docs/528

Wolczuk, Kataryna. 2002a. *The Moulding of Ukraine: The Constitutional Politics of State Formation*. Budapest: Central European University Press.

————. 2002b. The Constitutional Court of Ukraine: The Politics of Survival. In *Constitutional Justice, East and West: Democratic Legitimacy and Constitutional Courts in Post-Communist Europe in a Comparative Perspective*, ed. Wojciech Sadurski, 327–348. The Hague: Kluwer Law International.

LAWS OF UKRAINE [VERKHOVNA RADA UKRAINY]

Verkhovna Rada Ukrainy. 1989. Zakon Ukrainskoi Radianskoi Sotsialistychnoi Respubliky Ukrainy "Pro Movy v Ukrainskii RSR". [Law of Ukrainian SSR "On Languages in Ukrainian SSR"]. https://zakon.rada.gov.ua/laws/show/8312-11

————. 1992. Zakon Ukrainy "Про Конституційний Суд України". [Law of Ukraine "On the Constitutional Court of Ukraine".] https://zakon.rada.gov.ua/laws/show/2400-12

————. 1993. Zakon Ukrainy "Про міжнародні договори України". [Law of Ukraine "On International Treaties of Ukraine".] https://zakon.rada.gov.ua/laws/show/3767-12

————. 1996a. Zakon Ukrainy "Про Конституційний Суд України". [Law of Ukraine "On the Constitutional Court of Ukraine".] https://zakon.rada.gov.ua/laws/show/422/96-%D0%B2%D1%80/ed20170803

————. 1996b. "Konstitutsiia Ukrainy". [Constitution of Ukraine.] https://zakon.rada.gov.ua/laws/show/254%D0%BA/96-%D0%B2%D1%80

————. 2006. Zakon Ukrainy "Pro Vnesennia Zmin do Statti 17 Zakonu Ukrainy 'Pro Konstytutsiinyi Sud Ukrainy'". [Law of Ukraine "On Amending Article 17 of the Law "On Constitutional Court of Ukraine"."] https://zakon.rada.gov.ua/laws/show/73-16

76   A. NEKOLIAK AND V. PETTAI

————. 2012a. Zakon Ukrainy "Про засади державної мовної політики". [Law of Ukraine "On Principles of the State Language Policy".] https://zakon.rada. gov.ua/laws/show/5029-17

————. 2012b. Proekt Zakonu pro Vyznannia Takym, shcho Vtratyv Chynnist, Zakonu Ukrainy "Pro Zasady Derzhavnoi Movnoi Polityky". [Draft Law of Ukraine "On Annulling the Law 'On Principles of the State Language Policy'". http://w1.c1.rada.gov.ua/pls/zweb2/webproc4_1?pf3511=45291

————. 2016. Zakon Ukrainy "Pro Vnesennia Zmin do Deiakykh Zkoniv Ukrainy shchodo Chastky Muzychnykh Tvoriv Derzhavnoiu Movoiu u Prohramakh Teleradioorhanizatsii" [Law of Ukraine "On Amending Some Legislative Acts of Ukraine regarding Quota of Musical Production in Programs of Radio and TV-Organizations".] https://zakon.rada.gov.ua/laws/show/1421-19

————. 2017a. Zakon Ukrainy "Pro Vnesennia Zmin do Deiakykh Zakoniv Ukrainy shchodo Movy Audiovizualnykh (Elektronnykh) Zasobiv Masovoi Informatsii". [Law of Ukraine "On Amending Some Legislative Acts of Ukraine Regarding the Language of Electronic Mass Media".] https://zakon.rada.gov. ua/laws/show/2054-19

————. 2017b. Zakon Ukrainy "Pro Konstytutsiinyi Sud Ukrainy". [Law of Ukraine "On the Constitutional Court of Ukraine".] https://zakon.rada.gov. ua/laws/show/2136-19

————. 2017c. Zakon Ukrainy "Pro Osvitu". [Law of Ukraine "On Education".] https://zakon.rada.gov.ua/laws/show/2145-19

————. 2019. Zakon Ukrainy "Pro Zabezpechennia Funktsionuvannia Ukrainskoi Movy yak Derzhavnoi" [Law of Ukraine "On Provision of Functioning of Ukrainian Language as the Official Language."] https://zakon.rada.gov.ua/ laws/show/2704-19

APPEALS TO AND DECISIONS OF THE CONSTITUTIONAL COURT OF UKRAINE

Konstytutsyinyi Sud Ukrainy (KSU). 1997. Konstytutsyine Podannia pro Ofitsyne Tlumachenia Statti 10 Konstytutsyi Ukrainy sczodo Oboviazkovosti Ii Zastosuvannia. [Appeal to the Constitutional Court Regarding Official Interpretation of Article 10 of the Constitution]. http://www.ccu.gov.ua/ docs/406

————. 1999. Rishennia Konstytutsiynoho Sudu Ukrainy pro Ofitsyne Tlumachennia Polozhen' Statti 10 Konstytutsyi Ukrainy sczodo Zastosuvannia Derzhavnoi Movy Orhanamy Derzhavnoi Vlady,Mistsevoho Samovriaduvannia ta Vykorystannia Ii u Navchalniomu Protsesi v Navczal'nyvh Zakladakh Ukrainy (Sprava pro Zastosuvannia Ukrainskoi Movy) [Decision of the Constitutional Court of Ukraine Regarding Official Interpretation of the Article 10 of the Constitution (the Case on Application of Ukrainian language)]. https:// zakon.rada.gov.ua/laws/show/v010p710-99

3 NAVIGATING ETHNOPOLITICAL DISPUTES: UKRAINE'S CONSTITUTIONAL... 77

————. 2000a. Konstytutsyine Podannia sczodo Vidpovidnosti Konstytutsyi Ukrainy (Konstytutsyinosti) Zakonu Ukrainy "Pro Ratyficatsyiu Europeiskoi Hartii Rehionalnykh Mov abo Menshyn, 1992 r." [Appeal to the Constitutional Court of Ukraine Regarding Constitutionality of the Law "On Ratification of the European Charter for Regional or Minority Languages (1992)"]. http://www.ccu.gov.ua/docs/416

————. 2000b. Rishennia Konstytutsiynoho Sudu Ukrainy sczodo Vidpovidnosti Konstytutsyi Ukrainy Konstytutsyinosti) Zakonu Ukrainy "Pro Rratyficatsiiu Europeiskoi Hartii Rehionalnykh Mov abo Menshyn, 1992 r." (Sprava pro Ratyficatsyiu Hartii pro Movy) [Decision of the Constitutional Court about Constitutionality of the Law "On Ratification of the European Charter for Regional or Minority Languages (1992)" (the Case on Ratification of the Charter on Languages)]. https://zakon.rada.gov.ua/laws/show/v009p710-00

————. 2003. Uhvala Konstytutsiynoho Sudu Ukrainy pro Vidmovu u Vidkrytti Konstytutsiynoho Provadzhennia sczodo Vidpovidnosti Konstytutsyi Ukrainy (Konsytutsyinosti) Chastyny 3 Statti 10, Statti 14 Zakonu Ukrain'skoi RSR "Pro Movy v Ukrain'skiy RSR," punktu 4 Polozhennia pro Passport Hromadianyna Ukrayinu, Abzatsiv 5, 7, 9, 11 Opysu Pasporta Hromadianyna Ukrainy.[Decision of the Constitutional Court of Ukraine about Refusal to Open Constitutional Proceedings Regarding Constitutionality of Part 3, Article 10, and Article 14 of the Law of Ukrainian SSR "On Languages in Ukrainian SSR", article 4 of the Regulations on a Passport of a Citizen of Ukraine, Some Provisions of the Paragraphs on a Passport of a Citizen of Ukraine]. https://zakon.rada.gov.ua/laws/show/v024u710-03

————. 2004. Uhvala Konstytuciynoho Sudu Ukrainy pro Vidmovu u Vidkrytti Konstytuciynoho Provadzenia u Spravi pro Nadannia Vysnovku sczodo Vidpovidnosti Stattiam 157 i 158 Konstytutsyi Ukrainy Zakonproektu "Pro Vnesennia Zmin do Statti 38 Konstytutsyi Ukrainy," Podanoho do Verhovnoi Rady 165 Narodnymy Deputatamy Ukrainy. [Decision of the Constitutional Court of Ukraine about Refusal to Open Constitutional Proceedings Constitutionality of the Project of the Law "On Amending the Article 38 of the Constitution of Ukraine" (the Case on Russian Language as Official)]. https://zakon.rada.gov.ua/laws/show/v044u710-04

————. 2005. Konstytutsyine Podannia sczodo Vidpovidnosti Konstytutsyi Ukrainy (Konstytutsyinosti) Statti 15 Kodeksu Administratyvnoho Sudochynstva Ukrainy [Appeal to the Constitutional Court of Ukraine Regarding Constitutionality of Article 15 of the Code on Administrative Justice in Ukraine]. http://www.ccu.gov.ua/docs/528

————. 2006. Konstytutsyine Podannia sczodo Oficiynoho Tlumachenia Chastyny Druhoi Statti 14 Zakonu Ukrainy "Pro Kinematohrafiyu" [Appeal to the Constitutional Court of Ukraine Regarding Official Interpretation of Article 14 of the Law "On Cinematography"]. http://www.ccu.gov.ua/docs/560

———. 2007. Rishennia Konstytutsiynoho Sudu Ukrainy pro Ofitsyine Tlumachennia Polozhen' Czastyny Druhoi Statti 14 Zakonu Ukrainy "Pro Kinematohrafiyu" (Sprava pro Rozpovsiudzhennia Inozemnyh Filmiv) [Decision of the Constitutional Court of Ukraine about Official Interpretation of Article 14 of the Law "On Cinematography" (the Case on Distribution of Foreign Movies)]. https://zakon3.rada.gov.ua/laws/show/v013p710-07

———. 2008. Rishennia Konstytutsiynoho Sudu Ukrainy sczodo Vidpovidnosti Konstytutsyi Ukrainy (Konstytutsyinosti) Statti 15 Kodeksu Administratyvnoho Sudochinstva Ukrainy, Statti 7 Cyvilnoho Procesual'nohoKodeksu Ukrainy (Sprava pro Movu Sudochinstva) [Decision of the Constitutional Court of Ukraine about Constitutionality of Article 15 of the Code on Administrative Justice in Ukraine, Article 7 of the Civil Procedural Code of Ukraine (the Case on the Language of Justice)]. https://zakon.rada.gov.ua/laws/show/v008p710-08

———. 2009. Rishennia Konstytutsiynoho Sudu Ukrainy sczodo Vidpovidnosti Konstytutsyi Ukrainy (Konstytutsyinosti) Zakonu Ukrainy "Pro Vnesennia Zmin do Deyakykh Zakoniv Ukrainy" sczodo Povnovazhenn Konstytutsiynoho Sudu Ukrainy, Osoblyvostei Provadzhennia u Spravah za Konstytutsyinymy Zvernenniamy, ta Inshykh Polozhen' Zakonu Ukrainy "Pro Konstytuciynyi Sud" [Decision of the Constitutional Court of Ukraine regarding constitutionality of the Law of Ukraine "On Amending Laws of Ukraine Regarding Prerogatives of the Constitutional Court, Procedure of Reviewing Constitutional Requests", and Other Provisions of the Law "On Constitutional Court of Ukraine"]. https://zakon.rada.gov.ua/laws/show/v017p710-09/ed20100803

———. 2010. Konstytutsyine Podannia sczodo Vidpovidnosti Konstytutsyi Ukrainy (Konstytutsyinosti) Okremykh Polozhen' Zakonu Ukrainy "Pro Sudoustriy ta Status Suddiv," Kryminalno-Procesual'noho Kodeksu Ukrainy, Hospodars'ko-Procesual'noho Kodeksu Ukrainy, Cyvilnoho-Procesual'noho Kodeksu Ukrainy, Kodeksu Administratyvnoho Sudochynstva Ukrainy, Zakonu "Pro Vyshchu RaduYustytsii" [Appeal to the Constitutional Court of Ukraine Regarding Constitutionality of Some Provisions of the Law "On Judicial System and Status of the Judges", of the Criminal Procedural Code of Ukraine, of the Commercial and Procedural Code of Ukraine, of the Civil Procedural Code of Ukraine, of the Code on Administrative Justice in Ukraine, and of the Law "On Higher Council of Justice"]. http://www.ccu.gov.ua/docs/636

———. 2011. Rishennia Konstytuciynoho Sudu Ukrainy sczodo Vidpovidnosti Konstytutsyi Ukrainy (Konstytutsyinosti) Okremyh Polozhen' Zakonu Ukrainy "Pro Sudoustiy ta Status Suddiv," Kryminalno-Procesual'noho Kodeksu Ukrainy, Hospodars'ko—Procesual'noho Kodeksu Ukrainy, Cyvilnoho Procesual'noho Kodeksu Ukrainy, Kodeksu Administratyvnoho Sudochynstva Ukrainy. [Decision of the Constitutional Court of Ukraine about Constitutionality of Some Provisions of the Law "On Judicial System and

Status of the Judges", of the Criminal Procedural Code of Ukraine, of the Commercial and Procedural Code of Ukraine, of the Civil Procedural Code of Ukraine, of the Code on Administrative Justice in Ukraine]. https://zakon.rada.gov.ua/laws/show/v017p710-11

———. 2014. Konstytutsyine Podannia sczodo Nevidpovidnosti Konstytucyi Ukrainy (Nekonstytutsyinosti) Zakonu Uktainy "Pro Zasady Derzhavnoi Movnoi Polityky". [Appeal to the Constitutional Court of Ukraine Regarding Unconstitutionality of the Law "On Principles of the State Language Policy"]. Accessed July 23, 2019. http://www.ccu.gov.ua/docs/2056

———. 2017. Konstytutsyine Podannia sczodo Vidpovidnosti Konstytutsyi Ukrainy (Konstytutsyinosti) Zakonu Ukrainy "Pro Osvitu" [Appeal to the Constitutional Court of Ukraine Regarding Constitutionality of the Law "On Education"]. http://www.ccu.gov.ua/docs/2803

———. 2018. Rishennia Konstytutsiynoho Sudu Ukrainy sczodo Vidpovidnosti Konstytutsyi Ukrainy (Konstytutsyinosti) Zakonu Uktainy "Pro Zasady Derzhvnoi Movnoi polityky" [Decision of the Constitutional Court of Ukraine about Constitutionality of the Law "On Principles of the State Language Policy"]. https://zakon.rada.gov.ua/laws/show/v002p710-18

———. 2019a. Konstytutsyine Podania sczodo Vidpovidnosti Konstytutsii Ukrainy (Konstytutsiinosti) Zakonu Ukrainy "Pro Zabespechenia Funktsionuvannia Ukrainskoii Movy yak Derzhavnoi" [Appeal to the Constitutional Court of Ukraine Regarding Constitutionality of the Law "On Provision of Functioning of the Ukrainian Language as the State Language"]. http://www.ccu.gov.ua/sites/default/files/kp_51.pdf

———. 2019b. Rishennia Konstytutsiynoho Sudu Ukrainy sczodo Vidpovidnosti Konstytutsyi Ukrainy (Konstytutsyinosti) Zakonu Ukrainy "Pro Osvitu" [Decision of the Constitutional Court about Constitutionality of the Law "On Education"]. http://www.ccu.gov.ua/sites/default/files/docs/10_p_2019_zm.pdf

CHAPTER 4

Crimean Tatars and the Question of National and Ethnic Belonging in Ukraine

Alina Zubkovych

INTRODUCTION

Until 2014, the Soviet myth of Crimea as a place that symbolized "military glory" was predominantly the one reproduced by Russian, local Crimean, and Ukrainian post-Soviet authorities. Thus, the collective memory of ethnic minorities, such as Crimean Tatars, who were deported to Central Asia *en masse* in 1944 and only started repatriation at the beginning of the 1990s, lacked public and political support for more than 25 years (Bezverkha 2015). Ever since the annexation of Crimea by the Russian Federation in 2014, Kremlin officials have continued to promote the same rigid vision of Crimea (Grigas 2016). At the same time, the annexation has boosted mechanisms of national narrative re-actualization in mainland Ukraine (Onuch and Hale 2018). Previously oppressed memories received official support and have been utilized in recent constructed narratives on the image of Crimea. This study examines the

A. Zubkovych (✉)
Södertörn University, Stockholm, Sweden
e-mail: alina.zubkovych@nuforum.se

© The Author(s) 2020
H. Shelest, M. Rabinovych (eds.), *Decentralization, Regional Diversity, and Conflict*, Federalism and Internal Conflicts,
https://doi.org/10.1007/978-3-030-41765-9_4

81

post-Euromaidan dynamics of identity formation in Ukraine through the prism of a non-titular nation, namely Crimean Tatars.[1]

The "appearance" (not yet generally understood to be the "return") of Crimean Tatars in Crimea at the beginning of the 1990s had a predictable psychological impact on the peninsula's local population. Local political and economic elites revived Soviet myths, exploiting anti-Tatar prejudices that were still widespread and formed the core of the cliché (Shevel 2001). Breakaway from this cliché happened in 2014: with the annexation of Crimea and suppression of freedom of speech, a number of Crimean Tatars were forced to leave the peninsula and moved to Kyiv; a smaller number relocated to the western parts of Ukraine. In this chapter, we analyze how Crimean Tatars who resettled to Ukraine's mainland perceive themselves. The analysis is based on a series of in-depth semi-structured interviews with the settlers. The chapter aims to trace the way in which Crimean Tatars construct their identities, as well as dynamics of their national self-identification following the Euromaidan Revolution.

We argue that the construction of the new sense of "Ukrainness," incorporating Crimean Tatars, is based not on the ethnonational politics of belonging, but rather on political citizenship. A distinctive feature of this form of construction is a stronger inclusiveness towards ethnic minorities, replacing previously existing selectivity patterns—a phenomenon that requires further reflection and research (Uehling 2016). Thus, focusing on the dynamics of the Crimean Tatars' self-identification, this chapter seeks to contribute to this new strand of scholarship investigating a novel stage of national identity formation in Ukraine. Notably, as we will illustrate below, the emerging elements of a more inclusive politics of belonging do not display consistency in presenting Crimean Tatars and their culture as an integral part of Ukrainian collective memory. Rather, trying to come to grips with an inconsistent and fragmented process and product, academic discourse has tended to settle on a portrayal of identity in ethnonational terms. The reproduction and adaptation of such a discourse in non-academic discourses leads to a depiction of Ukraine as a multicultural, multi-religious, and ethnically vivid society without developing a nuanced understanding of the historical constitution of such features and the contemporary dynamics of identity formation.

In this vein, the chapter is structured as follows. First, it introduces a conceptual apparatus, focusing on the notions of ethnic and national

---

[1] On Euromaidan: see Chap. 1, fn 1.

identity, reflecting the primordialist and constructivist approaches respectively. Additionally, it demonstrates how the notions of "regional difference" and "regional diversity" attenuate those two approaches and play into the Ukraine's domestic debate on national identity. Based on these theoretical elaborations, the empirical section of the chapter analyses the dynamics of national identification in the case of Crimean Tatars. It uses in-depth interviews with Crimean Tatars who relocated to mainland Ukraine to demonstrate an extent to which the Euromaidan Revolution, followed by the annexation of Crimea by the Russian Federation in 2014 has led to the reconsideration of personal experiences, self-identification, and collective memory of the pre-annexation period.

The chapter is offering a nuanced insight into the post-2014 politics of belonging and the dynamics of identity formation in Ukraine, based on the example of the Crimean Tatar community.

I. Conceptual Foundations

1. Regional Difference vs Regional Diversity

Ukraine gained its independence in 1991, while the formation of its contemporary borders finished in 1954, when the Autonomous Republic of Crimea was transferred from the Russian Soviet Socialist Republic to the Ukrainian SSR. References to the etymological meaning of Ukraine as "borderland," and emphases on the complex historical and social-cultural constitution of its territory abound in historical texts. Indeed, the number and variety of the ethnicities and multiple identities that had a chances to impose and sustain historical change have inevitably nurtured the complexity of the regional structures in today's Ukraine. Hence, as underlined by Oksana Myshlovska in Chap. 2, regional diversity is concerned with a striking assortment of religious, ethnic, linguistic, and socioeconomic characteristics, and a range of differing historical collective memories and ideological traditions. An emphasis on regional differences is an important characteristic of contemporary Ukraine and its vision of itself as a state; while such an emphasis does not put the country's territorial integrity into question, it does provide a foundation for the regional factor to be manipulated. An important question that arises in this regard deals with terminology: should one speak of *regional differences* or of *regional diversity*? Do these terms have different connotations, and can selected terms influence our analysis of findings? Does *difference* stresses cleavages and otherness of the entities, whereas *diversity* has a pluralistic emphasis on the richness of variety?

The emphasis on regional differences has been predominantly made by scholars focusing on conflict potential, risks, and crisis. In this regard, Sasse's 2001 study might serve as an example. She identified Crimea, Donbas, and Zakarpattya as most prone to ethnoregional challenges, a consequence of the politicization of regional diversity in the territories (Sasse 2001, 70). Ethnicity is, hence, one of the cleavages prone to be politically mobilized at the regional level, though it can be also viewed as a means of attracting attention to more deeply rooted regional cleavages "such as multi-ethnicity, cultural or socio-economic factors that cross-cut ethnic markers" (Sasse 2001, 95). Summarizing key factors that have determined the peaceful overcoming of mobilized Russian nationalism in Crimea in 1993, Sasse concludes that the way that Ukraine "dealt with its ethnic and regional diversity and, above all, with its most precarious region, Crimea, belongs to its political achievements" (ibid. 96). Though contradicting the findings by Myshlovska presented in Chap. 2 (and, thus, pointing to the need for further research on pre-Euromaidan policies pertaining to regional diversity), these conclusions correlate with our intention to strongly differentiate between regional *difference* and *diversity* as terms having different connotations. Sasse (2001) explicitly uses "diversity" as a neutral fact of regional richness. Only when diversity starts to be exploited for political mobilization does the author focus on "differences." That is, context determines emphasis and the selection of a corresponding term.

In this vein, another terminological tangle concerning regional diversity in Ukraine arises from an unclear distinction between the concepts of ethnic and national identity. Sometimes these terms are applied as categories that do not require further explanation. However, empirical evidence demonstrates the opposite: the overlapping applications of the terms in respondents' statements suggest the need for a terminological reconsideration.

2. Ethnic Identity

The concept of ethnicity is one that is commonly used; however, it is interpreted in a different manner depending on the context and theoretical premises. The primordialist approach would generally emphasize ethnicity as a long-established bond granted with birth. As major representatives of such approaches, Edward Shills and Clifford Geerts connect ethnicity as a strongly ascribed category with blood, race, and language (Ibrahim 2011). Primordialism has been heavily criticized for failing to consider the flexibility of ethnic identity. Ibrahim (2011) gives an example of "Arabs" being thought to be a homogenous ethnic group to illustrate the inconsistency of such straightforward belief. The homogenous view does not take into account those who converted to Islam from Judaism and Christianity following the expansion of the Islamic empires in the seventh to tenth centuries; nor does it take into account groups that consider themselves politically as "Arabs," but speak Aramaic, Greek, Coptic or other languages. Examples like this demonstrate the weakness of the primordial approach to ethnic identity.

Instrumentalists and constructivists would rather view ethnic identity as a question of rational choice. Post-colonialist Homi Bhabha (1991, 1994) argues that ethnicity is a "cut and paste job": individuals will select that part of their identity from multiple variations, choosing what works best for them in their situation. Culture is another important factor in constructing stability in self-perception. Anthony D. Smith (2009) emphasized the role of symbols and myths in ensuring the continuity of ethnicity in the modern world. Finally, it is difficult to overestimate the impact of Benedict Anderson's (1991) seminal work on the understanding of nations as "imagined political communities," and the role of multi-ethnicity in the process of nation-building.

Inhabitants of countries and regions are presented as people aware of their ethnic backgrounds, and different factors will lead to their co-existence with others of similar or different backgrounds to be peaceful or a matter of clashes. The number and degree of religious, linguistic, and cultural differences tend to be cited as an explanation for peaceful or conflicting existence in the regions of Ukraine. Ethnic identity is a seemingly clearly defined category, one commonly reflected and described in literature on post-Soviet studies of Ukraine. Many scholars have speculated on a clear division between a regional and an ethnic identity prevailing there. In our view, such a division generates ideas of Ukrainian society divided into east and west in terms of language, history, protest participation, and habitus (Zhurzhenko 2002; Riabchuk 2015).

In constructivist terms, ethnicity, and its close relationship to language preferences, tends to be assumed to define the completeness and development of an identity. Consequently, the most widespread ethnicity is believed to construct the preconditions for the development of a national identity, grounded on a clear ethnic tradition, incorporating its cultural, territorial, and historical legacies (e.g., Smith 2009). Hence, over time, a dominant ethnic group develops into a titular nation, and its collective memory forms the background of the national narrative assumed to represent the country and to be shared by its inhabitants. In primordial terms, ethnicity is regarded as a self-evident and unproblematic category, with language as one of its important elements.

In the particular case of Ukraine, however, such self-evidence becomes most problematic. As underlined by multiple contemporary contributions in Ukrainian studies, the Euromaidan Revolution, the illegal annexation of Crimea by the Russian Federation, and the conflict in eastern Ukraine brought the problem of ethnicity and regional and national identity to the foreground. The flow of people forced to leave the Crimea and Donbas regions (referred to as "internally displaced persons" or IDPs) has considerably influenced the debate by restructuring the composition of regions' populations.

According to official figures, on January 2, 2019, the number of IDPs was 1.512 million (Ukraine Ministry of Social Policy 2019). The International Organization for Migration (IOM) reported that in March 2019 60 percent of the IDPs were displaced from Donetsk Oblast, 37 percent from Luhansk Oblast, and 3 percent from Crimea. Over 750,000 registered IDPs resided near the so-called "contact line," the boundary between government-controlled and uncontrolled territories of Ukraine (IOM 2019). The number of IDPs in the rest of Ukraine was: Kyiv city, 145,677 and Kyiv Oblast, 55,835; in eastern Ukraine, Kharkiv Oblast, 128,231 and Dnipropetrovsk Oblast, 68,271; and in southeastern Ukraine. Zaporizhzhya Oblast, 54,199 (IOM 2019). Notably, the number of displaced persons is still open to question due to the fact that official statistics does not cover those who did not register as IDPs, but live in mainland Ukraine, or left the country, or registered but continued to stay in the occupied territories (IDMC Ukraine). The last category is predominantly composed of retirees who registered as IDPs in order to get their pension benefits though continuing to reside in the occupied territories.

Here, it should be noted that measuring ethnic categories is usually a challenge for both statisticians and researchers. The complexity of Ukraine's territories' historical constitution and the multicultural co-existence of diverse nationalities in the territories of former multiethnic empires (Austro-Hungarian, Russian, Ottoman or the Kingdom of Poland) contributes to the challenging nature of this task. Hence, ethnicities' juxtaposition, shifting, overlapping, and permeability become an important point of analysis (Chandra 2012).

Although macro-data identifies the most salient ethnic groups in Ukraine, and still provides a useful broad picture of regional and national identities, the complexities outlined above make clear the usefulness of micro-level studies. The added value of micro-studies for empirical research lies in the fact that they enable a nuanced understanding of how both a respondent and an interviewer construct the ethnicity of the respondent. An output or a "clear variable" remains to be extracted from the usually complex uncertainty of multiple identities. Onuch and Hale (2018) demonstrate how different criteria of Ukrainian ethnicity lead to contradictory "findings": ethnicity can start to matter due to the design of a survey, or it can become irrelevant for the same reasons. Thus, in this study, one can see how the factor of ethnicity is represented as an important one in the context of the Euromaidan Revolution movement but becomes less evident when talking about support for NATO membership. Onuch and Hale (2018) conclude that such results crop up due to differences in the criteria selected to define ethnicity. To overcome such methodological subjectivity and to develop a more nuanced understanding of political effects produced by ethnicities, Onuch and Hale (2018) suggest supplementing the notion of ethnicity with more dimensions such as individual language preference, language embeddedness, ethnolinguistic identity, and nationality.

3. National Identity

In view of the above, it is important to underline that the discussion of regional diversity goes in line with understanding how ethnicities are reflected in, and related to, national self-perception. If the social construct of ethnicity is founded on fluctuating elements, what would be the constraints of perceiving the self as "Ukrainian" in terms of civic identification? Several surveys conducted in Ukraine by the University of St. Gallen may serve as a tool to both analyze national identification tendencies and to see the problematic spots that are left behind when surveys are made.

The first survey, conducted in 2015, covered all regions of Ukraine except the occupied Crimean peninsula and the occupied areas of Donetsk and Luhansk regions (Ukrainian Regionalism 2015). [2] When respondents

---

[2] Representative survey, $N = 6,000$ respondents, margin of error ≈ 2 percent.

were asked what their nationality was, the vast majority (88.6 percent) identified themselves as Ukrainians. No other nationality exceeded 7 percent, led by Russians (up to 6.9 percent), followed by undefined "mixed" (1.1 percent) and "other" (1.5 percent). Poles (0.7 percent), Belarusians (0.4 percent), Jews (0.4 percent), and Lithuanians (0.2 percent) were among other categories that were mentioned by respondents. However, since there are different types of identification, and people may not identify themselves by the defined national marker, questions like "To what extent do you feel yourself as..." enable the unveiling of more nuanced characteristics of self-identification. The recourse to the categories of gender/ occupation/ hobby/ local variations of identification and national identification as one of the possible choices in the formulation of a question serves to highlight the importance and topicality of national identity/ national identification as a category.

In a situation when a respondent has multiple choices, the category of "national identification" (counted on a scale between "1" to "5," where "1" means "absolute disagreement" and "5" "complete agreement") had the highest rate among respondents in 2015. A similar trend is evident for 2017 (Ukrainian Regionalism 2017): an association with the country got the highest average score (4.53); local and regional identifications were very close to the national identification figure (4.47); in 2015, local and national identification both scored 4.9. Identification with a particular generation (4.26), social stratum (3.97), and a profession (3.79) remain important factors in self-perception. Other possibilities of imagined forms of belonging such as being a European or an east Slav are shared to a lesser extent, with average scores of 2.88 and 2.79 respectively (Fig. 4.1).

Such data give an impression that there is a defined and non-problematic vision of national self-identification, whereby respondents can clearly identify themselves with one of the proposed categories of "Ukrainian," "Russian," and so on. However, if one takes the same survey and applies the advanced option of a "Story Map" that visualizes some of the answers given by the interviewees to the question: "To what extent do you feel Ukrainian?" the complexity of making the choice and deciding on the corresponding "answer" becomes more visible. The quotes presented below are taken from interviews conducted between 2012 and 2013 (Story Map: Ukrainian and Russian identities). Thus, they do not reflect the new connotations of "being Russian" or "being Ukrainian" that have been developing since 2013 as a consequence of the Euromaidan Revolution, the annexation of Crimea by the Russian Federation, and the conflict in

4 CRIMEAN TATARS AND THE QUESTION OF NATIONAL AND ETHNIC...

Fig. 4.1 Self-identification, Ukrainian Regionalism 2017. University of St. Gallen

eastern Ukraine. Nevertheless, the Story Map is illustrative of several crucial aspects of the complexity of national belonging and self-identification.

Notably, the Story Map demonstrates that the category "Being Ukrainian" tends to be addressed in ethnonational terms, and is easily applied in cases, when ethnicity corresponds to the national belonging. This is visible through such replies as (Lviv, 78, male, pensioner): "*I did not choose my nationality, I was born in a Ukrainian family*" ("*я не вибирав своєї національності, я народився в українській сім'ї*").[3] Another option is territorial determinism (Lviv, 44, male, taxi driver): "*Anyway, I live here, I was born here, no matter how it is, it is mine*" ("*але все таки, я тут живу, я тут народився, яке б воно не було - воно моє*").[4]

The post-colonial legacy inherited by respondents, visible through multiple ethnicities, makes it complex for respondents to make a clear choice. Such dilemmas are visible when a respondent in Crimea reflects whether he should define himself as a "Russian" or as a "Crimean Tatar," referring

---
[3] Story map: Ukrainian Identity, University of St. Gallen, Lviv, July–August 2012, Available at: https://uploads.knightlab.com/storymapjs/1523b6e328c2b6c9ecbffcb8a812c4c3/ukrainian-id/index.html.
[4] Ibid.

to the problem of his variegated family history (Simferopol, 25, male, financier): "*Honestly, difficult to say ... I do not ascribe myself to these or to others ... Maybe Russian. Well or yet, the Crimean Tatar ... Because Crimea, because still the history of ... my father, and this is the nationality of my relatives*" ("*Честно, затрудняюсь...не приписываю себя не к тем, не к другим...Может быть русский. Ну или, крымский татарин, все-таки...Потому что Крым, потому что, все-таки, история...моего отца, и этой национальности моих родных...*").[5] Or this kind of statement (Simferopol, 48, female, inspector): "*My mother is half-Polish, half-Ukrainian, my father is half-Ukrainian, half-Russian. Who am I? Ok, let's write 'Ukrainian'*" ("*У меня мама полуполька-полуукраинка, папа-полуукраинец-полурусский. Кто я? Ну давайте напишу «украинка»*").[6]

Similar multi-ethnic complexity is reflected in interviews from Donetsk, 2013 (Donetsk, 19, male, engineer): "*There are Ukrainians, Russians, Jews. And the Caucasian nationality. But there is no sharp division. Well, it seems to me that it does not exist in Ukraine anywhere*" ("*Украинцы, русские, евреи есть. И кавказской национальности. Но нету резкого такого деления. Ну, мнекажется, еговУкраиневообщенигдедонет*").[7]

Of course, reflection on multiple ethnicities is not the only way of thinking of the self. Mono-ethnic perception as a basis for national identification is another visible option. Such responses may serve as examples (Donetsk 2013, 61, male, watchman): "*Obviously [I'm Russian], because all my ancestors are Russians, all ancestors*" ("*Ну как, потому что все мои предки русские, все предки*").[8]

All the examples presented above illustrate the complexity of identification processes. A permanently shifting perception of "self" produces different interpretations of national belonging. External factors, such as a conflict or an occupation, may influence actualization of certain nodal points and suppression of others. The interviews presented above are

---

[5] Story map: Ukrainian Identity, University of St. Gallen, Crimea, June 2013, Available at: https://uploads.knightlab.com/storymapjs/1523b6e328c2b6c9ecbffcb8a812c4c3/ukrainian-id/index.html.

[6] Ibid.

[7] Story map: Ukrainian Identity, University of St. Gallen, Donetsk, April–May 2013, Available at: https://uploads.knightlab.com/storymapjs/1523b6e328c2b6c9ecbffcb8a81 2c4c3/ukrainian-id/index.html.

[8] Story map: Russian Identity, University of St. Gallen, Donetsk, April–May 2013, Available at:https://uploads.knightlab.com/storymapjs/1523b6e328c2b6c9ecbffcb8a812c4c3/russian-id/index.html.

illustrative of the complexity of the ways that people make their choices. They also demonstrate that such common ascriptions as "national" or "ethnic" belonging is an element of the multidimensional phenomena of the construction of ethnicity and national identity. The survey also demonstrates variation in both the criteria of measuring identity and the outcomes.

The annexation of Crimea and the conflict in eastern Ukraine made it highly topical to critically reconsider the politics of belonging in Ukraine. Such a search for redefinition is a result of several factors. Firstly, such redefinition serves as an immediate response to massive Kremlin hybrid media propaganda that, by using fake narratives, aims to simplistically distinguish Ukrainians into "Russian speaking," "Russia's compatriots," and "nationalistic" others. Secondly, an important reason for reconsidering the politics of belonging deals with the changes of regional landscape that have emerged as a result of the large number of IDPs forced to leave Crimea and certain parts of Donbas. In this context, Crimean Tatars who moved to mainland Ukrainian cities such as Kyiv, or to areas of western Ukraine, are of particular importance.

II. Empirical Findings Relating to Crimean Tatars' Identification Strategies

Despite being indigenous to Crimea, Crimean Tatars struggled for recognition during the Soviet era. Largely in view of Crimean Tatars' mass deportation from Crimea in 1944, their memory and rights were severely suppressed during the Soviet era. The memory of deportation, the Crimean Tatar language, the Crimean Tatar heritage in Crimea, toponymy, and other elements that constitute a national identity were banned. Thus, in addition to obliterating the very physical presence of the people by deporting them, the Soviet authorities also blurred their symbolic and historical presence. There were no references to the Crimean Tatars in the Soviet education program. The ethnic composition of post-1944 Crimea also changed: Slavic peasantry and retirees from the Soviet Navy were welcomed to stay in "leisure Crimea" (Shevel 2001; Sasse 2007; Williams 2016). After the disintegration of the Soviet Union, many Crimean Tatars returned to Crimea. This was the largest migration in the history of the Crimean Tatars, consisting of approximately 259,000 returnees—more than half of the entire nation (Williams 2016, 147).

For Crimean Tatars, the 1990s were marked by a continuous struggle for the restoration of collective rights, oppressed memory, and property rights (mainly with regard to the sale of land, rather than a restitution per se). Notably, the struggle for restoring Crimean Tatars' property rights was additionally aggravated by the emergence of stigmatization mechanisms, aiming at preserving ownership by "post-Soviet" inhabitants of Crimea and, to this end, excluding Crimean Tatars from the legal possibility to buy land in Crimea (Allworth 1998; Wilson 1998). The 2014 annexation of Crimea by the Russian Federation significantly changed an image of "Crimean Tatar," turning it into a designation of the main proponents of Ukrainian integrity in the peninsula (Uehling 2016).

Against this background, the self-perceptions of Crimean Tatars with regard to the categories of "ethnicity" and "nationality" were the central theme of our conversations with Crimean Tatars. We conducted 25 semi-structured, in-depth interviews with Crimean Tatars of different ages, occupations, and gender in Lviv (10 interviews) and Kyiv (15 interviews) between March 2017 and January 2018. There were 13 female and 12 male respondents. All were guaranteed anonymity. Ninety percent of the respondents had higher education and were involved into active Crimea-related initiatives as volunteers, directors of NGOs, or journalists, includingdirectors of Crimean Tatar media outlets and organizations that are now based in Kyiv or Lviv.

The selection was based on snowball sampling. In order to ensure the respondents' anonymity, all their names or places of their employment or study were removed. Instead, we applied a codification encompassing their sex, age, occupation, and place of residence. Each interview lasted around one hour. In some cases, conversation exceeded this time frame when there were advantageous conditions for that. Respondents shared their opinion on a set of questions that included such blocks as a reflection on self-identification, ethnicity, and national belonging, and thoughts on life in Crimea and regions of current settlement.[9] At first, I started with how respondents understood what it means for them to be Ukrainians. After the question was articulated in a similar manner, many of my respondents decoded the phrase "to be Ukrainian" as "to be a citizen of Ukraine." Such reaction contributed to the aforementioned statement on the

---

[9] All quotations from the respondents provided further in this chapter are translations from Ukrainian or Russian, the languages in which the interviews were conducted.

4 CRIMEAN TATARS AND THE QUESTION OF NATIONAL AND ETHNIC... 93

perception of the category "being Ukrainian" as merely ethnic. National belonging was reflected through the category of citizenship:

> *I am a citizen of Ukraine. I live where it is convenient for me. I like Ukrainians, they are mentally similar (ментально близки).* (Female, 43, self-employed, Kyiv)

Reflection on citizenship is also strongly connected to the experience of the Maidan protests in 2014:

> *For me, at that time* [before 2014], *it was inseparable: both to be the Crimean Tatar and the citizen of Ukraine. Politically, I perceived myself as a Ukrainian, ethnically I understood that I was a Crimean Tatar, but to be honest, there was no sentiment to the land on which I lived. I was considering the development of my career abroad. My entire perception changed in 2013, when the Maidan started. I came from Finland and stayed in Kyiv. I was in the night of dispersal of students, half an hour before dispersal, I went to sleep at some friends' house. In the morning, after I woke up, I saw an incredible pile of SMS and calls, and realized that something had gone wrong in this country. The same day I started working as a volunteer at the Hromadske[10] as an editor, and was on the square during the nights. Then I began to understand what the flag, the land, language, hymn meant to me.* (Female, journalist, 31, Lviv)

One should notice the double meaning here: "there was no sentiment to the land on which I lived." "Land" carries both connotations united together: Crimea and Ukraine.

> *I was on Maidan in Kyiv. I didn't throw any Molotov cocktails, I didn't perform any feats, but I had to be there with the [Crimean] Tatar flag (I keep it here; I will show it to you). I exercised my civil rights there simply as a citizen of Ukraine, it was not connected to our Crimean Tatar movement.* (Male, 48, entrepreneur, Kyiv)

Being Ukrainian in the majority of the responses means, first of all, to be a citizen, secondly, the respondents aged under 40 who were educated in Crimean schools, especially those who went through middle school and high school, also cited the Ukrainian language as an obvious determinant of their national belonging:

---

[10] Hromadske is the Ukrainian media outlet. It was heavily involved in streaming the Maidan protests of 2013–2014.

I am 21 years old, I was born in Crimea, in Simferopol, and I lived there all my life, never left for a long time, all my childhood I lived in Crimea, only occasionally [my childhood] took place in Turkey. The environment was Crimean Tatar and Ukrainian, because I studied at the Ukrainian gymnasium. [It was an] ordinary average family that is engaged in small business (we had a small hotel by the sea). (Female, 21, student, Lviv)

It is worth mentioning that the university education did not have such impact in relation to language and national identity as school education had. Also, reference to "Ukrainian schools" was made often by those who were less than 25 years, as well as parents who talked about their children of that age category. A "Ukrainian school" in this regard means that the educational program was conducted fully or partially in Ukrainian.

Reflection on national identity was sometimes mentioned in relation to religious background:

My mom taught me to honor all religions. I light a candle in the temple, and I read my prayer, if we say that God is one. I always considered myself a Ukrainian. A Crimean Tatar, a Muslim and a Ukrainian. Elementary—I have a Ukrainian citizenship. But six months ago I thought and did not know how to attribute myself. I do not know. Time must pass and I will understand who I am. (Female, 21, student, Lviv)

There are some conservative Tatars in Crimea. Many of them are covered in headscarves. This is a movement of Islam—the Crimean Tatars did not look like that, but they [adepts of the movement] believe that this is a return to religion. I celebrate Easter, last year I lit up the basket.[11] (Female, 21, student, Lviv)

Well, of course, I feel like a Crimean Tatar and, again, my religion is an inherent part of me, it is a part of my nationality. Here in Lviv I probably began to appreciate it more [Islam], because back in Crimea it was just a natural thing. (Male, 37, manager, Lviv)

A vision on the future of Ukraine's de-occupied Crimea in relation to the Crimean Tatars is repeatedly reflected through the idea of special priority for the indigenous population. These special rights are meant to strengthen Ukrainian—Crimean Tatar relations and secure the peninsula from different forms of separatism.

---

[11] The respondent used the word "koshik," the Ukrainian word for the basket used during the celebration of Easter by Christians. The original phrase was "Осветить кошик."

Ukraine is a big homeland and Crimea is a small one. We must be full masters (хозяева) in our small homeland. We must determine names of the villages, all of those that were completely renamed: Veselyye, Grushevki, Sadovyye and all other such names.[12] There should be our toponymy. We will be studying and restoring our language. Russian [language] is not under the threat, Ukrainian is protected by Ukraine and that is a right thing to do [to protect Ukrainian language]. In Crimea, the priority should be for the Crimean Tatars. Now if we become the owners there, we will be even greater patriots of Ukraine. If we would have access to the law enforcement system, judicial, to the state authorities [we would be greater patriots]. If we had this in the 1990s, believe me, such a situation would not have happened with Crimea. All this is because we had no one in the courts, no one in the armed forces. At the same time, we clearly position ourselves: we don't want to have a separate state, because it creates danger of situations when one would encroach on us and attack us all the time. We must live with mom Ukraine in one family and then you own what is your and understand that one should serve Ukraine and take the oath to Ukraine.
(Male, 48, entrepreneur, Kyiv)

Certain images are being suggested in the quoted paragraph and call for particular attention: "mom Ukraine," "small and big homeland" (Crimea and Ukraine), "masters of [small] land." They help to explain the symbolic relations between the Crimean Tatar and the Ukrainian identities. Such metaphors construct an image of the Ukrainian Crimean Tatar identity. These symbolic constructs were repeatedly mentioned by a number of respondents; such repetition indicates they are a part of the existing discourse on the self-identification and perception of Crimea.

The vision of self is also being constructed in relation to a distinction from others. Especially, when the distinction is projected by the Other to the Self. Collective prejudice is legitimized as a certain form of knowledge through the school system. The respondents, especially those aged 30 and older, mentioned cases from their childhood when they were stigmatized because of their ethnicity. The younger generation (20–30) did not recall such cases. That does not necessarily mean that such situations did not occur with them, but I expect that the intensity and a "normality" of such behavior declined aftere the 2000s. Also, those who were finishing high school in Crimea around 2014 might have developed stronger attachment

---

[12] The original phrase, "хер поймеш какие," is an obscene expression. Stylistically it was applied by the respondent to emphasize the village names' bankruptcy and his disagreement with the previously prevailing memory discourse in Crimea.

96 A. ZUBKOVYCH

to the re-emerged Ukrainian identity and therefore were more reluctant to recall conflict situations. However, one 30-year-old respondent mentioned several cases that I believe reveal the few important aspects that should be properly considered today by the policy makers and influencers.

In the following quotation, the respondent refers to the period of her matriculation in the mid-2000s:

> [...]about Lviv [...] we stood in line at the dean's office to submit the documents, we were not yet studying, I met a boy from Volhynia in a dormitory, but [what I intend to present] this is not discrimination and xenophobia, but rather "prejudice" [the term "prejudice" was said in English]. My mom and I stood in line and this boy from Volhynia [name and surname] stayed nearby and then he said to me [respondent switches to Ukrainian]: "And so, are you from Crimea, right? Are you Muslim? And I say "yes." He continues: "Do you know that all Muslims are terrorists? (Female, 31, photographer, Lviv)

This translation into English unifies the statements. Notably, original dialogues had rich multilingual switches, used by respondents to emphasize certain points (they not necessarily being aware of it). This phenomenon is especially visible in the response, quoted above. An interesting situation occurs when both sides of the conversation do not notice such multiple language switches and expect others to understand meanings of phrases said in different languages. More importantly, they expect others to share a similar knowledge of the contexts—i.e. of the common ground that brings together collective memories—and, hence, not to require additional reflection on why the entire conversation is not homogenized and is not reproduced through a single language. Explained by the richness of different contexts and a detailed nature of the rules an individual learns, reproduces, and transforms through being involved in a context, this phenomenon can be labelled as "banal multilingualism." The rationale for this is that a perception of some actions as "self-obvious" and "natural" implies a clear reference to the "banal nationalism" concept.

Michael Billig (1995) shed light on the existence of rituals and practice in Western democracies that became part of a nation's daily routines and, thus, turned to easily noticeable markers of the continuous performance of shared collective belonging. In its turn, "banal multilingualism" enables a researcher to trace complex dynamics of sociocultural processes in Ukraine, whereby the use of different languages reveals the multiplicity of performed identities.

The aforementioned aspect of stigmatization, rooted in the differences in religious background (even if neither side is a practicing believer) is mentioned as a strong prejudice of the pre-annexation era, when there was limited inter-regional cultural exchange. Another issue that was repeatedly referred to and requires reconsideration in collective memory terms deals with history education in Ukraine. One of respondents illustrated a problem of the inconsistency of the history education in a very clear way:

> *I had a discussion with the dean, he taught us history of Ukraine—the Cossack period. We had a discussion with him about the participation of the Crimean Khanate in Ukrainian history, because history was written very one-sidedly, and in general, Crimea or the Crimean Khanate in history books written by scholars is not perceived as an entity of the Ukrainian state. It is perceived as an enemy, an alien state, which was located on the territory of Crimea [...]. Yeah, perhaps it was so because there were different alliances. However, history should not be simply judged from what was "good" and what was "bad."[...] and all that narrative about the Tatars as invaders and barbarians who were raping women... Why are we not writing in the history schoolbooks about Cossacks who were raping women and robbing villages?* (Female, journalist, 31, Lviv)

Another respondent who expressed similar thoughts on the inconsistency of history books and history curricula, more generally, that lack critical reflection on Ukrainian Crimean Tatar history pointed out some progress since the annexation:

> *I am glad that interest [in learning more about Crimean Tatars] increases and intensifies. What impresses me is that there are more and more Ukrainians who start understanding that history of Crimea and Crimean Tatars is part of the history of the Ukrainians themselves. I am glad that Soviet historiography that existed before starts disappearing [...]. Unfortunately, there are not enough specialists today. We need specialists who read Arabic, Crimean Tatar, especially Old Crimean Tatar. There are so many moments when we do not know much about Crimean Tatar culture and heritage because everything was prohibited—such a nation simply did not exist [in the official discourse]. We cannot find in any source a ceramic vessel that was widespread among Crimean Tatars. Here, you have the object (vessel) but it does not have a name because it has not been studied. We should study all this.*
>   *Now I contribute to one of such projects, I hope that it will be implemented by Eurovision [2017 [...]] We expect to demonstrate that we [Ukrainians and Crimean Tatars] are not enemies as we were usually presented earlier, that we had a common past. We had a lot of trade and other types of relations, or look*

> *at the etymology of the "Maidan" word...Or why are 80 percent of the weapons from the Cossackhood era of Crimean Tatar origin? Or why did Cossacks use Turkic words for it[weapon]: they exchanged it.* (Male, 41, artist, Kyiv)

Here, it should be also mentioned that the respondents were unanimous in their evaluations of the situation when speaking about current life in Crimea and then opportunity to return there. Although using different words, all of them described post-annexation life in Crimea as marked by insecurity, censorship, self-censorship, a lack of freedom, and captivity. In this vein, one of the respondents talked about events that happened to his relatives following the annexation, consonant with multiple confessions, narratives, and reports on the use of law enforcement actions and actors for threats and intimidation:

> *While in Ukraine it was not "sweet" either—a lot of roads were constructed there, a lot was done for the city, not for people but for window dressing. Anyway, at least it became easier to get there. However, it remains difficult and dangerous for us—Crimean Tatar activists, representatives of the Crimean Tatar people, their families who have someone in Kyiv—to come there. Searches of houses do not stop for a very long time. They [local authorities] no longer pay attention to Ukrainian words, but at the level of power, they do not stop searches. This is scary. This is a tremendous stress for the people: you can be taken to jail at any moment for nothing! Personally to us, they came home twice, but my father was not at home. Once there was a grandfather, (He was an old man, 92 years old. He died this year and I went to the funeral). He told dad that he was so scared that he did not open the door and thought they would break it down. Dad looked at the camera and, in fact, they almost broke down the door. Such aggression in people. We will have to live with this for a long time.* (Female, Lviv, student, 21)

The respondent also emphasized the role of self-censorship:

> *One can start business there, one can make money on war. If you control yourself and say nothing, censor yourself in public life you can continue making money there. Life goes on, you can earn money. My aunt's spouse has a window business and it went up: the season lasts longer, the Russian market has opened, a lot of buildings are being built. What one should do? Children need to be fed. Nevertheless, their patriotism [to Ukraine] remains, they remain Ukrainians.* (Female, Lviv, student, 21)

4 CRIMEAN TATARS AND THE QUESTION OF NATIONAL AND ETHNIC...

The following quotation resonates with the previous one in terms of an emphasis on the pervasive controlling role of the police and at the same time it sheds light on some interesting nuances in the way the respondent becomes aware of the constructed images (prejudice) of others to her collective identity of "being Crimean Tatar" and uses the same constructed role to protect herself:

> *My father worked at a construction site. Something was making noise and a nasty Russian grandmother went to call the police. When the police came to my father, he came out with an axe and started saying something in Tatar. She angrily started saying: "According to the laws of the Russian Federation, you must speak the state language!" And my father, who looks so formidable, continues his talk in Tatar and brandishes an axe." The respondent laughs and continues: "He is hot-headed, he won't do anything, but he can scare one [with his look][...]We lived in a Russian district and they scoffed at us all the time. [...]* (Female, 43, entrepreneur, Lviv)

In this case, it is noticeable that the father made use of an image of an alien, a "barbaric medieval Tatar," a non-local person with whom communication is impossible due to different communication codes and collective norms. The Crimean Tatar's father had played with the harshest prejudice by performing as a stranger who could easily kill anyone with his axe—all this to prevent the local distrusted police performing their learned scenario. Such a logic of argumentation and interpretation is rooted in the ethno-methodological approach of Harold Garfinkel (1991), who made a significant contribution to the study of social order and the forms of rationality that help individuals to communicate. Hence, the Crimean Tatar father's attempt to "break" the orderliness of social life highlights the non-declared social norms shared by some of the local population and authorities in Crimea (the fear of Tatar-speaking persons).

In view of the decrease in freedom, distrust towards the post-annexation local authorities, and the prominence of politically motivated threats, our last set of questions dealt with respondents' reasons for remaining in Crimea and their plans for life, especially in relation to the geographies of life they envision for themselves. Reflection their responses enabled us to distinguish a couple of trends. Firstly, many Crimean Tatars believe that they ought to stay in Crimea. Whilst the current situation is labeled as "a hybrid deportation" (a definition recalling the 1944 deportation experience), remaining in Crimea is being considered to be a manifestation of a long-term struggle against occupation and neglected collective memory. Secondly, the vast majority of respondents expressed a wish to return to Crimea after de-occupation, with some of them proclaiming return as an irrevocable decision and others viewing it as one of several possibilities. Hence, an ideological necessity to stay in (or return to) Crimea can be articulated in different terms (yet, justified by similar values):

> *You know, our ancestors, our grandfathers, were not returning back to Crimea in order to leave from there en masse! My parents believe that they should remain in Crimea. Even my brother thinks so![13] He had the opportunity to leave, but he chose to stay. We are with all our hearts in Crimea, wherever we are [located]. Crimea is the most important thing for us. Of course, [it is the most important] after parents and family[…] I will definitely return to Crimea! This is about my family, my parents. I plan to build my family only with a Crimean Tatar and I want to live in Crimea.* (Female, journalist, 25, Kyiv)

I asked another respondent about his plans, as he strongly linked them to the de-occupation of Crimea.

> *I'm just thinking about that all the time. Staying here, I begin to grow into ties, deeds. They[ties] are also useful [to have] and they influence me. If it is necessary, I will be "a guide." If it is necessary, I will be here. Everything that we have done all this time there [in Crimea], works there and extols the annexation. Everything is been appropriated […], everything becomes Russian culture.[…] Here is an example. There is a mazanka[14] in a village, a Ukrainian village near Simferopol. An ethnographic expedition comes along and records some rituals—a funeral, if I am not mistaken. The ethnographer writes down everything and then asks [people]: "Whose traditions are these?" And they answer: "Russian." My respondent continues angrily: "How can it be Russian if you were singing in Ukrainian?! […] Ukrainians have lost their traditions and identify themselves as Russians."* (Male, 41, artist, Kyiv)

It also should be mentioned that it is a considerable (and potentially highly misleading) oversimplification to consider IDPs in Ukraine and Crimean Tatar inhabitants in Crimea as stable groups. Our interviews demonstrated that Crimean Tatars' personal geographies are dynamic. All of our respondents reported being in contact with relatives and friends who are in

---

[13] The reference to the brother is very important here because at the time of our conversation he was under arrest in Crimea as a result of a fabricated case.

[14] "Mazanka" is a Ukrainian word that refers to a house made of clay, bricks, or shrub covered with clay. Houses built in this way were widespread in the territories of steppe and forest-steppe Ukraine.

Crimea. Many tend to visit Crimea to see their friends and relatives; who in return visit them in mainland Ukraine. This dynamic, and the consequent complexity of possibilities can be traced in the following response:

I believe that there is no need to leave [Crimea]. If I had not needed to obtain higher education, I would not have left. If mom had not had a job issue—she would not have moved. It is not difficult to [physically] leave, but we are losing ourselves, our identity. But now [as I left] I do not know if I want to return. Yes I want to come back, but to MY Crimea. I am now living here [in mainland Ukraine] for the fifth year; other opportunities have appeared, and other horizons have expanded. [...] Once I was thinking about Crimea and imagined: I am in a car, surrounded by the mountains and nature—it is just magical. There is no magical nature like Crimea's! It is mine and everyone who lives there feels that it is his/hers. I do not have such feeling anywhere else, not in Lviv or in other places. Probably this can be called a feeling for the Motherland. (Female, Lviv, student, 21)

Previously, we, unfortunately, knew very little about each other, Crimea and Lviv are so far apart. When someone was coming to Crimea, it was to visit the sea, to swim, to sunbathe, and therefore they [inhabitants of Lviv] knew little about us. But here they began to learn more about it [Crimea and Crimean Tatars]. I know that now there exist about five music bands that enriched their repertoire by adopting Crimean Tatar songs. Hence, more people are starting to know more about us, of course. (Male, 39, manager, Lviv)

CONCLUSIONS

This analysis of the dynamics and challenges of Crimean Tatars' self-identification, their views on the current situation in Crimea, and its future is illustrative for the study of ethnic and national identities in flux in post-Euromaidan Ukraine. The interviews revealed that Crimean Tatars use different factors and experiences to construct their identities, including ethnicity, language, and educational experiences. These findings confirmed our theoretical assumption, according to which national identity is more fitted to capturing the complexities of one's self-identification, as compared to ethnic identity, since it enables respondents to refer to a broader range of categories. Thus, largely in consequence of the experiences of Euromaidan, the annexation, and subsequent intimidation by the occupation authorities, the category of "being Ukrainian" in Crimea is reflected not only in ethnonational terms, but also through citizenship, language, and "Ukrainian schools" experiences. Notably, the interviews enabled us to coin a concept of "banal multilingualism," signifying a communication practice that uses a switch from one language to another to underline particularities of the context, known to all participants of the conversation. In our view, "banal multilingualism" is illustrative of the contemporary sociocultural processes in Ukraine, when the use of multiple languages reflects the multiplicity of performed identities.

Importantly, in mainland Ukraine, Crimean Tatars are currently viewed as key proponents of Ukraine's territorial integrity, whereas Russian discourse in the annexed peninsula remains based on a rigid image of Crimean Tatars as "Tatar invaders," a perception inherited from early post-Soviet textbooks. Such an image is highly beneficial for the occupation authorities who continue to use collectively maintained prejudices to legitimize pressure on Crimean Tatars and any other inhabitants of the peninsula who do not support the annexation.

Even though the respondents unanimously characterize occupied Crimea as an insecure place, many of them link their identity to remaining at the peninsula or returning there after its de-occupation. Reflecting on the future of de-occupied Crimea, Crimean Tatars emphasize special (i.e. self-governance) rights to be granted to the indigenous population in order to strengthen Ukrainian–Crimean Tatar relations and secure the peninsula from different forms of separatism. In this regard, the metaphor of two types of homeland was reproduced, with Ukraine as a "big" homeland and Crimea as a "small" one.

In respondents' view, even though the Euromaidan, followed by the Russian Federation's annexation of Crimea, promoted the broadening and consolidation of "being Ukrainian" as a category, more effort is needed to ensure the consistency of history education in Ukraine. In particular, they advocate a more consistent conceptual reflection of the role of Crimea and Crimean Tatars in Ukraine's history, as part of a more ambitious effort to reconsider the politics of belonging in Ukraine. Many of the respondents have already actively engaged in developing platforms for public discussions of the above issues, as well as cultural initiatives. Under the general trend towards consolidation of the Ukrainian identity, interest by Crimea and Crimean Tatars is increasing, and manifests itself through the rise of cross-regional and cross-ethnic cultural cooperation, facilitated by the fact that Crimean Tatars in mainland Ukraine maintain active links with Crimea.

References

Allworth, Edward, ed. 1998. *The Tatars of Crimea: Return to the Homeland: Studies and Documents.* Durham: Duke University Press.

Anderson, Benedict. 1991. *Imagined Communities: Reflections on the Origin and Spread of Nationalism.* Revised and extended ed. London: Verso.

Bezverkha, Anastasia. 2015. Reinstating Social Borders between the Slavic Majority and the Tatar Population of Crimea: Media Representation of the Contested Memory of the Crimean Tatars' Deportation. *Journal of Borderlands Studies* 32 (2): 127–139.

Bhabha, Homi K. 1991. "Race," Time and the Revision of Modernity. *The Oxford Literary Review* 13: 193–219.

———. 1994. *The Location of Culture.* Routledge Classics.

Billig, Michael. 1995. *Banal Nationalism.* SAGE Publications.

Chandra, Kanchan. 2012. *Constructivist Theories of Ethnic Politics.* New York: Oxford University Press.

Garfinkel, Harold. 1991. *Studies in Ethnomethodology.* Polity City.

Grigas, Agnia. 2016. *Beyond Crimea: The New Russian Empire.* Yale University Press

Ibrahim, Vivian. 2011. Ethnicity. In *The Routledge Companion to Race and Ethnicity,* ed. Stephen M. Caliendo and Charlton D. McIlwain, 12–20. London: Routledge.

Internal Displacement Monitoring Centre (IDMC). Ukraine. http://www.internal-displacement.org/countries/ukraine.

International Organization for Migration (IOM). 2019. National Monitoring System Report on the Situation of Internally Displaced Persons. March 2019. http://ukraine.iom.int/sites/default/files/nms_round_13_eng.pdf

Onuch, Olga, and Henry E. Hale. 2018. Capturing Ethnicity: the Case of Ukraine. *Post-Soviet Affairs* 34 (2–3): 84–107.

Riabchuk, Mykola. 2015. "Two Ukraines" Reconsidered: The End of Ukrainian Ambivalence? *Studies in Ethnicity and Nationalism* 15 (1). (Special Issue: Nationalism and Belonging April): 138–156.

Sasse, Gwendolyn. 2001. The "New" Ukraine: A State of Regions. *Regional and Federal Studies* 11 (3): 69–100.

———. 2007. *The Crimea Question.* Harvard University Press.

Shevel, Oxana. 2001. Crimean Tatars and the Ukrainian State: The Challenge of Politics, the Use of Law, and the Meaning of Rhetoric. *Krimski Studii* 1 (7): 109–129.

Smith, Anthony D. 2009. *Ethno-Symbolism and Nationalism: A Cultural Approach.* Routledge.

Uehling, Greta. 2016. A Hybrid Deportation: Internally Displaced from Crimea in Ukraine. In *Migration and the Ukrainian Crisis: A Two-Country Perspective,* ed. Agnieszka Pikulicka-Wilczewska and Greta Uehling, 62–77. E-International Relations Publishing.

Ukraine Ministry of Social Policy. 2019. Oblikovano 1 512 435 Pereselentsiv. [1 512 435 Displaced Persons Were Registered]. https://www.msp.gov.ua/news/16534.html

University of St. Gallen. 2015. Ukrainian Regionalism. http://www.uaregio.org/images2/uaregio/methodology/2015.pdf

———. 2017. Ukrainian Regionalism. http://www.uaregio.org/en/surveys/data-visualisations/survey-infographics/identities/

———. n.d. Story Map: Ukrainian and Russian Identities. http://www.uaregio.org/en/surveys/data-visualisations/story-maps/

Williams, Brian G. 2016. *The Crimean Tatars: From Soviet Genocide to Putin's Conquest.* New York: Oxford University Press.

Wilson, Andrew. 1998. Politics in and Around Crimea: A Difficult Homecoming. In *The Tatars of Crimea: Return to the Homeland: Studies and Documents*, ed. Allworth Edward, 281–322. Durham: Duke University Press.

Zhurzhenko, Tatiana. 2002. The Myth of Two Ukraines. A Commentary on Mykola Riabchuk's "Ukraine: One State, two Countries"? *Eurozine.* https://www.eurozine.com/the-myth-of-two-ukraines/

PART II

The "Crisis In and Around Ukraine", Occupied Territories and their Reintegration: The Legal Dimension

CHAPTER 5

The Domestic Dimension of Defining Uncontrolled Territories and Its Value for Conflict Transformation in Moldova, Georgia, and Ukraine

Maryna Rabinovych

INTRODUCTION

Legal practitioners, politicians, or scholars seek to characterize the type of control exercised over territory or population by unrecognized political entities and develop and/or evaluate conflict transformation and resolution strategies (Coppieters 2018, 343). Hence, the violent conflict in eastern Ukraine that eventually led to the proclamation of the so-called Donetsk People's Republic ("DPR") and Luhansk People's Republic ("LFR") in 2014 gave rise to an intense debate on the conflict's standing

M. Rabinovych (✉)
University of Hamburg, Hamburg, Germany

© The Author(s) 2020
H. Shelest, M. Rabinovych (eds.), *Decentralization, Regional Diversity, and Conflict*, Federalism and Internal Conflicts,
https://doi.org/10.1007/978-3-030-41765-9_5

107

under international law,[1] as well as a legally accurate way to define such People's Republics. So far, the UN Security Council (SC) has been very cautious when addressing the nature of the conflict and avoided defining it in its official documents (UNSC 2014, 2015, 2018). By referring to the conflict as the "crisis in and around Ukraine," the OSCE hinted about the two-dimensional nature of the conflict without, however, specifying what the "around" dimension means (OSCE 2015). The International Criminal Court (ICC), for the present the only international adjudicator to opine on the events in eastern Ukraine from an international humanitarian law perspective, pointed to the parallel existence of "direct military engagement between the respective armed forces of the Russian Federation and Ukraine" and "the non-international armed conflict" in eastern Ukraine (International Criminal Court 2018, para. 72–73) with this opinion shared in a number of international law contributions on the conflict in eastern Ukraine (e.g. Korhonen 2015; Sayapin 2019).

In this context, the abovementioned ICC Report on Preliminary Examination Activities regarded the "DPR" and "LPR" as "armed groups," without referring to the status of uncontrolled territories[2] and their contested statehood (International Criminal Court 2018, para. 72–73). In our view, such a situation is most likely to be determined by the established practice of states' bilateral recognition of new members of the international community and the high degree of politicization of the recognition-related issues. However, the lawfulness of a new state's creation is "the first test of [its] ability to be recognized by other states" and the non-applicability of the "duty not to 'recognize as lawful'" under international law (Korotkyi and Hendel 2018, 148). Notably, determining the lawfulness of a new state's creation or, alternatively, the legal status of entities that exercise control over particular territory and population, requires, inter alia, an insight into the legislation of a "maternal state" (ibid.). Furthermore, examining the definitions of uncontrolled territories and political entities exercising factual control over them, recognition of control or influence by "maternal" states is an essential (and frequently overlooked) precondition for the international community to promote

---

[1] For the examples of international law-centered contributions on the conflict and the legal status of the "LPR" and "DPR," see, for instance: Korhonen (2015), Fabry (2017) and Korotkyi and Hendel (2018).

[2] For the purposes of this paper, we will use the term "uncontrolled territories," indicating that the governments of Moldova, Georgia, and Ukraine cannot exercise "effective control" over the whole of their territories in international humanitarian law (IHL) terms.

conflict transformation and resolution. The proliferation of unrecognized states in the post-Soviet space, extensively supported by the Russian Federation, makes comparative insights into the domestic legal definitions of uncontrolled territories and respective political entities especially valuable for the international community's efforts to transform such conflicts.

Against this background, this chapter is a comparative analysis of the domestic dimension of defining uncontrolled territories and political entities that control them in Moldova (Transnistria), Georgia (Abkhazia and South Ossetia), and Ukraine ("DPR" and "LPR") and its value for conflict transformation. Since Moldova and Georgia have lengthier experiences in dealing with uncontrolled territories, we will look at the lessons Ukraine can learn from them. The chapter has two substantial parts. Section "The 'Domestic Dimension' of Defining Uncontrolled Territories and Its Value for Conflict Transformation: The Cases of Moldova and Georgia" aims to trace the dynamics of defining uncontrolled territories and related political entities in Moldova and Georgia, and addresses the role of international actors in conflict transformation activities. Section "The 'Domestic Dimension' of Defining 'DPR' and 'LPR'—a Hybrid Model, Conflict Transformation and Lessons to Learn from Moldova and Georgia" focuses on Ukraine's domestic legislation pertaining to uncontrolled territories, the lessons it has learnt or may learn from the experience of Moldova and Georgia, and their value for conflict transformation. This discussion will incorporate a reflection on the recent "Steinmeier Formula" debate, illustrative of the role the domestic dimension may play in conflict transformation. The chapter concludes by emphasizing the importance of insights into "maternal" countries' domestic legislation for researching into unrecognized states and transforming conflicts underlying their establishment.

I. The "Domestic Dimension" of Defining Uncontrolled Territories and Its Value for Conflict Transformation: The Cases of Moldova and Georgia

Russia's foreign policy as it seeks to ensure the endurance of non-recognized states in the region has been receiving changed coverage in "maternal" countries' legislation over time. Firstly, as convincingly argued by Allison (2008), German (2009), and Souleimanov et al. (2018), unrecognized states are a crucial tool in Russia's "coercive diplomacy," exercised towards Georgia, Moldova, and Ukraine. There is ample proof of Russia's military presence in all the unrecognized states in question (Souleimanov et al. 2018, 73–74). In addition, extensive political and economic support is being channeled to state structures in non-recognized states. As confirmed by recent events in eastern Ukraine, a crucial component of Russia's strategy in unrecognized states is passportization (i.e. granting Russian citizenship to residents of the uncontrolled territories) (Ukraine Crisis Media Center 2019). Last but not least, in line with the literature on the dynamics of Russia's foreign policy, Russia's support to unrecognized states is a "moving target," difficult to "capture" in domestic legislation (e.g. Souleimanov et al. 2018, 73–74).

1. The Dynamics of Defining Transnistria and Its Regime in the Legislation of Moldova

Transnistria declared independence from the Republic of Moldova in September of 1990 (more than a year before the collapse of the USSR in December 1991) and proclaimed the Transnistrian Moldovan Republic (TMR). Rooted in the socioeconomic differentiation of the Soviet era and moderate interethnic cleavages, the confrontation between Moldovan and secessionist authorities escalated into a violent conflict in summer 1992 (Büscher 2016, 25–27). The ceasefire agreement, signed by the President of Moldova Mircea Snegur and Russian President Boris Yeltsin in July 1992, envisaged, inter alia, the creation of a trilateral peacekeeping force, the "Joint Control Commission," aimed at observing the ceasefire arrangements and demilitarization of the buffer zone (United Nations Security Council 1992). The ceasefire agreement also gave rise to the process of political negotiations on the status of Transnistria. According to the OSCE analysis, the key issues preventing the political settlement of the conflict included a language issue (despite the legal recognition of Russian as an interethnic language of communication); an idea of re-unification with Romania; Russia's continued military presence in the area; and the challenge of defining the legal status of Transnistria (OSCE Network 2016, 15–17, 23–24, 33–34).

Moldova's efforts to cope with the last of these challenges can be fitted into three periods:

1. Early period (1993–2005), preceding the adoption of the Law "On Fundamental Regulations of the Special Legal Status of Settlements on the Left Bank of the River Nistru (Transnistria)" (the "Moldovan Framework Law");
2. The consolidation of Moldova's domestic position on the legal status of Transnistria during the stalemate of the international talks on the status of Transnistria (2006–2011) and
3. The resumption of "5+2" talks[3] and the future of Transnistria's legal status (2011–present time).

1.1. Early Period (1993–2005) Preceding the Adoption of the Moldovan Framework Law

According to the OSCE, direct negotiations on the legal status of Transnistria between the governments of Moldova and the TMR at the beginning of 1993 could have been a success, if the TMR's Supreme Court had not blocked them by proposing a "draft treaty on the separation of powers between the subjects of the Moldovan confederation" (OSCE n.d., 5). Since the treaty virtually equated to granting Transnistria independence, Moldovan authorities opposed it, and requested the Commission on Security and Cooperation in Europe (CSCE) to launch a mission to contribute to the political settlement of the conflict (ibid.). Emphasizing the restoration of Moldova's territorial integrity as the primary settlement objective, the CSCE recommended decentralizing Moldova over the long term, thus rendering Transnistria's special status less singular (CSCE Mission to Moldova 1993, 1). At the same time, the commission pointed to the justifiability of Transnistria's special status, "differing from the constitutional condition of other parts of Moldova" and involving a considerable degree of self-rule" (e.g. the establishment of Transnistria's own legislative, executive and judicial bodies) (ibid., 2). Adopted in 1994, the Constitution of Moldova has, however, only referred to decentralization in the context of provision of public services (Art. 109). Moldova's Constitution (Art. 110(1)–111) defined another region—Gagauzia—as "an autonomous territorial-unit having a special statute and representing a form of self-determination of the Gagauzian

---

[3] "5–2" talks on Transnistria involve Moldova, Transnistria, Russia, Ukraine, and the OSCE, as well as the USA and the EU. Following the talks' stalemate in 2006, they were resumed in 2011 in Tiraspol.

people," constituting an "integral and inalienable part" of the Republic of Moldova. As opposed to the case of Gagauzia, the same Art.100 of the Constitution did not shed much light on the legal status of Transnistria, providing that "places on the left bank of the Dniester River may be assigned special forms and conditions of autonomy according to the special statutory provisions adopted by organic law." Notably, the Constitution also confirmed Moldova's neutrality (incorporating a prohibition of foreign troops' stationing on its territory) and the status of Moldovan (with Latin alphabet) as the state language (Art. 11 and Art. 13, respectively) (Moldova Parliament 2006).

Following the promulgation of Moldova's Constitution and before adoption of the respective law, there have been three attempts to define the status of the TMR: two memoranda proposed by the Russian Federation, and Joint Proposals by the OSCE, Russia and Ukraine. Signed by the representatives of Moldova, the Russian Federation and Transnistria (with Ukraine as a guarantor), the 1997 Memorandum on the Bases for Normalization of Relations between the Republic of Moldova and Transnistria (also referred to as the "Moscow" or "Primakov" Memorandum) confirmed the parties' commitment to the continuation of establishing state legal relationships between them (OSCE 1997). According to the 1997 memorandum, the document defining such relations and the legal status of Transnistria, shall be based "on the principles of mutually agreed decisions, including the division and delegation of competences and mutually assured guarantees" (with the Russian Federation and Ukraine acting as Guarantor States) (ibid.). Despite the fact that the Moscow Memorandum envisaged that the parties would proceed with the elaboration of the respective document immediately after the signing of the Memorandum, it never saw the light of day. The next loop of the labyrinth was the Memorandum on the Basic Principles of the State Structure of the United State (the "Kozak Memorandum"), suggested by the Russian Federation in 2003. According to this, "the final resolution of the Transnistrian problem should be realized through the transformation of the state structure of the Republic of Moldova with the goal of creating a united, independent, democratic state based on the federal principles with the borders of the Moldovan SSR on the 1 January 1990" (Regnum 2005). Notably, the "Kozak Memorandum" provided for Moldova's neutrality and demilitarization. It was envisaged that the Transnistrian Moldovan Republic would become a subject of the federation, authorized to form its own legislature (Supreme Council of the

TMR, executive (President and Government of the TMR) and judiciary. As opposed to the "Moscow Memorandum," the "Kozak Memorandum" defined the competencies of the federation and its subjects, as well as the foundations of the formation of federal and state budgets. Notwithstanding its elaborateness and Moldovan authorities' initial intention to sign it, the memorandum was rejected by the then President of Moldova, Vladimir Vororin, who argued that its adoption would contradict the Constitution of Moldova (Vahl and Emerson 2004, 173). The actual reason for the rejection is thought to be a lack of consensus among the key Western actors (the EU, the USA and the OSCE) about both the contents of the memorandum and the manner in which it was proposed (ibid.). Subsequently, the idea of Moldova's federalization was also reflected in the 2004, "Proposals and Recommendations of the Mediators from the OSCE, the Russian Federation and Ukraine" (OSCE 2004). Despite the fact that the proposals envisaged a far broader range of competencies for the federal state, as compared to "Kozak Memorandum," they were also rejected by the Moldova's leadership.

The first thirteen years of the Transnistrian case, after the conflict and the territory's factual breakaway from Moldova, went through the "ups and downs" of international political settlement talks with no domestic legislation defining the legal status of Transnistria and its relations with Moldova. This situation only changed in 2005, with the so-called "Ukrainian Plan" (Ukraine's proposal "Towards a Settlement through Democratization").

1.2. The Consolidation of the Moldovan Domestic Position Vis-à-vis Transnistria Under the Stalemate of International Settlement Talks (2005–2011)

Introduced by the then President of Ukraine, Victor Yushchenko, following intensive Ukraine—Moldova diplomatic communication at the summit of the GUAM (Georgia, Ukraine, Azerbaijan, Moldova) Organization for Democracy and Economic Development in Chisinau in spring 2015, Ukraine's proposal suggested solving the Transnistrian issue through democratizing Transnistria. Its major points addressed the creation of conditions for the development of democracy, civil society, and a multi-party system in Transnistria; the holding of free and democratic elections to the Transnistrian Supreme Council; the transformation of the peace-keeping operation in Transnistria into an international mission, composed of the military and civil observers; and setting up a special mission to prevent smuggling at the Moldova–Ukraine border (Protsyk 2004, 726–728). Although, in the view of the Moldovan leadership, the Ukrainian plan failed to reflect some of the important principles of settlement (e.g. the withdrawal of Russian troops, demilitarization), the Ukrainian initiative broke the stalemate and resulted in the formalization of Transnistria's "special status." While emphasizing "democratization" and "demilitarization" as key objectives of Moldova–Transnistria relations, Art. 1(1) of the Law "On Fundamental Regulations of the Special Legal Status of Settlements on the Left Bank of the River Nistru (Transnistria)" referred to the "reintegration policy" of Moldova. With this, Art. 1(1) positioned reintegration as an inevitable conclusion of negotiations, though providing for join negotiations on power-sharing. In this vein, Art. 3(1)(2) provided for the "setting" of Transnistria as a "special autonomous unit," constituting an "integral, component part" of the Republic of Moldova. Pursuant to Art. 4 of the Moldovan Framework Law, the Supreme legislative body of Transnistria is the Supreme Soviet (Council), with the elections of the first Supreme Soviet to be conducted by an International Election Committee (upon the OSCE's agreement). Notably, the Law granted Transnistria the right to "establish and maintain external contacts in economy, science, humanities," provided that the manner in which this right is exercised complies with the legislation of the Republic of Moldova (Parliament of Moldova, Art. 9). With regard to language, the law also opted for a compromise, nominating Moldovan, Russian, and Ukrainian as Transnistria's state languages. Notably, as opposed to all previous settlement proposals, including the "Ukrainian Plan," the 2005 Framework Law did not provide an option for Transnistria's secession.

According to Stephan Wolff, a more elaborate and realistic version of Moldova's domestic position is found in a 2007 package proposal for a "Declaration concerning principles and guarantees of the Transnistrian settlement," adopted after the 2006 referendum in Transnistria (in which 97 percent of voters opted for independence and "free association" with Russia (Wolff 2011). Compared to the 2005 Framework Law, the package proposal is marked by a milder stance towards reintegration and the rise of legal mechanisms aimed at ensuring adequate power-sharing and the solution of conflicts between Moldova and Transnistria (ibid.). Hence, the proposal included provisions on Transnistria's representation in Moldova's legislative and executive bodies, as well as the Constitutional and Supreme Courts, Security Council, and Prosecutor's General Office. Furthermore, contrary to the 2005 Framework Law, the 2007 package proposal envisaged a legal mechanism to solve disputes over competencies between the Republic of Moldova and Transnistria, as well as defining conditions of Transnistria's secession from Moldova (ibid.).

Even though Moldova opted for the rather mild 2007 proposal as a basis for a draft law on Transnistria's special status, such a law was never adopted. Instead, under the stalemate of international negotiations over Transnistria, the period in question has been marked by the emergence and consolidation of two "parallel universes" of regulation: the Moldovan, with Transnistria as its "integral, component part" (Parliament of the Republic of Moldova 2005), and the Transnistrian, avoiding even references to Moldova.

1.3. Resumption of the "5+2" Talks and the Future of Transnistria's Legal Status

Although a comparative insight into the nexus between the domestic dimension of defining uncontrolled territories and conflict transformation will be offered after section "The 'Domestic Dimension' of Defining South Ossetia and Abkhazia in Georgia's Legislation" analysis of the case of Georgia, the following paragraphs offer a brief overview of the progress of the "5+2" talks. As opposed to the "grand" political settlement proposals put forward at the end of the 1990s and the beginning of the 2000s, the concluding official documents of the 2012 "5+2" talks in Vienna emphasized "solidifying the positive results" achieved to that point in terms of the talks, building mutual trust and understanding, and small steps to be taken on the ground (OSCE 2012). Though referring to the comprehensive settlement agenda (including the clarification of Transnistria's legal status), the 2013 Odesa and Kyiv talks once again stressed "small steps" and focused on confidence-building and the free movement of people, respectively (OSCE 2013a, b). Confidence-building remained a focus of negotiations over the period from 2014 to 2016 (e.g. OSCE 2016). November 2017 was marked by the launch of the "1+1" Moldova–Transnistria talks that eventually led to the parties' agreement on a number of administrative and technical steps. Envisaging an increase in the capacity of the Gura Bicului–Bychok bridge across the river Dniester, and ensuring the functioning of Latin-alphabet schools administered by Moldova and the recognition of Transnistrian educational documents in Moldova, were beyond doubt measures consonant with the "grand" objective of political settlement (OSCE 2018). Another development that can be viewed as indirectly facilitating the settlement of the Transnistrian issue has been the breakaway state's authorities' decision to join the Deep and Comprehensive Free Trade Area (DCFTA) as a part of the EU–Moldova Association Agreement in 2016 after four years of consistently opposing it (Całus 2016). Although the Transnistrian leadership tried to advertise this step as the signing of the agreement, "separate from the DCFTA" (Całus 2016), scholars and analysts point to the implementation of regulatory changes under the DCFTA and closer links between Moldova and Transnistria as indications of progress in terms of supporting the successes of the "5+2" talks (e.g. Schleifer 2015; Van der Loo 2019).

Ultimately, under the continued existence of the "parallel universes" of regulation (including the lack of changes to the 2005 Moldovan Framework Law), the most recent period of conflict settlement efforts has been characterized as a policy of small steps, carefully shaped to contribute to the solution of most controversial issues (especially language) and facilitate business and people-to-people contacts.

2. The "Domestic Dimension" of Defining South Ossetia and Abkhazia in Georgia's Legislation

To elaborate on Georgia's legal thinking regarding the status of uncontrolled territories, we divide its evolution into two periods: (1) prior to the 2008 Russo-Georgian War; and (2) after the Russo-Georgian War, that eventually led to Russia's recognition of South Ossetia and Abkhazia as independent states, the severance of Russia–Georgia diplomatic relations, and its aftermath.

2.1. Prior to the 2008 Russo-Georgian War

South Ossetia declared its independence from Georgia in May 1992 as a consequence of the 1991–1992 South Ossetia War. The independence of Abkhazia was declared following its armed conflict with Georgia in 1992–1993. As noted by Dennis Sammut and Nikola Cvetkovski (1996), and Rachel Clogg (2008) in their papers on the Georgia–South Ossetia and Georgia-Abkhazia conflicts, both of these conflicts have been characterized by sharp interethnic cleavages, rooted in the pre-Soviet history of both regions rather than the socioeconomic differentiation of the Soviet era. Unlike the case of Transnistria, there was little progress towards political settlement immediately after a ceasefire under the Yeltsin–Shevarnadze Sochi Agreement of 1992 (United Nations Peacemaker 1992). Despite the fact that the Sochi Agreement provided for the launch of a Joint Control Commission (JCC) to facilitate political settlement in South Ossetia, it was only in 1995 that the JCC first met to discuss connectivity between Georgia and South Ossetia (Sammut and Cvetkovski 1996, 15–16). In contrast to the Sochi Agreement on South Ossetia, the Declaration on Measures for a Political Settlement of the Georgia–Abkhaz Conflict of April 4, 1994 stipulated parties' agreement on a number of political issues, such as the right of Abkhazia to its own Constitution and legislation (United Nations Security Council 1994, Annex I). Moreover, pursuant to the Declaration, "the parties have reached a mutual understanding regarding powers for joint action in the following fields: foreign policy and foreign economic contacts; border guard arrangements; customs; energy, transport and communication" and agreed "to continue active efforts to achieve a comprehensive settlement" (ibid.).

Notwithstanding the above, Art. 1 of the 1995 Constitution of Georgia defined Georgia as "an independent, unified and indivisible state, as confirmed by the Referendum of 31 March 1991, held throughout the country, including the Autonomous Soviet Socialist Republic of Abkhazia and the Former Autonomous Region of South Ossetia" (The Parliament of Georgia 1995, Art. 1). Hence, in contrast to the Constitution of Moldova, the Constitution of Georgia did not provide for the autonomy of breakaway regions, linking the determination of the territorial state structure of Georgia with "the complete restoration of the jurisdiction of Georgia over the whole territory of the country" (ibid., Art 2(3)). However, as can be seen in Georgia's 2001 draft law on amending the 1999 Constitution of Abkhazia, by the beginning of 2000s Georgia regarded the breakaway regions as autonomous, even though they constituted "an inalienable part of Georgia" (Parliament of Georgia 2001).

Like the 2005 Moldovan Framework Law's provisions on the Supreme Council of Transnistria, the 2001 draft law referred to the Supreme Council of Abkhazia as the legislative body empowered to adopt laws in terms of the competences defined by the Constitution of Georgia and the Constitution of Abkhazia (ibid., Art. 8). Respective draft laws also referred to the Constitution of Georgia and the authorities of Georgia's higher state bodies in relation to the application of Abkhazia's Constitution, the functioning of the executive branch, and budgetary issues (ibid, Art. 6, Part B). However, an insight into the Constitutions of Abkhazia and South Ossetia testifies to the existence of two parallel regulatory universes in Georgia prior to the start of the Russo-Georgian War (i.e., the

118   M. RABINOVYCH

Constitutions of Abkhazia and South Ossetia not even mentioning Georgia) (Abkhaz World 2008). Here it should be mentioned that conflicts in Abkhazia and South Ossetia have been a much more difficult cases for international settlement efforts than that in Transnistria, given the Russian Federation's comprehensive control over the security sector and confidence-building in the breakaway regions.

2.2. The Russo-Georgian War and Its Aftermath

Whilst Georgia's relations with Abkhazia and South Ossetia were marked by stalemate until 2004, Mikheil Saakashvili's coming to power as a result of the Rose Revolution in Georgia in 2005 marked the start of Georgia's attempts to reintegrate the breakaway regions. Georgia's reintegration efforts had both a diplomatic dimension (e.g. Saakashvili's suggestion of a peace settlement to South Ossetia at the Parliamentary Assembly of the Council of Europe) and a policing/ military dimension (e.g. disarmament of the paramilitary leader Emzar Kvitsiani and the restoration of Georgian jurisdiction in Kodori, Abkhazia, in 2006) (Mitchell 2009, 175–176). A number of factors, including Russian opposition to Georgia's efforts to reintegrate the breakaway regions and its aspiration to join NATO, led to the five-day border conflict in Tskhinval in August 2008 known as the Russo-Georgian War.

Whilst the question "Who started the war?" is highly politicized and difficult to answer in the context of the relations between Russia, Georgia, Abkhazia, and South Ossetia (Cheretian 2009, 155), it is beyond the doubt that the armed conflict had multiple implications for the future of Georgia and its breakaway territories. In particular, Georgia's military defeat solidified Russia's power in the breakaway regions (including its military presence), creating, according to some experts, barely surmountable barriers to Georgia's NATO accession (Friedman 2008). Naturally, the 2008 war and Georgia's defeat also led to Georgia's reconsideration of its domestic legislation on uncontrolled territories.

Hence, in contrast to Moldovan domestic legislation that never openly referred to Russia's role in Transnistria, the 2008 Law of Georgia "On Occupied Territories" stipulated the aim of defining "the status of territories that have been occupied as a result of military aggression by the Russian Federation, and to establish a special legal regime for these territories" (Parliament of Georgia 2008, Art. 1). According to Art. 3 of this law, such "emergency rule and special legal regime implies, inter alia, restrictions on free movement (primarily applicable to foreign nationals and stateless persons (Art. 4)), the conduct of transactions relating to real property and economic activities. Pursuant to Art. 6 of the Law "On Occupied Territories." The restriction on the conduct of economic activity is applicable to a broad range of actions, including all the activities whose conduct requires obtaining approval documents under Georgian legislation, or involves the use of public resources, or the arrangement of money transfer. Furthermore, in line with the Hague Conventions of 1907 and the Fourth Geneva Convention, the law declared all human rights violations in the occupied territories "the responsibility of the Russian Federation, as a state carrying out military occupation" (ibid., Art. 7). Last but not least, Art. 8 of the law pointed to the illegal nature of official bodies in the occupied territories, if not created under the Georgian legislation.

This brief overview of the 2008 Georgia's Law "On Occupied Territories" displays a sharp contrast to both Georgia's pre-conflict legal framing of uncontrolled territories and the case of Transnistria. Thus, the law's definition of South Ossetia and Abkhazia as "occupied territories" and of Russia as an occupying power, presupposes an application of international humanitarian law (IHL) that regards a territory occupied, "when it is placed under the authority of a host army" (Second International Peace Conference 1907, Art. 42). This, in turn, leads to numerous consequences, such as a "maternal state's" application of numerous restrictions vis-à-vis occupied territories and its expectation of the occupation's condemnation and the application of sanctions to an occupying force by its international partners (as exemplified by Art. 9 (2) of the Law "On Occupied Territories"). Moreover, as we will demonstrate in section "The 'Domestic Dimension' of Defining Uncontrolled Territories and Its Nexus with Conflict Transformation", a "maternal state's" legal definition of uncontrolled territories as "occupied" has a considerable impact on conflict transformation.

3. The "Domestic Dimension" of Defining Uncontrolled Territories and Its Nexus with Conflict Transformation

3.1. Defining Conflict Transformation

As noted by Thania Paffenholz (2009) in her overview of peace-building theories, "building peace is in itself one of the most intricate enterprises of human beings," giving rise to and, subsequently, embedding numerous schools of thought, such as conflict resolution, management and transformation (3–4). As opposed to conflict resolution (aiming to solve a conflict and rebuild the relationships between the parties) and conflict management (limiting negative aspects of the conflict and emphasizing positive ones), the first step towards conflict transformation lies in comprehending the conflict as a "socially constructed cultural event" (Lederach 1996, 9). Hence, from a social constructionist perspective, conflicts emerge "through an interactive process of the search for and the creation of shared meaning" (ibid.). Subsequently, the transformation of a conflict requires transforming perceptions of the conflict itself and a subject matter it refers to or, in other words, a creation of the new meaning, genuinely shared by involved stakeholders. Notably, conflict transformation practice envisages the construction of new meanings at three levels: the top level (state bodies, big business, political parties), the mid range (local government, local media, research centers and think tanks, and even organized crime networks) and grassroots level (family and community-based groups) (Lederach 1997, 91–92). Moreover, according to the Berghof Foundation for Peace Support, advocating systemic conflict transformation, successful transformation of a conflict requires not only the multilevel shaping of a shared meaning by its parties, but the consolidation of a shared meaning by the international community (of donors) (Körppen et al. 2008, 22). The above brushstrokes, drawing the picture of conflict transformation, also clearly illustrate the reason why we chose to focus on conflict transformation: debating and construing shared meanings is about definitions. Hence, a conflict transformation's focus on the construction of shared meanings enables one to trace the nexuses between dynamics of different actors' positions on conflicts/ uncontrolled territories, a creation of joint meanings, and practical steps they agree on.

Before proceeding with the analysis of relationship between Moldova's and Georgia's domestic definitions of uncontrolled territories, and respective conflict transformation processes, we will refer to the conceptions of conflict transformation utilized by key regional peace and security actors: the EU and the OSCE. Tending to use the concept of "transformation" in the context of the promotion of fundamental values (i.e. democracy, human rights, and the rule of law) and the promotion of regional integration, EU official documents primarily refer to conflict resolution, rather than transformation (e.g. Council of the European Union 2018). At the same time, as can be proved by a number of contributions on the EU's role in dealing with conflicts in its immediate neighborhood (Deiana et al. 2019; Tocci 2008), the EU's understanding of conflict transformation is close to its vision of transformation. In particular, it is marked by considering conflict transformation in a broader context of political development (transformation) and the deployment of all available EU instruments, as underlined by the EU Integrated Approach to External Conflicts and Crises (Council of the European Union 2018). Moreover, driven by its own experience of using integration as a means to promote peace, the EU emphasizes cooperation between conflicting parties as a means of transforming conflict (here being close to the conflict-management school of thought, based on stressing positive aspects of the relationships between conflict parties; Deiana et al. 2019, 530–533). On top of that, an important component of the EU conflict-transformation strategy is the engagement with local civil society that, even though less organized and professional than the NGOs with which the EU usually works, may have strong legitimacy in the conflict context (Tocci 2008, 6).

Like the EU, the OSCE characterizes its engagement in conflicts as "management" and "resolution", rather than "transformation". However, in comparison to the EU, the OSCE's approach to dealing with conflicts links less with political development, broadly defined. It is, instead, more conflict context-focused, and utilizes "dialogue facilitation, mediation and confidence-building activities between conflict-affected societies and communities" and the monitoring of security situation and the implementation of peace arrangements on the ground (OSCE 2017, 9–10).

Based on the above overview, the analysis will continue with an examination of the role domestic definitions of uncontrolled territories play in conflict-transformation activities by international actors.

3.2. Domestic Definitions of Uncontrolled Territories and Conflict Transformation in Transnistria, and Abkhazia and South Ossetia

It is clear that the conflicts in Transnistria, Abkhazia, and South Ossetia share numerous characteristics, such as their outburst in the post-Soviet space, the pivotal role of language and identity issues, Russian military engagement and support of one of the parties to the conflict, and the eventual emergence of the *de facto* states. However, since the ceasefires of the 1990s, the transformation of conflicts in Transnistria, and Abkhazia and South Ossetia have taken different trajectories.

Foremost, as has been explained, prior to the adoption of the Moldovan Framework Law in 2005, the Russian Federation, Ukraine, and the OSCE repeatedly suggested plans that envisaged a comprehensive political settlement of the Transnistrian situation. As noted by the OSCE, the situation has been quite different for South Ossetia and Abkhazia, where "there have never been substantive discussions between the sides on concrete options for a political resolution," but only the Geneva International Discussions (GID), dealing with risk-reduction and humanitarian issues, rather than the politics of conflict (OSCE Network 2016, 12). Whilst the OSCE does not offer an explanation of this "no-talks" phenomenon, it seems reasonable to assume that it has its origin in the more radical nature of the confrontation in the South Ossetian and Abkhazian cases, and the contiguity of Russia with Abkhazia and South Ossetia, facilitating its immediate control over their foreign and security policies.

Subsequently, following a stalemate in international efforts to resolve the Transnistrian conflict in 2006–2011, the resumption of the "5+2" talks and direct Moldova–Transnistria talks has led to progress. As was mentioned when analyzing the case of Transnistria, progress encompasses a number of "small steps," consonant with the "grand" political settlement objective (e.g. the improvement of connectivity between Chisinau and Tiraspol, the recognition of Transnistrian educational documents in Moldova) and the very fact of direct talks between the parties (OSCE 2018). Despite being characterized as small, respective steps can be definitely attributed to the change in the parties' social construction of the conflict from a perception of a situation of the stalemate and no-dialogue to its perception as one being addressed through dialogue on specific steps and facilitating cooperation. Here it has to be noted that, participating in the "5+2" format and making best use of its political and economic leverage, and "soft" power in Moldova, the EU has played a considerable role in the transformation; further, the conflict transformation is being extensively supported by the OSCE (Beyer and Wolff 2016, 335–336).

Referring to the "domestic dimension" of defining uncontrolled territories, it can and should be argued that it has been of significant importance at different stages of the conflict and its transformation. Over the period from 1992 until 2005 (the introduction of the Moldovan Framework Law), the lack of Moldovan domestic legislation on the status of uncontrolled territories left open a space for many varied political settlement suggestions, each of which would have required specific changes to be introduced into Moldovan legislation. Also, as convincingly illustrated by John Beyer and Stefan Wolff (2016), the notorious "Kozak Plan" was very close to being approved due to the absence of detailed regulations on the legal status of uncontrolled territories in Moldovan legislation (340). Hence, in view of the proliferation of "grand" settlement scenarios between 1992 and 2005, an important function fulfilled by the Moldovan Framework Law has been a "solidification" of the status-quo and Moldova's attitude to it. Later on, the rather soft stance of the Moldovan Framework Law, and its absence of any reference to Russia's role in the conflict, has served as one of the factors enabling the parties to launch talks on "small steps." Whilst the talks would be hardly possible without the relatively low level of societal radicalization in the Transnistrian case, parties' political commitment, and international support, one role of the Moldovan Framework Law has been to provide Moldova's and international observers' and mediators' positions in negotiations with legal backing and, most probably, set the "red lines" beyond which Moldova will not go in political settlement negotiations.

As noted above, the trajectory of the conflict and its transformation in South Ossetia and Abkhazia has been very different from the Transnistrian scenario; similarly, striking differences can be distinguished in the role played by respective domestic regulations in conflict transformation. While in the Moldovan case the absence of framework regulations on Transnistria has created favorable ground for multiple settlement proposals, this was not the case for Georgia, where "no substantive discussions" were held. Moldova's "soft" stance in domestic legislation and cooperation between Moldova and breakaway regions were favorable to the resumption of political settlement talks, whereas the 2008 Georgian Law "On Occupation" cemented political stalemate. Hence, as noted by Madalina Dobrescu and Tobias Schumacher (2020), and Julian Bergmann (2020), the conflicts in South Ossetia and Abkhazia are challenging for international transformation and management efforts. It should be emphasized that the challenge does not arise from the 2008 Law "On Occupation," but from the situation it addresses, exemplified by the extraordinary depth of South Ossetia's and Abkhazia's "economic, intergovernmental, technocratic and social links with Russia," which undermine their autonomy (Gerrits and Bader 2016).

According to the 2019 US Statement at the GID on the conflict in Georgia, the lack of cooperation by the Abkhazian and South Ossetian *de facto* authorities remains a crucial concern, especially in light of the parties' "failure to fully implement the ceasefire agreement" (U.S. Mission to International Organizations in Geneva 2019). Hence, the GID currently focus on ensuring the non-use of force and humanitarian issues, rather than a political settlement or even small steps towards cooperation. At the same time, whilst informal trade between Georgia and its breakaway regions and between Abkhazia and third states is on the rise, there is a belief that the talks on mutually beneficial commerce between Georgia and its breakaway regions "could open the lines of communication long cemented shut" (International Crisis Group 2019). The opening of such talks and the formalization of respective commercial activities would, however, evidently require changes to the 2008 Law "On Occupation" that currently imposes numerous restrictions on movement, economic activity, and property titles in the occupied territories (Art. 4–6) (Parliament of Georgia 2008). Therefore, the example of trade talks illustrates that, despite its importance for applying IHL to qualify the conflict, the provisions of the 2008 Law "On Occupation" may constitute an obstacle to conflict transformation through cooperation.

Ultimately, analysis reveals that the transformation of conflicts in Transnistria, and South Ossetia and Abkhazia went in different directions, with much more progress on transformation, i.e. the creation of new meanings, achieved in Transnistria. It also transpires that domestic regulations on uncontrolled territories (as well as their absence) may fulfil several functions with regard to conflict transformation: leaving the space open or opening up space for international talks on conflict settlement; defining the "red lines" a "maternal state" may not cross in the context of international peace talks; promoting a particular qualification of the conflict and uncontrolled territories under international law (e.g. occupation); and promoting or hindering conflict transformation through different forms of cooperation, such as trade and investment.

II. The "Domestic Dimension" of Defining "DPR" and "LPR"—a Hybrid Model, Conflict Transformation and Lessons to Learn from Moldova and Georgia

The history of the "DPR" and "LPR" dates back to Russian-sponsored protests in southeastern Ukraine in early 2014, with protesters claiming threats to Russian-speaking population were being exerted by Ukraine's post-Euromaidan authorities. A crucial impetus to the protests was given by the 2014 decision of the Verkhovna Rada of Ukraine to repeal the Law of Ukraine "On the Foundations of State Language Policy" (also known as the "Kivalov–Kolesnichenko Law")[4] that provided for the broad application of the so-called "regional languages" (Verkhovna Rada 2012). Even though this decision was eventually vetoed by the acting President of Ukraine, the protesters refused to acknowledge the new authorities in Kyiv and demanded Ukraine's federalization. Importantly, as demonstrated by empirical research into identities in Donbas by Elise Giuliano (2018) and Gwendolyn Sasse and Alice Lackner (2018), the protesters were motivated by their feeling of abandonment from Kyiv and Kyiv's lacking attention towards local concerns, rather than by the language problem.

Against this background, the sequence of events preceding the declaration of independence by the "People's Republics" was as follows. Starting in February 2014, rallies were followed by protesters' seizure of public buildings in March–April 2014 (e.g. the seizure of the Donetsk Oblast Council and the Security Service of Ukraine (SBU) in Luhansk on April 6, 2014). In Donetsk, protesters formed a "Supreme Council" on April 7, 2014 that on the same date adopted a Declaration of Sovereignty of the "Donetsk People's Republic," an Act Declaring Independence of the "Donetsk People's Republic," and an Appeal to the President of the Russian Federation, Vladimir Putin.[5] It is of interest that, substantiating the "DPR's" move for independence, these documents referred to two groups of reasons: the illegal nature of the new authorities in Kyiv and the way they came to power; and foreign policy issues, namely "the factual leadership of the country by the USA and Europe" and the deterioration of "century-long relations with Slavic peoples, the peoples that comprise the Commonwealth of Independent States (CIS)" (Komitet Izbiratelei Donbasa 2014). Such a strong emphasis on foreign policy issues distinguishes the conflict in eastern Ukraine from the cases of South Ossetia and Abkhazia, and is largely explicable by more than two decades of Ukraine's independent foreign policy experience prior to the start of the Donbas–Kyiv standoff. As compared to South Ossetia, Abkhazia, and Transnistria, a peculiarity of the declarations of independence by the "DPR" and "LPR" has been the inclusion of an Appeal to the President of the Russian

---

[4] The Kivalov–Kolesnichenko Law was eventually declared unconstitutional, based on the decision of the Constitutional Court of Ukraine of February 28, 2018 in case 1-1/2018.

[5] To access the abovementioned documents (in Russian), visit: http://komitet.net.ua/article/120042/.

Federation, reflecting an initial ambition (or hope) to eventually join the Russian Federation (ibid.).

The non-recognition of the new Kyiv authorities, disagreement with Kyiv's foreign policy vector, and demands for federalization and close ties with the Russian Federation were also cited by separatist leaders to substantiate their seizure of public buildings in Yenakiive, Mariupol, Sloviansk, Gorlivka, and Kramatorsk. In May 2014, the creation of the "DPR" and "LPR" was consolidated by "referenda" on the self-determination of the republics, with 89 percent of voters supporting self-determination in the "DPR" and 96.2 percent in "LPR" (with a claimed voter turnout of around 75 percent in both) (BBC 2014). Importantly, such "referenda" were illegal *a priori* in light of Ukrainian domestic legislation that did not provide for local referenda (Verkhovna Rada 2013). Additionally, the legally void status of the "referenda" can be substantiated by multiple flaws in their organization and conduct, such as the non-systemic nature of the voting, and threats, reported by pro-Ukrainian inhabitants of the Donetsk and Luhansk oblasts. As subsequent sections of the chapter will highlight, the seizure of public buildings across Donbas in April 2014 and the "referenda" on the self-determination of the "DPR" and "LPR" marked the advent of a highly complex conflict, notably in the context of its regulation in domestic legislation.

2. Ukraine's Domestic Regulations on the Conflict and Uncontrolled Territories: A Hybrid Model and its Nexus with Conflict Transformation (2014–2019)

Based on comparative legal analysis, this section characterizes Ukraine's domestic regulations on uncontrolled territories as both sharing some of the approaches with Georgian and Moldovan models but featuring a number of important legislative novelties. As will be illustrated later, such novelties are inextricably linked to ongoing international conflict-transformation efforts (importantly, as opposed to the cases of Transnistria, Abkhazia, and South Ossetia, the case of eastern Ukraine is marked by the existence of an international agreement on comprehensive political settlement, adopted in Minsk in February 2015 (UN Peacemaker 2015).

2.1. Two Groups of Regulations on Uncontrolled Territories

The complexity and "hybridity" of Ukraine's domestic regulations on uncontrolled territories is determined by the simultaneous operation of two intertwined groups of legal acts, regulating the "special status" of the uncontrolled territories in the context of the Minsk Agreements, and their "reintegration," involving action by the Armed Forces of Ukraine. The first group of legal acts comprises the Law of Ukraine "On the Special Order of Local Self-Government in Certain Districts of Donetsk and Luhansk Oblasts" of September 16, 2014 (with multiple amendments, further referred to as the "Special Status" Law) (Verkhovna Rada 2014a), the Law of Ukraine "On the Creation of the Necessary Conditions for the Peaceful Resolution of Situation in Certain Areas of Donetsk and Luhansk Oblasts" of October 6, 2017 (prolonging the period of application of the former Law by a year) (Verkhovna Rada 2017) and the Law of Ukraine "On the Amendments to Art. 1 of the Law of Ukraine 'Interim Self-Government Order in Certain Areas of Donetsk and Luhansk Oblasts" of October 4, 2018 (Verkhovna Rada 2018a).

In its turn, the "reintegration" group encompasses the Law of Ukraine "On Peculiarities of the State Policy on Guaranteeing State Sovereignty of Ukraine on the Temporarily Occupied Territories of Donetsk and Luhansk Oblasts" of January 18, 2018 (Verkhovna Rada 2018b) and the Law of Ukraine "On Ensuring the Rights and Freedoms of Citizens and the Legal Regime on the Temporarily Occupied Territory of Ukraine" of April 15, 2014 that the former Law refers to (Verkhovna Rada 2014b). The simultaneous existence of respective groups of legislation, reflecting the dual (and potentially contradictory) Ukrainian domestic policy vis-à-vis uncontrolled territories can be attributed to the long-lasting stalemate in the implementation of the 2015 Minsk-II Agreement that repeatedly referred to the Law of Ukraine "On Interim Self-Government Order in Certain Areas of Donetsk and Luhansk Oblasts" (e.g. with regard to conducting local elections in the uncontrolled territories (UN Peacemaker 2015).

2.2. The "Special Status Group and the Minsk-II Agreement
The 2014 Law of Ukraine "On Interim Self-Government Order in Certain Areas of Donetsk and Luhansk Oblasts" highlights details of the "special self-government order" in certain areas of Donetsk and Luhansk oblasts to be ensured following the fulfilment of a number of conditions, in line with the Minsk Agreements (Verkhovna Rada 2014b). Hence, pursuant to Art. 10(4) of the Law of Ukraine in question, such conditions encompass, inter alia, the conduct of snap, general, equal, free, and transparent local elections, based on the Ukrainian Constitution and international agreements entered into by Ukraine; the engagement of international impartial

observers (including the OSCE and the Congress of Local and Regional Authorities of the Council of Europe), and the "complete withdrawal of all illegal armed groups, their military equipment, militants and mercenaries" (ibid.).

Despite sharing the key message/ task of the 2005 Moldovan Framework Law, i.e. a peaceful transfer from a *de facto* statehood to an autonomy/ special status *within* a "maternal" state, a "special self-government order" for certain areas of Donetsk and Luhansk oblasts is quite different to "autonomy" under Moldovan Framework Law. The key difference lies in the fact that, while the autonomy of Transnistria under the 2005 Framework Law envisages election of a Supreme Council and a negotiation of its competencies with the authorities of Moldova (Parliament of Moldova, Art. 4), a "special status" only applies to the local self-government bodies. Moreover, according to Art. 5 of the Law of Ukraine "On Interim Self-Government Order in Certain Areas of Donetsk and Luhansk Oblasts," the local-self-government bodies are to observe the Constitution and legislation of Ukraine. In contrast, Transnistria's autonomy under the 2005 Framework Law included the adoption of Transnistria's own Fundamental Law (that cannot, however, contradict the Constitution of the Republic of Moldova) and own legislation in respective areas of competence (ibid., Art. 4(3)). Importantly, whilst the 2005 Framework Law granted the Russian language official status in Transnistria, along with Moldovan, Ukraine's 2014 "Special Status" Law referred to the "right of linguistic self-determination" of each citizen in certain areas of Donetsk and Luhansk areas and "free use of Russian or any other language in societal or private life," but with Ukrainian remaining the only official language in the country (Verkhovna Rada 2014a, Art. 4(3)). Finally, yet importantly, initially conceived as a part of 'grand' political settlement, the Law of Ukraine "On Interim Self-Government Order in Certain Areas of Donetsk and Luhansk Oblasts" provides for the non-application of criminal prosecution measures to participants in the conflict (ibid., Art. 3).

The analysis reveals that, as compared to the case of Moldova's domestic regulations, Ukraine's 2014 "Special Status" Law reflects Ukrainian authorities' ambition to reintegrate the breakaway territories under a lesser degree of their autonomy. Notwithstanding the above, the "Special Status" Law fulfils at least four functions pertaining to conflict transformation in terms of the Minsk-II process. Firstly, repeatedly referred to by the Minsk-II Agreement, the Law sets the legal framework for Ukraine's fulfilment of (at least a part of) its commitments under the agreement and, thus, serves as a point of reference in international negotiations. Secondly, being a part of comprehensive political settlement efforts, the law stipulates that, according to Ukraine's official position, transforming the conflict and ensuring the breakaway regions' transfer from the *de facto* statehood to a "special status" under Ukraine's jurisdiction (ibid., Art. 10) will be allowed. Thirdly, this allows the law setting "red lines" that Ukraine may not cross when agreeing to the new settlement scenarios, as well as providing any opposition or civil society with a point of reference, if such changes take place. In general, it can be argued that, providing for the contested territories' "special status" and different forms of the government's support to them, the law is conducive to the dialogue on conflict transformation.

Before we proceed with analyzing the "reintegration category of Ukraine's domestic legislation, two remarks have to be made. First of all, since Minsk II initially obliged Ukraine to conduct the decentralization-cantered constitutional reform by 2015, the adoption of the "Special Status" Law cannot be alone regarded as Ukraine's fulfilment of its obligations under the Minsk-II Agreement (UN Peacemaker 2015). Secondly, as is currently being proven by the debate on the implementation of Minsk-II and the notorious "Steinmeier Formula,"[6] the settlement of the ongoing conflict remains highly politicized and, subsequently, the value of domestic legislation vis-à-vis new grand deals must not be overestimated.

2.3. Legislation on "Reintegration" and Conflict Transformation

Another reason why the value of Ukraine's 2014 "Special Status" Law ought not to be overestimated is the parallel application of the 2018 Law of Ukraine "On Peculiarities of the State Policy on Guaranteeing State Sovereignty of Ukraine on the Temporarily Occupied Territories in Donetsk and Luhansk Oblasts" (also known as the "Reintegration" or "De-occupation" Law). Since the "Reintegration" Law refers to uncontrolled territories as "temporarily occupied by the Russian Federation" (Verkhovna Rada 2018b, Preamble, Art. 1), both its spirit and substance are much closer to the previously analyzed 2008 Law of Georgia "On Occupation," than to the 2014 "Special Status" Law or 2005 Moldova's

---

[6] For the controversies surrounding the "Steinmeier Formula" see, for instance: Surnacheva and Honcenko (2019) and Deutsche Welle (2019).

Framework Law. Adopted in the context of continued armed conflict and Ukraine's officially expressed disillusionment with the progress of international political settlement, the "Reintegration Law" does not refer to either the Minsk Agreement or the "Special Status" law. Notwithstanding the above, when introducing the newly signed "De-occupation" Law, the then President of Ukraine, Petro Poroshenko, claimed the law's full compliance with Ukraine's international obligations, including the Minsk Agreements (Ukrayinska Pravda 2018a). The law was, however, criticized by the Ukraine's Opposition Block party and the Russian Federation as respectively undermining the implementation of the Minsk Agreements and leading to the escalation of the conflict (Ukrayinska Pravda 2018b). The "Reintegration Law" also received much criticism from human rights organizations, arguing that, under Russia's sole responsibility for the situation at the uncontrolled territories, citizens would be deprived of assistance and any kind of compensation granted by Ukrainian authorities (Zmina 2018). Furthermore, human rights organizations were reported as being against the expansion of authorities of the military personnel and law enforcement agencies (ibid.). The observation of human rights in the uncontrolled territories remains a grave concern.

Referring to the substance of the legal document, it is worth stressing that the law manifests a transfer from a legal uncertainty about the current regime of the uncontrolled territories (generated by the "Special Status" Law due to the non-fulfilment of requirements, stipulated by its Art. 10) to their regime as "temporarily occupied territories." Despite the official statements of President Poroshenko, lawyers have debated whether such a change of uncontrolled territories' legal regime is in line with the Minsk Agreements, the "Special Status" Law, and whether it would impede the conflict settlement (e.g. Gromad'ske Radio 2018). In our view, for the interests of the legal certainty and a stronger interplay between international and domestic law, it would have been useful for the "Reintegration" Law to refer to the Minsk Agreements and the "Special Status" Law and to clarify its relation to them. However, the "Special Status" Law provides not for the *actual*, but the *potential (aspired)* legal regime of these territories, conditional upon the fulfilment of specific conditions by a number of actors (Verkhovna Rada 2018b, Art. 10). Hence, since the respective conditions have not been fulfilled to date, it can be argued that the "Reintegration" Law filled the existing lacuna, rather than coming into contradiction with the Minsk Agreements or the "Special Status" Law. Moreover, it should not be forgotten that the Minsk Agreements do not represent an international treaty in the sense of Art. 2(1)(a) of the Vienna Convention on the Law of Treaties (United Nations 1969), and, thus, cannot be viewed as prevailing on Ukraine's domestic legislation as allowed by the Constitution. What can, however, be deemed to be unclear from a lawyer's viewpoint is the relation between the "Reintegration" Law and martial law to be introduced by the President of Ukraine in line with the Constitution of Ukraine and the Law of Ukraine "On the Legal Status of Martial Law" in the event of a threat to Ukraine's independence or territorial integrity (Verkhovna Rada 2015).

Given the "Reintegration" Law's strong stance on Russia's involvement in the conflict, many voices argued that it would negatively affect conflict transformation in line with the Minsk Agreements by provoking Russian retaliatory measures. However, apart from the Russian Federation's immediate official reactions, the "Reintegration" Law has not been much referred to in press releases pertaining to the Minsk process (Ukrayinska Pravda 2018b). Furthermore, as opposed to the Georgia's Law "On Occupation," the "Reintegration" Law does not provide for restrictions that may legally impede cooperation between Ukraine and its breakaway territories as a means of conflict transformation. On the contrary, Art. 6 of the "Reintegration" Law stipulates a number of aspects of protecting civilians' rights in the occupied territories, including the provision of humanitarian and legal assistance and the promotion of the preservation of cultural links. Moreover, virtually equating territories in eastern Ukraine with Crimea, annexed by the Russian Federation, the "Reintegration" Law provides for expanding the scope of application of the Ukrainian Law "On Ensuring the Rights and Freedoms of Citizens and the Legal Regime on the Temporarily Occupied Territory of Ukraine" to uncontrolled territories in eastern Ukraine (Verkhovna Rada 2014b). In turn, the law provides for both Ukraine's "taking all necessary measures" to ensure observance of the rights of Ukrainian citizens living in the occupied territories, and its obligation to preserve and ensure economic, financial, political, social, information, and cultural links with the citizens of occupied territories (ibid., Art. 5). However, since both the "Reintegration" Law and the Law of Ukraine "On Ensuring the Rights and Freedoms of Citizens and the Legal Regime on the Temporarily Occupied Territory of Ukraine" stipulate Russia's sole responsibility for occupation in line with international law (Verkhovna Rada 2018b, Art. 2; Verkhovna Rada 2014b, Art. 3), Ukrainian citizens living in the occupied territories are not entitled to any monetary compensation from the Ukrainian side for the infringement of their rights. Together with significant authorities of the military and law enforcement agencies, an absence of a legal pathway or acquiring compensation for human rights' violations in the occupied territories from Ukraine is viewed by human rights organizations as the key problem of the "reintegration" legal regime (Zmina 2018).

Ultimately, the analysis substantiates the "hybridity" of the domestic dimension of defining the legal status of contested territories in Ukraine, caused by the parallel application of the "Special Status" Law and the "Reintegration" Law. Even though the spirit and substance of the "Special Status" Law is close to the 2005 Moldova Framework Law, while the "Reintegration" Law is comparable to the 2008 Georgia's Law "On Occupation," the laws on both the special status and reintegration are marked by peculiarities, absent in both Georgia's and Moldova's legislation. In particular, the uniqueness of the "Special Status" Law lies in stipulating conditions to be fulfilled by other international actors to make this "special status" functional. Thus, apart from promoting conflict transformation by the very fact of its existence, the "Special Status" Law presents certain "red lines" Ukraine would not cross in terms of international political settlement. In turn, despite multiple concerns regarding its impact on implementation of the Minsk Agreements, the "Reintegration" Law does not seem to have impeded the international peace processes. A potential source of legal uncertainty is, however, the lack of provisions highlighting the relation between the Minsk Agreements, the "Reintegration" Law, and the "Special Status" Law.

3. Ukraine's Domestic Legislation and the "Steinmeier Formula"

This section focus on the nexus between Ukraine's domestic legislation on the legal status of uncontrolled territories and the so-called "Steinmeier Formula" that occupied international and Ukrainian newspapers' headlines in autumn 2019. Before proceeding with the analysis, the highly politicized and controversial nature of the situation surrounding the "Steinmeier Formula" should be stressed. It envisages that a special status can start functioning after the OSCE confirms the legitimacy of elections in the uncontrolled territories, and the possibility of its incorporation into the "Special Status" Law, including stakeholders' highly divergent perceptions of its meaning and consequences. The analysis here concerns solely the developments that took place before October 25, 2019, and acknowledges the situation's proneness to further changes, also in light of the upcoming Normandy Four summit. At this stage, it may be argued that, as presented in the letter from Ukraine's representative on the Trilateral Contact Group (TCG), Leonid Kuchma, to the OSCE Special Representative, Martin Sajdik (112 UA 2019), the "Steinmeier Formula" brightly exemplifies the importance of domestic regulations for conflict transformation.

As published on October 2, 2019, "Steinmeier Formula" suggests amending the "Special Status" Law, so that it [provisionally] enters into force "at 20:00 local time of the day of voting in elections in certain areas of Donetsk and Luhansk regions, scheduled and held in accordance with the Constitution of Ukraine and the special law of Ukraine regulating the holding of elections in the mentioned districts" (ibid.). It is envisaged that the "Special Status" Law will act on a provisional basis until the publication of the final report of the OSCE/ODIHR [Office for Democratic Institutions and Human Rights] Election Observation Mission, in accordance with established OSCE/ODIHR practice (ibid.). It will continue acting on a regular basis, if the OSCE/ODIHR Report "concludes in accordance with established OSCE/ODIHR practice that early local elections in certain areas of Donetsk and Luhansk regions were generally held in accordance with the OSCE and Ukrainian standards" (ibid.). Notably, while not referring to the withdrawal of troops and exchange of prisoners, provided for in the Minsk Agreements and Art. 10 of the "Special Status" Law, the text of the "Steinmeier Formula" attributes several crucial functions to Ukraine's domestic legislation. Firstly, the very fact that the "Formula" was conceived as a modification of final clauses of the "Special Status Law," rather than the international law document, testifies to the pivotal role domestic legislation is to play in defining the status of uncontrolled territories. Secondly, pointing to the Constitution of Ukraine and "the special law of Ukraine regulating the holding of elections in the mentioned districts" as benchmarks for deciding on the regular application of the "Special Status" Law, Ukraine's domestic legislation lies at the heart of the transfer from the ongoing conflict to the territories' "special status."

Notably, the incorporation of the "Steinmeier Formula" into the new "Special Status" Law to start operating in 2020 led to intense debate and protests in Ukraine, with participants blaming current President of Ukraine, Volodymyr Zelenskyy, of "capitulation" and "betrayal" (Surnacheva and Homenko 2019). In this vein, the most common concern about the "Steinmeier Formula" has been the sequencing of the disengagement, withdrawal of troops, and transfer of control over the border to Ukraine, on the one hand, and the incorporation of the "Steinmeier Formula" into the legislation of Ukraine. Whilst Art. 10 of the current version of the "Special Status" Law referred the removal of all unlawful armed formations and the prevention of armed formations' intrusion into the election processes as preconditions of "special status," such preconditions are not envisaged by the "Steinmeier Formula." Another important concern about the "Formula" is its recourse to "the special law of Ukraine regulating the holding of elections in the mentioned districts," the reasons for non-applying current Ukraine's legislation on elections and the extent to which such a "special law" would be different from existing legislation (ibid.).

Moving beyond the solely legal concerns, surrounding the "Formula," it is crucial to point to its diverse and contradictory reflections in discourses of the key actors, engaged in the conflict in eastern Ukraine and its transformation. In his explanation of the suggested "Formula," German President Walter Steinmeier emphasized the importance of small steps, such as granting uncontrolled territories temporary "special status" before the results of early elections are determined (Ukrinform 2019). Even though referring to the adoption of the "Steinmeier Formula" as a "technical step" on the way to comprehensive political settlement, President Zelenskyy stressed a ceasefire and prisoner exchange as political conditions of its incorporation (TSN UA 2019). Kremlin welcomed the signing of the "Formula," though expressing concerns about the opposition forces' reaction to it (Surnacheva and Homenko 2019). Hence, in its recent statement, the political party "European Solidarity," led by the former president Petro Poroshenko, pointed to the danger of inverting the "security" and "political" blocks of the Minsk Agreements (European Solidarity 2019). Last but not least, the leaders of the so–called "DPR" and "LPR" equated signature of the "Steinmeier Formula" to Ukraine's "acknowledging the special right of Donbas people to the independent determination of its destiny," (TASS 2019). Arguing that "we will define ourselves, which language to speak, how our economy will look like, how our court system will form…and how we will integrate with Russia," the leaders of "DPR" and "LPR" evidently overestimated both the power of the "Steinmeier Formula" and the scope of the "Special Status Law" (TASS 2019).

To sum up, conceived as an amendment to the Ukraine's "Special Status" Law, the "Steinmeier Formula" attributes a crucial role to Ukraine's domestic legislation in both defining "special status" and conducting conflict transformation. At the same time, the case of the "Steinmeier Formula" testifies to the fact that, tightly intertwined with the complex political settlement process, a domestic law on "contested territories" may become a crucial source of controversy, as well as political and legal uncertainty in conflict transformation.

CONCLUSION

Against the background of the predominance of international law perspective in the analysis of the so-called post-Soviet conflicts and a legal status of the "contested territories," the aim of this chapter has been threefold. Firstly, it aimed to analyze the "domestic dimension" of defining a status of the "contested territories." Secondly, it looked at the role domestic rules actually or potentially may play with regard to conflict transformation. Based on the above insights, the analysis proceeded with the case of Ukraine, including the novel debate on the "Steinmeier Formula."

We found that the 2005 Moldovan Framework Law and the 2008 Georgian Law "On Occupied Territories" adopt very different approaches to determining the legal status of the "contested territories," reflecting opposite trends in the transformation of conflicts in Transnistria, Abkhazia, and South Ossetia, respectively. Hence, the 2005 Moldovan Framework Law introduces Transnistria as an "autonomy," enjoying a broad array of rights, without referring to the role the Russian Federation continues to play in the region. On the contrary, the 2008 Georgian Law "On Occupied Territories" regards Abkhazia and South Ossetia as territories occupied by the Russian Federation, and introduces numerous restrictions pertaining to free movement and conducting economic activities there. In this vein, we found the Moldovan Framework Law to be conducive to conflict transformation through cooperation in terms of "5+2" and "1+1" talks. In its turn, the stipulation of multiple restrictions in the 2008 Georgia's Law "On Occupied Territories" impedes the application of such an approach, along with the ongoing Geneva International Discussions.

Being shaped by numerous factors (e.g., the degree of radicalization of a particular conflict, the status quo of the international political settlement efforts), domestic laws on a status of the contested territories may fulfil several functions with regard to conflict transformation. They include, among others, leaving the space open or opening up the space for international talks on conflict settlement; defining "red lines" a "maternal state" may not cross in the context of international peace talks; promoting a

136 M. RABINOVYCH

particular qualification of the conflict and contested territories under international law; and promoting or hindering conflict transformation through different forms of cooperation, such as trade and investment.

Applying the above insights to the case of Ukraine, the chapter established that the "domestic dimension" of defining uncontrolled territories in Ukraine is marked by a "hybridity." Such a "hybridity" is manifested by the parallel application of "Special Status" and "Reintegration" legislation that, in turn, stems from Ukraine's profound disillusionment with the progress of the Minsk process in 2018. It was established that, even though the "Special Status" Law is rather close to the 2005 Moldovan Framework Law, and the spirit of the "Reintegration" Law is close to the 2008 Georgia's Law "On Occupation," both legal acts of Ukraine are considerably different from the respective legislation of Moldova and Georgia. Such differences include, amongst others, much narrower competencies of local political entities under the "Special Status" Law, compared to the Transnistria's autonomy; the conditional nature of "special status"; and an absence of cooperation-related restrictions in the "Reintegration" Law. The "Special Status" Law was shown to be conducive to conflict transformation, since it demonstrates Ukraine's readiness to compromise with the breakaway territories. Sequentially, despite such allegations in the media, the "Reintegration" Law appears to impede conflict transformation, with the key threat to it created not by the provisions of the "Reintegration" Law itself, but legal uncertainty surrounding its interplay with the Minsk Agreements and the "Special Status" Law. The chapter's insight into the substance of the "Steinmeier Formula," conceived as an amendment to the "Special Status" Law, detected and made manifest a significant role attributed to Ukraine's domestic law in defining the status of these territories and accompanying the conflict-transformation process, within the international peace process. This case also illustrated the high degree of political controversy and legal uncertainty domestic legislation is prone to create, being highly intertwined with the dynamics of political settlement.

Overall, the analysis testifies to the multiplicity of nexuses between the "domestic dimension" of the defining uncontrolled territories, on the one hand, and international political settlement and conflict transformation efforts, on the other. Thus, we call for researchers' to pay particular attention to the legislation of "maternal" states and its role in, and interplay with international settlement talks and the overall dynamics of conflict transformation.

REFERENCES

112 UA. 2019. Ukraine Publishes Text of Steinmeier Formula, October 2. https://112.international/conflict-in-eastern-ukraine/ukraine-publishes-text-of-steinmeier-formula-44132.html.

Abkhaz World. 2008. Constitution of the Republic of Abkhazia. https://abkhaz-world.com/aw/reports-and-key-texts/607-constitution-of-the-republic-of-abkhazia-apsny.

Allison, Roy. 2008. Russia Resurgent? Moscow's Campaign to 'Coerce Georgia to Peace'. *International Affairs* 84 (6): 1145–1171.

BBC. 2014. V Donecke Obnarodovany Rezultaty 'Referenduma' [The Results of Referendum Are Published in Donetsk]. https://www.bbc.com/ukrainian/ukraine_in_russian/2014/05/140511_ru_s_donbass_referendum.

Bergmann, Julian. 2020 (forthcoming). *The European Union as International Mediator: Brokering Stability and Peace in the Neighbourhood*. Basingstoke: Palgrave Macmillan.

Beyer, John, and Stefan Wolff. 2016. Linkage and Leverage Effects on Moldova's Transnistria Problem. *East European Politics* 32 (3): 335–354.

Büscher, Klemens. 2016. The Transnistria Conflict in Light of the Crisis over Ukraine. In *Not Frozen! The Unresolved Conflicts over Transnistria, Abkhazia, South Ossetia and Nagorno-Karabakh in Light of the Crisis over Ukraine*, ed. Sabine Fischer, 25–43. Berlin: SWP.

Całus, Kamil. 2016. The DCFTA in Transnistria: Who Gains? New Eastern Europe. http://neweasterneurope.eu/old_site/articles-and-commentary/1861-the-dcfta-in-transnistria-who-gains.

Cheretian, Vicken. 2009. The August 2008 War in Georgia: From Ethnic Conflict to Border Wars. *Central Asian Survey* 28 (2): 155–170.

Clogg, Rachel. 2008. The Politics of Identity in Post-Soviet Abkhazia: Managing Diversity and Unresolved Conflict. *Nationalities Paper* 36 (2): 305–329.

Coppieters, Bruno. 2018. 'Statehood', 'de facto Authorities' and 'Occupation': Contested Concepts and the EU's Engagement in Its European Neighbourhood. *Ethopolitics* 17 (4): 343–361.

Council of the European Union. 2018. Conclusions on the Integrated Approach to External Conflicts and Crises, 5413/18 of January 22.

CSCE Mission to Moldova. 1993. Report No 13. https://www.osce.org/moldova/42307?download=true.

Deiana, Maria-Adriana, Milena Komarova, and Cathal McCall. 2019. Cross-Border Cooperation as Conflict Transformation: Promises and Limitations in EU Peacebuilding. *Geopolitics* 24 (3): 529–540.

Deutsche Welle. 2019. MID FRG: "Formula Shtajnmajera"—Eto Tolko Odin Fragment Pazla [Steinmeier's Formula Is Just One Piece of a Puzzle]. https://www.dw.com/ru/мид-фрг-формула-штайнмайера-это-только-один-фрагмент-пазла/a-50683234.

138   M. RABINOVYCH

Dobrescu, Madalina, and Tobias Schumacher. 2020. The Politics of Flexibility: Exploring the Contested Statehood-EU Actorness Nexus in the Georgia. *Geopolitics* 25(2): 407–427.

European Solidarity. 2019. Ne Mozhna Pidpysuvaty Formulu Putina, Yaka Zrujnuye Ukrayinsku Derzhavu—Zayava Frakciji 'Yevropejska Solidarnist'. [It Is Not Allowed to Sign Putin's Formula, Which Will Destroy Ukrainian State], October 1. https://eurosolidarity.org/не-можна-підписувати-формулу-путіна-я/.

Fabry, Mikulas. 2017. Whose International Law? Legal Clashes in the Ukrainian Crisis. In *Triangular Diplomacy among the United States, the European Union, and the Russian Federation. Responses to the Crisis in Ukraine*, ed. Vicki Birchfield and Alasdair R. Young, 169–188. London and New York: Routledge.

Friedman, George. 2008. The Russo-Georgian War and the Balance of Power (Blair's Blog). http://blog.cafewall.com/wp-content/uploads/2008/09/rus-v-geo-analysis.pdf.

German, Tracey. 2009. David and Goliath: Georgia and Russia's Coercive Diplomacy. *Defence Studies* 9 (2): 224–241.

Gerrits, Andre, and Max Bader. 2016. Russian Patronage Over Abkhazia and South Ossetia: Implications for Conflict Resolution. *East European Politics* 32 (3): 297–313.

Giuliano, Elise. 2018. Who Supported Separatism in Donbas? Ethnicity and Popular Opinion at the Start of the Ukraine Crisis. *Post-Soviet Affairs* 34 (2–3): 158–178.

Gromad'ske Radio. 2018. Chy vidpovidayut' Minski Domovlenosti Ukrayinskomu Zakonodavstvu? Komentuyut' Eksperty? [Does the Minsk Agreement Correspond to Ukrainian Legislation?]. https://hromadske.radio/news/2018/02/12/chy-vidpovidayut-minski-domovlenosti-ukrayinskomu-zakonodavstvu-komentuyut-eksperty.

International Criminal Court. 2018. Report on Preliminary Examination Activities. https://www.icc-cpi.int/itemsDocuments/181205-rep-otp-PE-ENG.pdf.

International Crisis Group. 2019. Report No 249. Abkhazia and South Ossetia: Time to Talk Trade. https://www.crisisgroup.org/europe-central-asia/caucasus/georgia/249-abkhazia-and-south-ossetia-time-talk-trade.

Komitet Izbiratelei Donbasa [Committee of Donbas' Voters]. 2014. 'Russkaya Vesna' v Dokumentah. Kakie Akty Prinyala Doneckaya Narodnaya Respublika ['Russian Spring' in Documents. Which Acts Did the Donetsk People's Republic Adopt?]. http://komitet.net.ua/article/120042/.

Korhonen, Outi. 2015. Deconstructing the Conflict in Ukraine: The Relevance of International Law to Hybrid States and Wars. *German Law Journal* 16 (3): 452–478.

Korotkyi, Tymur, and Nataliia Hendel. 2018. The Legal Status of the Donetsk and Luhansk Peoples' Republics. In *The Use of Force Against Ukraine and*

International Law, ed. Serhii Sayapin and Evhen Tsybulenko, 145–170. London and New York: Routledge.

Körppen, Daniela, Beatrix Schmelzle, and Oliver Wils (eds.). 2008. Berghof Handbook 'A Systemic Approach to Conflict Transformation. Exploring Strengths and Weaknesses.' https://core.ac.uk/download/pdf/71733139.pdf.

Lederach, John Paul. 1996. *Preparing for Peace. Conflict Transformation across Cultures*. New York: Syracuse University Press.

———. 1997. *Building Peace: Sustainable Reconciliation in Divided Societies*. Washington, DC: United States Institute of Peace Press.

Mitchell, Lincoln A. 2009. Compromising State-Building in Saakashvili's Georgia. *Central Asian Survey* 28: 171–183.

Moldova Parliament. Moldova (Republic of)'s Constitution of 1999 with Amendments through 2006. Constitute Project. https://www.constituteproject.org/constitution/Moldova_2006.pdf.

OSCE 1997. Memorandum on the Basis for Normalization of Relations between the Republic of Moldova and Transdniestria. https://www.osce.org/moldova/42309?download=true.

———. 2004. Proposals and Recommendations of the Mediators from the OSCE, the Russian Federation, Ukraine with Regards to the Transdniestrian Settlement.

———. 2012. Participants in Talks on Transdniestrian Settlement Review 2012 Progress. https://www.osce.org/cio/97712.

———. 2013a. Latest Round of Talks in Transdniestrian Settlement Process Concluded in Odesa with Agreement on Confidence-Building Measure. https://www.osce.org/cio/101928.

———. 2013b. Transdniestrian Settlement Talks in Kyiv Conclude with Decisions on Freedom of Movement, Pensions and Social Assistance, Waste Facilities Reconstruction. https://www.osce.org/cio/108960.

———. 2015. OSCE Response to the Crisis in and Around Ukraine. https://www.osce.org/home/125575?download=true.

———. 2016. Renewed Transdniestrian Settlement Talks Provide Impetus for Real Progress in the Coming Weeks. https://www.osce.org/cio/244651.

———. 2017. Mediation and Dialogue Facilitation in the OSCE. Reference Guide. https://www.osce.org/secretariat/126646?download=true.

———. 2018. Commitment to Finalize All the Aspects of the 'Package of Eight' Makes This Year Historic for Chisinau and Tiraspol, Says OSCE Special Representative. https://www.osce.org/chairmanship/382879.

———. n.d. Transdniestrian Conflict. https://www.osce.org/moldova/42308?download=true.

OSCE Network of Think Tanks and Academic Institutions. 2016. Protracted Conflicts in the OSCE Area. Innovative Approaches for Cooperation in the

140 M. RABINOVYCH

Conflict Zones. http://osce-network.net/file-OSCE-Network/documents/ Protracted_Conflicts_OSCE_WEB.pdf.

Paffenholz, Tanja. 2009. Understanding Peacebuilding Theory: Management, Resolution and Transformation. *New Routes* 14 (2): 3–6.

Parliament of Georgia. 1995. The Constitution of Georgia. http://www.parliament.ge/files/68_1944_951190_CONSTIT_27_12.06.pdf.

———. 2001. Ob Izmeneniyah v Konstitucii Avtonomnoj Respubliki Abhaziya [On Amendments to the Constitution of the Autonomous Republic of Abkhazia]. https://matsne.gov.ge/ka/document/view/1921803?publication=0.

———. 2008. Law of Georgia 'On Occupied Territories'. https://matsne.gov. ge/en/document/download/19132/5/en/pdf.

Parliament of the Republic of Moldova. 2005. Law 'On Fundamental Regulations of the Special Legal Status of Settlements on the Left Bank of the River Nistru (Transnistria)'. https://www.osce.org/pc/16208?download=true.

Protsyk, Oleh. 2004. Democratization as a Means of Conflict Resolution in Moldova. *European Yearbook of Minority Issues Online* 4 (1): 723–737.

Regnum. 2005. Memorandum Kozaka: Rossijskij Plan Obedineniya Moldovy i Pridnestrovya ['Kozak Memorandum': Russian Plan of Uniting Moldova and Transnistria]. https://regnum.ru/news/458547.html.

Sammut, Dennis, and Nikola Cvetkovski. 1996. Confidence-Building Matters. The Georgia-South Ossetia Conflict. http://www.vertic.org/media/ Archived_Publications/Matters/Confidence_Building_Matters_No6.pdf.

Sasse, Gwendolyn, and Alice Lackner. 2018. War and Identity. The Case of the Donbas in Ukraine. *Post-Soviet Affairs* 34 (2): 139–157.

Sayapin, Serhii. 2019. The End of Russia's Hybrid War against Ukraine? Opinio Juris. http://opiniojuris.org/2019/01/04/the-end-of-russias-hybrid-war-against-ukraine/.

Schleifer, Marc. 2015. Can Closer Economic Ties with Moldova Resolve the Transnistrian Frozen Conflict? CIPE Blog. https://www.cipe.org/ blog/2015/12/09/can-closer-economic-ties-with-moldova-resolve-the-transnistrian-frozen-conflict/.

Second International Peace Conference. 1907. Hague Convention (IV) Respecting the Law and Customs of War on Land and its Annex: Regulations Concerning the Laws and Customs of War on Land. https://ihl-databases.icrc.org/ihl/ INTRO/195.

Souleimanov, Emil Aslan, Eduard Abrahamyan, and Huseyn Aliyev. 2018. Unrecognized States as a Means of Coercive Diplomacy? Assessing the Role of Abkhazia and South Ossetia in Russia's Foreign Policy in the South Caucasus. *Journal of Southeast European and Black Sea Studies* 18 (1): 73–86.

Surnacheva, Elizaveta, and Sviatoslav Homenko. 2019. 'Zrada Sluchilas': v Chem Vinyat Zelenskogo Protivniki 'Formuly Shtajnmajera' ['Betrayal Happened':

What the Opponents of 'Steinmeier Formula' Blame Zelenskyy For?]. *BBC Kyiv*, October 2.

TASS. 2019. Glavy DNR i LNR Sdelali Sovmestnoe Zajavlenie po Podpisaniju 'Formuly Steinmeira' [Heads of DPR and LPR Made a Shared Statement on the Signing of 'Steinmeier Formula'], October 2. https://tass.ru/mezhdunarodnaya-panorama/6951739.

Tocci, Nathalie. 2008. The European Union, Civil Society and Conflict Transformation. *MICROCON Policy Working Paper 1*. https://core.ac.uk/download/pdf/6993307.pdf.

TSN UA. 2019. Zelenskyy Poyasnyv, za Yakyh Umov Vidbudetsya Rozvedennya Syl na Donbasi i Implementaciya 'Formuly Steinmeiera' [Zelenskyy Explained the Conditions, Under Which the Disengagement in Donbas and the Implementation of 'Steinmeier Formula'] Will Take Place, October 16. https://tsn.ua/politika/zelenskiy-poyasniv-za-yakih-umov-vidbudetsya-rozvedennya-sil-na-donbasi-y-implementaciya-formuli-shtaynmayera-1427628.html.

U.S. Mission to International Organizations in Geneva. 2019. US Statement at the Geneva International Discussions on the Conflict in Georgia. https://geneva.usmission.gov/2019/04/04/u-s-statement-at-the-geneva-international-discussions-on-the-conflict-in-georgia/.

Ukraine Crisis Media Center. 2019. Economic Blackmail, Passportization as Occupation: What Putin Is Actually Saying to Zelensky, May 3. http://uacrisis.org/71789-economic-blackmail-passportization-occupation-putin-actually-saying-zelenskyi.

Ukrayinska Pravda. 2018a. President Pidpysav Zakon pro Reintegraciyu Donbasu [President Signed the Law on Donbas' Reintegration], February 20. https://www.pravda.com.ua/news/2018/02/20/7172270/.

———. 2018b. V Rosiyi Vidreaguvali na Zakon pro Reintegraciyu Donbasu [Russia Reacted to the Law on Donbas' Reintegration], January 18. https://www.pravda.com.ua/news/2018/01/18/7168820/\.

Ukrinform. 2019. Steinmeier Explains His 'Formula'. https://www.ukrinform.net/rubric-polytics/2794744-steinmeier-explains-his-formula.html.

United Nations. 1969. Vienna Convention of the Law of Treaties. 1155 U.N.T.S. 331, 8 I.L.M. 679.

United Nations Peacemaker. 1992. Agreement on Principles of Settlement of the Georgian-Ossetian Conflict ('Sochi Agreement'). https://peacemaker.un.org/sites/peacemaker.un.org/files/GE%20RU_920624_AgreemenOnPrinciplesOfSettlementGeorgianOssetianConflict.pdf.

———. 2015. Package of Measures for the Implementation of the Minsk Agreements. https://peacemaker.un.org/ukraine-minsk-implementation15.

United Nations Security Council. 1992. Note Verbale dated 31 July 1992 from the Permanent Mission of Moldova to the United Nations Addressed to the

142   M. RABINOVYCH

Secretary—General, S/24369*, August 06. http://www.onu.mfa.md/img/docs/S-24369-of-6-august-1992.pdf.

———. 1994. Letter Dated 5 April 1994 from the Permanent Representative of Georgia to the United Nations Addressed to the President of the Security Council. Accessed October 26, 2019. https://peacemaker.un.org/sites/peacemaker.un.org/files/GE_940404_DeclarationOnMeasuresForPoliticalSettlementGeogianAbkhazConflict.pdf.

———. 2014. Resolution 2166, Adopted by the Security Council at Its 7221st meeting, on 21 July 2014. S/RES/2166(2014). https://www.securitycouncilreport.org/atf/cf/%7B65BFCF9B-6D27-4E9C-8CD3-CF6E4FF96FF9%7D/s_res_2166.pdf.

———. 2015. Resolution 2202, Adopted by the Security Council at Its 7384th meeting, on 17 February 2015. S/RES/2202(2015). https://www.securitycouncilreport.org/atf/cf/%7B65BFCF9B-6D27-4E9C-8CD3-CF6E4FF96FF9%7D/s_res_2202.pdf.

———. 2018. Statement by the President of the Security Council, 6 June. S/PRST/2018/12. https://undocs.org/S/PRST/2018/11.

Vahl, Marius, and Michael Emerson. 2004. Moldova and the Transnistrian Conflict. In *Europeanization and Conflict Resolution. Case Studies from the European Periphery*, ed. Bruno Coppieters, Michael Emerson, Michel Huysseune, Tamara Kovziridze, Gergana Noutcheva, Nathalie Tocci, and Marius Vahl. Ghent: Academy Press.

Van der Loo, Gillaume. 2019. Law and Practice of the EU's Trade Agreements with Disputed Territories: A Consistent Approach? In *The Interface between EU and International Law: Contemporary Reflections*, ed. Ingre Govaere and Sacha Garben. London: Bloomsbury Publishing.

Verkhovna Rada. 2012. Pro Zasady Derzhavnoyi Movnoyi Polityky [On the Foundations of State Language Policy], July 3. https://zakon.rada.gov.ua/laws/show/5029-17.

———. 2013. Pro Vseukrainc'kyi Referendum [On a Ukraine-wide Referendum], November 6. https://zakon.rada.gov.ua/laws/show/5475-17.

———. 2014a. Pro Osoblyvzj Poryadok Miscevogo Samovryaduvannya v Okremyh Rajonah Doneckoyi ta Luhanskoyi Oblastej [On the Special Order of Local Self-Government in Certain Districts of Donetsk and Luhansk Oblasts], September 16. https://zakon.rada.gov.ua/laws/show/1680-18.

———. 2014b. Pro Zabezpechennya Prav i Svobod Gromadyan ta Pravovyj Rezhym na Tymchasovo Okupovanij Teritoriyi Ukrayiny [On Ensuring the Rights and Freedoms of Citizens and the Legal Regime on the Temporarily Occupied Territory of Ukraine], April 15. https://zakon.rada.gov.ua/laws/show/1207-18.

———. 2015. Pro Pravovyj Rezhym Voyennogo Stanu [On the Legal Status of Martial Law], May 12. https://zakon.rada.gov.ua/laws/show/389-19.

. 2017. Pro Stvorennya Neobhidnih Umov dlya Myrnogo Vregulyuvannya Sytuaciyi v Okremyh Rajonah Doneckoyi ta Luhanskoyi Oblastej [On the Creation of the Necessary Conditions for the Peaceful Resolution of Situation in Certain Areas of Donetsk and Luhansk Oblasts], October 6. https://zakon.rada.gov.ua/laws/show/2167-19.

. 2018a. Pro Vnesennya Zmin do Statti Zakonu Ukrainy 'Pro Osoblyvzj Poryadok Miscevogo Samovryaduvannya v Okremyh Rajonah Doneckoyi ta Luhanskoyi Oblastej, October 4. https://zakon.rada.gov.ua/laws/show/2588-19?lang=en.

. 2018b. Pro Osoblyvosti Derzhavnoyi Polityky iz Zabezpechennya Derzhavnogo Suverenitetu Ukrayini na Timchasovo Okupovanyh Teritoriyah u Dcneckij ta Luhanskij Oblastyah [On the Peculiarities of State Policy on Guaranteeing State Sovereignty of Ukraine on the Temporarily Occupied Territories in Donetsk and Luhansk Oblasts], January 18. https://zakon.rada.gov.ua/laws/show/2268-19.

Wolff. Stefan. 2011. A Resolvable Frozen Conflict? Designing a Settlement for Transnistria. European Centre for Minority Issues Issue Brief #26. http://edoc.vifapol.de/opus/volltexte/2013/4777/pdf/brief_26.pdf.

Zmina. 2018. Pravozahysnyky Prosyat' Poroshenka Povernuty na Povtornyj Rozglyad Zakon pro Reintegraciyu Donbasu [Human Rights Defenders Ask Poroshenko to Return the Law on Donbas Reintegration for the Second Hearing]. https://zmina.info/news/pravozahisniki_prosjiat_poroshenka_povernuti_na_povtornij_rozgljiad_zakon_pro_reintegracijiu_donbasu-2/.

CHAPTER 6

The Reintegration of Donbas Through Reconstruction and Accountability. An International Law Perspective

Tomasz Lachowski

INTRODUCTION

The Ukrainian Revolution of Dignity (2013/2014), also known as the Euromaidan Revolution (Wynnyckyj 2019), resulted not only in the ousting of president Viktor Yanukovych and changes in the internal and foreign politics of Kyiv—becoming more pro-Western—but also led to the Russian aggression against the Ukrainian state and the outbreak of an ongoing armed conflict in and around Ukraine (Bertelsen 2017). As a result, the Russian Federation annexed Crimea and provided military and financial assistance for the creation of unlawful proto-states within Ukrainian territory—the "Donetsk People's Republic" (DPR) and the "Luhansk People's Republic" (LPR).

This chapter analyzes the extent to which the peace-building and transitional justice approaches under international law can set "normative"

T. Lachowski (✉)
Department of International Law and International Relations, University of
Lodz, Łódź, Poland
e-mail: tlachowski@wpia.uni.lodz.pl

© The Author(s) 2020   145
H. Shelest, M. Rabinovych (eds.), *Decentralization, Regional
Diversity, and Conflict*, Federalism and Internal Conflicts,
https://doi.org/10.1007/978-3-030-41765-9_6

146   T. LACHOWSKI

and "policy" frameworks (Koskenniemi 1990, 10–11) for the reintegration efforts of the authorities in Kyiv (as well as the international community), aimed at restoring Ukraine's jurisdiction over its territories in Donbas. In this vein, this chapter will revolve around a number of key international law issues pertaining to the conflict, such as the Russian Federation's legal responsibility for its military aggression, creating and supporting DPR/LPR; individual accountability for crimes committed during the bloodshed in the Donets Basin; and extra-judicial instruments for ensuring truth and reconciliation in a (post-)violence society.

Importantly, the chapter covers the period between 2014 and 2019—just slightly touching on the post-2019 presidential and parliamentary elections in Ukraine. The analysis is based on legal methodology (normative and explanatory approaches, and—to some extent—the legal dogmatics model), supplemented by field research, including expert interviews conducted by the author.

I. "Donetsk" and the "Luhansk People's Republic(s)" as New Quasi-States in the Post-Soviet Space

"Donetsk" and "Luhansk People's Republic(s)" are new examples of so-called quasi-states, named also *de facto* regimes, proto-states, or unrecognized states in post-Soviet space (Pegg 1998; Kolstø 2006, 747). Since their formation in 2014, DPR and LPR "joined the club" of other pro-Russian *de facto* regimes in the former Soviet Union like Transnistria (Moldova), Abkhazia, South Ossetia (Georgia) or Nagorno-Karabakh (Azerbaijan, factually an Armenian-backed proto-state). These *de facto* states emerged in the early 1990s during the dissolution of the USSR. It is important to note that the issue of unrecognized regimes is not limited solely to the post-USSR region. The Ankara-backed Turkish Republic of Northern Cyprus and Somaliland in the northeast of Africa are partly relevant in the analysis of the current Ukrainian case, and the Republic of Serbian Krajina in eastern Croatia, which existed between 1991 and 1995 during the armed conflict in the territory of the former Yugoslavia, is another good example (Kolstø 2006, 750).

Undoubtedly, there are common features that unite these examples of *de facto* states and they might be divided into two interrelated groups based on legal and political factors.

Concerning the legal category, unrecognized states are located beyond any normative legal system, and thus are not international law subjects. Moreover, even though quasi-states base their factual, (semi-)independent existence on the claim of a right to self-determination, international law does not provide a unilateral right to secede without the clear consent of the *de iure* state. As *de facto* states' very appearance on the international arena is, hence, unlawful, *de facto* regimes tend to be classified as an integral part of the respective maternal state. Furthermore, as can be argued from a legal point of view, the reference to "remedial secession" (Buckheit 1978, 222), which is based on the claim that secession "remedies" the violation of a people's right to (internal) self-determination as an instrument of last resort, cannot be applied to the above-mentioned examples of quasi-states (see Supreme Court of Canada 1998).[1]

Given the cause of their formation—an armed conflict, supported in most of the cited cases by a third state, leading to the infringement of another state's territorial integrity—there is an argument to be made that Russia's support for DPR/LPR or Turkey's backing of the Turkish Republic of Northern Cyprus should be treated as acts of aggression. International law sets a clear obligation of non-recognition of an unlawful situation. In other words, legal rights cannot derive from illegal acts (*ex iniuria ius non oritur*; ICJ 1971; Dawidowicz 2010, 676–686). In this regard, an act of aggression constitutes a violation of the fundamental norms of the international legal system (*ius cogens*). Such norms bind states to refrain from any formal act of recognition (such as the illegal annexation of Crimea by the Russian Federation; ILC 2001, Article 41 (2)). As a result, proto-states infringing the territorial integrity or sovereignty of a given state must not be recognized by any subject of international law (Caspersen 2013, 77–101). Nonetheless,

---

[1] A valuable legal framework was established by the Supreme Court of Canada in 1998, regarding the legality of the possible secession of Quebec from the Canadian state. The Supreme Court in Ottawa held that in order to recognize the right to self-determination beyond the colonial sense, Quebec, as any other entity, would have to meet the requirements of three inter-related prerequisites: (1) people living in a such entity form a "nation"; (2) this nation is subjected to human rights violations and repressive policies by the *de iure* state; and (3) there is no other possible way to secure the rights of a "nation" than the creation of an independent state. DPR and LPR do not represent any other nation than Ukraine or Russia (which already possess their own states). Moreover, it cannot be proven that Ukraine has violated fundamental human rights of Donbas's residents, especially in a structural or systematic way. Lastly, a military response and a subsequent creation of the *de facto* regime without Kyiv's consent cannot be said to be the only possible way of "securing the rights" of people living in the Donets Basin.

148 T. LACHOWSKI

treating the existence of unrecognized regimes as a state of occupation is still problematic. Firstly, according to international humanitarian law, a state of occupation is linked to a situation of an ongoing international armed conflict. How do we reconcile this phrase with the notion of "frozen conflict" associated with quasi-states in the post-Soviet region? Secondly, on the basis of Article 2 common to all four Geneva Conventions of 1949, occupation is conducted by a state on the territory of another state. This principle does not mention the role of non-state actors (as a proto-state's representatives will be characterized in this chapter). Therefore, in order to be able to define the above-mentioned cases as cases of occupation by another state, we need to refer to the direct presence of a third state in the form of illegal stationing of Russian troops in Transnistria, Abkhazia, South Ossetia, or DPR/LPR against the will of Moldova, Georgia, or Ukraine.

As for the political features of quasi-states, British scholar Scott Pegg offered one of the first definitions. In particular, he stressed the factual capacity of *de facto* authorities to govern a certain territory with the support of local people. This state of affairs enables the formation of a secessionist entity, but with no chance of getting legitimacy irrespectively of its effectiveness (Pegg 1998). Undoubtedly, unrecognized regimes do look like normal states, possessing an identified territory, population and a center of power. Such resemblance underpins Pål Kolstø's (2006) notion of "state-like entities" (751–752). That being said, such entities lack the ability to enter into relations with other members of the international community (Bryant 2014, 125). Most importantly, all *de facto* regimes would not be sustainable without a strong protector state, providing military, political, and financial assistance (i.e. the Russian Federation in the cases of Transnistria, Abkhazia, South Ossetia, and both "Donbas republics"). Significantly, a protector state (especially in Russia's case) attempts to position itself as a "mediator" trying to "solve a dispute," thereby presenting the conflict as an "internal conflict" between a legal government and secessionist "authorities." Last but not least, a powerful protector state—if needed from the political point of view to destabilize the *de iure* state— can easily freeze a conflict in order to form "a situation in which active armed conflict has ended but there is no possibility to solve the root of the conflict" (Legucka 2017, 82).

DPR and LPR fit the above definition of quasi-states. In short, they are *de facto* exercising sovereignty, but at the same time lack sovereignty *de iure.* Both proto-states emerged on the wave of the so-called "Russian spring" in 2014, often understood as a response of the pro-Russian residents in Eastern Ukraine to the outcomes of the Revolution of Dignity and a new post-Maidan government in Kyiv. However, this interpretation is deeply flawed, as it overlooks the role of the Kremlin in inspiring, stimulating, and supporting the separatist revolt, which brings us to the conclusion that "the problem of separatism in the East" was artificially created by the Russian Federation (Kravchenko 2019b).[2] Interestingly, this factor has been emphasized even by scholars who assert the internal character of the conflict in Donbas (Katchanovski 2016, 480).

On April 7, 2014, the DPR proclaimed its independence. On April 27, 2014, leaders of the LPR emulated their counterparts in Donetsk. Two "referenda," held on May 11, 2014, resulted in almost 90 percent of the votes in DPR and 96 percent in LPR being cast in favor of secession from Ukraine. On May 24, 2014, in Donetsk's Hotel Shakhtar, leaders of both breakaway republics signed a document founding "Novorossiya" (New Russia), a confederation consisting of DPR and LPR, aiming to join the Russian Federation (Nemtsova 2014; Coyle 2018, 112–113). However, for now "Novorossiya" remains more a theoretical and ideological project than a real political entity, while Russia is not willing to "openly" absorb the eastern part of Ukraine (O'Loughlin et al. 2017, 124–144). Thanks to Moscow's support, DPR and LPR have succeeded in consolidating their factual presence with durable *de facto* authority and borders shaped by constant military actions (Mitrokhin 2015, 221–242; Legucka 2017, 81). As in the cases of Transnistria, Abkhazia, and South Ossetia, Russia's interest is to maintain the status quo and freeze an armed conflict without a clear intention of incorporating DPR/LPR into the Russian Federation.[3] Essentially, the Kremlin seeks to destabilize the internal politics of Kyiv and deepen social polarization among Ukrainians, which would facilitate Ukraine's return to Russia's sphere of influence (Malyarenko and Wolff 2018).

---

[2] What is more, the Russian aggression contributed to consolidating Ukrainian society in spite of cultural differences (e.g. linguistic). For instance, the Ukrainian voluntary units on the front line comprised mostly Russophone Ukrainians (Riabchuk 2015, 138–156).

[3] Clearly, the annexation of Crimea constitutes an exception. It is noteworthy that in April 2019 the Kremlin offered a facilitated process for residents in the seized parts of Donbas to obtain Russian citizenship. Arguably, this might be seen as a step towards Russia's 'creeping annexation' of Ukraine's eastern regions.

II. Ukraine's Response to the Establishment of DPR/LPR in a War-torn Environment

Soon after the outbreak of the armed conflict in Donbas, Ukrainian authorities adopted a number of diplomatic and judicial measures aimed at, firstly, ending the hostilities, and secondly, establishing the official narrative of Ukraine being a victim of Russian aggression.

Importantly, this narrative, directly based on arguments derived from international law, was especially prominent during Petro Poroshenko's term as President of Ukraine. He managed to consolidate the international coalition of states supporting Kyiv, for instance, through the application of sanctions against the Russian Federation by, inter alia, the United States and the European Union (EU). Sanctions were perceived as means of bringing the Kremlin to face responsibility for its violations of international law in its relations with Ukraine, and as restrictive measures that put political and economic pressure on the Russian President, Vladimir Putin, to stop infringing the territorial integrity and sovereignty of Ukraine (Zadorozhnii 2016, 313–315). Post-2014 diplomatic actions undertaken by the Ukrainian authorities resulted in the adoption of numerous resolutions by different international organizations and institutions (i.e. the Parliamentary Assembly of the Council of Europe (PACE); the EU; the OSCE Parliamentary Assembly) that qualified the situation in Ukraine as "Russian military aggression in Ukraine," "the ongoing Russian war against Ukraine," and "and the occupation of the territory of Ukraine by the Russian Federation" (a list of these documents can be found in Sayapin 2019). In addition, in 2014 the Russian Federation was suspended from PACE as a result of its illegal annexation of Crimea. Bearing in mind the fact that the Russian Federation is a permanent member of the United Nations Security Council (UNSC), the adoption of a similar resolution in the forum of the UNSC was impossible. Nevertheless, according to the UN Charter of 1945, a UNSC resolution determining an act of aggression is merely of declaratory, not constitutive, character. In spite of its quite successful efforts in the field of foreign politics, Ukraine adopted a binding normative act in its domestic legislation naming the Russian Federation as an "aggressor" and "occupier" only on January 18, 2018 (when the Verkhovna Rada enacted the law "On the peculiarities of state policy on ensuring Ukraine's state sovereignty over temporarily occupied territories in Donetsk and Luhansk regions," hereinafter called "the law on de-occupation and reintegration of Donbas into Ukraine"). This law was the legal basis for the transformation of the Anti-Terrorist Operation (ATO), launched by the Ukrainian authorities on April 13, 2014, into the Joint Forces Operation (JFO) on April 30, 2018.

It is important to underline that the limited, though visible, success in the area of diplomatic efforts in maintaining the interest of the world in the "Ukrainian case" did not result in ending the armed conflict in Donbas. The "Normandy format" (with the participation of Ukraine, Russia, France, and Germany), together with the Tripartite Contact Group (Ukraine, Russia, the OSCE, joined by the so-called leaders of DPR/LPR), led to the adoption of two "Minsk accords"—"Minsk-I" on September 5, 2014 and "Minsk-II" on February 12, 2015. The two accords, however, did not manage to finally end the hostilities. "Minsk-II," a political instrument, not a binding international treaty, is now perceived as far from perfect, though it was the main measure securing a ceasefire and bringing peace in the eastern Ukraine (Wittke 2019). Needless to say, since it calls for the de-escalation of hostilities, disarmament, unconditional amnesty for all (pro-Russian) "protesters," as well as further constitutional and national dialogue in Ukraine,[4] it is often seen as a necessary evil by different scholars (Hurak 2015, 124–140).

The current Head of the Ukrainian state, Volodymyr Zelenskyy, is more reluctant to openly name Russia as an aggressor, which affects the modalities of diplomatic negotiations over the "Donbas issue," particularly the "Normandy format" (Pifer 2019).[5] On October 1, 2019, Zelenskyy announced that Ukraine had agreed on a road map to ending armed conflict, the so-called "Steinmeier Formula," This calls for the organization of local elections and the special status of the Donbas region—fully in the spirit of the "Minsk accords." Even so, Ukrainian representatives argue that in the case of the failure of implementation of the peace road map, the "Steinmeier Formula" should be abandoned, as it may strongly affect the reintegration process and functioning of Ukraine in the aftermath of the conflict (Lynch 2019) in two important ways. Firstly, by the inclusion of all illegal militants and the so-called leaders of DPR/LPR, covered by blanket amnesty provisions, into post-conflict Ukrainian society. Secondly, the special status of the Donbas region,

---

[4] The question remains: "with whom?" The illegal entities of DPR/LPR? Such a presumption is definitely in line with the interests of the Kremlin, not Kyiv.

[5] The strongest speech of Volodymyr Zelenskyy about the Russian Federation seems to be the one he delivered at the 74th session of the UN General Assembly in September 2019, when he called out "Russian aggression" and "occupation of Ukrainian territories" by the Kremlin (President of Ukraine 2019).

152 T. LACHOWSKI

which the formula requires to be granted by Ukrainian legislation, may create a pro-Russian "Trojan horse" within the state, permanently opposing the pro-European aspirations of Kyiv. Nonetheless, the discussions of the "Steinmeier Formula" clearly demonstrate the growing expectations of Western states (mainly Germany and France) of an end to the conflict in Donbas and the re-opening of their relations with the Kremlin. What is more, Russia was reintegrated into PACE on June 24, 2019, as Szymon Kardaś and Jadwiga Rogoża rightly point out (2019), "without having made any concessions, including any modification of its aggressive policy towards Ukraine." The decision of PACE needs to be recognized as a political success for the Kremlin and another sign of a possible turn in the politics of several European states towards Russia.

With regard to judicial means, Ukraine has resorted to different international courts to counter the outcomes of Russia's aggression and the ongoing armed conflict. It is important to pay particular attention to the Ukrainian application against the Russian Federation lodged in 2017 in the International Court of Justice (ICJ 2019), and the eight interstate complaints against Russia lodged in the period between 2014 and 2018 before the European Court of Human Rights (ECtHR) over numerous violations of the European Convention on Human Rights (ECHR) by the Kremlin.[6] Moreover, the Verkhovna Rada issued two ad hoc resolutions on the basis of Article 12 (3) of the International Criminal Court (ICC) Rome Statute to pursue individual accountability for crimes under international law committed in Donbas (and Crimea) since the beginning of hostilities (Marchuk 2016).[7] Finally, as a result of an incident in the Kerch Strait (connecting the Black Sea and the Sea of Azov) on 25 November 2018,[8] when Russia for the first time openly attacked and seized three

[6] The ECtHR has associated itself with complaints concerning the events in Crimea. The same has been done with complaints regarding possible human rights violations in Donbas. One complaint was withdrawn by the Ukrainian authorities.

[7] The first, of February 25, 2014, was related to the "Maidan events" (already dropped by the ICC Prosecutor; ICC 2015, para. 95), while the second, from February 4, 2015, accepted the jurisdiction of the Hague-based Court over crimes against humanity and war crimes allegedly committed in Crimea and Donbas, starting from February 20, 2014 (with no closing date). The ICC Prosecutor decided to open a preliminary examination. Ukraine is still not a party to the Rome Statute, although this may change in coming years, at least according to debates in the Verkhovna Rada.

[8] As a result of the events in the Kerch Strait, the Ukrainian parliament approved a presidential decree to introduce martial law in ten oblasts of Ukraine for a period of 30 days lasting until December 26, 2018. In spite of the political discussions, experts underlined that the

Ukrainian military vessels, Ukraine brought an action against the Russian Federation before the International Tribunal for the Law of the Sea (ITLOS).

It has to be stressed that in its actions on the "judicial frontline" Ukraine is limited by the specifics of each legal instrument applied. As an example, Kyiv has brought an action before the ICJ claiming that the Russian Federation has violated the International Convention on the Elimination of All Forms of Racial Discrimination of 1965 (by infringing the rights of the Crimean Tatars) as well as the International Convention for the Suppression of the Financing of Terrorism of 1999 (by supporting the acts of terrorism committed by pro-Russian separatists in Donbas). Interestingly, in its complaint, Ukraine does not request the Hague-based Court to rule on the issue of the Russian aggression or unlawful occupation (likewise, the status of Crimea); nonetheless, the ICJ may still define Russia's responsibility for its illegal interference in the domestic affairs of a sovereign country.[9] Similarly, the ECtHR can deliver a judgment determining the "effective control" exercised by Kremlin over the seized parts of Donbas (likewise the illegal administration of DPR/LPR). However, most probably it would not refer to the issue of "aggression" or "occupation" per se, a consequence of the structure of the human rights system under the ECHR.

Last but not least, the Kremlin arbitrarily refuses to enforce the judgments of international tribunals—for instance, in April 2017 the ICJ issued provisional measures, obliging Russia to refrain from violating the rights of Crimean Tatars; however, the Russian Federation failed to implement the ICJ order. Moreover, in 2016 the Russian Constitutional Court issued a first judgment stating that any decision of the ECtHR which stands in contradiction to the constitution of the Russian Federation shall not be executed by the Russian authorities. This approach is assessed as the violation of international law, namely the Vienna Convention on the Law of Treaties of 1969 (Fleig-Goldstein 2017). As might be expected, any judgment of the ECtHR that determines Russian responsibility for human rights violations in Donbas would be blocked from enforcement by the authorities in Moscow. Even when the Kremlin agrees to comply

---

martial law was a useful instrument to enhance the combat readiness and mobility of the Ukrainian army in anticipation of a possible open attack by Russian forces (Tymchuk 2018).

[9] In the judgment of November 8, 2019, the ICJ determined its jurisdiction in the case and declared the Ukrainian application admissible (ICJ 2019).

154 T. LACHOWSKI

with the order of an international tribunal, it does so solely for strictly political reasons. Such was the case for the return of captured vessels and Ukrainian sailors (in accordance with the order of the ITLOS of May 25, 2019), paving the way to the next meeting of the "Normandy format" at the end of 2019.

III. Legal Qualification of Russia's Incursion into Ukraine

According to the 2019 report issued by the Office of the High Commissioner for Human Rights (OHCHR), since the beginning of the bloodshed more than 13,000 people have been killed (at least 3,321 civilians) and around 27,500–30,000 have been injured. In addition, we can point to over 1.3 million registered internally displaced persons (IDPs). Needless to say, these numbers are still growing (OHCHR 2019). It has to be stressed that international public perception of the armed conflict in and around Ukraine remains rather blurred due to the effective policy of disinformation conducted by the Kremlin, especially in Western European societies (i.e. the notion of a "civil war" in Ukraine), based on the so-called hybridity of the conflict aimed at discrediting Ukraine in the eyes of Western partners as a "failed state" (Mahda 2018, 179–202; Tymchuk 2018).

It is important to note that a state of war against Russia has never been declared by Kyiv; just the ATO (and JFO later on) (see Romanchuk 2017). Interestingly, in the aftermath of World War II the notion of "war" was generally abandoned by international law. Different post-war treaties replaced it with the term "use of force," embodied in the UN Charter (Sassòli 2007, 241–264), and the phrase of "armed conflict" that might be either "international" (interstate) or "non-international" (intrastate; with government forces fighting against an organized armed group; ICTY 1995, para.70). The possibility of a subsequent internationalization following third-state interference began to be regulated by humanitarian law (the four Geneva Conventions of 1949).

International law does not set a formal condition for the official declaration of a "state of war" issued by one state against another state to classify ongoing hostilities as an example of "use of force" and/or an "armed conflict." Moreover, both indicated notions have a broader scope than the concept of "war." They refer to different aspects of military activities: *ius ad bellum*, which sets the legal criteria for entering into war ("use of force") and *ius in bello*, concerning the question whether military actions are being conducted justly or unlawfully. An infringement of the criteria set out by *ius ad bellum* may constitute an act of aggression. By contrast, *ius in bello* relates to the possible commitment of war crimes or flagrant violations of humanitarian law in a situation of an "international" or "non-international armed conflict." As Marco Sassòli remarks, "[a]lthough international armed conflicts are prohibited (*ius ad bellum* perspective), they still occur (*ius in bello* framework)." Thus, the separation of these two branches of international law is still relevant (Sassòli 2007, 244).

From the perspective of *ius ad bellum*, Russia's activities in Crimea and Donbas infringed Article 2(4) of the UN Charter, which sets a prohibition on the use of force. Moreover, such activities constitute an act of aggression in the light of international law, as stipulated by UN General Assembly (UNGA) Resolution No. 3314 of 1974 (even though a resolution itself is not binding, it should be construed as a reflection of binding norms of customary international law, one of the primary sources of international law (Czapliński et al. 2017). The UNGA Resolution defines aggression as "the use of armed force by a State against the sovereignty, territorial integrity or political independence of another State, or in any other manner inconsistent with the Charter of the United Nations" (Article 1), which clearly corresponded to the Russian conduct towards Ukraine in the aftermath of the Revolution of Dignity, especially the illegal annexation of Crimea. Moreover, the Russian Federation violated the 1994 Budapest Memorandum on Security Assurances. This memorandum was supposed to provide an additional guarantee of the sovereignty, political independence, and territorial integrity of the Ukrainian state in "exchange for" Kyiv's abandoning the nuclear arsenal. The memorandum itself was "merely" a non-binding document (not an international treaty); however, interpreted in the light of Article 2(4) of the UN Charter (setting a clear prohibition of the use of force "against the territorial integrity or political independence of any state"), it constitutes a fully binding norm of international law. What is more, in 1970 the UNGA adopted its "Declaration on Principles of International Law concerning Friendly Relations and Co-operation among States," which can be characterized as "the main source of generally accepted international law that codifies its principles" (Zadorczhnii 2016, 224). Russia's activities in Ukraine were openly against the most fundamental principles of international order binding all members of the international community on the ground of customary international law.

By supporting the illegal referendum held in Crimea on March 16, 2014, Russia also violated the provisions of the Ukrainian–Russian bilateral international treaties concluded in 1997 and 2010 securing the Russian presence in Crimea (likewise the Treaty on Friendship, Cooperation, and Partnership between Ukraine and the Russian Federation of 1997 that eventually expired in April 2019). Inter alia, these treaties concerned the division of the Black Sea Fleet and the principle of non-interference in domestic affairs. Eventually, the conduct of the so-called "little green men" (unmasked soldiers, in fact members of the Russian Special Forces) may be attributed to Russia on the grounds of Article 8 of the Draft Articles on the Responsibility of States for Internationally Wrongful Acts (DARSIWA) of 2001 (reflecting the binding customary international law on the matter). Similarly, the military operations observed in Donbas can be also assessed using the same paradigm—as a combination of direct aggression and indirect aggression. Direct aggression is reflected in all the documented cases of bombardment of Ukrainian territory and in the direct presence of Russian troops in Ukraine without the country's consent. Indirect aggression relates to the fact that pro-Russian militants act under the direction or control of Russian military leaders. Last but not least, the incident observed in Kerch Strait should be construed as an another example of an ongoing act of aggression. This is because the 1974 UNGA resolution stipulates that "the first use of armed force by a State in contravention of the (UN) Charter shall constitute prima facie evidence of an act of aggression." This is exactly what happened on February 26, 2014, when Russian troops and militants started to control the area of Sevastopol (Sayapin 2019). As a consequence, an act of aggression of the Russian Federation triggered Ukraine's inherent right of self-defense, enshrined in Article 51 of the UN Charter and customary international law.

The Russian leadership tried to justify the use of force on the basis of alleged threats to ethnic Russians and Russian-speakers, and on the grounds of supporting the right to self-determination of the Crimean Peninsula. In particular, it framed its actions through the principle of intervention by invitation and the "responsibility to protect" (R2P) doctrine to protect "*Russkiy mir's*" (the "Russian world's") residents from the "oppressive Ukrainian state" (Yakubova 2018). As convincingly argued by Veronika Bílková, all such arguments "either have an unclear status under international law or the conditions for their application were not met in Crimea" (Bílková 2015, 49). Undeniably, the same can be said about the

Russian-speaking residents of Donbas, who have never been systematically persecuted by Ukrainian authorities (Kersten 2014).

Agnieszka Szpak suggests that we should distinguish the situation witnessed in Crimea after the annexation from the one observed in Donbas on the basis of international humanitarian law (Szpak 2017, 261). Article 2(2) common to the four Geneva Conventions of 1949 says: "the present Convention shall apply to all cases of declared war or of any other armed conflict which may arise between two or more of the High Contracting Parties, even if the state of war is not recognized by one of them. The Convention shall also apply to all cases of partial or total occupation of the territory of a High Contracting Party, even if the said occupation meets with no armed resistance." Undoubtedly, this provision, irrespective of the lack of military resistance or low intensity of hostilities, is applicable to the situation of Crimea (Szpak 2017, 272–273) since the very beginning of the Russian special operation in Crimea, February 26, 2014 (ICC 2018). By incorporating the Crimean Peninsula, Russia violated Article 43 of the Annex to the IV Hague Convention (Laws and Customs of War on Land) of 1907, which imposed an obligation on the occupying power to "respect the laws in force in the country" and to preserve the status quo of the occupied territory.

As for the situation in Donbas, the hostilities met the requirements set by Article 3, common to all four Geneva Conventions of 1949, which stipulates a situation of non-international armed conflict (a state of affairs existing in the Donets Basin since April 30, 2014, at the earliest; (ICC 2018)). As a matter of fact, pro-Russian militants can be identified as well-organized armed group with a hierarchical structure. Furthermore, to the extent that it can be proven that there are Russian troops on Ukraine's territory, and that pro-Russian separatists' actions are being conducted under the control or instructions of Russian military leaders (as during the Battle of Ilovaisk in August 2014; see Mitrokhin 2015; Tymchuk et al. 2016; Coyle 2018, 96–100), then the situation amounts to an international armed conflict and a corresponding state of occupation exercised by the Russian Federation. As a consequence, all examples of Russo-Ukrainian relations covered by the provisions of international humanitarian law, such as the event in the Kerch Strait, are clear emanations of an international armed conflict (Korotkyy 2019, 139). None the less, from the strictly legal point of view (especially in the light of an issue of legal responsibility), the situation of an international armed conflict—with the Russian troops or Russian military leaders directly involved in hostilities—needs to be distinguished from all clashes of pro-Russian militants, acting without (or beyond) any instructions or control of the Russian military leadership, and the Ukrainian army. Therefore, the situation of international armed conflict in Donbas exists in parallel to a non-international armed conflict, which may be assessed in detail only on a case-by-case basis by a relevant court, for instance the ICC. While this assessment can be found in three annual reports by the ICC Prosecutor (2016–2018), the text did not refer to the situation observed in Donbas as a state of occupation (ICC 2018, paras 68; 72–73).

To sum up this section, it has to be underlined that the legal classification of Russia's unlawful incursion into Ukraine has several implications for the process of reintegration of Donbas exercised through the means of post-conflict justice and accountability. First of all, since February 26, 2014, we have observed an act of aggression by the Russian Federation against Ukraine—that is why, legally speaking, all its outcomes, including the establishment of DPR/LPR, are null and void, therefore they cannot be recognized by the international community. Secondly, in the light of international humanitarian law, Russian activities in the Ukrainian territory, witnessed not only in the illegally annexed Crimea, but also in Donbas, should be named as a situation of international armed conflict. Therefore, it precludes the validity of the Kremlin argument of a "civil war" in Ukraine. Lastly, from the political point of view, the international character of hostilities justifies the internationalization of the process leading to the solution of "the Donbas issue," for instance by the deployment of a UN peacekeeping mission.

IV. Responsibility for the "Donbas Events" under International Law

Setting the responsibility for an unlawful act or omission and, as a result, clarifying the duty to repair the prior violation of a legal obligation, are the immanent features of each normative system (PCIJ 1928). As for the main research question, on the Ukrainian efforts to reintegrate the seized parts of Donbas after the armed conflict comes to an end, setting the responsibility for "the Donbas events" directly affects the modalities of process leading to the restoration of a full jurisdiction of Kyiv over the temporarily lost parts of the Donets Basin.

6 THE REINTEGRATION OF DONBAS THROUGH RECONSTRUCTION... 159

There are two key conditions of the process: Firstly, exclude the perpetrators of international crimes (coming either from DPR/LPR or Russia) from the peace negotiations process and the subsequent reintegration strategy. Such individuals shall be held accountable by an Ukrainian domestic court, or the ICC. Secondly, it has to be underlined that if the Russian Federation is officially held responsible for its unlawful acts committed on the Ukrainian soil by a relevant international tribunal, it shall not be treated as a neutral mediator invited to solve the issue, but as a party to the international armed conflict. As a result, a legal path is opened for Kyiv to seek reparations from Russia on the grounds of international law and so not be obliged to bear all costs of the reintegration of Donbas.

Therefore, considering the human rights violations and grave breaches of international humanitarian law that have occurred in Donbas (and are still being witnessed at the time of writing), committed either by Russia, or by pro-Russian militants, and the necessity to define the parallel obligations of the Ukrainian state, it is essential to provide a three-fold legal analysis on the basis of: general international law; international human rights law; and international criminal law.

With reference to the first dimension, activities of a quasi-state (i.e. a non-state actor) cannot be assessed as actions of organs of a state protector *de iure* or *de facto*, unless the complete dependence of a quasi-state on a supporting third state can be proven (Milanović 2009, 310–311). In order to attribute acts committed by representatives of the unrecognized regimes of DPR/LPR to Russia, it is necessary to demonstrate that their conduct meets the requirements stipulated by Article 8 of DARSIWA ("the person or group of persons is in fact acting on the instructions of, or under the direction or control of, that State in carrying out the conduct"). In this respect, it is worth recalling the International Court of Justice (ICJ) judgment in the case of *Nicaragua v. USA* (ICJ 1986), regarding the potential US responsibility for the violations committed by Washington-backed *contras* (guerrillas) in Nicaragua, in which the Court set a test of an "effective control." This test was repeated later on by the ICJ in the case of *Bosnia v. Serbia* (ICJ 2007), which concerned, inter alia, the Srebrenica massacre. In in the eyes of the Court, "effective control" assumes that a third state must exercise a significant degree of control over non-state actors' *concrete operations* leading to the violation of international law. From this perspective, military, financial, or logistical support is not sufficient to attribute militants' conduct to a state protector. It should be underlined that this approach was criticized by some scholars, who argued that the ICJ wrongly

160 T. LACHOWSKI

applied Article 8 of DARSIWA. For instance, Griebel and Plücken claim that a non-state actor, whose acts or omissions are attributable to a certain state (protector), shall be automatically treated as an organ thereof *de facto* (2008, 601–622). Some other experts underline the problem of "the responsibility gap" by adopting this approach and propose to broaden the scope of the attribution of a conduct of a non-state actor to a state on the additional ground of "complicity" (Lanovoy 2017, 563–585). Otherwise, it might be problematic to successfully apply a test of an "effective control" in practice. As a result, Griebel and Plücken emphasize, the ICJ fails to satisfy the present needs of the international community, which can have some implications also for the analyzed "Donbas events." Having in mind Ukraine's application filed against the Russian Federation before the ICJ in 2017—part of which is related to the possible support by the Kremlin of the acts of terrorism committed by pro-Russian separatists in Donbas, including the shooting-down of Malaysia Airlines Flight MH17 and the shelling of civilians in several Ukrainian cities—in assessing the possible attribution of the rebels' conduct to Russia, the Court would most probably rely again on its "effective control" test.

Taking into consideration the human rights paradigm and the system of the European Convention on Human Rights (ECHR), the European Court of Human Rights (ECtHR) repeatedly ruled that a primary obligation of a member state to protect human rights must be exercised within its territory (ECtHR 2001). None the less, in special circumstances the scope of this duty may be broadened beyond its territorial jurisdiction (ECtHR 2005). Needless to say, a jurisdiction is a first step in setting the responsibility of a state party for violation of an international obligation derived from the Convention. However, these two notions cannot be considered as synonyms (Orakhelashvili 2003, 545). Moreover, states' obligations under ECHR are divided into two categories, "negative" and "positive," meaning that a state is not only obliged not to violate human rights by its own conduct, but also to create an efficient system of securing people's rights and freedoms against infringement by non-state actors (including a legal duty to investigate, prosecute, and punish all cases of rights violations). What is significant for the "Donbas events," is that human rights are still applicable in the situation of an armed conflict or a state of occupation; this has become an immanent feature of the relevant case-law of the ICJ (see the 2004 *Israeli Wall Advisory Opinion*) or ECtHR (*Isayeva v. the Russian Federation* of 2005).

6 THE REINTEGRATION OF DONBAS THROUGH RECONSTRUCTION... 161

The first time the ECtHR was confronted with the issue of a state protector's responsibility for a quasi-state's conduct resulting in the violation of the ECHR was with the Turkish Republic of Northern Cyprus. In *Loizidou v. Turkey* (ECtHR 1995) and *Cyprus v. Turkey* (ECtHR 2005) the Court in Strasbourg determined Turkey's jurisdiction, thereby finding the country responsible for numerous violations of human rights. In particular, Turkey's military presence and strong political support created a situation of "effective overall control" exercised by Turkey over a quasi-state's conduct infringing the ECHR.

It is necessary to stress that the "effective overall control" test crafted by the ECtHR does not require a state protector to directly control every action leading to the concrete violation. In this regard, its threshold is much lower than in the "effective control" test shaped by the ICJ, analyzed above. Furthermore, the Court in Strasbourg is very pragmatic in its attitude towards the protection of human rights guaranteed by the ECHR. Therefore, the control of a state over a certain territory is a matter of fact rather than law (i. official determination of a state of occupation is not necessary). This is what matters for admitting the jurisdiction and further responsibility of the Russian Federation for its activities in Donbas under ECHR (in the light of humanitarian law, "'effective control' is a *conditio sine qua non* of belligerent occupation"; Dinstein 2019, 48).

Later on, in the cases of *Ilaşcu v. Moldova and Russia* (ECtHR 2004) and *Catan v. Moldova and Russia* (ECtHR 2012), the ECtHR determined the parallel jurisdiction of Moldova (state *de iure*) and the Russian Federation (a state protector) over the conduct of the *de facto* regime of Transnistria leading to the violations of the ECHR. The court reiterated the basic principle of securing people's human rights under the territorial jurisdiction of a member state. The latter, however, may be limited as a result of the lack of factual control exercised over some part of its territory (although not fully excluded). The ECtHR stated that Moldova "still has a positive obligation under Article 1 of the Convention to take the diplomatic, economic, judicial or other measures that are in its power to take and are in accordance with international law to secure to the applicants the rights guaranteed by the Convention" (ECtHR 2004, para.331). Nevertheless, the examination of responsibility of the *de iure* state shall be always conducted on a case-by-case basis. In parallel, the court found that, by exercising control over the *de facto* regime, the Russian Federation possessed (extraterritorial) jurisdiction and might be held responsible for the human rights violations in Transnistria. Next, concerning the human

162   T. LACHOWSKI

rights violations witnessed in Nagorno-Karabakh in two cases of *Sargsyan v. Azerbaijan* and *Chiragov v. Armenia* (ECtHR 2015a, b), the ECtHR found that Azerbaijan as the state *de iure* is still obliged to protect rights on its territory, while Armenia—exercising overall control over Nagorno-Karabakh (jurisdiction)—may be also responsible for human rights violations in the quasi-state.

The ECtHR has already examined Ukraine's potential responsibility concerning human rights violations observed in DPR/LPR. In the cases of *Khlebik v. Ukraine* (concerning the Luhansk district; ECtHR 2017) and *Tsezar v. Ukraine* (concerning Donetsk; ECtHR 2017)), the Court found no violation of the ECHR, since "the domestic (Ukrainian) authorities have done all in their power under the circumstances to address the applicant's situation" (ECtHR 2017, para.79). The ECtHR stated also that the DPR/LPR are not controlled by Ukraine. As a result, authorities in Kyiv have no negative obligations with reference to this territory. Nonetheless, under different circumstances, a potentially inadequate Ukrainian response towards the infringement of rights occurring in DPR/LPR, the ECtHR may still find Ukraine responsible under ECHR (the "positive obligations" principle; see Grant 2014).[10] It is necessary to remember that there are currently more than 4,360 individual complaints concerning the events in Donbas (and Crimea), of which just 150 have been communicated by the ECtHR. Moreover, 3,000 cases are filed against Ukraine (mostly by the Ukrainian soldiers who were captured in the aftermath of the Battle of Ilovaisk in August 2014 and held unlawfully by the DPR "administration"), about 1,000 against the Russian Federation and Ukraine, and around 400 just against Russia (Lishchyna 2018). The first applications considering Russia's possible jurisdiction and subsequent responsibility, lodged in 2014, were communicated by the Court in Strasburg on 9 January 2018. They are still under examination at the time of writing (ECtHR 2018a, b).

Last but not least, as a result of the ICC involvement in Ukraine, the Hague-based court may determine the individual criminal accountability

---

[10] On June 10, 2015, Ukraine officially notified the Secretary General of the Council of Europe that due to the armed conflict in Donbas it was derogating from certain obligations coming from the ECHR. Kyiv took similar action with reference to obligations under the International Covenant on Civil and Political Rights (ICCPR) on May 21, 2015. However, firstly, these derogations cannot be applied retrospectively, and, secondly, most of the rights and freedoms guaranteed by the ECHR or the ICCPR, such as freedom from torture, are non-derogable rights (Milanović 2015).

of persons who committed crimes against humanity or war crimes on Ukraine's territory (in the form of, inter alia, killings, destruction of civilian objects, torture/ ill-treatment or disappearances, as indicated in ICC 2017, paras. 104–110), starting from February 20, 2014 (set by the Verkhovna Rada in its ad hoc resolution of September 8, 2015), regardless of their nationality or official positions held within a given state structure. However, in order to prosecute and punish the representatives of the Russian Federation, the ICC needs to classify hostilities observed in the east of Ukraine as an international armed conflict (in reports of 2016, 2017 and 2018, the ICC Prosecutor has noticed such a possibility). The process whereby an internal conflict becomes internationalized takes place under the "overall control" test, formulated in the case of *Tadić* by the Appeal Chamber of the International Criminal Tribunal for the former Yugoslavia (ICTY) in its judgment of 1999. The ICTY stated that in addition to financial or military aid, a state protector had to play an important role in the coordination or management of the factual functioning of a non-state actor. However, there is no requirement of commanding the concrete operation of a guerrilla movement as was ruled by the ICJ in the "effective control" test (Cassese 2007, 649–668). Moreover, in order to prosecute the pro-Russian rebels for international crimes, there is no need to legally determine a situation of an international armed conflict. On the contrary, a situation of a non-international armed conflict is sufficient to bring to justice pro-Russian militants before the ICC (which is much easier from the strictly evidential point of view). Furthermore, the ICC (or the Ukrainian domestic courts) may also prosecute members of the Ukrainian forces (either the regular army, or military voluntary units) for committing war crimes or crimes against humanity (Amnesty International 2014). However, the ICC adheres to the principle of complementarity in its work. In this respect, it cannot assess the situation as a substitute for the Ukrainian authorities. That being said, it worth stressing that the Ukrainian state does not possess enough institutional capacity and experience in prosecuting international crimes by domestic means (Polunina 2016, 6). Nonetheless, in April 2015 the parliament adopted an amendment to the Criminal Code of Ukraine, increasing the state's legal responsibility for war crimes. Undoubtedly, the strict cooperation of the Ukrainian prosecutors and the ICC will improve the domestic justice system in Ukraine and serve as a guarantee that perpetrators of the most heinous crimes will be brought to justice.

This analysis demonstrates possible legal paths to setting the responsibility of the Russian Federation for the "Donbas events," as well as the individual accountability of either the representatives of Russia, or the pro-Russian militants for international crimes committed on the Ukrainian territory. It is important to recall that the Ukrainian authorities decided to use most of the existing instruments under international law. As a result, it can be argued that Kyiv has tried to adopt a comprehensive strategy on the "judicial frontline," most visible in the field of human rights. Undoubtedly, a binding judgment of a relevant international tribunal finding Russia to have violated international law in relation to events and actions in Ukraine can lead to at least two inter-related effects that can contribute to the successful reintegration of Donbas into Ukraine (Lachowski 2018, 48–51). Firstly, strictly normatively, such a decision would open the possibility of Kyiv seeking reparations (including financial compensation, but also satisfaction as a form of remedy) from the Kremlin. Secondly, from a non-normative standpoint, such a decision would be a powerful weapon to counter Russia's policy of propaganda and disinformation on the "Donbas events" (Zolotukhin 2018).

V. Reintegration of Donbas into Ukraine— Peacebuilding and Transitional Justice Perspectives

This section attempts to determine the mechanisms for the possible reintegration of the seized parts of the Donets Basin into Ukraine, which at the same time would entail the dismantling of the illegal entities of DPR/LPR. It takes into consideration a two-fold approach: a peacebuilding approach (including the potential establishment of a UN peacekeeping mission) and a transitional justice perspective that acknowleges the regional diversity of Ukrainian citizens.

The adoption of a satisfactory solution to the ongoing armed conflict in and around Ukraine and the illegal annexation of Crimea remains one of the most important challenges for Ukrainian authorities. Needless to say, even though a majority of Ukrainians agree on the necessity of settling the conflict in Donbas, most surveys reveal a lack of consensus among Ukrainian citizens on the shape of Ukraine's policy towards the seized territories (Lyubashenko 2017, 119–125; Razumkov Centre 2019; Sasse 2019). For example, particularly controversial are issues such as whether the restoration of Ukraine's jurisdiction over Donbas should be exercised through military means (supported mostly in western and central regions of the country) or via a peaceful resolution, federalization, and blanket amnesties (which is unpopular even in southern and eastern regions), or a strong retributive policy towards pro-Russian militants with no compromises (which tends to be rejected in the south and east of Ukraine). According to one recent survey, support for the establishment of an international peacekeeping mission in Donbas is generally high (60 percent). The same survey confirmed that the highest percentage of support in south is gained by the variant "Successful restoration of prosperous life in the Ukraine-controlled areas of Donbas" (41.7 percent), as an action that should be taken to establish peace in Donbas. However, there are significant regional divergences, with almost 80 percent of the positive attitude concentrated in western regions compared to just 33 percent in the east, where almost 40 percent of respondents expressed a negative attitude to the introduction of international peacekeeping forces in Donbas (Ilko Kucheriv 2018). Moreover, the majority of Ukrainians (56 percent) are against a special status for Donbas (just 10 percent opt for autonomy) and the implementation of the so-called Steinmeier Formula as an element of the peace process covered by the Minsk accords (Razumkov Centre 2019). What is interesting, according to the recent surveys, most of the residents of DPR/LPR are in favor of staying within Ukraine (55 percent, in comparison with 45 percent who want to join the Russian Federation), however just 31 percent call for a special status for Donbas (Sasse 2019).[11]

1. Post-Conflict Peacebuilding with Regard to Donbas

Since the 1992 Agenda for Peace issued by former UN Secretary-General, Boutros Boutros-Ghali, the organization's role in peacekeeping (or peacebuilding), alongside its roles in preventive diplomacy and peace-making efforts, has been constantly revised (Boutros-Ghali 1992, paras. 20–22). As a result, these days UN missions in conflict or post-conflict zones tend to be equipped with more robust mandates than in the past. Such mandates may include the active promotion of human rights, capacity-building efforts to strengthen local institutions, and the reintegration of former combatants into society (UNSG 1998, para. 63). Other tasks include conducting investigations into serious violations of human rights, which are

---

[11] Moreover, the majority of people currently living in the self-proclaimed republics still define themselves as residents of Donets Basin with a mixed Russian–Ukrainian ethnic and regional identity, just as was the case prior to the 2014 events (Sasse 2017).

166 T. LACHOWSKI

treated not only as a means to delivering justice in a criminal law case, but also as a peacebuilding tool (UNSG 2000, para.13; Jenkins 2012).

With this in mind, the UN Security Council (SC) under Chapter VII of the UN Charter (which implies a legally binding status) have established UN transitional administrations. Unlike "classic" peacekeeping operations, such transitional administration are not formed in response to a given state's consent. In particular, the main function of such international interim administrations is to assist a (post-)conflict society in strengthening the capacity of state institutions and eventually transferring full sovereignty to a given community (Stahn 2008, 44). The most influential transitional administrations in recent history—such as those established for Cambodia (UNTAC) in 1992, Eastern Slavonia, Baranja, and Western Sirmium (UNTAES) in 1996, Timor-Leste (UNTAET) and Kosovo (UNMIK) in 1999—possessed mandates which included a variety of activities related to post-conflict reconciliation and transitional justice. To give a few examples, the retributive special panels in Kosovo were responsible for prosecuting and punishing war criminals. The same applies to the restorative Truth and Reconciliation Commission in East Timor (Stahn 2001, 105–183). Significantly, these experiences might provide valuable models for Ukraine.

Among different peacebuilding operations established in (post-)conflict environments, UNTAES seems to offer the most fitting experience that could apply to the Ukrainian case. First of all, it functioned in a (post-)conflict zone, where a self-proclaimed proto-state (Republic of Serbian Krajina) was established with the political, economic, and military assistance of a third state, namely Serbia (at that time, the Federal Republic of Yugoslavia). Moreover, the UNTAES had to operate in compliance with the ICTY, which may be compared with ICC interference in the "Ukrainian situation" and the possible cooperation of the Hague-based court with a peacekeeping mission in Donbas (Gowan 2015, 519–531). The process of reintegration of Eastern Slavonia, Baranja, and Western Sirmium included some components of the institutional reform toolkit, namely the reform of police so that the force operated on the basis of dualism (consisting of representatives of both communities: Croats and Serbs). Nonetheless, the (geo)political conditions for UNTAES and a potential mission in Donbas differ greatly, thus presenting important limitations largely of a political character: pro-Russian militants in Donbas are being supported by a UNSC permanent member, and Ukraine does not possess a the kind of strong military position towards separatists that the Croatian army did vis-à-vis Serbs in Eastern Slavonia (Gowan 2018, 9–10). In sum, without the strong support of the international community Ukraine cannot deploy military or political resources strong enough to force the Russian Federation to cease its ongoing act of aggression.

Since the beginning of the conflict, authorities in Kyiv made an effort to convince the international community of the significant contribution that a UN peacekeeping mission could make toward stopping the violence, enforcing a ceasefire, and creating a framework for the subsequent reintegration of Donbas into Ukraine (Coyle 2018, 91). Despite initial hesitation, in September 2017 Vladimir Putin announced his possible agreement to the creation of such peacekeeping mission. However, his consent would be conditional upon including a Russian contingent as part of the mission. Moreover, by limiting the peacekeepers' mandate to the demarcation line, Moscow's proposal effectively would exclude the Russia–Ukraine border from the jurisdiction of the UN mission. Clearly, this perspective is at odds with Kyiv's interest (Strzelecki et al. 2017).

In February 2018 a report on the creation of a peacekeeping mission in Donbas was prepared by UN expert Richard Gowan. He emphasized the necessity of crafting a robust mandate for the mission in eastern Ukraine. In his view, such mission should include at least 20,000 personnel and be divided into military, police, and civilian components. Moreover, the mission should be administered by non-NATO European states, such as Sweden, Finland or Austria, as well as countries with close ties with Russia such as Belarus or Kazakhstan. Finally, the mission as a whole should be monitored by the EU, through the creation of a Special Representative (Gowan 2018).

2. Transitional Justice in Post-Maidan Ukraine in the Light of an Ongoing Armed Conflict

A successful resolution of the conflict in Donbas and completion of the post-conflict reconciliation process requires that post-Maidan Ukrainian authorities assemble and apply a broader transitional justice toolkit (Lyubashenko 2017; Martynenko 2018). Needless to say, Ukraine probably serves as the first example in history of a state that simultaneously adopts transitional justice mechanisms aimed at rejecting the Soviet legacy (and likewise the legacy of Viktor Yanukovych's regime) while being forced—as a result of Russian external aggression—to shape its politics towards the application of post-conflict justice and reconciliation in the process of reintegration of previously lost territory (Donbas). These two dimensions are inter-related, so instruments directed at dealing with the past as decommunization or lustration while strengthening national identity, as via the Ukrainian language law of 2019, affect the pillars of post-conflict justice and reconciliation and cannot be treated as separate.

Transitional justice refers to the introduction of a combination of both judicial and non-judicial instruments, such as individual criminal prosecutions (conducted either on an international, or purely domestic level), truth-seeking and truth-telling mechanisms, institutional reforms, vetting, and dismissals or reparations, by post-authoritarian or post-conflict societies to address historical injustices and deal with massive structural historical abuses ("a backward-looking justice"; UNSG 2004, para. 8; Teitel 2000, 6–9). In post-communist (or post-Soviet) Central and Eastern European states, such instruments as decommunization and lustration became the visible core of transitional justice efforts (Stan 2009). From the very start, transitional justice was rooted in international law and the human rights paradigm by the presumption that transition from an authoritarian rule to democracy, or from war to peace, should lead to the establishment of a democratic state based on rule of law principles, and not a political revenge against the representatives of the ancien régime (Arthur 2009). In the last two decades, transitional justice has started to be implemented not only *in the aftermath* of a conflict, but also *during* bloodshed. The ultimate goal is to create a future framework capable of increasing accountability, building civic trust in state institutions, and ensuring an official truth and reconciliation process that could potentially be accepted by the conflicting parts of a divided society ("a forward-looking justice"; Engstrom 2013, 59). In other words, the standard transitional justice toolkit as a comprehensive strategy may need to be slightly changed to fit the Ukrainian case.

Taking into account the regional diversity of Ukrainian citizens and their attitude towards the interpretation of Ukraine's history, some researchers opt for the adoption of truth-telling or truth-seeking mechanisms (Kemp and Lyubashenko 2018, 349–350), potentially set in a framework of a truth and reconciliation commission, in the post-conflict reconstruction of Donbas (Nuzov 2017, 150–153). Mykola Riabchuk draws attention to the fact that in 1991 independent Ukraine emerged as a common state of both "Soviet" and "non-Soviet Ukrainians," with different historical experiences and expectations for the future of their own state (Riabchuk 2015, 142). According to Riabchuk, the biggest failure of the post-1991 Ukrainian authorities (regardless of their concrete political fractions) was "the inability of consecutive national governments to address the problem of and offer a comprehensive policy for national integration" (2015, 144). From this perspective, all internal "divisions" (e.g. Ukrainophones/ Russophones)[12] are a consequence, not the root cause, of the "different" (complex) Ukrainian identities. Bearing in mind, for instance, the post-Maidan Ukrainian politics of history (a backward-looking justice), it is clear that the activities promoted by the Ukrainian Institute of National Remembrance (UINR) were definitely based on the "non-Soviet Ukrainians" legacy, which implied a complete rejection of Russian ("Russkiy mir") dominion over Ukraine. In turn, this approach based on the policy of decommunization directly affected the modalities of the reintegration process (a forward-looking justice), as it was rejected not only by residents of DPR/LPR but also a part of the Ukrainian society remaining in the territory controlled by Kyiv (Kasianov 2018, 147–152). Nonetheless, treating the regional diversity of Ukrainian citizens as an obstacle to implement transitional justice in the aftermath of the Revolution of Dignity and the context of an ongoing armed conflict, is a false assumption. On the contrary, a properly crafted transitional justice strategy might contribute to the consolidation of the diverse Ukrainian society. The regional diversity of Ukraine might be reflected, for instance, in a more open way of conducting politics of memory (not "nationalist-centered" as is the charge sometimes laid against UINR), although still strictly in compliance with the current post-Maidan policy of decommunization (Kozyrska 2016) that would cover Donbas and Crimea both *de iure* and *de facto* after their reintegration. The UINR seems to understand the situation, since its proposals, for instance, to rename various locations covered by the scope of the decommunization laws (cities, streets, squares etc.) are often based on the historical names of such locations (prior to the Soviet era) or refer to the neutral names without any political context—this is also an example to the seized parts of Donbas (Shpak 2019). Nonetheless, the concept of decommunization itself, the central instrument of the "dealing with the past" compartment of the transitional justice toolkit, is a sovereign choice of post-Maidan Ukraine trying to come to terms with its totalitarian Soviet past. It is even more defensible when one bears in mind the ongoing external aggression of the Russian Federation—the continuation state of the USSR and the executor of the "Russkiy mir" ideology—against Ukraine.

---

[12] The "traditional," but not necessarily correct, division of Ukrainians into Ukrainophones and Russophones, or the more Western-oriented west and pro-Russian east, are mostly outdated in the aftermath of the Russian aggression, as Riabchuk argues convincingly (2015, 139–140).

The same applies to the issue of language policy. The newly adopted law of April 25, 2019 securing Ukrainian as the state language (Verkhovna Rada 2019) cannot be seen as an instrument of oppression directed against the Russian-speaking or ethnic Russian population in Ukraine. Rather, it should be treated as a nation-building tool in a war-torn environment. (…) what was noticed by the Venice Commission. Experts of the Commission underlined: "the language policy is an extremely complex, sensitive and highly politicized issue in Ukraine, especially in the context of the ongoing conflict with Russia. In view of the particular place of the Russian language in Ukraine, as well as the oppression of the Ukrainian language in the past, the Venice Commission fully understands the need to promote the use of Ukrainian as the State language" (Venice Commission 2019). Therefore, in the specific situation of Ukraine, the language law may be assessed as a part of the transitional justice efforts observed in the post-Maidan era. Although some voices that identify the current language policy as a new instrument of dividing Ukrainians might be noticed too (Huba 2019), according to various experts their objections can be overcome by the creation of a State Institute of Ukrainian Russian (Hnatovsky 2019) that would "take full control of Ukrainian Russian (…) that reflects the country's cultural, political and social specificities" (Kamusella 2019). By these actions, the Ukrainian authorities may fully secure the rights of minorities, comply with human rights standards, and consolidate the diverse society of Ukrainian citizens.

Nonetheless, as it was stated before, transitional justice, with its "normative anchor" obliging states to prosecute and punish the perpetrators of the most heinous crimes, cannot be limited solely to extra-judicial means of reconciliation. Therefore, criminal response is a necessary measure applied in a transitional (post-conflict) justice strategy, if a state is willing to act fully in compliance with international law. With regard to criminal prosecutions of "Donbas crimes," it is worth stressing that these were proceeded solely in domestic courts in Ukraine (in spite of ICC interference). Several hundred cases of "terrorism" are being investigated or have been already transferred to Ukrainian courts since the outbreak of conflict (Bachmann and Lyubashenko 2017, 310). Occasionally, proceedings have also dealt with the crime of aggression committed by the representatives of the Russian Federation (Sayapin 2018, 1093–1104). Additionally, Ukrainian authorities are planning to put in place instruments aimed at reintegrating into Ukrainian society ex-combatants from Donbas. Amnesty is one such instrument, although blanket amnesties are prohibited by international law. However, allegedly perpetrators of war crimes will be exempted from amnesty and held accountable either before Ukrainian courts, or the ICC (Lachowski 2017, 41–43), which may be assessed as fully lawful under international law.

Last but not least, restoration of full jurisdiction and control over the seized parts of Donbas should be included in the wider process of decentralization in Ukraine. This process implies a transfer of government power and funds from the central level to the level of local communities, a means of enhancing self-rule (Pryshchepa 2019, 89–95). This might satisfy the needs of regional diversity without a federalization of Ukraine, a policy which Russia has actively promoted as a part of its foreign policy towards its nearest neighbors (Dascalu 2019). Undeniably, institutional pro-democratic reforms and strengthening rule of law in Ukraine may attract people living in the so-called DPR/LPR. Residents in Eastern Ukraine are being exposed to Kremlin propaganda of a "neo-Nazi junta in Kyiv" (Tymchuk 2018; Yakubova 2018). Pro-democratic reforms may contribute to convincing residents in Donbas that only in a democratic Ukraine they will be able to fully exercise their rights and freedoms (Kravchenko 2019a, b). Lastly, it is worth mentioning that the law on special status of Donbas of September 16, 2014 (Verkhovna Rada 2014), adopted in the aftermath of "Minsk-I," has formally entered into force (and is constantly prolonged by the Ukrainian authorities), without any real legal effect on changing the situation of Donbas in Ukrainian legislation. This is a direct consequence of the conduct of DPR/LPR against the "Minsk accords," for instance, by organizing illegal elections in the two self-proclaimed republics without Kyiv's consent. The current discussions of the implementation of the "Steinmeier Formula" and, as a result, granting Donbas special status in the aftermath of hostilities seem to be an example of an attempt to federalize Ukraine, against the interest of Kyiv.

3. Ukrainian Attempts to Form a Strategy of Post-conflict Peace-building and Transitional Justice

The liquidation of DPR/LPR requires the decisive response and proposals issued by the government and expert circles. In this respect, the legacy of other post-violence societies appears invaluable (for example, the experience of reintegrating former IRA-fighters in Northern Ireland; Tuka 2013). On 18 January 2018 the Verkhovna Rada enacted the law on de-occupation and reintegration of Donbas, which came into force on 24 February 2018 (Verkhovna Rada 2018). In addition to its primary goals of regaining the full control over the lost territories, first, the law named the Russian Federation as the aggressor and occupant (according to the law, this would entail having to bear the responsibility for all damages that occurred during the conflict in Donbas). Secondly, it abandoned the formula of ATO (transformed into the JFO). Thirdly, it vested the president with additional powers regarding the format of military operations, conducted under the united command of Ukraine's Armed Forces Joint Operative Headquarters. The law on de-occupation and reintegration of Donbas strengthened the position of Ukrainian authorities towards not only the pro-Russian separatists, but also the Kremlin itself, however as Mykola Hnatovsky convinces, rather in a form of securing the (right) narrative of Ukraine being a victim of the Russian external aggression than in a strictly legal manner (2019). In this respect, it is worth mentioning the "Waiting for You Home" program, run by the Secret Service of Ukraine (SBU). The latter assists pro-Russian militants or DPR/LPR "authorities" in returning to a peaceful life under the condition of reporting the committed offences. However, as already mentioned, the perpetrators of serious violations of human rights or grave breaches of humanitarian law cannot be released from the criminal liability (SBU 2018).

All further ideas to formulate a comprehensive reintegration strategy—like Arsen Avakov's (Minister of Internal Affairs) "Small steps mechanism" (Avakov 2018) or the report by the Centre for Research of Donbas Social Perspectives (2018)—call for the establishment of the UN peacekeeping mission and a broad policy of transitional justice. These include the criminal responsibility of DPR/LPR leaders, conditional amnesties to reintegrate ex-militants into Ukrainian society and the law on collaboration, which restricts the right to be elected or hold public office for all those "who held key positions in the quasi-public bodies in the occupied territories of the Donetsk and Luhansk oblasts after April 14, 2014" (CRDSP 2018). In the aftermath of the 2019 early parliamentary elections, a group of Ukrainian NGOs issued an open letter to the newly elected deputies of the Verkhovna Rada to form a common strategy leading to reintegration of Donbas and Crimea. This strategy envisaged an establishment of a new ministry of reintegration and national identity, created through the amalgamation of the Ministries of Temporarily Occupied Territories, of Information Policy and Veterans, supposed to closely cooperate with the civil society organizations (Ilko Kucheriv 2018, 2019). What is more, the Ukrainian NGOs are putting a constant pressure on the state authorities to finally ratify the ICC Rome Statute and adopt a law that harmonizes the criminal legislation with the provisions of international law to ensure the domestic efforts in prosecuting the wrongdoers under Ukrainian law (what corresponds to the "complementarity principle" set in the Rome

Statute; Zmina 2019). Eventually, on 30 October 2019, President Volodymyr Zelenskyy called for the creation of the comprehensive transitional justice strategy for post-conflict Ukraine at the state level (Ukrainian News 2019).

The above-mentioned efforts are a noticeable step in the process of formulating an all-embracing strategy of ending the armed conflict and implementing post-war reconstruction. Nonetheless, some crucial elements—like the balance between retributive and restorative response towards the atrocities witnessed in Donbas or the inclusion of truth-telling and truth-seeking initiatives—still require additional improvements by the authorities in Kyiv.

CONCLUSION

Undoubtedly, the conduct of the Russian Federation leading to the illegal annexation of Crimea and the outbreak of an armed conflict in Donbas can be classified as an act of aggression under international law. Therefore, all members of the international community must refrain from any act of formal recognition of such unlawful situation, including the existence of the unrecognized regimes of DPR/LPR (including, for instance, "passportization" in the seized parts of Donbas by the Russian Federation in April 2019). Increasing Russia's responsibility under international law would definitely support Ukraine's claim on the international character of the conflict and strengthen its position in coping with the effects of Kremlin's propaganda. Eventually, it can contribute to the strategy of de-occupation and reintegration of Donbas at the end of hostilities.

In sum, this chapter attempted to present the possible legal and political instruments available to Ukrainian authorities to facilitate the process of reintegrating Donbas into Ukraine. Therefore, Ukraine's reintegration efforts should be based on the following parallel aspects under international law. First of all, the so-called leaders of DPR/LPR shall be held accountable by a relevant domestic court, or the ICC, but not covered by the blanket amnesty provisions proposed by the "Minsk accords." Thus, it is necessary for Ukraine to ultimately ratify the Rome Statute, since the ICC interference can enhance the reform of the Ukrainian judicial system and strengthen the capacity of domestic courts in prosecuting the cases of international crimes. Secondly, in order to consolidate a post-violence society in the aftermath of a conflict, Kyiv should create conditions for those pro-Russian militants who did not commit war crimes or other grave breaches of humanitarian law to reintegrate within Ukrainian society, for instance, on the basis of conditional amnesties or other non-judicial remedies. At the same time, it would entail the final liquidation of DPR/LPR. Thirdly, in shaping its reintegration strategy, the Ukrainian authorities shall take into consideration the inclusion of the different regional perspectives, which should be incorporated into the decentralization process, while rejecting Kremlin-sponsored proposals of federalization. Moreover, a strong transitional justice pillar inclusive of a retributive and a restorative character (eg. truth-seeking and truth-telling mechanisms)—alongside significant cooperation of the government with civil society organizations—can contribute to the process of restoring the Ukrainian jurisdiction over the seized parts of the Donets Basin. Lastly, the analyzed process of reintegration may become internationalized, for instance, through the establishment of a UN peacekeeping mission. However, no leading role should be given to the Russian Federation, which needs to be defined not as a mediator, but as an aggressor and a party to the ongoing international armed conflict in and around Ukraine, and, as a result, held responsible for its violations of international law by a relevant international tribunal.

References

Amnesty International. 2014. Ukraine: Mounting Evidence of War Crimes and Russian Involvement. September 7, 2014. All websites cited in this article were accessed November 25, 2019. https://www.amnesty.org/en/latest/news/2014/09/ukraine-mounting-evidence-war-crimes-and-russian-involvement/.

Arthur, Paige. 2009. How "Transitions" Reshaped Human Rights: A Conceptual History of Transitional Justice. *Human Rights Quarterly* 31 (2): 321–367.

Avakov, Arsen. 2018. Strategy of Restoration of the Integrity of Ukraine and De-occupation of the Donbas. Small Steps Mechanism. June 7, 2018. https://avakov.com/strategy-of-restoration-of-the-integrity-of-ukraine-and-de-occupation-of-the-donbass-small-steps-mechanism.html.

Bachmann, Klaus, and Igor Lyubashenko. 2017. The Puzzle of Transitional Justice in Ukraine. *International Journal of Transitional Justice* 11 (2): 297–314.

Bertelsen, Olga, ed. 2017. *Revolution and War in Contemporary Ukraine. The Challenge of Change*. In *Soviet and Post-Soviet Politics and Society* 161, general ed. Andreas Umland. Stuttgart: Columbia University Press.

Bílková, Veronika. 2015. The Use of Force by the Russian Federation in Crimea. *Heidelberg Journal of International Law* 75: 27–50.

Boutros-Ghali, Boutros. 1992. *An Agenda for Peace*. New York: United Nations.

Bryant, Rebecca. 2014. Living with Liminality: De Facto States on the Threshold of the Global. *The Brown Journal of World Affairs* 20 (2): 125–143.

Buckheit, Lee C. 1978. *Secession: The Legitimacy of Self-Determination.* New Haven: Yale University Press.

Caspersen, Nina. 2013. *Unrecognized States: The Struggle for Sovereignty in the Modern International System.* Cambridge: Polity Press.

Cassese, Antonio. 2007. The Nicaragua and Tadić Tests Revisited in Light of the ICJ Judgment on Genocide in Bosnia. *European Journal of International Law* 18 (4): 649–668.

Centre for Research of Donbas Social Perspectives. 2018. Introduction of the International Provisional Administration in the Temporarily Occupied Territories of the Donetsk and Luhansk Oblasts as Part of a Peacekeeping Strategy for Ukraine. Kyiv.

Coyle, James J. 2018. *Russia's Border Wars and Frozen Conflicts.* Palgrave Macmillan.

Czapliński, Władysław, Sławomir Dębski, Rafał Tarnogórski, and Karolina Wierczyńska. 2017. *The Case of Crimea's Annexation Under International Law.* Warszawa: Scholar.

Dascalu, Diana. 2019. Frozen Conflicts and Federalization: Russian Policy in Transnistria and Donbas. *Journal of International Affairs,* May 22. https://jia.sipa.columbia.edu/online-articles/frozen-conflicts-and-federalization-russian-policy-transnistria-and-donbass.

Dawidowicz, Martin. 2010. The Obligation of Non-Recognition of an Unlawful Situation. In *The Law of International Responsibility,* ed. James Crawford, Alain Pellet. and Simon Olleson, 676–686. Oxford: Oxford University Press.

Dinstein, Yoram. 2019. *The Law of the Belligerent Occupation.* Cambridge: Cambridge University Press.

Engstrom, Par. 2013. Transitional Justice and Ongoing Conflict. In *Transitional Justice and Peacebuilding on the Ground: Victims and Ex-Combatants,* ed. Chandra Lekha Sriram, Jemima García-Godos, Olga Martin-Ortega, and Johanna Herman, 41–61. London: Routledge.

Fleig-Goldstein, Rachel M. 2017. The Russian Constitutional Court versus the European Court of Human Rights: How the Strasbourg Court Should Respond to Russia's Refusal to Execute ECtHR Judgments. *Columbia Journal of Transnational Law* 56: 172–218.

Gowan, Richard. 2015. United Nations Transitional Administration for Eastern Slavonia, Baranja and Western Sirmium (UNTAES) and UN Civilian Police Group in Croatia (UNPSG). In *The Oxford Handbook of United Nations Peacekeeping Operations,* ed. Joachim A. Koops, Norrie MacQueen, Thierry Tardy, and Paul D. Williams, 519–531. Oxford: Oxford University Press.

176 T. LACHOWSKI

———. 2018. Can the United Nations Unite Ukraine? Hudson Institute, February. https://s3.amazonaws.com/media.hudson.org/files/publications/UkraineJan29.pdf.

Grant, Thomas D. 2014. Ukraine v. Russian Federation in Light of Ilaşcu: Two Short Points. *EJIL: Talk!*, May 22. https://www.ejiltalk.org/ukraine-v-russian-federation-in-light-of-ilascu-two-short-points/.

Griebel, Jörn, and Milan Plücken. 2008. New Developments Regarding the Rules of Attribution? The International Court of Justice's Decision in Bosnia v. Serbia. *Leiden Journal of International Law* 21 (3): 601–622.

Huba, Roman. 2019. Why Ukraine's New Language Law will Have Long-term Consequences. *Open Democracy*, May 28. https://www.opendemocracy.net/en/odr/ukraine-language-law-en/.

Hurak, Ihor. 2015. The Minsk Agreement of 2015: A Forced Step or Small Achievement of the Ukrainian Side within the Diplomatic Confrontation around the War in Donbas. *The Copernicus Journal of Political Studies* 7 (1): 124–140.

Ilko Kucheriv. 2018. Democratic Initiatives Foundation / Razumkov Center Sociological Service. The Future of Donbas: Public Opinion in Ukraine and its Regions, July 20. https://dif.org.ua/en/article/the-future-of-donbas-public-opinion-in-ukraine-and-its-regions.

———. 2019. Democrativ Initiatives Foundation. Daĭ p'iat'! Eksperty proponuiut' uhodu z novym parlamentom dlia povernennia Krymu i Donbasu. July 24. Kyiv. https://dif.org.ua/article/day_pyaty_experty_proponuyti_krym_donbas?fbclid=IwAR0vYaxDArnE8W6t-FBvhQCLwTJXxCOTRM4SU0zlbs-mNeqam42nWZ6SLK8E#.XTqz84CgUiA.facebook.

Jenkins, Robert. 2012. *Peacebuilding: From Concept to Commission*. London: Routledge.

Kamusella, Tomasz. 2019. After Ukraine's New Language Law, it is High Time for Ukrainian Russian. *New Eastern Europe*, August 7. https://neweasterneurope.eu/2019/08/07/after-ukraines-new-language-law-it-is-high-time-for-ukrainian-russian/.

Kardaś, Szymon, and Joanna Rogoča. 2019. Russia Returns to the Council of Europe. *OSW Analyses*, May 20. https://www.osw.waw.pl/en/publikacje/analyses/2019-05-20/russia-returns-to-council-europe.

Kasianov, Georgiy. 2018. *Past Continuous: Istorychna Polityka 1980-kh–2000-kh: Ukraïna ta Susidy*. Kyiv: Laurus, Antropos-Lohos-Film.

Katchanovski, Ivan. 2016. The Separatist War in Donbas: A Violent Break-up of Ukraine? *European Politics and Society* 17 (4): 473–489.

Kemp, Gerhard, and Igor Lyubashenko. 2018. The Conflict in Ukrainian Donbas: International, Regional and Comparative Perspectives on the Jus Post Bellum Options. In *The Use of Force against Ukraine and International Law: Jus Ad*

Bellum, Jus In Bello, Jus Post Bellum, ed. Sergey Sayapin and Evhen Tsybulenko, 329–354. The Hague: T. M. C. Asser Press / Springer.

Kersten, Mark. 2014. Does Russia have a 'Responsibility to Protect' Ukraine? Don't Buy It. *The Globe and Mail,* March 4. https://www.theglobeandmail.com/opinion/does-russia-have-a-responsibility-to-protect-ukraine-dont-buy-it/article17271450/.

Kolstø, Pål. 2006. The Sustainability and Future of Unrecognized Quasi-States. *Journal of Peace Research* 43 (6): 747–764.

Korotkyy, Tymur. 2019. Kvalifikatsiya Porushen' RF Zhenevskykh Konventsii vid 12 serpnia 1949 r. shchodo Zakhoplenykh Ukraïnskykh Moriakiv [The Qualification of the Breaches of Geneva Conventions of 12 August 1949 Concerning Captive Ukrainian Sailors]. *Ukrainian Journal of International Law* 3: 139–140.

Koskenniemi, Martii. 1990. The Politics of International Law. *European Journal of International Law* 4 (1): 4–32.

Kozyrska. Antonina. 2016. Decommunisation of the Public Space in Post–Euromaidan Ukraine. *Polish Political Science Yearbook* 45: 130–144.

Kravchenko, Valeriy. 2019a. Mozhlyvosti Prymyrennia na Donbasi: v Poshukakh Limitiv Kompromisu. *PolUkr.net,* February 25. http://www.polukr.net/uk/blog/2019/02/mozlivosti-primrienia-na-donbasi/.

———. 2019b. Security Passport: Case Study of Hybrid Warfare Techniques in Ukrainian Regions. Diagnosis before Prevention. Lecture Delivered on the Conference 'Hybrid Warfare: Phenomenon and Reaction'. L'viv, Ukraine, June 11.

Lachowski, Tomasz. 2017. Transitional Justice in Ongoing Conflicts and Post–War Reconstruction: Reintegrating Donbas into Ukraine. *Polish Political Science Yearbook* 46 (2): 36–54.

———. 2018. Prawo Międzynarodowe Praw Człowieka jako Instrument Przeciwdziałania Skutkom Poważnego Naruszenia Prawa Międzynarodowego Publicznego—Analiza Wybranych Aspektów Przypadku Agresji Federacji Rosyjskiej wobec Ukrainy (w latach 2014–2018) [International Human Rights Law as an Instrument to Counteract the Consequences of Serious Violations of International Public Law—Analysis of the Selected Aspects of the Case of Aggression of the Russian Federation against Ukraine (2014–2018)]. *Wschodni Rocznik Humanistyczny* 15 (4): 25–58.

Lanovoy, Vladyslav. 2017. The Use of Force by Non-State Actors and the Limits of Attribution of Conduct. *European Journal of International Law* 28 (2): 563–585.

Legucka, Agnieszka. 2017. Frozen and Freezing Conflicts in Eastern Europe and South Caucasus: Implications for Regional Security. *Yearbook of the Institute of East-Central Europe* 15 (2): 79–97.

Lynch, Justin. 2019. Zelenskyy Flounders in Bid to End Ukraine's War. *Foreign Policy*, October 11. https://foreignpolicy.com/2019/10/11/zelensky-pushes-peace-deal-ukraine-war-russia-donbass-steinmeier-formula/.

Lyubashenko, Igor. 2017. *Transitional Justice in Post-Euromaidan Ukraine: Swimming Upstream*. Peter Lang Pub Inc: Frankfurt am Main.

Mahda, Yevhen. 2018. *Russia's Hybrid Aggression: Lessons for the world*. Kyiv: Kalamar.

Malyarenko, Tatyana, and Stefan Wolff. 2018. The Logic of Competitive Influence-Seeking: Russia, Ukraine, and the Conflict in Donbas. *Post-Soviet Affairs*. https://doi.org/10.1080/1060586X.2018.1425083.

Marchuk, Iryna. 2016. Ukraine and the International Criminal Court: Implications of the Ad Hoc Jurisdiction Acceptance and Beyond. *Vanderbilt Journal of Transnational Law* 49 (2): 323–370.

Milanović, Marko. 2009. State Responsibility for Acts of Non-state Actors: A Comment on Griebel and Plücken. *Leiden Journal of International Law* 22 (2): 307–324.

———. 2015. Ukraine Derogates from the ICCPR and the ECHR, Files Fourth Interstate Application against Russia. *EJIL: Talk!*, October 5. https://www.ejiltalk.org/ukraine-derogates-from-the-iccpr-and-the-echr-files-fourth-interstate-application-against-russia/.

Mitrokhin, Nikolay. 2015. Infiltration, Instruction, Invasion: Russia's War in the Donbass. *Journal of Soviet & Post-Soviet Politics & Society* 1 (1): 219–249.

Nemtsova, Anna. 2014. Who Will Be the President of Novorossiya? *Foreign Policy*, April 29. https://foreignpolicy.com/2014/04/29/who-will-be-the-president-of-novorossiya/.

Nuzov, Ilya. 2017. The Dynamics of Collective Memory in the Ukraine Crisis: A Transitional Justice Perspective. *International Journal of Transitional Justice* 11: 132–153.

O'Loughlin, John, Gerard Toal, and Vladimir Kolosov. 2017. The Rise and Fall of "Novorossiya": Examining Support for a Separatist Geopolitical Imaginary in Southeast Ukraine. *Post-Soviet Affairs* 33 (2): 124–144.

Orakhelashvili, Alexander. 2003. Restrictive Interpretation of Human Rights Treaties in the Recent Jurisprudence of the European Court of Human Rights. *European Journal of International Law* 14 (3): 529–568.

Pegg, Scott. 1998. De Facto States in the International System. Working Paper No. 21 (Institute of International Relations The University of British Columbia, February).

Pifer, Steven. 2019. How to End the War in Ukraine. What an American-Led Peace Plan Should Look Like. *Foreign Affairs*, November 21. https://www.foreignaffairs.com/articles/ukraine/2019-11-21/how-end-war-ukraine.

Polunina, Valentyna. 2016. Between Interests and Values Ukraine's Contingent Acceptance of International Criminal Justice. In *After Nuremberg. Exploring Multiple Dimensions of the Acceptance of International Criminal Justice*, ed.

Susanne Buckley-Zistel, Friederike Mieth, and Marjana Papa. Nuremberg: International Nuremberg Principles Academy. http://www.nurembergacademy.org/fileadmin/media/pdf/acceptance/Ukraine.pdf.

President of Ukraine. 2019. Statement by President of Ukraine Volodymyr Zelenskyy at the General Debate of the 74th session of the UN General Assembly, September 25. https://www.president.gov.ua/en/news/vistup-prezidenta-ukrayini-volodimira-zelenskogo-na-zagalnih-57477.

Pryshchepa, Kateryna. 2019. The State of Decentralization in Ukraine. *New Eastern Europe* 35 (1): 89–95.

Razumkov Centre. 2019. Hromadska Dumka pro Sytuatsiiu na Donbasi ta Shliakhy Vidnovlennia Suverenitetu Ukraïny nad Okupovanymy Terytoriiamy, October 11. http://razumkov.org.ua/napriamky/sotsiologichni-doslidzhennia/gromadska-dumka-pro-sytuatsiiu-na-donbasi-ta-shliakhy-vidnovlennia-suverenitetu-ukrainy-nad-okupovanymy-terytoriiamy.

Riabchuk, Mykola. 2015. 'Two Ukraines' Reconsidered: The End of Ukrainian Ambivalence? *Studies in Ethnicity and Nationalism* 15 (1): 138–156.

Romanchuk, Oleh. 2017. Viïna Rosiï proty Ukraïny. Chomu Rechi ne Nazyvaiut' Svoïmy Imenamy? *Radio Svoboda*, January 3. https://www.radiosvoboda.org/a/28211790.html.

Sasse, Gwendolyn. 2017. The Donbas—Two Parts, or Still One? The Experience of War through the Eyes of the Regional Population. *ZOiS Report* 1. https://www.zoisberlin.de/fileadmin/media/Dateien/ZOiS_Reports/ZOiS_Report_2_2017.pdf.

———. 2019. Most People in Separatist-held Areas of Donbas Prefer Reintegration with Ukraine—New Survey. *The Conversation*, October 14. http://theconversation.com/most-people-in-separatist-held-areas-of-donbas-prefer-reintegration-with-ukraine-new-survey-124849.

Sassòli, Marco. 2007. Ius ad Bellum and Ius in Bello—The Separation between the Legality of the Use of Force and Humanitarian Rules to Be Respected in Warfare: Crucial or Outdated? In *International Law and Armed Conflict: Exploring the Faultlines. Essays in Honour of Yoram Dinstein*, ed. Michael N. Schmitt and Jelena Pejic, 241–264. Leiden and Boston: Martinus Nijhof Publisher.

Sayapin, Sergey. 2018. A Curious Aggression Trial in Ukraine. Some Reflections on the Alexandrov and Yerofeyev Case. *Journal of International Criminal Justice* 16: 1093–1104.

———. 2019. The End of Russia's Hybrid War against Ukraine? *Opinio Iuris*, January 4. http://opiniojuris.org/2019/01/04/the-end-of-russias-hybrid-war-against-ukraine/.

Shpak, Alina. 2019. Summary of De-communization in Ukraine, Lecture delivered at the Eastern Europe Initiatives Congress, Lublin, Poland, September 23.

So-called "DNR Minister" decides to use SBU Program "Waiting for You at Home". 2018, August 28. https://ssu.gov.ua/en/news/1/category/21/view/5146#.nMDWJ2n5.dpbs.

Stahn, Carsten. 2001. The United Nations Transitional Administration in Kosovo and East Timor: First Analysis. *Max Planck Yearbook of United Nations Law* 5: 105–183.

———. 2008. *The Law and Practice of International Territorial Administration: Versailles to Iraq and Beyond*. Cambridge: Cambridge University Press.

Stan, Lavinia. 2009. *Transitional Justice in Eastern Europe and the Former Soviet Union: Reckoning with the Communist Past*. New York and London: Routledge.

Strzelecki, Jan, Wojciech Konończuk, and Tadeusz Iwański. 2017. Russia's ploy with UN forces in the Donbas. *OSW Analyses*, September 6. https://www.osw.waw.pl/en/publikacje/analyses/2017-09-06/russias-ploy-un-forces-donbas.

Szpak, Agnieszka. 2017. Legal Classification of the Armed Conflict in Ukraine in Light of International Humanitarian Law. *Hungarian Journal of Legal Studies* 58 (3): 261–280.

Teitel, Ruti. 2000. *Transitional Justice*. Oxford: Oxford University Press.

Tymchuk, Dmytro, Iuriï Karin, Konstiantyn Mashovets', and V"iacheslav Husarov. 2016. *Vtorhnennia v Ukraïnu: Khronyka rosiïs'koï ahresiï*. Kyïv: Braït Star Pablyshynh.

Venice Commission, Report on the State Language Law of Ukraine, 6 December 2019, https://search.coe.int/directorate_of_communications/Pages/result_details.aspx?ObjectId=09000016809933ef.

Wittke, Cindy. 2019. The Minsk Agreements—More than "Scraps of Paper"? *East European Politics* 35 (3): 264–290.

Wynnyckyj, Mychailo. 2019. *Ukraine's Maidan, Russia's War: A Chronicle and Analysis of the Revolution of Dignity*. Ibidem Press.

Yakubova, Larysa. 2018. *"Russkyĭ mir" v Ukraïni: na Kraiu Prirvy*. [Russian World in Ukraine: On the Edge of an Abyss]. Kyïv: Vydavnytsvo "Klio".

Zadorozhnii, Oleksandr. 2016. *International Law in the Relations of Ukraine and the Russian Federation*. Kyiv: K.I.S.

"Zelenskyy Lists Four Elements For Reintegration Of Donbas And Crimea". 2019. *Ukrainian News*, October 30. https://ukranews.com/en/news/662778-zelenskyy-lists-four-elements-for-reintegration-of-donbas-and-crimea.

Zmina. 2019. The Coalition for the ICC and its Members Sent a Letter to the President of Ukraine, Volodymyr Zelenskyy, Calling for Prompt Ratification of the ICC Rome Statute and Commitment to Fight Impunity Domestically, October 1. https://org.zmina.info/en/statements-en/joint-letter-to-the-president-of-ukraine-on-icc-rome-statute-ratification/.

6 THE REINTEGRATION OF DONBAS THROUGH RECONSTRUCTION... 181

CASE LAW

European Court of Human Rights (ECtHR). 2001. Banković and Others v. Belgium and 16 Other States, Application no. 52207/99, December 12.

ECtHR, Catan v. Moldova and Russia, Application no. 43370/04, 19 October 2012.

ECtHR, Chiragov v. Armenia, Application no. 13216/05, 16 June 2015.

ECtHR, Cyprus v. Turkey, Application no. 25781/94, 10 May 2001.

ECtHR, Ilaşcu v. Moldova and Russia, Application no. 48787/99, 8 July 2004.

ECtHR, Khlebik v. Ukraine, Application no. 2945/16, 25 July 2017.

ECtHR, Lefter v. Ukraine and Russia, Application no. 30863/14, communicated on 9 January 2018.

ECtHR, Loizidou v. Turkey, Application no. 15318/89, 23 March 1995.

ECtHR, Öcalan v. Turkey, Application no. 46221/99, 12 May 2005.

ECtHR, Sargsyan v. Azerbaijan, Application no. 40167/06, 16 June 2015.

ECtHR, Tsezar v. Ukraine, Application no. 73590/14, 13 February 2018.

International Criminal Court (ICC), Report on Preliminary Examination Activities 2015, 12 November 2015, https://www.icc-cpi.int/iccdocs/otp/OTP-PE-rep-2015-Eng.pdf.

ICC, Report on Preliminary Examination Activities 2017, 4 December 2017, https://www.icc-cpi.int/itemsDocuments/2017-PE-rep/2017-otp-rep-PE_ENG.pdf.

ICC, Report on Preliminary Examination Activities 2018, 5 December 2018, https://www.icc-cpi.int/itemsDocuments/181205-rep-otp-PE-ENG.pdf.

International Court of Justice (ICJ), Judgment on the application of the International Convention for the Suppression of the Financing of Terrorism and of the International Convention on the Elimination of All Forms of Racial Discrimination (Ukraine v. Russian Federation), 8 November 2019.

ICJ, Legal Consequences for States of the Continued Presence of South Africa in Namibia (South West Africa), ICJ Reports 1971, Advisory Opinion of 21 June 1971.

ICJ, Bosnia v. Serbia, ICJ Reports 2007, 26 February 2007.

ICJ, Nicaragua v. the United States of America, ICJ Reports 1986, 27 June 1986.

International Law Commission (ILC), Draft Articles on Responsibility of States for Internationally Wrongful Acts, Supplement no. 10 (A/56/10), November 2001.

International Criminal Tribunal for the former Yugoslavia (ICTY), Prosecutor v D. Tadić (Decision on the Defence Motion for Interlocutory Appeal on Jurisdiction), 2 October 1995.

International Tribunal for the Law of Sea (ITLOS), Ukraine v. the Russian Federation, 25 May 2019.

182 T. LACHOWSKI

Permanent Court of International Justice (PCIJ), The Chorzów Factory case, PCIJ 1928, Ser. A, no. 17, 13 September 1928.

Office of the High Commissioner for Human Rights (OHCHR), Report on the human rights situation in Ukraine 16 November 2018 to 15 February 2019, 21 March 2019, https://www.ohchr.org/Documents/Countries/UA/Repor tUkraine16Nov2018-15Feb2019.pdf.

Report of the UN Secretary-General (UNSG), Brahimi Report, UN Doc A/55/305-S/2000/89 (2000).

Report of the UNSG, Causes of conflicts and promotion of durable peace and sustainable development in Africa, UN Doc A/52/871-S/1998/318 (1998).

Report of the UNSG, The rule of law and transitional justice in conflict and post-conflict societies, UN Doc S/2004/616 (2004).

Supreme Court of Canada, Reference Re Secession of Quebec, 2 S.C.R. 217, 20 August 1998.

DOMESTIC LAWS OF UKRAINE

Verkhovna Rada. 2014. Pro Osoblyvzj Poryadok Miscevogo Samovryaduvannya v Okremyh Rajonah Doneckoyi ta Luganskoyi Oblastej [On the Special Order of Local Self-Government in Certain Districts of Donetsk and Luhansk Oblasts], September 16. https://zakon.rada.gov.ua/laws/show/1680-18.

———. 2015. Pro Vnesennia Zminy do Kryminal'noho Kodeksu Ukrainy Shchodo Perevyshchennia Viĭskovoiu Ssluzhbovoiu Osoboiu Vlady Chy Sluzhbovykh Povnovazhen, April 7, http://zakon.rada.gov.ua/laws/show/290-19.

———. 2018. Pro Osoblyvosti Derzhavnoyi Polityky iz Zabezpechennya Derzhavnogo Suverenitetu Ukrayini na Timchasovo Okupovanyh Teritoriyah u Doneckij ta Luganskij Oblastyah [On the Peculiarities of State Policy on Guaranteeing State Sovereignty of Ukraine on the Temporarily Occupied Territories in Donetsk and Luhansk Oblasts], January 18. https://zakon.rada. gov.ua/laws/show/2268-19.

———. 2019. Pro Zabezpechennia Funktsionuvannia Ukraïnckoï Movy yak Derzhavnoï, April 25. https://zakon.rada.gov.ua/laws/show/2704-19.

INTERVIEWS

With Hnatovsky, Mykola. 2019. The First Vice-President of the Ukrainian Association of International Law and Chairman of the European Committee for the Prevention of Torture and Inhuman or Degrading Treatment, August 27, Kyiv.

With Lishchyna, Ivan. 2018. Deputy Minister of Justice of Ukraine—Government Commissioner for European Court of Human Rights, June 1, Kyiv.

With Martynenko, Oleg. 2018. Chief of the Analytical Department of Ukrainian Helsinki Human Rights Union, November 28, Kyiv.

With Tuka, Heorhiy. 2018. Deputy Minister for the Temporarily Occupied Territories and Internally Displaced Persons of Ukraine, January 18, Kyiv.

With Tymchuk, Dmytro. 2018. A military Expert, the Coordinator of the "Information Resistance", November 28, Kyiv.

With Zolotukhin, Dmytro, 2018. Deputy Minister of Information Policy of Ukraine, November 27, Kyiv.

PART III

Federalization / Decentralization as a Tool of Conflict Resolution: Discursive and Foreign Policy Perspectives

CHAPTER 7

Three Faces of Federalism in the Foreign Policy: Russian and German Approaches to the "Ukraine Crisis"

Nadiia Koval

INTRODUCTION

Since the end of the Cold War and even more in the 2000s, "the boom in the study of federalism is accompanied by growth in its applied side" (Erk and Anderson 2009, 1). International organizations often propose federalism as a remedy for ethnic divisions and internal conflict. Sometimes, the federal system of government is deemed conducive to less aggressive behavior of the state both in internal politics and internationally. Further, federalism is also believed to be an instrument of good governance that contributes to a prosperous, just, and democratic society. Thus, the belief in federalism as a universal recipe for political improvement explains its important place in the political debate, especially for countries going through a transition and/or a conflict.

During the independence period, an open-ended post-Soviet transition, federalism clearly was not on the governmental agenda in

---

N. Koval (✉)
Foreign Policy Council "Ukrainian Prism", Kyiv, Ukraine

© The Author(s) 2020   187
H. Shelest, M. Rabinovych (eds.), *Decentralization, Regional Diversity, and Conflict*, Federalism and Internal Conflicts,
https://doi.org/10.1007/978-3-030-41765-9_7

Ukraine—"unitarianism has proved to be the most popular credo among Ukraine's elites" (Kuzio 1998, 69). The unitary post-Soviet state was very resistant to any loosening of centralization, so a few attempts for the so-called "administrative reform" were weak and half-hearted. In general, Ukraine has survived two and a half decades as a unitary state with the only autonomous republic—the Autonomous Republic of Crimea.

Nevertheless, since the conflict with Russia in 2014 started with an occupation and an illegal annexation of the very autonomous republic, the topic of federalism came to the fore in the international arena—be it direct ultimata of the Russian government, an elaborated reform advocated by partners, or sophisticated conflict-resolution plans advanced by various think tanks and commentators. Using to the full the variability of federalism theory and practice, "federalism," "federalization," or "decentralization" were suddenly being touted as the most effective cure for most of Ukraine's problems—achieving internal stability, implementing democratization and a reform agenda, or even treating it as the first step to building the new regional/ world order.

In order to understand how different facets of federalism theory and practice are interconnected in the context of hybrid war waged by Russia against Ukraine, the chapter will focus on foreign policy uses and abuses of federalism. It will first turn to the theoretical background, identifying three relevant narratives in federalism theory, and then explore their usage in discourse of two key external actors—Russia and Germany. The choice of Russia is obvious, as this state put the federalization of Ukraine in the center of its strategy and launched federalization-related discourse internationally. Germany, on the other hand, is one of the most important international partners involved in conflict resolution, one with a long tradition of federalism who sought to include some federalism-related instruments into its conflict-resolution strategy and actively supported decentralization reform. The key data for this chapter are speeches, articles, and positions of the ministries of foreign affairs of the two countries, supplemented by the texts from other governmental institutions.

I. Three Faces and One Paradox: Exploring Federalism Theory

Federalism theory most often distinguishes between federalism, the principle or ideological inclination, and a federation, the institutional arrangement of a given state. In the discourse around Ukraine, however, the most frequently used term is "federalization," the process of turning a unitary state into a federal one. In other words, the Ukrainian case is about so-called "devolutionary federalism" or, employing the distinction proposed by A. Stepan, a model of creating a "holding together" federation (1999).

In the setting of political transition and conflict resolution, it is possible to outline three dimensions of devolutionary federalism in the international context. First, devolutionary federalism has been imposed by external players as a means to pacify a defeated aggressor and to prevent it from aggressive behavior in the future. The classical example is that of Nazi Germany and the solution, introduced at the Yalta Conference and beyond, was to give significantly more power to the regions (the initial idea was to dismember Germany into many small states). A more recent case would be a federalization of Iraq, enshrined in the 2005 Iraqi Constitution as an alternative to a highly centralized, oppressive, and aggressive regime of Saddam Hussein.

The 1940s and 1950s witnessed attempts by failing empires to achieve a more favorable settlement in post-colonial nation-states, a movement which engendered suspicion towards federalism even in ethnically diverse states like Indonesia. Michael Collins defines post-1945 British initiatives for federal governments in former colonies "as a way of maintaining British influence in particular parts of the empire, a way of reconfiguring the politics of collaboration so as to defy the logic of nationalism with its fetishisation of sovereign territoriality, and hence to maintain key British spheres of influence" (2013, 24). The key reason for imposing federalism would be something that Kenneth Wheare noted long ago: "federalism and a spirited foreign policy go ill together" (1953, 196). In other words, the adoption of federalism could limit a state's foreign policy options.

Second, and probably a much more common situation since the end of the Cold War, is the attempt to apply federalism as an instrument of (post-) conflict resolution in the aftermath of internal conflicts, especially in the case of strongly displayed ethnic diversity. In this case, federalization is used as a substitute for secession and is associated with power sharing and the empowerment of distinct ethnic or national communities. The normative inviolability of borders in a post-colonial world after World War II, and the exponential rise of intrastate conflicts in multiethnic societies, contributed to making federalism a popular solution for taming conflicts and avoiding outright secession.

This kind of federalism is actively encouraged by international organizations. "It is often international development and peacebuilding practitioners that offer up federalism as an option for state-building in post-conflict contexts, rather than the citizens of those post-conflict countries," states an analytical report on federalism as peace model, referring to institutions like the United Nations Department of Political Affairs (UNDPA) and the UN Development Programme (UNDP). The report also concedes that "of all the policy choices available, federalism tends to be the most popular among policymakers" (Salisbury 2015, 5). The emblematic case in which federalism intended for conflict resolution has been directly imposed with diverse international sponsorship, is that of Bosnia and Herzegovina.

The key to employing federalism as a conflict-resolution instrument is identity. It is applicable when some ethnic group is geographically concentrated, and/or the society is deeply divided along linguistic, ethnic, or sectarian lines. Anderson and Keil (2017) speak of plurinational countries as prone to "holding together" federalism and they elaborate a theory of multinational federalism (another term in use is ethnofederalism).

As regards identity-based conflicts, the paradox of federalism, however, remains unresolved. The essence of the paradox is that on the one hand, federalism is used to prevent secession and create stability, and on the other, applying federal solutions may, in fact, provoke further secession (Anderson 2010). The reasons for this are that radical reforms of governance can provoke further unrest, and introducing independent institutional and infrastructural arrangements, e.g. local militias or taxation systems, may provide further opportunities to secessionist groups to impose their agenda on a population through the local state apparatus. All in all, not only does federalism protect identities, it also amplifies and even constructs them. This makes the practical problem-solving impact of identity-driven federalism rather ambiguous.

The third dimension of federalism is its relation to the promotion of democracy, which was concisely formulated by Ivo Duchacek as "federalism is simply a territorial twin of democracy" (1991, 3). Thus, devolution is reported to be conducive to good governance, subsidiarization, and thriving local communities. This process can be internally driven: limited decentralization reform is a path many unitary states, such as Poland or France, have taken in recent decades. It is even more common in developing or transitioning states with the help and support of international players. In the case of decentralization, identity issues are rather irrelevant and the whole process can be more technical and symmetrical.

A number of works make a clear distinction between federalism and decentralization, up to the point that the processes can even be stated to be unrelated (there are some very centralized federations and some extremely decentralized unitary states). However, others use the terms interchangeably, The latter is often strikingly true in the case of political discourse. In the "Ukraine crisis" case, the confusion of federalization and decentralization is deliberate and exploited by the different players. While Russia generally advocates deep federal solution via constitution/ referendum, it underlines that the term itself is of secondary importance; the Minsk Agreements contain clear elements of asymmetrical federalism, but use the decentralization denominator; Ukraine itself, while acknowledging the Minsk Agreements, concentrates predominantly on the decentralization reform agenda devoid of compromises on the unitary nature of the state; and Germany, too, speaks mostly of decentralization, though it supports elements of a federal solution as well.

This deliberate lack of terminological clarity is further assisted by the fact that the distinction between the three dimensions of federalism is purely analytical, and they are often intertwined in the real world. The link between federalism as an internal instrument of conflict resolution and federalism as promotion of good governance is that decentralized and democratic societies are believed to be not only more striving but also more stable and peaceful than the centralized ones. There is a "[w]idely shared belief that centralised systems of government make autocratic and anti-democratic behaviour easier, while federalism 'protects liberalism and enhances markets' by fostering political and economic competition" (Salisbury 2015, 5). Thus, decentralization is supposed to bring about both peace and prosperity, whereas centralization leads to more aggressive behavior, ineffective use of resources, and lack of democratic control.

While the first dimension of federalism in the international framework is related to *realpolitik* thinking (e. g. weakening a state and/or creating instruments to influence its politics) and is mostly presented as a pragmatic policy solution, the two other dimensions are hugely influenced by a normative approach, given the desirability of both internal peace and functional democracy. This more plausible normative meaning becomes a favorite explanation even for *realpolitik* cases: when defending German federalism, emphasis is more often given to the "coming together" history of the German state in the nineteenth century, than to the calculations of the great powers in the 1940s. In Iraq, the democratization agenda and the empowering of minorities are no less important explanation than prevention of further conflict. In Indonesia, the initial non-acceptance of an imposed federal system has gradually shifted to a discussion about the most just and effective state structure.

A final observation is that the effect of federalism in any given case is highly context-dependent, yielding illustrations both of stunning success and complete failure. Of course, the failures can be explained by the argument that federalism's prerequisites were not met, or that it is less federalism per se that achieves its goals but more so the structure it creates that makes those goals achievable (Neumann 1955). Still, the scholars who tried to study the conducive contexts have found neither statistically significant correlations nor robust regularities. For this reason, many researchers and practitioners emphasize that rather than a rigorously proven consequential theory federalism is a political belief, a "promise of striking a balance between unity and diversity"(Hueglin and Fenna 2015, 1) or a very general principle, claiming there are as many federalisms as there are federations (Salisbury 2015, 4). Whether federalism can actually deliver on the promise of conflict stabilization or it does the opposite remains an open question. Notwithstanding this ambiguity, federalism persists as "everybody's second choice of institutionalized conflict management in cases of deeply divided societies" (Elazar 1994, 21–25; Cameron 2009, 1).

Being both versatile and encompassing, the concept of federalism grows even more problematic if combined with the concept of hybrid war. To begin with, "hybrid war" is under-conceptualized, to the extent that some authors (Van Puyvelde 2015) even think that the phenomenon does not exist. Indeed, the most general definition of hybrid warfare—combining military and non-military actions in order to achieve certain political aims—is vague and can be applied to the widest range of conflicts throughout the history of humanity (Williamson and Mansoor 2012). Studying the instruments of the hybrid war is also tricky as they are constantly evolving and context tailored in each and every circumstance (McCulloh and Johnson 2013, 3), using the specific weaknesses of the attacked and exploiting to the most the strengths of the attacker, thus resisting plausible generalizations.

Consequently, it is more promising to study hybrid war through the prism of the aims that one state is trying to achieve over the other. Here I follow Alexander Lanoszka, who regards hybrid warfare as a strategy rather than a new type of warfare: "it is a strategy because it deliberately integrates the use of various instruments of national power so as to achieve foreign policy objectives in the light of the believed goals and capabilities of the adversary (2016, 178)." Similarly, Bettina Renz and Hanna Smith argue that "the idea that Russia is conducting 'hybrid warfare' against the West is highly problematic, as it tells us nothing about the possible goals and intentions of such a presumed approach. The idea also overemphasises change and novelty in Russian intentions and capabilities, whilst at the same time underestimating continuity"; they propose a "complex study of Russian goals and intentions instead" (2016, 1). In this vein, the following section treats the federalization of Ukraine as one of Russia's foreign policy aims, and the following analysis intends to explain why Russia is so adamant about it and how federalism is used by Russia to achieve its bigger political goals in the post-Soviet area. Section "Roaming Between Deterrence, Dialogue and Reform Agenda: The German Case" looks into how Germany, a key international player involved in conflict resolution, reacts to this Russian agenda and how it frames three conceptual dimensions of federalism to shift the conflict dynamics. Section "Conclusions: Ukraine and International Uses of Federalism: A Shadow of Limited Sovereignty" draws conclusions on the larger consequences for Ukraine of the multifaceted usage of federalism in the international arena.

II. Imposed Federalism and the Case for Neutrality: The Russian Approach

While more or less unequivocal examples of Russian demands for federalization have been observed throughout the history of independent Ukraine,[1] never have they been as persistent, vocal, and even central to Russian policy towards Ukraine, as around and after the attack on Crimea in February 2014. A statement on the necessity of Ukrainian federalization by the representative of the Russian Ministry of Foreign Affairs (MFA) at a conference in Kyiv on February 14, 2014 was sufficiently blunt to elicit an official protest from President Yanukovych's administration (MFA 2014a). In addition, a number of related statements and publications were issued at this point by various Russian politicians (e.g. Glaz ev 2014).

---

[1] An eminent Ukrainian strategist, Volodymyr Horbulin, notes that the first official scenario for the federalization for some of the states of the Commonwealth of Independent States was published in a report by the Russian Foreign Intelligence Service "Russia-CIS: Should the Position of the West be Corrected?" ("Россия—СНГ: Нуждаетсялив к оррективровкепозиция Запада?") back in 1994 (Horbulin 2016).

Immediately after the invasion and occupation of Crimea, Russian federalization discourse moved into the international limelight. On March 10, 2014 the Russian MFA distributed a paper to international partners, including the BRICS states, explicitly stating a set of demands to Ukraine that were to be implemented through an all-encompassing constitutional reform, recounted and detailed on numerous occasions throughout the first half of 2014 (MFA 2014f, h, q). They were publicized on the MFA website, mentioned in multiple interviews of Foreign Minister Lavrov, and via individual government-oriented expert contributions (Migranyan 2014).

Summarizing the Russian vision as presented by MFA, the desired state of affairs for Ukraine was as follows:

1. Ukraine to become a federal state with its constituencies having broad competences in the spheres of economy, finance, culture, language, education, foreign economic relations, cultural ties with the neighboring regions and minorities' rights. Every region was to elect both its executive and legislative institutions, to drastically limit Kyiv's control. A key demand in this regard had been traditionally, and remained, for Ukraine to give an official, preferably state, status for the Russian language (MFA 2014d, h, i).

2. Ukraine to become an officially neutral state in the widest possible interpretation. The usual starting point was denying any rapprochement with Western security organizations. After all, the extremely hostile attitude of Russia to Ukraine's pro-NATO course and the EU's eastern enlargement had been apparent for years, and there was a predictable line about threats arising from Ukraine's non-neutrality for current conflict resolution (MFA 2014j, k) or even the whole system of European security (MFA 2014q). Even more important was Russian opposition to Ukraine's participation in European political and economic integration, characterizing the whole Eastern partnership project as "an instrument of fevered exploitation of the geopolitical space," ignoring the "legitimate interests" of Russia (MFA 2014c), or "unrestrained impulse... to irrevocably involve Ukraine in the 'Western orbit'" (MFA 2014d). Thus, the desire to prevent the signing of the Association Agreement and establish the Deep and Comprehensive Free Trade Area (DCFTA) between the EU and Ukraine, to renegotiate its conditions or to delay ratification, became an important part of the Russian agenda after late 2013.

Federalism and neutrality, in the Russian view, were to be adopted constitutionally via a referendum, followed by countrywide presidential and parliamentary elections as well as by direct elections of regional councils and governors, resetting the whole Ukrainian political system. A referendum would be needed to guarantee that the changes would be permanent. On March 17, the day after a bogus "referendum" in Crimea, the Russian MFA issued a statement in which it demanded from Ukraine the establishment of a constitutional assembly with equal representation of all regions to formulate and unanimously endorse a federation- and neutrality-themed draft constitution, and to put it to a referendum (MFA 2014b). The demand was rejected both by Ukraine and its international partners.

For this double scenario to gain ground, the Kremlin simultaneously created and supported two different discourses for the needs of their hybrid strategy.

Pushing for the federalization agenda, it strove to present the conflict as a solely internal Ukrainian crisis, and Russia as a benevolent power with special interests, reframing the Crimean annexation as an act of assistance rather than as a self-interested military-political action. Thus, Russia brushed off the Western idea of negotiating with Ukraine in the framework of a "contact group," suggesting instead the creation of a support group of Russia, the United States and the European Union to assist Ukraine to conduct a national dialogue, which would eventually produce a new constitution of a neutral federated state, guaranteeing the rights of the Russian language (MFA 2014d, e, q). The idea was to induce Ukrainians to endorse the "national dialogue and constitutional process" concurrently avoiding describing the conflict as a Russo-Ukrainian one (MFA 2014h, j, k), and to promote federalization in a second sense—as a conflict-resolution mechanism.

At the same time, introducing the neutrality discourse Russia (once again) strove to initiate a discussion on future European (or Eurasian) security order, or even creating a kind of multilateral world order. While in the initial phase of the conflict, Russia concentrated on criticism of supposed Western infringement—military, political, economic—into its perceived sphere of influence, it gradually switched to proposals and ideas on how to rework regional arrangements and overall positioning on the international arena (President of Russia 2014; *Financial Times* 2019). Those proposals included negotiating arrangements with the EU about the "common neighborhood," reviving the discourse of a common security architecture, and rebalancing global powers via, for example, by introducing China and India into the G7–G10 formats.

While contradictory, both lines of reasoning were intended to severely limit the sovereignty of Ukraine both in its domestic (unobstructed choice of the state organization) and foreign affairs (freedom to form alliances). The seriousness of the claim was backed up by the positive vote for the "right" of the Russian army to interfere, passed in the Russian parliament on March 1, 2014, and threats to attack Ukraine repeated on some further occasions (Lavrov 2014). A few weeks later, though, the stakes rose higher: the inciting and support for the fighting in Ukraine's east began. Russia started to supplant the general logic—Ukraine needs to federalize and become neutral as a unitary state, and a pro-Western orientation is unacceptable—with a more specific logic—presenting the fighting as an uprising of "federalization supporters," whom the central government did not listen to and severely repressed (MFA 2014n, o). Russia tried to present these ideas as emanating from the Ukrainian Party of the Regions, unsuccessfully striving to involve its representatives in international negotiations (MFA 2014h, j, k).

In parallel, Russia worked on international recognition of its idea of federalization as a conflict-resolution instrument in different forums, starting with the talks in Geneva on April 17, where the final statement, agreed by all the parties, stated that "The announced constitutional process will be inclusive, transparent and accountable. It will include the immediate establishment of a broad national dialogue, with outreach of all of Ukraine's regions and political constituencies." Russia insisted that all regions of Ukraine should be monitored and indeed, the OSCE Special Monitoring Mission (SMM) was established in nine regions in May 2014 (Interestingly, Russia bemoaned that OSCE SMM would allegedly hide the facts on the true on-the-ground support for federalization (MFA 2014s). Russia insisted that both the Geneva statement and the OSCE roadmap share its view as to federalization. To further this agenda, "referenda" were held in the occupied parts of Donetsk and Luhansk regions in mid-May 2014 and military support continued. At the same time, Russia insisted that all Ukraine's decentralization attempts, launched since April 2014, were insufficient, non-inclusive, secret, non-transparent, and did not involve the "representatives of the regions" in the process (MFA 2014d, e, m; Permanent Mission of the RF to the UN 2016, etc.). Nevertheless, while Russia succeeded in promoting part of its pro-federalism thinking into international discourse, it failed to achieve its immediate aim, namely a change to Ukraine's Constitution and a referendum before the 2014 presidential and parliamentary elections, which the Kremlin had declared indispensable on several occasions (MFA 2014l; Lavrov 2014).

The next important developments for Ukraine's federalization agenda were brought by mediated agreements: Minsk-I (Protocol on the Results of Consultations of the Trilateral Contact Group, September 5, 2014) and Minsk-II (Package of Measures for the Implementation of the Minsk Agreements, February 12, 2015), which codified political demands for conflict resolution and were validated by UN SC resolution 2202 (2015). Both were adopted after direct interventions by the Russian army in August 2014 and in January–February 2015 respectively, and put the emphasis on the special status for parts of Donetsk and Luhansk regions, thus laying the ground for the asymmetrical federalization. As the "Minsk-II" text states:

> *Carrying out constitutional reform in Ukraine with a new Constitution entering into force by the end of 2015, providing for decentralization as a key element (including a reference to the specificities of certain areas in Donetsk and Lugansk regions, agreed with the representatives of these areas), as well as adopting permanent legislation on the special status of certain areas of the Donetsk and Lugansk regions in line with measures as set out in the footnote until the end of 2015.*

The mentioned footnote referred to "linguistic self-determination," "participation of organs of local self-government in the appointment of heads of public prosecution offices and courts," "creation of the local people's police," etc.

While the Minsk Agreements hardly speculated about neutrality, the Minsk-II footnote referred to "support by central government authorities of cross-border cooperation in certain areas of Donetsk and Lugansk regions with districts of the Russian Federation," creating the clear link with the first dimension of federalization as discussed in this chapter— influencing foreign policy choices. Neither of the Minsk Agreements mentioned Crimea, thus dividing the conflict into sub-conflicts, weakening its international dimension, and framing it as an internally Ukrainian conflict that could, therefore, be resolved through federalization mechanisms.

Since then, "Minsk" has become the key framework for the conflict resolution, and Russia has insisted that the "political" part of Minsk (namely, the decentralization/ federalization agenda) should precede the "security" part (military disengagement) and regards the agreements as marking the onset of federalization onset. In 2018, when the international peacekeeping force was discussed as a way to guarantee security, Lavrov fumed about the unacceptability of the proposal:

> [...]having a status that guarantees (this is literally written in the Minsk Agreements) the Russian language, culture, special ties with Russia, [...] their own voice in appointing judges, prosecutors, having their own people's police [...] That is, federalisation in the normal sense. You can call it decentralisation, as everyone is afraid of the word "federalisation." But when they tell us that they will do all this—grant an amnesty, give special status, organize elections, but first it is necessary to give the entire region to this international force to run the show, this will not work. (MFA 2018)

All in all, while the Minsk-centered approach has gradually become the primary conflict-resolution method in theory, but has stumbled in practice, Moscow has begun to invest in developing better relations with the key countries of the EU and worldwide, in order to renegotiate the regional and (hopefully) world order. Thus, the Russian approach could be characterized as the one hugely exploiting the *realpolitik* cause for federalization, with the strategic aim of regaining power and influence in the former Soviet republics, which is supported by its policy of suggesting federalization in the cases of Moldova and Georgia, coming most closely to the post-colonial framework of imposed federalism. The continuity of the Russian policies in different parts of the post-Soviet space, suggesting similar federalization-related guidelines and direct military pressure, as well as an intensive negotiating track with key Western powers leaves no doubt as to the primacy of foreign policy considerations. In this case, federalization of Ukraine plays rather a tactical role, with a blocking vote for the devolved regions being able to prevent Ukraine's geopolitical realignment. Finally, the democratization agenda of federalization has virtually no place in Russian discourse, and non-federalizing, symmetrical decentralization of the country is regarded as contrary to the coveted form of federalism.

III. Roaming Between Deterrence, Dialogue and Reform Agenda: The German Case

From the very beginning of the conflict the position of international partners had two well-defined tracks. The first track was that of *deterrence*. In March 2014, most leaders of the Western states strongly condemned Russian behavior, insisting on its unacceptability. In her Bundestag speech in March 2014 German Chancellor Angela Merkel expressed one of Germany's strongest objections to Russia's actions in the entire course of the conflict:

> It is in this context, fellow members of this House, first in Georgia back in 2008 and now in the heart of Europe, in Ukraine, that we are witnessing a conflict about spheres of influence and territorial claims, such as those we know from the 19th and 20th century but thought we had put behind us. [...] The law of the strong is being pitted against the strength of the law, and one-sided geopolitical interests are being placed ahead of efforts to reach agreement and cooperation. (FFO 2014a)

Not only did Merkel note the continuity of Russian deeds, but she also underlined the readiness of the EU to sign the Association Agreement with Ukraine in the near future, thus limiting Russian claim to decide about the "common neighborhood." Yet, in the same speech, she reiterated that the Eastern Partnership is not directed against anyone, and invited Russia to discuss the issues of trade in the triangle the EU–Russia–Ukraine, opening the path for limited political compromise. That laid ground for the second, *dialogue* track, which gained ground throughout the conflict.

While in Germany most political players tried to combine deterrence and dialogue, the partners within the ruling coalition had explicitly different emphases. Chancellor Merkel, representing the CDU/CSU conservative block, was advocating a more hardline approach, whereas the Social Democratic Party, especially its Foreign Affairs Minister (2013–2017) Frank-Walter Steinmeier, espoused a more conciliatory attitude towards Russia. He was an early advocate of keeping the dialogue and communication lines with Russia open in order to reach political solution of the conflict, which, in his view, would spare Germany and the EU from military hostilities, a new Cold War, and would help to uphold the newly fragile European security order. Steinmeier justified his approach as follows:

Seventy years after the end of the Second World War in Europe, we cannot start revising Europe's borders. This cannot be allowed to happen. And 25 years after German and European reunification, we must not pave the way for a new division in Europe either. [...] The two things go hand in hand: political and economic pressure, where necessary, along with keeping the channels of communication open and returning to the negotiating table. (FFO 2014d)

As the evolution of Steinmeier's discourse in spring and summer 2014 shows, the dialogue component in dealing with Russia was about a more cautionary approach in sanctions policy, declaring diplomacy and politics the only possible solution to the crisis, and putting increasing emphasis on initiatives related to federalization and/or decentralization in Ukraine. While the very word federalization was not often uttered, with the course of time German attention to Russian arguments on the political resolution of the conflict became apparent, supported by traditional German perceptions of the benefits of decentralization in general.

Thus, as early as May 2014, Steinmeier stated (FFO 2014b) that national dialogue was "absolutely vital" for the proper conduct of elections in Ukraine, and could be organized in the form of the conferences of mayors and governors from all the parts of Ukraine, supplemented by round-table discussions mediated by the OSCE (former German diplomat Wolfgang Ischinger was appointed as a co-facilitator for these round tables). Steinmeier stated "we need to launch a process of a constitutional reform, in which all regions of the country feel properly represented within the institutions debating it." Even in August 2014, the German foreign minister was still talking about national dialogue, the need to resume the round tables and that "constitutional reform on decentralisation and the rights of linguistic minorities needs to take shape" (Steinmeier 2014b).

What also facilitated his acceptance of the mixed conflict-resolution mechanisms was a specific interpretation of Ukraine's past and present, as a country internally prone to conflict. According to Steinmeier, "in 1991, Ukraine inherited a difficult legacy with its independence. It lies on the border between East and West, with regions that have completely different histories, with a plethora of unresolved ethnic, religious, social and economic conflicts. It does not surprise me that when the pressure in the pot rises, it would erupt" (Steinmeier 2014a).

The closest the German government approached open support for Ukraine's federalization at this point was an interview of the vice-chancellor, Sigmar Gabriel (also a SDP member): "The territorial integrity of Ukraine can only be maintained if an offer is made to the areas with a Russian majority […] A clever concept of federalization seems to be the only practicable way" (Chambers 2014). After a great deal of negative response to the interview in Ukraine, chancellor Merkel tried to explain in a press conference that federalization has different meanings in Germany and Ukraine, and that vice-chancellor Gabriel had been referring to "decentralization." This explanation, however, was barely convincing. The distinction between federalization and decentralization in German discourse was indeed blurred, as this case exemplified. Often, the one meant the other, and conflict resolution was treated as a logical continuation of the promotion of good governance.

With the signing of the Minsk Agreements, especially the "Protocol" of February 2015, German discourse became firmly Minsk-centered: the agreements were routinely proclaimed "the only viable way for the country to regain sovereignty over its territory" (Steinmeier and Ayrault 2016). The key innovation was the linking of sanctions to advancement in the Minsk process, creating predictability and sense of control over the situation on the ground and shifting the resolution mechanisms to the internal political situation in Ukraine. Since then, giving life and impetus to the Minsk process has become the key objective of conflict resolution as viewed by Germany. Local elections in the occupied territories as well as constitutional amendments "paving the way for special arrangements for local self-government in eastern Ukraine" were a crucial policy objective of German mediation in the crisis (FFO 2015). Another idea was the gradual removal of sanctions against Russia in response to small steps in the progress toward a political settlement along Minsk lines, or at least designing criteria for easing of those sanctions (Steinmeier 2014c).

In October 2016, the so-called "Steinmeier formula" was introduced with the sponsorship of the German foreign minister in order to relaunch the stalled Minsk process via a small-steps approach. The key element here was the swift legislative approval of "special status" for the occupied parts of Donetsk and Luhansk oblasts, first provisionally and later on a permanent basis, provided that subsequent elections in the area would be considered to be free and fair by the OSCE ODIHR. An agreement incorporating this formula was officially signed in Minsk on October 1, 2019.

Finally, since 2014, supporting decentralization reform *sensu stricto* has officially been touted as a priority area for German–Ukrainian cooperation. As in the case of the round tables in May 2014, Germany appointed a reform envoy—Georg Milbradt—to support changes in this sphere (FFO 2019a; Milbradt 2019). And indeed, in five years Germany has invested considerable resources in decentralization-related initiatives.[2] All in all, the five most important points as to peace and stability in Ukraine defined by the German government were: (1) implementing the Minsk Agreements; (2) not tolerating infringements of international law; (3) strengthening and protecting OSCE observers; (4) assessing deployment of blue helmet troops; and (5) supporting reforms in Ukraine, including "greater decentralisation" (FFO 2018). Thus, the double federalism/decentralization track could be considered as the linchpin of German foreign policy towards Ukraine.

As to the foreign policy dimension of the federalization process, it is almost non-existent in official German discourse, as is direct support for Ukraine's neutrality. Still, with the dialogue trend gradually gaining ground (supported by lobbying ambitious German-Russian projects such as Nord Stream 2 pipeline, demands for the lessening of sanctions, and the renewal of economic and security cooperation) the idea of constructive relations with Russia, including some compromises about "common neighborhood" gained a place. The election of Donald Trump to the post of US president, which gradually put severe strain on the transatlantic relationship, only induced a desire to cooperate with Russia on the wide range of economic and security questions. Steinmeier and Gabriel had already initiated intensification of economic and civic ties between Germany and Russia despite sanctions, reasoning that Russia is a very important player to deal with problems on the world stage and for regional security. This dialogue trend peaked under the current minister of foreign affairs, Heiko Maas. In speeches in 2019, in stark contrast to the Merkel speech cited at the beginning of this section, he spoke of "trust," "shared interests," and "joint action," claiming that "Germany and Russia—despite some differing interests—are collaborating constructively." He has met with Russian minister of foreign affairs Lavrov intensively, celebrated the strengthening of economic cooperation and contributed to renewal or initiating of different bilateral formats with Russia. He even announced a new European Ostpolitik, of which the core element "is, naturally, our relationship with Russia" (FFO 2019b).

---

[2] See for example: Support to the decentralisation reform in Ukraine. https://www.giz.de/en/worldwide/39855.html.

Because of that and the policy of avoiding a too-provocative stance towards Russia, Germany frames and actively supports the pro-European policy of the Ukrainian government much more as an attempt at modernization and reform, rather than integration into the EU. Germany is also traditionally unenthusiastic about not only Ukraine's NATO membership, but also the increased military presence of NATO in Central European member states since 2016, labeled by Steinmeier as "saber-rattling," meaning excessively provocative towards Russia. Thus, while a very important partner, Germany has also been one of the key European states restraining Ukraine's aspirations for rapid European integration once agreements strengthening links with the EU (the Association Agreement, free trade area, liberalized visa regime) had materialized. This has been reflected in its position of including a phrase about Ukraine's European aspirations in common EU–Ukraine documents, or the explicitly limited ambitions of the Eastern Partnership since the Riga Summit in 2015, which resulted in the total absence of a 10th anniversary Eastern Partnership summit in 2019 (now expected in 2020 in Berlin). Surely, this cannot be solely attributed to partial accommodation to Russian demands: the consequences of the refugee crisis and the call for internal EU reform before further enlargement were no less important. However some signs of more openness to Russian ideas of new security architecture for Europe can be detected here.

Interestingly, the largely non-existent federalism–neutrality link in official government discourse occupies an important place in the German think tank community, which often treats federalism and neutrality as a solution for Ukraine in a highly detailed manner. Two examples among plenty are very telling. In late March 2014, Gwendolyn Sasse, currently the director of the Center for East European and International Studies (ZOiS), published a text under the bold title "The Crimea Crisis Should Mark the Beginning of a Federal State for Ukraine" (Sasse 2014) and has continued to research related questions ever since. The second example would be "Foresight Ukraine" (2017), a project by the regional office in Vienna of the Friedrich Ebert Stiftung (a German foundation linked to the Social Democratic Party). The authors aimed to resolve "the crisis of international dialogue with Russia" via drafting four scenarios for the future development of Ukraine; the only two positive scenarios combine decentralization and neutrality.

All in all, the German support for federalism in Ukraine remains apparent, in both the conflict resolution dimension, and in support for

204 N. KOVAL

decentralization reform. The international dimension of federalization appears to have had lesser importance for Germany, officially, though it remains a topic of research in expert circles.

CONCLUSIONS: UKRAINE AND INTERNATIONAL USES OF FEDERALISM: A SHADOW OF LIMITED SOVEREIGNTY

This chapter has described the three ideas of federalism as applied to the first five years of the hybrid conflict between Russia and Ukraine, described officially by OSCE as "conflict in and around Ukraine." The chapter considers the "around" part, paying particular attention to Russian and German visions, analyzing their official discourse as to the three dimensions of imposed/ sponsored federalism: federalism as a means of influencing a country's foreign policy choice; federalism as a means of resolving internal conflicts; and federalization/ decentralization as a way to create a just and democratic political system in a given state.

For Russia the federalization of Ukraine is a long-term primary strategic goal, regarded as a means of regaining lost influence in the post-Soviet states; at minimum limiting their integration into Western political and security institutions. Russia entered the conflict with a prepared set of demands to Ukraine, corresponding to the tactics earlier employed in other post-Soviet states, like Georgia and Moldova. Playing on the first two dimensions, it generally ignored promotion of good governance via federalization, or even criticized it as irrelevant and distracting.

Germany did not have any ready-made plans for Ukraine's federalization, but having a historic legacy of federalism, strong belief into nonmilitary methods of conflict resolution, and its own vision of regional security, it invested heavily in federalism as a conflict-resolution mechanism and decentralization as a means to promote democracy in Ukraine. At the same time, aiming to further deepen relations with Russia, out of strategic concerns, Germany is contributing indirectly to the fulfilment of the Russian aim of creating a grey zone of security and economic cooperation in Eastern Europe. It also tends to ignore the continuity of federalism instruments in Russian policy and prefers to separate the question of Crimea (a non-recognition policy) from that of Donbas (a political resolution with elements of federalism).

This international promotion or imposition of federalism has several consequences for Ukraine. First, federalism is perceived extremely negatively both by the country's elites and the general public, as Russian attempts to impose a form of federalism have irreparably corrupted the idea. Second, the links between federalization and neutrality further spoil the prospects of the idea, as does the absence of Crimea in any federalization equations. Thirdly, it raises the question of limited sovereignty, as its employment by international actors has already been sufficiently extensive to cross this line. These are the factors that academics and analysts who study federalism for Ukraine in an internal policy framework need to take into account.

References

Anderson, Lawrence M. 2010. Towards a Resolution of the Paradox of Federalism. In *New Directions in Federalism Studies*, ed. Jan Erk and Wilfred Swenden, 144–155. London: Routledge.

Anderson, Paul, and Soeren Keil. 2017. Federalism: A Tool for Conflict Resolution?', 50 Shades of Federalism. 50 Shades of Federalism. http://50shadesoffederalism.com/federalism-conflict/federalism-tool-conflict-resolution/.

Renz, Bettina, and Hanna Smith. 2016. Russia and Hybrid Warfare—Going Beyond the Label. Kikimora Publications at the Aleksanteri Institute, University of Helsinki, Finland, No. 1 https://helda.helsinki.fi/bitstream/handle/10138/175291/renz_smith_russia_and_hybrid_warfare.pdf?sequence=1.

Cameron. David. 2009. The Paradox of Federalism: Some Practical Reflections. *Regional and Federal Studies* 19 (2): 309–319.

Chambers, Madeline. 2014. Germany's Vice-Chancellor Backs 'Federalization' in Ukraine. *Reuters*, August 23. https://www.reuters.com/article/us-ukraine-crisis-germany-gabriel/germanys-vice-chancellor-backs-federalization-in-ukraine-idUSKBN0.

Collins, Michael. 2013. Decolonisation and the 'Federal Moment'. *Diplomacy & Statecraft* 24 (1): 21–40.

Duchacek, Ivo D. 1991. Perforated Sovereignties: Towards a Typology of New Actors in International Relations. In *Federalism and International Relations: The Role of Subnational Units*, ed. H.J. Michelmann and P. Soldatos. Oxford: Clarendon Press; New York: Oxford University Press.

Elazar Daniel J. 1994. *Federalism and the Road to Peace*. Kingston, Institute of Intergovernmental Relations, Queen's University.

Erk, Jan, and Lawrence Anderson. 2009. The Paradox of Federalism. Does Self-Rule Accommodate or Exacerbate Ethnic Divisions? *Regional & Federal Studies* 19 (2): 191–202.

FFO (German Federal Foreign Office). 2014a. Policy Statement by Federal Chancellor Angela Merkel on the situation in Ukraine. German Bundestag, March 13. https://www.auswaertiges-amt.de/en/newsroom/news/140314-merkel-ukraine/260760.

———. 2014b. Speech by Foreign Minister Frank-Walter Steinmeier to the German Bundestag on the situation in Ukraine, May 5. https://www.auswaertiges-amt.de/en/newsroom/news/140507-bm-bt-ukraine/262002.

———. 2014d. Speech by Foreign Minister Frank-Walter Steinmeier at the German Bundestag Debate on the Federal Foreign Office Budget, September 11. https://www.auswaertiges-amt.de/en/newsroom/news/140911-bm-bt-hh/265174.

———. 2015. Ukraine Conflict: Discussion of the Political Process, July 30. https://www.auswaertiges-amt.de/en/aussenpolitik/laenderinformationen/ukraine-node/supportukraine/150729-bm-ambmorel/273660.

———. 2018. Five Points for Peace in Ukraine. Germany's Strategy in the Ukraine Conflict, November 30. https://www.auswaertiges-amt.de/en/aussenpolitik/laenderinformationen/ukraine-node/supportukraine/five-points-for-peace-in-ukraine/2166708.

———. 2019a. Ukraine. German Ministry of Foreign Affairs, January 4. https://www.auswaertiges-amt.de/en/aussenpolitik/ukraine/228182.

———. 2019b. Speech by Foreign Minister Heiko Maas at the New Year reception of the German Eastern Business Association (OAOEV), January 10. https://www.auswaertiges-amt.de/en/newsroom/news/new-year-reception-german-eastern-business-association/2177446.

Financial Times. 2019. Vladimir Putin Says Liberalism Has 'Become Obsolete', June 27. https://www.ft.com/content/670039ec-98f3-11e9-9573-ee5cbb98ed36.

Foresight Ukraine. Scenario Group Ukraine 2027. Four Scenarios for the Development of Ukraine. 2017. Vienna: Friedrich-Ebert-Stiftung, Regional Office for Cooperation and Peace in Europe. http://library.fes.de/pdf-files/bueros/wien/13723.pdf.

Glaziev, Sergei. 2014. Federalizatsiya—Uzhe ne Ideya, a Ochevidnaya Neobkhodimost. By Sergey Sidorenko. Kommersant, February 6. https://www.kommersant.ru/doc/2400532.

Horbulin, Volodymyr. 2016. Thesis to the Second Anniversary of the Russian Aggression against Ukraine. Ukraine Crisis Media Center, February 18. http://uacrisis.org/40347-gorbulin-tezy.

Hueglin, Thomas O., and Alan Fenna. 2015. *Comparative Federalism: A Systematic Inquiry.* University of Toronto Press.

Kuzio, Taras. 1998. *Ukraine: State and Nation Building.* Routledge.

Lanoszka, Alexander. 2016. Russian Hybrid Warfare and Extended Deterrence in Eastern Europe. *International Affairs* 92 (1): 175–195.

Lavrov, Sergey. 2014. Americans are "running the show" in Ukraine. By Sophie Shevardnadze. Russia Today, April 23. https://www.rt.com/shows/sophieco/154364-lavrov-ukraine-standoff-sophieco/.

McCulloh, Timothy, and Richard Johnson. 2013. *Hybrid Warfare. JSOU Report*, August 4. The JSOU Press Mac Dill Air Force Base, Florida.

MFA (Ministry of Foreign Affairs of the Russian Federation). 2014a. Otvet Zamestitelya Direktora Departamenta Informatsii i Pechati MID Rossii M.V. Zakharovoy na Vopros «RIA Novosti» o Vyzove v MID Ukrainy Sovetnika-Poslannika Posol'stva Rossii v Kiyeve [Answer by Maria Zakharova, Deputy Director of the Information and Press Department of the Russian Ministry of Foreign Affairs, to the Question from RIA Novosti Regarding the Summoning of the Minister-Councillor of the Russian Embassy in Kiev to the Ukrainian Ministry of Foreign Affairs], February 14. http://www.mid.ru/web/guest/maps/ua/-/asset_publisher/ktn0ZLTvbbS3/content/id/76518.

———. 2014b. Zayavleniye MID Rossii o Gruppe podderzhki dlya Ukrainy [Statement on Support Group for Ukraine], March 17. http://www.mid.ru/web/guest/maps/ua/-/asset_publisher/ktn0ZLTvbbS3/content/id/70394.

———. 2014c. Interv'yu Ministra Inostrannykh Del Rossii Sergeya Lavrova Programme «Vesti v Subbotu s Sergeyem Brilovym». [Interview given by the Russian Foreign Minister Sergey Lavrov to the programme "Vesti v Subbotu s Sergeem Brilyovim", Moscow], March 29. http://www.mid.ru/web/guest/foreign_policy/news/-/asset_publisher/cKNonkJE02Bw/content/id/68466.

———. 2014d. Interv'yu Ministra Inostrannykh Del Rossii S.V. Lavrova Programme «Voskresnoye Vremya», Moskva, 30 marta 2014 goda [Interview by the Russian Foreign Minister Sergey Lavrov, Given to the Programme "Voskresnoye Vremya" Moscow], March 30. http://www.mid.ru/web/guest/foreign_policy/news/-/asset_publisher/cKNonkJE02Bw/content/id/68426.

———. 2014e. Kommentariy i Otvety na Voprosy SMI Ministra Inostrannykh Del Rossii S.V. Lavrova po Itogam Peregovorov s Gosudarstvennym Sekretarem SSHA Dzh. Kerri, Parizh. [Commentary and Answers to Media Questions from Russian Minister of Foreign Affairs Sergey Lavrov Following Negotiations with US Secretary of State J. Kerry, Paris], March 30. http://www.mid.ru/web/guest/maps/us/-/asset_publisher/unVXBbj4Z6e8/content/id/68378.

———. 2014f. Zayavleniye MID Rossii o razvitii situatsii na Ukraine [Statement by the Russian Ministry of Foreign Affairs Regarding the Development of the Situation in Ukraine], April 7. http://www.mid.ru/web/guest/maps/ua/-/asset_publisher/ktn0ZLTvbbS3/content/id/66982.

————. 2014h. Interv'yu Ministra Inostrannykh Del Rossii S.V. Lavrova v Spetsyalnom Vypuske Programmy "Voskresny Vecher s Vladimirom Solovyovim" na Telekanale "Rossiya 1". [Interview by the Russian Foreign Minister, Sergey Lavrov, in a Special Edition of the Programme "Voskresny Vecher s Vladimirom Solovyovim" on the "Russia 1" TV Channel, Moscow], April 11. http://www.mid.ru/web/guest/foreign_policy/news/-/asset_publisher/cKNonkJE02Bw/content/id/66102.

————. 2014i. Otvet Ministra Inostrannykh Del Rossii S.V. Lavrova na Vopros Gazety «Argumenty i Fakty», Opublikovannyy 16 aprelya 2014 goda. [Answer by the Russian Foreign Minister, Sergey Lavrov, to the Question from the Newspaper "Argumentii Fakti" [Arguments and Facts]], April 16. http://www.mid.ru/web/guest/maps/ua/-/asset_publisher/ktn0ZLTvbbS3/content/id/65318.

————. 2014j. Vystupleniye i Otvety na Voprosy SMI Ministra Inostrannykh Del Rossii S.V. Lavrova po Itogam Vstrechi Predstaviteley ES, Rossii, SsHA i Ukrainy, Zheneva, April 17. http://www.mid.ru/web/guest/maps/ua/-/asset_publisher/ktn0ZLTvbbS3/content/id/64910.

————. 2014k. Geneva Statement of April 17, 2014, April 18. https://mfa.gov.ua/en/press-center/comments/1050-zhenevsyka-zajava-vid-17-kvitnya-2014-roku.

————. 2014l. Vystupleniye i Otvety na Voprosy SMI Ministra Inostrannykh Del Rossii S.V. Lavrova v Khode Pervogo Foruma Molodykh Diplomatov Stran SNG, Moskva. [Speech and answers to questions by Minister of Foreign Affairs Sergey Lavrov during the First Forum of CIS Young Diplomats], April 25. http://www.mid.ru/web/guest/integracionnye-struktury-prostranstva-sng/-/asset_publisher/rl7Fzr0mbE6x/content/id/63438.

————. 2014m. Otvety zamestitelya Ministra Inostrannykh Del Rossii S.A. Ryabkova na Voprosy Agentstva «Interfaks» v Svyazi s Vvedeniyem SSHA Antirossiyskikh Sanktsiy [Answers by the Russian Deputy Foreign Minister, Sergey Ryabkov, to the Questions from Interfax Agency Regarding Introduction of Anti-Russian Sanctions by the United States], April 28. http://www.mid.ru/web/guest/maps/us/-/asset_publisher/unVXBbj4Z6e8/content/id/63070.

————. 2014n. Zayavleniye MID Rossii o tragicheskikh sobytiyakh v Odesse [Statement by the Russian Ministry of Foreign Affairs Regarding the Tragic Events in Odessa], May 5. http://www.mid.ru/web/guest/maps/ua/-/asset_publisher/ktn0ZLTvbbS3/content/id/62122.

————. 2014o. O Telefonnom Razgovore Ministra Inostrannykh Del Rossii S.V. Lavrova s Ministrom Inostrannykh Del FRG F.-V. Shtaynmayyerom. [Phone Conversation Between the Russian Foreign Minister, Sergey Lavrov, and the German Foreign Minister, Frank-Walter Steinmeier], May 8. http://

www.mid.ru/web/guest/telefonnye-razgovory-ministra/-/asset_publisher/KLX3tiYzsCLY/content/id/61330.

———. 2014q. Interv'yu Ministra Inostrannykh Del Rossii S.V. Lavrova Telekanalu «Blumberg», Moskva, 14 maya 2014 goda—Glavnyye novosti. [Interview of the Russian Foreign Minister Sergey Lavrov to "Bloomberg TV", Moscow], May 14. https://brazil.mid.ru/glavnye-novosti/-/asset_publisher/fQhQyFywI7xQ/content/interv-u-ministra-inostrannyh-del-rossii-s-v-lavrova-telekanalu-blumberg-moskva-14-maa-2014-goda?inheritRedirect=false.

———. 2014s. Otvety Ministra Inostrannykh Del S.V. Lavrova na Voprosy SMI «naPolyakh» Sankt-Peterburgskogo Mezhdunarodnogo Ekonomicheskogo Foruma, 23 maya 2014 goda [Answers to Questions from the Mass Media by the Russian Foreign Minister, Sergey Lavrov, on the Side-lines of the St. Petersburg International Economic Forum], May 23. http://www.mid.ru/web/guest/foreign_policy/news/-/asset_publisher/cKNonkJE02Bw/content/id/59026.

———. 2018. Foreign Minister Sergey Lavrov's Interview with *Kommersant* Newspaper, January 21. http://www.mid.ru/web/guest/foreign_policy/news/-/asset_publisher/cKNonkJE02Bw/content/id/3026359.

Migranyan, Andranik. 2014. A Way Out of the Ukraine Crisis. A Negotiated Solution Now Is Preferable to Chaos Late., National Interest, March 27 http://nationalinterest.org/commentary/way-out-the-ukraine-crisis-10135.

Milbradt, Georg. 2019. Decentralization Cannot Be Rolled Back Because Reform Is Too Popular Among People. By Ilona Sologoub, Olena Shkarpova, and Yar Batoh. *VOX Ukraine*, July 1. https://voxukraine.org/en/decentralization-cannot-be-rolled-back-because-the-reform-is-too-popular-among-people/.

Neumann, Franz L. 1955. Federalism and Freedom: A Critique. In *Federalism: Mature and Emergent*, ed. A.W. Macmahon. Garden City, NY: Doubleday.

President of Russia. 2014. Zasedaniye Mezhdunarodnogo Diskussionnogo Kluba «Valday». [Meeting of the Valdai Discussion Club], October 24. http://kremlin.ru/events/president/news/46860.

Salisbury, Peter. 2015. Why Federalism? Federalism as a Model for Peace and Statebuilding. In *Federalism, Conflict and Fragmentation in Yemen* (report). Safeworld, October.

Sasse, Gwendolyn. 2014. The Crimea Crisis Should Mark the Beginning of a Federal State for Ukraine, March 21. Quartz. https://qz.com/190731/the-crimea-crisis-should-mark-the-beginning-of-a-federal-state-for-ukraine/.

Sergei Glaziev. 2014. Federalizatsiya—Uzhe ne Ideya, a Ochevidnaya Neobkhodimost. By Sergey Sidorenko. Kommersant, February 6. https://www.kommersant.ru/doc/2400532.

Steinmeier, Frank-Walter. 2014a. I Can Understand Why People Are Afraid. By Nikolaus Blome. *Speigel Online*, April 28. https://www.spiegel.de/international/europe/frank-walter-steinmeier-talks-about-the-ukraine-crisis-and-russia-a-966493.html.

———. 2014b. Quoted in We Are Not Naive. By Peter Carstens. *Frankfurter Allgemeine Sonntagszeitung*, August 3. https://www.auswaertiges-amt.de/en/newsroom/news/140803-bm-fasz/264108.

———. 2014c. Quoted in We Must Not Ignore Russia. By Norbert Wallet. *Stuttgarter Zeitung*, November 2. https://www.auswaertiges-amt.de/en/newsroom/news/141102-bm-st-ztg/266662.

Steinmeier, Frank-Walter, and Jean-Marc Ayrault. 2016. Fateful Days on the Dnieper. *Frankfurter Allgemeine Zeitung*, February 22. https://www.auswaertiges-amt.de/en/newsroom/news/160222-faz-ukraine/278794.

Stepan, Alfred C. 1999. Federalism and Democracy: Beyond the U.S. Model. *Journal of Democracy* 10 (4): 19–34.

Van Puyvelde, Damien. 2015. Hybrid War—Does It Even Exist? *NATO Review Magazine*, May 7. http://www.nato.int/docu/review/2015/also-in-2015/hybrid-modern-future-warfare-russia-ukraine/EN/index.htm.

Wheare Kenneth, Clinton. 1953. Federal Government, 196. Cited via *"The Impact of Treaties on Australian Federalism"* by Brian R. Opeskin and Donald R. Rothwell, 27 Case W. Res. J. Int'l L. 1, 1995

Williamson, Murray, and Peter R. Mansoor, eds. 2012. *Hybrid Warfare: Fighting Complex Opponents from the Ancient World to the Present.* Cambridge University Press.

CHAPTER 8

The Dark Side of Decentralization Reform in Ukraine: Deterring or Facilitating Russia-Sponsored Separatism?

Jaroslava Barbieri

INTRODUCTION

Over the last 15 years, the Kremlin has consistently stoked separatist sentiment as a destabilizing tool in Ukraine. The most common tactic has been the instrumentalization of the ethnic Russian and/or Russian-speaking population, often through passportization policies (Grigas 2016, 42). To this end, as far back in the late 1990s the Russian leadership created the legal basis for cementing its stronghold in the post-Soviet region. Shevel (2011) showed that by eclectically combining ethnic, linguistic, civic, religious, and historical-cultural connotations, the deliberately "fuzzy" definition of "compatriots" [*sootechestvenniki*] incorporated into the 1999

J. Barbieri (✉)
University of Birmingham, Birmingham, UK

© The Author(s) 2020
H. Shelest, M. Rabinovych (eds.), *Decentralization, Regional Diversity, and Conflict*, Federalism and Internal Conflicts,
https://doi.org/10.1007/978-3-030-41765-9_8

211

212   J. BARBIERI

citizenship law[1] enabled the Russian leadership to promote simultaneously a number of ad-hoc policies targeting various groups residing in the territory of the former Soviet Union. Critically, such ambiguity allowed post-Soviet Russian leaders to avoid fully committing to a nation-building agenda defined either in territorial or ethnic terms, thereby opening the door to potential irredentism at their discretion (ibid., 180).

Against this background, in order to justify its "deniable" intervention in Ukraine in 2014 the Kremlin framed its actions as a case of humanitarian intervention on the basis of alleged threats to ethnic Russians and Russian speakers (Allison 2014, 1259). By creating artificial divisions and fueling internal discord, this tactic has proved to be successful in impairing Ukraine's state capacity. At its core is the attempt to portray Ukraine's regional differences as an insurmountable impediment to its viability as a state. Further, as argued below, Russia's attempts to destabilize its neighbor from within are not confined to this tactic.

With this in mind, the aim of this chapter is to gauge the extent to which the ongoing decentralization reform in Ukraine has been effective so far in curbing Russia-sponsored separatism. The latter includes activities deliberately intended to undermine Ukraine's constitutional order that rely on the mobilization of economic grievances and/or historical-cultural narratives by regional and local elites with the assistance of Kremlin-linked individuals. In particular, I look at the destabilizing effect produced by so-called "fake" territorial communities (henceforth fake *terhromady*) and "special economic zones" (SEZs) as symptomatic of the failure of the decentralization reform thus far to contain Russia-sponsored separatism.

Existing publicly available investigations show that since the beginning of the conflict in the east and the launch of decentralization reform in 2014, "fake" terhromady have been established all over the country. Essentially, these entities appropriate and twist the vocabulary and tools derived from decentralization reform to put in place a parallel system of power. In fact, they operate alongside, but in opposition to, the official

---

[1] "Compatriots" are defined as: first, citizens of the Russian Federation permanently residing abroad; second, individuals and their descendants who live outside its territory and are connected to peoples that have historically resided on the territory of the Russian Federation; third, individuals who made a free choice in favor of a spiritual, cultural, and legal connection with Russia; fourth, individuals whose direct ancestors used to be residents of the USSR or are currently residing in states that were part of the USSR; and finally, émigrés who either became citizens of another state or became stateless persons (President of the Russian Federation 1999).

territorial communities established as part of the ongoing reform (hence their denomination as "fake"). At the same time, by demanding regional autonomy to some degree, the promotion of SEZs risks consolidating trends that the decentralization reform is supposed to combat in the first place. Critically, these entities have been promoted with the assistance of individuals linked to Viktor Medvedchuk[2] and Russian security services. As shown below, Medvedchuk, leader of the NGO "Ukrainian Choice" and co-chairman of the pro-Russian party of the "Opposition Platform—For Life,"[3] has been an unwavering advocate of federalization in Ukraine for years.[4] These connections have led observers to believe that while relying on self-serving local and regional elites, these separatist projects have the Kremlin's blessing, if not its direct involvement. More critically, I argue that the Russian leadership will find fertile ground for promoting separatist projects during the transition period leading up to the completion of the decentralization reform.

In the context of the Minsk peace talks, given the link created between the decentralization process and the implementation of a "special status" (i.e. autonomy) in Donbas, I also analyze the potential threats to Ukraine's national security derived from the latter. Fake terhromady, SEZs, and "special status" in Donbas are treated as different yet inter-related projects reflecting Russia's effort to recruit regional and local elites in order to stoke separatist sentiment and, ultimately, weaken Ukrainian statehood in the post-2014 period. In fact, these projects are given legitimacy through the discreditation of national-level institutions and the dismissal of the viability of Ukraine as an independent state. In light of these considerations, I argue that the devolution of powers to the local level in the form promoted by Kyiv (with the West's blessing) can carry as many risks to the unity of the state as Moscow's ambition to federalize the country.

So far, there has been little academic debate on the implications of these three phenomena to Ukraine's territorial sovereignty and social cohesion. For this reason, this chapter relies extensively on non-academic sources. After this introduction, the chapter is structured in five sections. In Section "Background Before 2014", I examine how the domestic debate in Ukraine

---

[2] As is well known, the Russian President is godfather to Medvedchuk's daughter.

[3] In the 2019 parliamentary election, the party came second in the vote with 13.05 percent through party lists, gaining 37 seats (plus six in single-mandate electoral districts) (24 Kanal 2019).

[4] In March 2014, the movement announced on its website the launch of the "Concept" for federalization reform in Ukraine (Ukrayins'kyi Vybir 2014).

on alternative territorial-administrative systems evolved over time. Here I also highlight the most important separatist projects of the pre-2014 period. Section "Russia's Exploitation of Ukraine's Weak National Institutions and Existing Cracks in the Decentralization Process After 2014" illustrates why the decentralization reform launched in 2014 has failed to contain Russia-sponsored separatism. Section "Decentralization: A Faulty Panacea to Russia-Sponsored Separatism" has three sub-sections: first, an overview of the legislation behind the reform; second, an account of the instruments adopted by fake terhromady to undermine Ukraine's constitutional order and thus promote separatism; third, an account of the same undermining in relation to SEZs. In section "Granting 'Special Status' to Donbas: A threat to Ukraine's National Security", I offer a summary of Ukraine's legislation towards the non–government-controlled areas (NGCAs) and show how offering autonomy might exacerbate rather than solve Russia-sponsored separatism in the east. Finally, I provide some concluding remarks in light of President Volodymyr Zelenskyy's coming to power.

I. Background Before 2014

In order to make the argument that the ongoing decentralization process can carry as many risks to Ukraine's territorial sovereignty as Moscow's calls for federalizing its neighbor, a point of clarification is required. The model of federalization promoted by Russian President Vladimir Putin and his close associate Medvedchuk envisages a type of redistribution of powers aimed at irreversibly weakening the Ukrainian state by fragmenting the country into several "quasi-states." According to this model, Ukraine's southern and eastern regions should be allowed to pursue independent foreign and trade policies, have autonomy on matters such as education and language, and hold referenda to decide on these issues (a prerogative ideally to be extended to all regions).[5] This model underlies Moscow's request to grant "special status" to Donbas. Critics perceive

---

[5] As noted by both Western and Russian commentators, Putin's model prescribes the transition towards a confederation rather than a federation. In fact, a federal arrangement envisages power-sharing between the national government and subnational units, while foreign and trade policy remain a prerogative of the former. In this respect, Putin's notion that subnational units should be entitled to have political leverage over the central government misrepresents how federal states are conventionally organized. See Youngs (2014) and Ryzhkov (2014).

such federative arrangement as a deliberate instrument aimed at neutralizing the country's Euro-Atlantic aspirations and a catalyst for the eventual dismantling of the Ukrainian state (Samokhvalova 2012).

In contrast, the ongoing decentralization reform started in Ukraine in 2014 envisages the distribution of decision-making *across* levels of government. Specifically, the combination of territorial-administrative reorganization and fiscal decentralization is presented as a "vaccination" against Kremlin-sponsored separatism (Sultanova 2015). In support of this claim, two aspects stand out.

The first aspect relates to the gradual *diffusion of political and fiscal influence*. Prior to the reform, political and financial resources were concentrated at the regional level. This state of affairs led to the consolidation of regional "fiefdoms" in the hands of powerful oligarchs and their clientelistic networks, whose resources provided the incentives to fuel secessionist aspirations. In this respect, the lack of a strong state policy precipitated centrifugal tendencies easily exploitable by the Kremlin (especially in Ukraine's southern and eastern regions). Against this background, the opportunity for district [*rayon*] and local community [*hromada*] authorities to establish a direct relationship with the central government and no longer be dependent on regional [*oblast'*] authorities should act as a deterrent to secessionism.[6] Supposedly, the empowerment of lower levels of government facilitates the dismantling of existing avenues for rent-seeking, thereby hindering Russia's ability to drive wedges in Ukrainian society.

The second aspect is more straightforward and relates to *size*. Compared to oblasts, hromadas cover a much smaller territorial area. In theory, their separatist ambitions should shrink accordingly.[7] At the same time, this new administrative map of Ukraine would prevent the Kremlin from carving out entire regions for the creation of separatist entities with "credible" and "sustainable" autonomist claims.

---

[6] This point was emphasized by Volodymyr Parkhomenko, Deputy Direction of the Analytical Centre for the Association of Ukrainian Cities, and Anatoliy Tkachuk, Director of Science and Development at the Civil Society Institute. See "Vostok + Zapad: Detsentralizatsiya—'Mify o Detsentralizatsii' [East + West: Decentralization—"Myths about Decentralisation"], YouTube video, "Unian," 10.00 and 17.48, February 28, 2015, https://www.youtube.com/watch?v=b7bXiM2XA4I&list=PLW_5Md4I65ArL5ja_Vhrhx9XVXiWQDjXs&index=1.

[7] This argument was presented by Yuriy Hanushchak, Director of Territorial Development. Ibid., 19.45.

There appears to be consensus among political elites in Ukraine and the West that the combined effect of these two developments is to "gradually eliminat[e] effective entry points for Russian subversive measures aimed at destabilization and separation of entire regions" (Umland 2019). This chapter presents empirical evidence that fundamentally questions this overly optimistic premise. As already mentioned, since the launch of the decentralization reform Russian "curators" have successfully managed to exploit local elites' vested interests to promote projects such as "fake" terhromady, SEZs, and autonomy in Donbas. What these separatist projects have in common is an effort to weaken Ukraine's territorial sovereignty, cripple its economy, and disseminate the idea that the formation of Ukraine as an independent state was an historical accident. The idea of federalizing Ukraine is presented as the optimal territorial-administrative structure for "holding" the country together.

That said, it would be inaccurate to portray the idea of federalization as an exclusively Russia-driven process. In fact, after the collapse of the Soviet Union Ukraine's future territorial-administrative model became the subject of intense domestic debate. Contrary to the highly centralized system inherited from Soviet times, Ukraine's pre-Soviet historical legacy included federalism and decentralization (Wolczuk 2002, 69). Against this background, with the emergence of the new Ukrainian state national democrats viewed federalism as a viable (and even preferable) alternative to a more centralized model. In particular, Viacheslav Chornovil, the leader of the national democratic movement, *Rukh*, was convinced that it would be economically beneficial *over the long run* for Ukraine to adopt a federal system in the form of "regional-land self-government" [*regional'ne zemel'ne samoupravlinnya*]. His model envisaged, nonetheless, the preservation of a unitary Ukrainian state, thereby rejecting the prospect of giving these "lands" [*zemli*] state-like prerogatives.[8] In this respect, Chornovil's federalist model considerably differs from Medvedchuk's proposals.

It is worth mentioning that national democrats' initial advocacy for a federal model was based on perhaps naïve but understandable assumptions. First, in post-communist countries unitarism has had a negative connotation, as it evoked the Soviet legacy of centralization; second, in the eyes of regional elites, a more centralized system carried the risk of

---

[8] "Ukrayinu Mohla Vryatuvaty Federalizatsiya [Federalization Could Have Saved Ukraine]/ Vyacheslav Chornovil," YouTube video, "ukrmemorial UA," 1.30, January 25, 2015, https://www.youtube.com/watch?v=y5h8lubkedk.

simply transferring the all-powerful authority from Moscow to Kyiv; third, a federal arrangement could accommodate Ukraine's economic and cultural regional differences, thus providing a panacea against centrifugal tendencies (Androshchuk 2010, 23). However, separatist tendencies in Crimea and Donbas[9] over the period 1991–1994 exposed the weakness of Kyiv's control over peripheral regions, thereby discrediting the idea of federalism once and for all (Sasse 2001, 80). As a result, national democrats fell back on the notion that only a strong center would act as "an engine of the state-building project" (Wolczuk 2002, 82). These tensions in the early stages of Ukraine's independence are reflected in the eventual adoption of "a hybrid territorial-administrative system—a unitary state with a federal component, Crimea" (ibid., 78). Here it is important to emphasize that Chornovil criticized the political autonomy offered to the Crimean Peninsula.[10] In his view, this move gave legitimacy to the separatist tendencies promoted by Russia-supported local communists while aggravating the isolation of Crimean Tatars (Derevinskyy 2018, 48).

Russia's active support of separatist projects in eastern Ukraine gained momentum during the Orange Revolution in 2004 (Honchar 2016, 74). In reaction to the annulment of the results of the second round of the presidential election by the Ukrainian parliament, local authorities in eastern Ukraine organized rallies in support of the pro-Russian candidate Viktor Yanukovych. On November 28, 2004, the First All-Ukrainian assembly of members of parliament and deputies of local councils was organized in Severodonetsk (Luhansk oblast) on the initiative of the oblast councils of Crimea, Dnipropetrovsk, Donetsk, Kharkiv, Kherson, Luhansk, Mykolaïv, Odesa and Zaporizzhya, plus the Sevastopol City Council. A prominent role was played by Yevhen Kushnariov, the Governor of Kharkiv oblast. On this occasion, participants floated the idea of creating a "South-East Ukrainian Autonomous Republic." However, the project was aborted shortly after (Todorov 2019). Ukrainian analysts pointed to the participation of then Moscow mayor, Yuriy Luzhkov, as an indicator of the Kremlin's direct involvement (Vynohradov 2016).

---

[9] In March 1994, a local referendum was held in Donets'k and Luhans'k oblasts in parallel with the parliamentary elections. Reportedly, 80 percent of the local population voted in favor of federalization (Kazanskyi 2014).

[10] For a detailed overview of the events leading to the institutionalization of Crimean autonomy in the early 1990s, see Sasse (2001, 91–94).

218   J. BARBIERI

A second assembly took place in Severodonetsk in March 2008. Alongside Luzhkov, the Russian delegation also included Konstantin Zatulin, then First Deputy Chairman of the Russian State Duma Committee for CIS Affairs and Relations with Compatriots and head of the Institute of CIS Countries. The Institute has been considered a key platform for Russia's soft power projection in the post-Soviet region (Polegkyi 2011, 17). On this occasion, Zatulin called for the federalization of Ukraine and, while addressing the local audience using the term "compatriots," he reportedly declared that "Russia has always been, is and will be with you" (quoted in Moser 2013, 192). Interestingly, in 2010 the Institute of CIS Countries organized an international conference in Odesa in which representatives from the institute and the Russian nationalist party *"Rodina"* urged the city to become "the center of Ukrainian federalism" (Censor.net 2010). These few examples manifest the presence of recurrent Russian individuals and institutions tasked with establishing contacts with local and regional elites in Ukraine. Most importantly, they point to the Kremlin's direct involvement in the promotion of separatist projects in Ukraine.

That said, there is an argument to be made that at that point in time Russia was not "ready" to resort to military action. As a result, irredentist scenarios were confined to the rhetoric of Russian nationalist elite circles. To give an example, during an online press conference on the website of Putin's "United Russia" party in January 2009, Zatulin reportedly declared that "when the time is right," Russia would just have to "send the signal" and Ukraine's southern and eastern regions would take the decision to join the Russian Federation (Unian 2009). Overall, prior to Putin's third presidential term, Russia lacked the willingness and capacity to intervene militarily in Ukraine. Supporting separatist sentiment among the local elite was considered a sufficiently effective destabilizing tool to maintain Ukraine within its sphere of influence.

II. Russia's Exploitation of Ukraine's Weak National Institutions and Existing Cracks in the Decentralization Process After 2014

The events of 2014 were a tragic demonstration of how Ukraine's central institutions are strong more on paper than in reality. Early on, observers emphasized that in light of the loss of control over Crimea and parts of Donetsk and Luhansk oblasts, rapid decentralization posed non-negligible risks, as the state appears "too fragile to bear any such process" (Youngs 2014). From this perspective, an exclusive focus on decentralization lacking a parallel effort to strengthen national-level institutions in a country as large and diverse as Ukraine "could inadvertently increase the risk of break-up" (Bond 2014).

Nonetheless, the Ukrainian government dismissed such concerns as misplaced, while portraying the reform as an unequivocal "success story." In August 2019, an article was published on the official website dedicated to the reform with the intention of reassuring those who saw the required constitutional changes as "dangerous" "in the face of war, political instability and immaturity, [and a] fragmented society" (Decentralization 2019). According to the article, such fears were overblown as the country would necessarily go through a "transition period" lasting for years, which would require "align[ing] the legislation with the new [constitutional] rules." However, one could argue that precisely this unavoidable transition period could offer a window of opportunity for the Kremlin to promote separatist projects by exploiting existing cracks in the decentralization process.

The institution of prefects, which is supposed to progressively replace regional and district state administrations, is a case in point. This institution adopts the French model, in which prefects embody the role of state oversight over local government bodies. In order to avoid the old risk of clientelistic networks and political favors between local political and business elites, the prefects will rotate every three years. However, prefects can formally be established only following the elimination of local state administrations and the adoption of decentralization-related constitutional amendments (Minregion 2015).

In this respect, the merging of the decentralization process with the request to grant "special status" to the occupied areas as part of the Minsk peace process indefinitely postpones decentralization-related constitutional amendments (including the institution of prefects). This delay leaves a situation of ambiguity, which can be exploited by Russia's hybrid aggression to threaten Ukraine's national security (Fluri and Badrack 2017, 25). As pointed out by Ivan Lukeriya, an expert from the Reanimation Reform Package, for the time being "there is no comprehensive legal control over decisions made by local authorities" (Holub 2019). As prefects would be tasked with notifying the President of acts adopted by local authorities that might threaten Ukraine's territorial integrity or national security, the risk of separatism cannot be overstated.

Hennadiy Zubko, Ukraine's former Minister of Regional Development and Deputy Prime Minister, warned that even if the relevant constitutional amendments were to be passed, the creation of a training program for new prefects would require a long period of time (Skorokhod 2019). As a result, it remains unclear how state authorities will be able to monitor local government bodies to make sure that they comply with Ukraine's laws and Constitution. This lack of state oversight during the transition period raises concerns about possible external attempts to instigate separatist sentiment.

This possibility suggests that there is a "dark side" to decentralization reform, which has been unduly neglected. While failing to recognize the legitimacy of local and national authorities, the self-proclaimed "representatives" [*upovnovazheni*] or "registrators" [*reyestratory*] of fake terrhromady unlawfully act on behalf of entire villages, cities, or even oblasts, through illegitimate practices involving the appropriation of state authority. These include issuing so-called "passports of persons" [*pasporty lyudyny*], vehicle registration number plates, certificates to so-called "national entrepreneurs" [*narodni pidpryyemsti*] (who refuse to pay taxes), occasionally even their own currency. Fake terrhromady have also been accused of confiscating communal property and establishing local courts and law-enforcement agencies. While preaching populist ideas on "self-government" with the assistance of Kremlin-connected individuals, the promoters of fake terrhromady rely on arbitrary interpretations of Ukraine's Constitution to justify these unlawful activities.

During a press conference dedicated to the phenomenon of fake terrhromady understood as a "threat to national security," Anatoliy Tkachuk argued that these individuals seek to sow chaos with the ultimate goal of corroding Ukraine's social fabric and unravelling Ukraine as a state (UCMC 2017). As a result, fake terrhromady have become an important target for the Security Service of Ukraine (SBU). As emphasized by Andriy Levus, former Deputy Chief of the SBU, at their core these illegitimate practices aim to subvert Ukraine's constitutional order (Texty.org.ua 2016a).

At the same time, the demand for regional autonomy underlying the promotion of SEZs contradicts the goal of the decentralization reform to contain centrifugal tendencies. A distinct, yet related issue is the granting of "special status" to the occupied areas in Donbas. Significantly, Russia portrays divisions within Ukrainian society as home-grown and pre-existing the conflict in and around Ukraine rather than being artificially amplified by Moscow to destabilize the country. As argued in section "Granting 'Special Status' to Donbas: A threat to Ukraine's National Security", such framing allows the Kremlin to promote local self-governance as a way to contain (if not solve) those allegedly long-neglected divisions, while *de facto* consolidating local pro-Russian sentiment.

II. DECENTRALIZATION: A FAULTY PANACEA TO RUSSIA-SPONSORED SEPARATISM

1. Ukraine's Decentralization Reform: Key Legislation

One common misunderstanding is that the decentralization reform started under Western pressure within the framework of the Minsk Agreements. This is inaccurate, as there had been earlier attempts (see Leitch 2015). However, it was only after the Euromaidan revolution and President Petro Poroshenko's coming to power that the process was set into motion in a systematic way.

As explained in a recent report by the German Institute for International and Security Affairs, the territorial-administrative structure inherited from the Soviet times suffered from a number of problems. First, it faced an "accountability deficit." Although local councilors were elected, they formally shared power with centrally appointed administrators at the district and regional level, who, *de facto*, set the agenda. Significantly, state administrators were accountable to the central government rather than to the local electorate. The same applied to elected councilors in settlements below the district level (Dudley 2019, 7–8). Second, in light of this formal power-sharing, "duplication of responsibilities" between state administrators and local councilors was a recurrent problem. Such overlapping of tasks led to inefficient provision of local services (ibid., 8). Third, the old system relied on a "trickle-down system of fiscal transfers," whereby the capital negotiated and dispensed budgets exclusively to regions, each of which arbitrarily decided how to allocate the funds to various districts, which gave out the remaining resources to the villages and settlements within their remit. As a result, communities at the lowest level were left with very scarce resources (ibid., 9).[11] The ongoing decentralization reform is meant to rectify these important shortcomings.

---

[11] It is worth mentioning that Cities of Regional Significance (CRSs) represented an exception. In fact, their mayors and councils were democratically elected and directly accountable to their electorate. Moreover, a separate portion of the state budget was allocated to and directly negotiated with CRSs, whose councils enjoyed some degree of fiscal autonomy. However, these privileges also enabled local political elites in cahoots with local business tycoons to capture key assets in CRSs in exchange for political loyalty to the capital (ibid., 8, 10).

Ukraine's decentralization process kicked off in April 2014 with the adoption of the "Concept of the Reform of Local Government and Territorial Organization of Power" (Verkhovna Rada 2014a). This text set out the main target goals of the reform, namely, to create and sustain genuine living conditions for citizens, provide high-quality and accessible public services, establish institutions of direct democracy, and align the interests of the government with those of territorial communities. To the extent that communities have a better sense of local issues and citizens' needs on the ground, the transfer of administrative and budgetary responsibilities from national and regional authorities to the community level is seen as an unequivocally positive development.

Thus, the Ukrainian Parliament [*Verkhovna Rada*] approved the Law "On Cooperation of Territorial Communities" in mid-June 2014 (Verkhovna Rada 2014b) and the Law "On Voluntary Amalgamation of Territorial Communities"(ATCs) in February 2015 (Verkhovna Rada 2015a). The first bill clarified the issues on which these new entities would cooperate. The second bill enabled the incorporation on a voluntary basis of several settlements into the territorial communities. As of January 2020, 1029 ATCs have been created, corresponding to 33.3 percent of the total Ukrainian population and covering 44.2 percent of the total territory of Ukraine (excluding the occupied territories) (Decentralization 2020).

In April 2015, the government approved the "methodology" which would provide the "mechanisms and conditions" for the formation of capable territorial communities. Interestingly, the text specifies that the amalgamation process must take into consideration the "historical, geographical, socio-economic, cultural characteristics" of the administrative and territorial units in question (Cabinet of Ministers 2015). A later amendment added additional criteria, namely "natural, ecological, *ethnic*" characteristics (Cabinet of Ministers 2017). This is a very important point when discussing the potential of the decentralization process for containing secessionist aspirations. In this respect, Zubko pointed out that the amalgamation of communities from different ethnic backgrounds would create a "preventing mechanism against separatist sentiment" (Skorokhod 2019).

The amalgamation process increases not only the institutional, but also the financial capacity of local self-government bodies. To this end, in November 2015 the Rada passed amendments to the budget and the tax codes (Verkhovna Rada 2015b). This was a necessary step to proceed with fiscal decentralization, which is said to have already brought about positive results. Hromadas now receive additional tax payments and are entitled to directly manage their budget to improve local infrastructure, healthcare, and education.

It is worth noting that Ukraine is still formally using an administrative-territorial system established back in 1981. As of April 2020, the basic law on the territorial-administrative structure of Ukraine had not entered into force. [12] The new structure would envisage a three-tier system: regional level [oblasts plus the Autonomous Republic of Crimea], district level [rayons] and basic level [hromadas]. As explained by Zubko, the bill aims to eliminate duplication of powers and improve the quality of service provision by increasing the funding of local self-government budgets, with education and healthcare progressively becoming an *exclusive* function of the ATCs (TSN 2018). The minister expected the draft law to be passed by the end of 2019 (Ukrinform 2019).

As already mentioned, the implementation of the provisions outlined in the concept required constitutional amendments. These concerned especially the definition of the community [hromada] as a legitimate political-administrative sub-level, namely the "primary unit" [*pervynna odynytsya*] in Ukraine's administrative-territorial structure (article 133); the establishment of executive bodies accountable to district and regional councils (article 140); and the transformation of state administrations at lower levels of government into a watchdog and supervisory authority (i.e. prefects), responsible for ensuring that local self-government bodies comply with the laws and the Constitution (article 118–9) (Verkhovna Rada 2015c).

At the end of August 2015, the Rada passed amendments in the first reading following the approval of the Constitutional Court of Ukraine and the Venice Commission (Council of Europe 2014). However, a controversial provision ("[s]pecifics of local self-government in certain districts of Donetsk and Luhansk regions are determined by a separate law") was swiftly added to the amendments. This provision caused violent protests to erupt outside the parliament building, which led to the death of four guardsmen in a grenade attack. Opponents feared that the amendments would give political legitimacy to Moscow-supported separatist forces and, ultimately, veto power over Kyiv's decisions. In the face of a lack of domestic consensus around this topic, the process was halted (Korrespondent 2015).

---

[12] The draft law was submitted to parliament in February 2018 (Verkhovna Rada 2018a).

As emphasized by the German government's special envoy for decentralization and good governance, the decentralization reform thus continued in the absence of constitutional amendments "*because* it was mixed up with the Minsk process" (Sologoub et al. 2019). For the time being, progress with the decentralization reform remains fragile. In the absence of constitutional changes, "decentralization will always be an unfinished reform" (Cabinet of Ministers 2019), as the latter proceeds on the basis of simple laws that could be reversed at any time.

2. Fake Terhromady: A Bottom-up Model to Bring the Ukrainian State Down

Supporters of the reform claim that by disempowering regions and districts, the decentralization process weakens the traditional target of Russia's subversive operations. While providing original insights, this argument fails to address the danger represented by actors who distort the vocabulary and tools derived from decentralization reform to promote separatist activities against the Ukrainian state.

The phenomenon of "national entrepreneurs" is particularly noteworthy. The so-called "representatives" of terhromady effectively seize tax powers and divert tax revenues from Ukraine's state coffers, whereas individuals "registered" as "national entrepreneurs" engage in tax evasion. More critically, this unlawful practice may be "weaponized" against Ukrainian institutions. There is concern among Ukrainian security services that "registrators" might store a "dossier" for each "national entrepreneur" in a given *terhromada*. Should there be a desire to replicate the scenario that led to the creation of the so-called "Donetsk and Luhansk People's Republics" ("DPR"/"LPR") elsewhere, Tkachuk argued in an interview, these dossiers could be used to blackmail tax evaders, forcing them to "storm" local state administrative buildings in hopes of heading off criminal prosecution (Protsyuk 2016).

What most of these cases have in common is their leaders' connection to Medvedchuk's NGO "Ukrainian Choice." It is worth mentioning that in February 2019, the Prosecutor General's Office of Ukraine opened criminal proceedings against Medvedchuk for "treason" and "encroachment on the territorial integrity and inviolability of Ukraine" (RFE/RL 2019). The phenomenon was aptly captured by journalist Kataryna Handzyuk. In her article "Medvedchuk Hides in the Details" she describes activities behind the terhromada in the village of Stara Zburivka in southern Kherson oblast. Her investigation illustrates how self-appointed "representatives" informed locals that carrying a "person's passport" would give them immunity against Ukraine's laws and grant them tax exemption (Handzyuk 2016). The self-proclaimed "representative" of this terhromada was Sergey Ryabov,[13] a former supporter of anti-Maidan protests.

An important thing to note is that these entities have been emerging *before* the beginning of the decentralization reform and are *not* confined to Ukraine's southern and eastern regions, which are usually associated with separatist sentiment. One of the oldest reported cases dates back to 2007. At the time, an "independent state" under the name of "Chernihiv Southern Realm" [*Chernihivs'ke Pivdenne Sudarstvo*] had been created in Bakayivka village in Chernihiv oblast in the north of the country. The entity was established by two residents, who announced the creation of "the Titular Sovereign People of Ukraine" [*tytul'nyy suverennyy narod Ukrayiny*] (Potapchuk 2016). According to one Ukrainian investigation, its leader proclaimed himself "emperor," whilst his two main collaborators were former Russian citizens and graduates from two Russian military academies.[14] In 2016, the SBU opened criminal proceedings against the members of the organization. The evidence found suggests that they had refused to comply with Ukrainian conscription laws and managed to establish local self-government bodies, courts, law enforcement agencies, even financial institutions. The self-proclaimed "realm" issued banknotes, driving licenses, car registration number plates, and so-called "passports of the indigenous people of Ukraine." Whoever possessed this identity document allegedly gained immunity from Ukraine's judicial authorities and was granted exemption from paying taxes and utility bills (Texty.org. ua 2016b).

Perhaps the most cited case with regards to "national entrepreneurs" is the terhromada created in Khmelnytskyy (Western Ukraine) by Pavlo

---

[13] "Zibrannya Starozbur'yivchan 03.11.2013" [Meeting of StaraZburivka Residents November 3, 2013], "paysonkrays," 58.28, November 7, 2013, https://www.youtube.com/watch?v=4gP6uHZAnW4.

[14] "Separatysts'kyy Proekt Medvedchuka. Rozsliduvannya Diyal'nosti 'Terytorial'nykh Hromad' (Video)" [Medvedchuk's Separatist Project. Investigation of 'Territorial Communities' (Video)], "Censor.net," 23.31, December 12, 2016, https://censor.net.ua/blogs/1103928/separatistskiyi_proekt_medvedchuka_rozslduvannya_dyalnost_teritoralnih_gromad_vdeo.

Bilets'kyy, a local entrepreneur, and Ol'ha Uhrak,[15] former assistant to Communist MP Volodymyr Novak (2002–2006). Reportedly, Bilets'kyy gave out car registration plates, while encouraging local residents not to register their car in the state vehicle register or pay taxes (Kazanskyi 2019). In order to obtain a certificate granting the status of "national entrepreneur," apparently it was sufficient to sign a contract with the community in question on condition of withdrawing one's name from state fiscal records (Terhromada.blogspot.com 2016). In March 2017, the local court arrested Bilets'kyy and Uhrak's property. The police found copies of the certificates distributed to so-called "national enterprises," "passports of persons," and seals with the inscription "Territorial community of Khmelnytskyy city" (Depo.ua 2017).

Back in 2016, then Prosecutor General Ihor Lutsenko explicitly accused Medvedchuk of orchestrating the registration of such terhromady and declared that the self-proclaimed "representative" of Khmelnytskyy would be charged with treason (*Ukrayins'ka Pravda* 2016). In response, Medvedchuk's "Ukrainian Choice" published a statement on its website in which it rejected all accusations. Against all evidence of its involvement, the movement took the opportunity to present a constitutionally enshrined federal structure as the only solution to the separatist sentiment of which terhromady is an obvious symptom (Ukrayinskyi Vybir 2016). This is an interesting twist: the NGO instigates these secessionist entities and then exploits their destabilizing potential as an argument to promote federalization as a panacea.

Liudmyla Lyubovetska also appears as one of the self-proclaimed "representatives" of the terhromada in Khmelnytskyy.[16] According to one investigation, Lyubovetska supports the "Union of Creators of Holy Russia," a Russian nationalist organization advocating the creation of the

---

[15] In this documentary, in her speech in front of the Khmelnytskyi City Council, Uhrak relies on a populist reading of Article 5 of the Constitution of Ukraine to justify the establishment of terhromada in Khmelnytskyi: "In Ukraine people are the transmitter of sovereignty and the unique source of power. People carry out power directly and through public authorities and organs of local self-government". See "Separatysts'kyy Proekt Medvedchuka," 6.07.

[16] "Pravookhorontsi Prodovzhuyut' Shukaty Dokazy Nezakonnoyi Diyal'nosti Narodnykh Pidpryyemtsiv" [Law enforcement Agencies Continue to Look for Evidence of Illegal Activity of National Entrepreneurs], YouTube video, "UA:PODILLYA," 0.50, May 25, 2016, https://www.youtube.com/watch?v=6phCg9RmY9A.

"Divine Monarchy of Holy Russia" in Ukraine, Belarus, and Russia.[17] In a video uploaded on the website of "Ukrainian choice," Lyubovetska refers to Article 69 of the Constitution of Ukraine: "The expression of the will of the people shall be exercised through elections, referenda and other forms of direct democracy." Through use of populist rhetoric, this Article is being exploited to give an appearance of legitimacy to the creation of terhromady as an example of such alternative forms of direct democracy. Interestingly, Lyubovetska displays the signed agreement which allegedly established the terhromada.[18] At the end of her speech, she claims that should a "person of the Ukrainian people" be unsatisfied with national state institutions or local government bodies, then the Ukrainian Constitution grants this person the opportunity to exert power directly through the creation of a terhromada based on such an agreement.[19] From this perspective, terhromady represent a particular type of separatism, one that cultivates disloyalty to national-level institutions in the name of "the sovereign people."

In this respect, one investigation shows that self-appointed "representatives" found a clever way of circumventing the law on the voluntary amalgamation of hromadas. All they needed to do was find three residents in a single community and ask them to sign an "Agreement" (Texty.org.ua 2016a). As noted by Anatoliy Tkachuk, current Ukrainian legislation does not list "territorial communities" as a legal entity of public law (by law, such legal entities cannot be arbitrarily established by private citizens).[20]

[17] "Feykovaya Detsentralizatsiya: Novyy Plan Separatistov—Sekretnyi Front" [Fake Decentralization: Separatists' New Plan—Secret Front], YouTube video, "Telekanal ICTV," 5.50, December 14, 2016, https://www.youtube.com/watch?v=O6L9Tj6nEas.

[18] "'Ukrayins'kyyVybir' u Khmel'nyts'komu Proviv Zustrich z Predstavnykamy Terytorial'noyi Hromady Mista" [Ukrainian Choice in Khmel'nytskyy Met with Representatives of the Territorial Community of the City], "Ukrayinskyi Vybor," 3:27, January 27, 2014, http://vybor.ua/video/grazhdanskoe_obschestvo/ukrayinskiy-vibir-u-hmelnicko nu-proviv-zustrich-z-predstavnikami-teritorialnih-gromad-mista.html. In the same video, Vasyl' Nimchenko, a representative from Medvedchuk's NGO "Ukrainian Choice," argues that the amalgamation process among communities will "enable them to protect their property rights over the land" (1:26). According to this narrative, the state "usurped" power because at no point was the land "transferred" to the state—the people "own" the land (1.50).

[19] Ib d., 6.15.

[20] "Feykovi Hromady—Nova Zahroza Natsional'niy Bezpetsi Ukrayiny? UKMTS 23.05.2017" [Fake Terhromady—New Threat to Ukraine's National Security? UCMC May 23, 2017]." YouTube video, "Ukraine Crisis Media Center," 10.01, May 23, 2017, https://www.youtube.com/watch?v=8AoWYFX2vik.

Yet another case was registered in the city of Ternopil in western Ukraine. Reportedly, by September 2019 the terhromada had illegally seized local lands and issued as many as 150 certificates of "national entrepreneurs," all effectively engaging in tax evasion (Chasopys 2019). According to Ihor Huskov, advisor to the central command of Ukraine's SBU, there is evidence indicating that Russian security services are behind these entities (Segodnya 2017). In April 2017, the SBU liquidated the terhromada that had been operating in Sumy, a northern city close to the border with Russia. Allegedly, its organizers had attempted to establish illegal governing bodies, take over the functions of the local state authorities and get hold of buildings owned by the municipality. They had also registered around thirty "national entrepreneurs" (Sluzhba Bezspeky 2017). According to a local investigation, the terhromada's page on the Russian social network "Vkontakte" had a direct link to the Russian movement "Kursom Pravdy i Yedineniya"[21] [The Course of Truth and Unity], which advocates the re-establishment of the USSR.[22] According to another investigation, representatives from "Kursom Pravdy i Yedineniya" had been organizing events all around the country, calling for the seizure of power in Ukraine.[23] Interestingly, there is a homonymous party in Russia, which on its website mentions the "Public Safety Concept" [*Kontseptsiya obshchestvennoy bezopasnosti*], published on the Kremlin's website on November 20, 2013 during the outbreak of the Euromaidan protests (Kremlin 2013). On his Vkontakte page, the self-proclaimed "representative" of Sumy, Volodymyr Oliynyk, also refers to the "Public Safety Concept."[24] In an interview, Oliynyk mentioned that their coordinates are known to someone named Serhiy Danilov,[25] who is now a member of the "working group" advising the so-called "DPR authorities."[26] Such net-

---

[21] Its website is no longer accessible.

[22] "Separatyzm u Sumakh | Pid Prytsilom" [Separatism in Sumy | Under fire], YouTube video, "UA: Sumy," 1.06, May 5, 2017, https://www.youtube.com/watch?v=faww6SWV-DA. Allegedly, all references to "Kursom Pravdy I Yedineniya" had been taken down after the end of the investigation in June 2015 (ibid., 5.20). Interestingly, the Ukrayins'kyy Vybir website published an article on the nature of these (fake) *terhromady* (ibid., 4.43). However, the article is no longer accessible.

[23] "Separatysts'kyy Proekt Medvedchuka," 29.55.

[24] Separatyzm u Sumakh | PidPrytsilom" [Separatism in Sumy | Under fire], Youtube video, "UA: Sumy," 1.06, May 5, 2017, https://www.youtube.com/watch?v=faww6SWV-DA, 2.22.

[25] Ibid., 3.15.

[26] "Separatysts'kyy Proekt Medvedchuka," 29.55.

works indicate that the various fake terhromady reflect a systematic effort to challenge Ukraine's territorial sovereignty by putting in place a parallel system of power and spreading separatist sentiment among the local population.

3. *"Special Economic Zones": Russia-sponsored Federalization in Disguise*

In addition to terhromady, the promotion of so-called SEZs is also being suspected of covering up subversive operations. This phenomenon has been identified in Dnipropetrovsk (renamed Dnipro since 2016) and Kharkiv (eastern Ukraine), Zaporizzhya and Odesa (southeastern and southwestern Ukraine respectively), and Zakarpattya (western Ukraine).

It is worth mentioning that the phenomenon of SEZs is far from new. In the early 1990s, the Rada introduced legislation that allowed for the creation of so-called "Free Economic Zones" (FEZs). The aim was to attract foreign investment and promote local infrastructure and socioeconomic development. As a result, a number of FEZs were established across the country. Overall, SEZs and FEZs produced mixed and often suboptimal results and were seen to serve the interests of local and regional business and political elites rather than the national interest, which is why the International Monetary Fund pressurized Ukrainian authorities into liquidating them as a condition for renewing its financial assistance (UCIPR 2000). The establishment of SEZs and so-called "territories of priority development" in Donetsk and Luhansk oblasts in 1999 is a case in point. At that time, the Donetsk "clan" demanded favorable legislative regimes from the central authorities in exchange for approving the closure of coal mines as part of a World Bank restructuring program (Swain and Mykhnenko 2007, 39; see also Kuromiya 2002, 473). In fact, mines were a major source of revenues for local business tycoons and provided employment to the local population. In this respect, miners also constituted the electoral basis of local political elites.

What distinguishes these first experiments from the recently resumed demands in favor of SEZs across Ukraine is the involvement of Russian "curators" on a wave of reaction to the creation of the "DPR"/"LPR" in Donbas. A recent report on *The Surkov Leaks* provided evidence of how Putin's former top aide and spin-doctor, Vladislav Surkov, had been managing networks of activists and politicians to destabilize Ukraine. Critically, the authors showed how the leaked emails point to Russia's direct involvement in the projects in Zakarpattya, Odesa Dnipro, Zaporizzhya, and Kharkiv (Shandra and Seely 2019, 56–62).

In September 2015, the so-called "Public Council of Dnipropetrovsk Region" was created on the initiative of members of local councils. Their mandate was to develop legislation aimed at strengthening the region's powers (112.ua 2015). In a promotional video,[27] its leader, Serhiy Shapran, advocated the creation of the "Dnipropetrovsk People's Economic Republic" [*Dnipropetrovs'ka Narodno-Ekonomichna Respublika*]. The name dangerously echoed the "DPR"/"LPR" in the east of Ukraine. Formally, the Dnipropetrovsk Republic would seek "economic autonomy" for the region to escape the country's dire economic situation (Dyachenko 2015). It is important to stress that Shapran was the leader of Medvedchuk's "Ukrainian Choice" office in Dnipro.[28]

Around the same time, Serhiy Kivalov, the head of the Ukrainian Maritime Party and former MP for the Party of Regions, submitted an electronic petition on the President's website.[29] The petition proposed the creation of a "free economic zone" ("Porto-Franco") in Odesa which would introduce duty-free import and export of goods as well as extend prerogatives for the Odesa City Council (Electronic petitions 2015).[30] According to a local activist, the proposal aimed to destabilize the situation not only in Odesa but also in Mykolaïv and Kherson (Depo.Odesa 2016a). First, Ukraine's state coffers would take a hit, as all the maritime trade passing through the Odesa port would be-tax-free. Second, local officials would consolidate Odesa as a regional fiefdom increasingly isolated from the capital and thus vulnerable to Russia-sponsored separatist activities (Depo.Odesa 2016b).

For a while, it seemed that the project had been abandoned. However, in April 2019 Odesa's mayor, Hennadiy Trukhanov, posted on the city

[27] "Otkrytiye Priyemnoy GRD" [Opening of the Reception of PCD]. YouTube video, "Rada Dnepropetrovsk," November 22, 2015, https://www.youtube.com/watch?v=AKOm8OeVu5U.

[28] In an interview on the "Ukrainian Choice" website, Shapran parrots Medvedchuk's idea that federalization will help keep the country together: "Komanda Viktora Medvedchuka. Sergey Shapran" [Viktor Medvedchuk's Team: Sergey Shapran], "Ukrayinskyy Vybor," 3.30, May 1, 2015, http://vybor.ua/video/Persons_and_personalities/komanda-viktora-medvedchuka-sergey-shapran.html.

[29] It is worth noting that Kivalov lost the 2019 parliamentary election to a representative of the Party of the Servant of the People.

[30] Interestingly, students from the National University "Odesa Law Academy" complained of being forced to sign Kivalov's petition (Depo.Odesa 2015).

council's website an amendment to an existing order on the creation of a working group in charge of expanding the SEZ.[31] According to a local journalist, the problem with the proposal is that it seeks to expand this special regime to the *entire* Odesa oblast (Mazur 2019). An additional risk is that Ukraine's Law on SEZs, to which the updated order refers, also grants enormous prerogatives to local authorities.[32] Most importantly, any resulting secessionist attempts may cost Ukraine access to Odesa ports, a vital economic and strategic asset (Kolibelkin 2016).

The co-chair of the revived working group is Sergiy Grinevetsky, former Governor of Odesa Region (1998–2005). In 2015, Grinevetsky advocated fiscal autonomy when he wrote that SEZs would be successful provided that local authorities were solely responsible for considering and approving investment projects. Moreover, his original proposal to the Azarov government on reviving the special regime was accompanied by a draft bill which sought to expand the territory of the SEZ (Grinevetsky 2015).[33]

It is worth mentioning that back in April 2016, parents of school pupils in Odesa complained about the handbook on the history of Odesa sponsored by Trukhanov. In it, Odesa is referred to as the "capital of Novorossiya," and an important part of the text is dedicated to the "Porto-Franco" experience dating back to the nineteenth century. Interestingly, among the authors we find Oleh Bryndak, the current deputy chairman of the "Porto-Franco" working group and a member of Odesa City Council. The founders of the publishing house are the Mazurenky brothers: Volodymyr Mazurenky used to be a member of Medvedchuk's Social Democratic Party of Ukraine, while Valentyn Mazurenky was associated with the same party as a member of Odesa City Council (Depo. Odesa 2016c).

In December 2015, Alla Aleksandrovskaya, leader of the "Slobozhanshchina" movement and former MP for the (now banned) Communist Party, organized a round table in Kyiv to discuss a bill on the establishment of a "special region of Slobozhanshchina" in Kharkiv oblast. This special regime envisaged the establishment of strong trade relations with Russia. Two other issues were raised: first, increasing the region's budget and, second, electing governors in Ukraine. At the meeting,

---

[31] https://omr.gov.ua/ua/acts/mayor/173243/.

[32] See articles 9–11 (Verkhovna Rada 2006).

[33] The proposal was largely ignored by the Azarov and Yatsenyuk governments.

Aleksandrovskaya commented that "if a 'special regime' is being considered for Odesa then why not consider it also for Kharkiv region?" (Golos. ua 2015). The proposal was also supported by Vasyl Nimchenko, Deputy Chairman of Medvedchuk's NGO "Ukrainian Choice," an MP from Medvedchuk's "Opposition Platform," and First Deputy Head of the Parliamentary Committee on Legal Policy. It is worth mentioning that he was also present at the event set up by "Ukrainian Choice" dedicated to the terhromada in Khmelnytskyy.[34] In June 2016, the SBU detained Aleksandrovskaya for allegedly attempting to bribe local deputies in Kharkiv to vote in favor of federalization (Prestupnosti.NET 2016).

Around the same time, the SBU disbanded a prospective meeting in the southern city of Zaporizzhya, where allegedly it was planned to announce a "special status" for the region (TSN 2015). The event was put together by the organization "Sotsial'noe Zaporozzhya" [Social Zaporizzhya], which former SBU director Vasyl Hrytsak listed as one of the entities bankrolled by Moscow's "curators" involved in promoting "hidden federalization" (*Ukrayins'ka Pravda* 2017).

Hrytsak's list included also the NGO "Zakarpats'kyi Kray" [Zakarpattya region]. Significantly, in mid-February 2016, its leader conducted a roundtable discussion in which he described the existing overly centralized system in Ukraine as the major source of the economic crisis in the region. He advocated granting the entire region "special status" to attract investment. To this end, the NGO claimed to be preparing relevant amendments to Ukraine's legislation and Constitution. Participants supported the idea of having an elected governor accountable to the local population rather than centrally appointed prefects (Ihnat 2016). Significantly, these proposals echoed those already presented in the context of the Kharkiv experiment.

As argued by Russia observer Lilia Shevtsova, by 2015, it became clear to the Kremlin that it had overestimated its ability to successfully fuel pro-Russian secessionist movements in other regions beyond Donbas. The realization of this miscalculation caused Russian officials to bury the "Novorossiya" projecting Donetsk and Luhansk oblasts (news.online.ua 2016). However, there is an argument to be made that the prospect of autonomy for the occupied areas in Donbas offers Russia new venues to destabilize Ukraine from within.

[34] See note 18.

III. Granting "Special Status" to Donbas: A threat to Ukraine's National Security

1. Ukraine's Legislation on Donbas under President Poroshenko

From the onset of the peace process, granting "special status" to non-government-controlled areas (NGCAs) has been a key political provision in the Minsk Agreements (*Financial Times* 2015). Signed in February 2015 by the Trilateral Contact Group (TCG), which brought to the table Ukraine, Russia, and the Organization for Security and Cooperation in Europe (OSCE) (plus the "representatives" of "DPR"/"LPR"), the agreements were intended to revive the Minsk Protocol ceasefire signed in September 2014, but which failed in early 2015.

The 2015 version proposed implementing an immediate ceasefire, to be followed by the withdrawal of heavy weaponry by both sides. Then Ukraine would have to authorize local elections to be held in the occupied territories "in accordance with Ukrainian legislation." Crucially, provision 9 states that Ukraine would regain full control of its state border only the day *after* local elections. According to provision 11, by the end of 2015 Ukraine would be required to implement constitutional amendments to allow for decentralization (including a reference to the "special status" of the occupied territories) and to adopt permanent legislation on the "special status" of these areas.

Provisions 11 and 12 state that Ukraine must agree the special regime and issues related to local elections "with representatives of certain areas of the Donetsk and Luhansk regions." From the beginning of the conflict, Russia has insisted on promoting direct negotiations between the Ukrainian central authorities and the self-proclaimed leaders of "DPR"/"LPR." Fundamentally, this strategy aims to legitimize the role of separatists at the negotiating table as autonomous actors and that of Russia as a mediator rather than a direct party to the conflict.

In analyzing potential threats to Ukraine's national security derived from granting "special status" to Donbas, two additional provisions are particularly noteworthy. Ukraine must adopt an amnesty law for individuals fighting on the side of Russia-backed militants (provision 5). Moreover, both sides are required to pull out all foreign armed formations (including mercenaries) and disarm illegal groups (provision 10). Neither of these provisions indicates an explicit timeframe for their implementation.

On September 16, 2014, Ukrainian lawmakers adopted the law "On the Special Order of Local Self-Government in Certain Districts of Donetsk and Luhansk oblasts" (often referred to as the "law on special status") (Verkhovna Rada 2014c). Although for the limited period of three years, the law identified the necessary steps for organizing local self-government with the aim of stabilizing the situation, restoring the rule of law and citizens' constitutional rights and freedoms, facilitating the return and reintegration of internally displaced people, and enabling the resumption of normal life in the NGCAs. These steps included granting amnesty to those who fought on the side of Russia-supported separatists (article 3),[35] the right to linguistic self-determination (article 4), the participation of local representatives in appointing the heads of courts and prosecutors' offices (article 5), a special economic regime (article 7), "cross-border cooperation" with Russia (article 8), and the power by local councils to create "people's militia" units, to be formed "on a voluntary basis" and tasked with protecting public order (article 9).

Among the amendments adopted on March 17, 2015 (Verkhovna Rada 2015d), Article 10 laid out a list of preconditions before the special regime can enter into force: presence of and safe working conditions for international electoral observers during local elections; withdrawal of all illegal armed formations, weaponry, and mercenaries from Ukraine's territory; prohibition of illegal interference in local elections (including by illegal armed formations); ensuring political pluralism and a multi-partisan system; restoration of Ukrainian television, radio broadcasting, and printed media in the NGCAs; guarantees for free expression of will and secret ballot; right to vote for internally displaced people; transparency in the vote count and declaration of electoral results. To this day, these preconditions have not been satisfied.

---

[35] On the same day, the Rada also passed the law "On Preventing Persecution and Punishment of Participants of Events on the Territories of Donetsk and Luhansk Oblasts" (Verkhovna Rada 2014d). The law was meant to pardon "members of armed groups" and those who "participated in the activities of the self-proclaimed bodies". Yet, it was not extended to individuals involved in the downing of the MH17 flight in July 2014. In the end, the law never entered into force. At the time, legal experts pointed out that it would be impossible to enforce the law in practice (Bludsha 2014). Moreover, Amnesty International warned that the law risked enabling people guilty of torturing prisoners to avoid criminal responsibility (Interfax 2014). It is worth mentioning that in late August 2019, deputies from the Opposition Bloc presented a new draft law on amnesty (Verkhovna Rada 2019a).

On October 5, 2017, President Petro Poroshenko submitted two bills to the Rada. The draft law "On Creating the Necessary Conditions for the Peaceful Resolution of the Situation in Certain Districts of Donetsk and Luhansk Oblasts" mentioned the request to the UN Security Council and Council of the European Union to establish an international peacekeeping operation (Verkhovna Rada 2015e) and extended by one year the effect of the above-mentioned "law on special status" originally adopted on September 16, 2014 (which would have expired on October 18, 2017). The next day the bill was adopted (Verkhovna Rada 2017).

The draft law "On the Aspects of State Policy on the Restoration of the State Sovereignty of Ukraine over the Temporarily Occupied Territory of Donetsk and Luhansk Oblasts" is more commonly known as the "Donbas reintegration bill." The text declared Russia to be an "aggressor state" and gave the NGCAs the official status of "occupied territories." The law was adopted on January 18, 2018 (Verkhovna Rada 2018b). The final version describes Russian military aggression as relying on the assistance of Russian regular troops, special formations, advisors, instructors, illegal armed forces, armed gangs, and mercenaries. "DPR"/"LPR" are referred to as representatives of the "occupying administration of the Russian Federation." Moreover, several MPs insisted on setting the annexation of Crimea as the starting date of the occupation of Ukraine. While no specific date is mentioned, the text makes reference to the 2014 Crimean law, which dates the annexation to February 20, 2014 (Verkhovna Rada 2015f).

This bill is significant because hitherto there had been no law that explicitly referred to Russia as an aggressor state. According to one commentator, Western partners might have talked Kyiv out of enshrining into law such an explicit accusation, as this would have further obstructed the already difficult negotiations (Hromadske 2017). Unsurprisingly, Russian Foreign Minister Sergei Lavrov accused the Donbas reintegration bill of violating the Minsk Agreements (Unian 2018a). The Russian Ministry insinuated that the overlap between the approval of the law and the US decision to supply Ukraine with lethal weapons[36] was not coincidental (Unian 2018b).

---

[36] In December 2017, the US administration approved the largest sale of weapons to Ukraine since 2014. While Congress had authorized such sales back in 2014 with the Ukraine Freedom Support Act, the Obama administration refrained from actively supplying the Ukrainian military with lethal weapons (Rogin 2017).

2. The Steinmeier Formula: A Tool to Legalize Russian-Installed Separatist Entities?

From a legal point of view, strictly speaking the Minsk Agreements should be considered nothing more than a declaration of intent.[37] The resulting ambiguity gave rise to incompatible interpretations on the Russian and Ukrainian side with regards to the *sequencing* for implementing the relevant security and political provisions. Such a clash of interpretations translated into ill-defined commitments for the negotiating parties, providing the opportunity to avoid responsibilities (Peters and Shapkina 2019, 3; Sargsyan 2019, 3). The Kremlin demands that Ukrainian authorities prioritize decentralization and local elections in the NGCAs, whereas Kyiv maintains that the stabilization of the security situation (namely full demilitarization and restoration of control over the state border) must precede the implementation of the political provisions.

In theory, the so-called Steinmeier Formula was meant to provide a solution to such a stalemate. At the Normandy summit (which brought together the leaders of France, Germany, Russia, and Ukraine) on October 2, 2015, then German Foreign Minister Walter Steinmeier advanced a proposal which was intended to clarify *exclusively* the steps for the implementation of the special regime for the NGCAs. According to the formula, as a first step Ukraine was required to adopt a special law on holding local elections in the NCGAs. In this respect, observers have emphasized that this proposal unequivocally favored Russia's interpretation of the Minsk Agreements, as it envisaged the implementation of the political provisions prior to stabilizing the security situation.

Unsurprisingly, this version was never accepted under Poroshenko's presidency. For a few years, it seemed that the negotiating parties had abandoned the original formula. However, Ukraine's new Foreign Minister, Volodymyr Prystayko, caused public outcry when he announced that on September 2, 2019 Normandy Four advisers had reached an agreement on the wording of the Steinmeier Formula, later to be discussed by the TCG (Unian 2019). Significantly, Moscow had demanded Ukraine's commitment to the Steinmeier Formula in written form as a

---

[37] In both Ukrainian and Russian legislation, only the head of state has the prerogative to sign legally binding international treaties on behalf of the state (Peters and Shapkina 2019, 3). However, the Minsk Agreements do not bear the signatures of the heads of states, but rather those of diplomats representing the participants in the TCG.

precondition for holding the next Normandy summit (Korrespondent 2019a).[38]

Initially, the spokesperson for Leonid Kuchma (former President and Ukraine's current representative to the TCG) declared that although in principle Ukraine has no objections to the formula, Ukraine's acceptance of local elections would be conditional upon the realization of a number of points, which essentially echoed those listed under article 10 of the law "on special status." These include allowing the participation of international electoral observers, withdrawing all illegal armed formations, weaponry, and mercenaries from Ukraine's territory, prohibiting illegal interference and vote rigging in local elections, ensuring political pluralism and free expression, restoring Ukrainian media in the NGCAs, and guaranteeing voting rights to internally displaced people (Korrespondent 2019b).

Despite these initial tensions, on October 1, 2019 Russian media circulated the final text with the signatures of the TCG members plus the "representatives" of "DPR"/"LPR" (Kommersant 2019). Unlike the original version from 2015–2016, the updated version of the Steinmeier Formula mentions that elections must "comply with Ukraine's Constitution and law on special status" (Ukrainian Weekly 2019). The text specifies that the law "on special status" would enter *provisionally* into effect at 20:00 on the election day. It would enter into force on a *permanent* basis if and only if the official report of the OSCE's election observation mission (EOM) confirms that the elections complied with the OSCE's standards.

The law "on special status" was due to expire on December 31, 2019; on December 12, 2019 the Rada extended it for another year, to December 31, 2020. The Rada is currently drafting a new law, the text of which, at the time of writing, has not been made publicly available. At a press briefing, Zelenskyy stated that the new law would "not cross any red lines"[39] and would put in place effective "preventing mechanisms"[40] to ensure that full demilitarization and restoration of control over the border remain preconditions for elections to be held.

As a result, a number of Ukrainian experts argue that the main responsibility for avoiding Ukraine's "capitulation" to Russia's demands based

---

[38] The last meeting of the Normandy format was on October 2016.

[39] "Ekstrennyi Bryfinh Volodymyra Zelens'koho 01.10.2019" [Emergency Briefing by Vladimr Zelenskyy 01.10.2019], 3.15, "Ukrayins'ka Pravda," October 1, 2019, https://www.youtube.com/watch?v=XSW0g1ON1KM.

[40] Ibid., 8.25.

on the Steinmeier Formula lies with the Rada. In fact, *only* the law "on special status" can regulate the modality of holding elections and establishing local self-governance (Nayem 2019; Zholobovych 2019). Significantly, the formula itself does *not* mention the withdrawal of Russian troops and restoration of control over the border as necessary requirements for the organization of local elections. As already mentioned, the formula is meant to specify *exclusively* the steps for the implementation of the law "on special status." All the other provisions listed in the Minsk Agreements remain fundamentally disputed. In this respect, it is up to the Rada to enshrine in the new law the "preventive mechanisms" already in place under article 10 of the existing law (Polishchuk 2019).

Unlike the 2014 Minsk Protocol and the 2015 Minsk Agreements, the updated version of the Steinmeier Formula does not envisage a single document inclusive of all the TCG members' signatures. Instead, the formula was agreed by all the parties with separate letters to the OSCE. Once again, this allows the various negotiating parties to apply their own arbitrary interpretation to the text. In this respect, the formula replicates the ambiguity it was supposed to solve.

3. Risks Associated with Granting "Special Status" to Russia-Occupied Territories

Some skeptical observers have dismissed public concerns over the Steinmeier Formula as exaggerated. Arguably, the latter has no legal obligations attached to it and hardly adds anything new to existing legislation (Spirin 2019). Nonetheless, there is an argument to be made that unless the Rada establishes strong preventive mechanisms in the new legislation, the formalization of "special status" to the NGCAs may foster rather than contain secessionist tendencies in Donbas (Kompaniiets 2018, 7). It is important to note that the "representatives" of "DPR"/"LPR" immediately qualified the agreed formula as being synonymous with obtaining formal recognition of their right to autonomy and thus with legalizing their power: "We will decide by ourselves which language to speak, what our economy will look like, how our judicial system will be formed, how our people's militia will protect our citizens and how we will integrate with Russia" (RBK 2017).

Under the present circumstances, the implementation of a special regime in the NGCAs following the Steinmeier Formula presents a number of risks to Ukraine's national security.

First, should local elections fail to meet the OSCE's standards, the law on special status would nonetheless still *temporarily* apply to the NGCAs for the period leading up to the release of the OSCE's report. This means that the central government would be formally obliged to recognize and interact with the new local "government." One non-negligible risk is that the OSCE's EOM may choose to downplay electoral violations that occurred in constituencies to which access was denied, thereby allowing the law "on special status" to enter into force on a permanent basis in order to achieve formal progress in the peace negotiations (Zolkina and Sydorenko 2019). To reduce such danger, the mission of international observers deployed in Donbas should have the *mandate* and the *capabilities* to not only engage in electoral monitoring, but also manage local militias and demand access to the entire occupied territory (ibid.). In fact, "DPR"/"LPR" militias have consistently denied the OSCE's Special Monitoring Mission access to certain parts of the NGCAs.

Second, the existing self-proclaimed "authorities" in "DPR"/"LPR" will be allowed to hold office and therefore be legalized if amnesty is granted to individuals who contributed to creating these entities. The reintegration of Donbas under these conditions would potentially turn Russia-backed separatist forces into veto players in the Rada, obstructing the country's Euro-Atlantic aspirations.

Third, if local elections are held prior to completing the demilitarization process, the presence of illegal armed formations currently on the ground would be legitimized. Once again, in the absence of timely investigations, amnesty would only facilitate this process. On multiple occasions Ukrainian authorities have stressed that amnesty will not be extended to individuals who have engaged in war crimes. However, if elections are held before any meaningful investigations are carried out (which may take years) then individuals who have committed war crimes might end up in local government. More critically, article 9 of the existing law "on special status" could transform these illegal armed formations into local police (Peters and Shapkina 2019, 5). Essentially, local government would be able to create its own power structures which would operate outside the control of central authorities (Fluri and Badrack 2017, 33), thereby creating a "Russian enclave" within Ukraine (ibid., 35).

Fourth, once "DPR"/"LPR" authorities' control of these areas is legitimized, it is difficult to imagine that Russia would allow Ukraine to regain control over the border. As already mentioned, the Minsk Agreements state that Ukraine would regain control over the border on the first day *following* elections and the implementation of constitutional amendments. Unsurprisingly, Medvedchuk argued that Zelenskyy's promise to hold local elections only *after* the restoration of control over the border contradicts the Minsk Agreements (Censor.net 2019). Moreover, Russia is unlikely to withdraw its troops, as doing so would equate to admitting its direct involvement in the conflict, something that the Kremlin denies to this day.

Fifth, as a result of the loss of control over the border, the central government's inability to monitor the flow of weapons into Ukraine's territory would persist. This would create additional risks for public safety across the country. Arguably, "special status" risks amplifying illicit cross-border trade under the guise of "cross-border cooperation" with Russia.

Sixth, autonomy in language and education risks radicalizing secessionist sentiment. It has been reported that since 2015, Ukrainian language has been progressively sidelined in schools in NGCAs and Russia has been transporting in its "humanitarian convoys" tons of Russian school textbooks which target the new generation with pro-Russian patriotic sentiment (Durnev 2019). More recently, the self-proclaimed leader of "DNR" suggested introducing amendments to the "DNR Constitution" in order to strip Ukrainian of the status of state language and declare Russian "the only *state language* in the republic" as part of the "intensive integration process of the DPR into the Russian Federation" (TASS 2019). Critically, such initiatives betray local elites' intention to attribute state-like properties to the rebel regions and thus undermine Ukraine's territorial sovereignty. This is also exemplified by the law "On the State Border of the DPR" adopted in late November 2019. The law defines the new "state border" of the self-proclaimed republic along the pre-2014 administrative boundaries of the *entire* Donetsk oblast, thus incorporating the government-controlled areas into "DPR" (RIA Novosti 2019).

Seventh, the Minsk Agreements and the existing law "on special status" place the exclusive burden of post-conflict reconstruction onto Kyiv.[41]

---

[41] Interestingly, the Russian Ministry of Finances has excluded from the 2018 federal budget as well as the 2019–2020 budget cycle "humanitarian support" to "separate territories," which allegedly is a term Surkov came up with to refer to entities such as "DPR"/"LPR" without having to mention them explicitly (RBK 2017). Although it remains unclear what "humanitarian support" exactly stands for (thus suggesting that there might be alternative channels of Russian assistance that need not be suspended), Moscow is trying to find an uneasy balance between making these regions politically loyal to Moscow and economically dependent on Kyiv.

Even if the transformation of the occupied territories into "quasi-states" were to fail, their reintegration would add prohibitive costs to Ukraine's state coffers for demining the area and addressing a number of environmental hazards created by the war (Hamilton 2019).[42]

Eighth, it would be unwise to underestimate the impact that pardoning people who had a direct involvement in combat operations would have on Ukrainian society at large. As stressed by Roman Bezsmertnyy, former Ukraine's representative in the Minsk political subgroup, Russia is benefitting from the growing tensions within Ukrainian society created by Zelenskyy's acceptance of the Steinmeier Formula (Novosti 2019). Public outrage might increase the risk of lynching [*samosud*]. Russian propaganda has consistently portrayed the conflict as a "civil war" to cover up its military aggression and confuse people's understanding of the situation on the ground. Paradoxically, the literal implementation of the Minsk Agreements in Russia's favor might throw the country into a "real civil war" (Brunson 2019).

Ninth, selling autonomy to Donbas as a conflict-resolution tool legitimizes Russia's narrative of the conflict. The general assumption is that granting autonomy can settle competing (territorial) claims in an internal ethnic conflict (Wolff and Weller 2005). However, it would be inaccurate to portray the war in eastern Ukraine as an internal conflict triggered by grievances along ethnic lines. As pointed out by Wilson (2016), identity factors, economic interdependence with Russia, and a long-simmering alienation from the capital since the 2004 Orange revolution were necessary but not sufficient conditions for the outbreak of the conflict in Donbas. Ultimately, a fully-fledged war would have not been possible without Russia's military and financial assistance as well as the support of Russia-oriented local elites. In this respect, granting "special status" to Donbas de-responsibilizes Russia for its role in escalating the conflict.

Last but not least, we should not underestimate the destabilizing impact on Ukraine's sovereignty resulting from a possible "domino effect." As noted by one Ukrainian analyst, it is entirely possible that cities such as Kharkiv or Odesa might wish to imitate the Donbas scenario and demand a similar "special status." In turn, this would increase the risk of "unravelling" the Ukrainian state (Minakov 2019). Under Zelenskyy's leadership,

---

[42] These include the contamination of water supply to the region as a result of flooded mines, dumped radioactive waste, chemical pollution of the soil, air contamination, and deforestation.

the Rada's recent approval in its first reading of the "law on the city of Kyiv" is a case in point (Verkhovna Rada 2019b). Here Kyiv City Council is given prerogatives that are typical of a federalist unit: it would have its own electoral system as well as the ability to sign international treaties, while members of Kyiv City Council would work on a permanent basis (at present, only members of parliament earn a salary, whereas deputies in local councils work on a voluntary basis) (Honcharenko 2019). If permanently adopted, other cities may wish to emulate the capital's example, thereby creating a domino effect with detrimental implications for the unity of the state.

CONCLUSION

This aim of this chapter was to challenge the prevailing argument that the ongoing decentralization reform in Ukraine can act as a powerful deterrent to Russia-sponsored separatism. It can be debated whether the proliferation of fake terhromady and SEZs with the assistance of individuals linked to Viktor Medvedchuk reflects clumsy and largely inconsequential destabilizing attempts or systematic efforts orchestrated by Russian "curators" to undermine Ukraine's constitutional order. That said, it is hardly deniable that the absence of appropriate state oversight of local government bodies (i.e. "prefects") during the transition period leading up to the completion of the decentralization process creates favorable conditions for the promotion of destabilizing activities.

Due to the connection established between the decentralization reform and "special status in Donbas" as part of the Minsk peace process, this chapter also addressed the potential risks to Ukraine's national security associated with offering autonomy to the occupied territories. In opposition to Poroshenko's militaristic rhetoric, Zelenskyy's commitment to reach significant progress opened a window of opportunity for the Russian leadership to reboot the Minsk process to its own advantage. In particular, Moscow is capitalizing on the new Ukrainian leadership's inexperience on the one hand, and a growing desire in Western Europe to "normalize" relations with Russia on the other (Socor 2019). Possibly, formal progress in the Minsk talks might put Russia in a positive light and lead to the lifting of a portion of the sanctions currently in operation.

Essentially, everything will depend on the ability of Zelenskyy's leadership to uphold its promises. However, one element of concern is that thus far Zelenskyy's government style has shown a propensity to take decisions behind closed doors. Regardless of Russia's destabilizing operations, this leaves observers wonder whether Ukraine's sovereignty might be endangered from within as well. In one scene from Zelenskyy's "Servant of the People" TV series, the new "President" was confronted with a map of Ukraine, fragmented into several "independent states."[43] It remains to be seen whether the TV series was meant to be a parody or a premonition.

REFERENCES

"Free Economic Zones in Ukraine: Genesis, Trends and Prospects". *UCIPR (Ukrainian Center for Independent Political Research)* 6, no. 189 (October 2, 2000). http://pdc.ceu.edu/archive/00001290/.

112.ua. 2015. Deputaty Mistsevykh Rad Stvoryly 'Hromads'ku Radu Dnipropetrovshchyny' [Deputies from Local Councils Created the "Public Council of the Dnipropetrovs'k Region"], September 17. https://ua.112.ua/polityka/deputaty-mistsevykh-rad-stvoryly-hromadsku-radu-dnipropetrovshchyny-259053.html.

24 Kanal. 2019. Ofitsiyni Rezul'taty Parlaments'kykh Vyboriv 2019 za Partiynymy Spyskamy [The Official Results of the 2019 Parliamentary Elections Based on Party Lists], August 3. https://24tv.ua/parlamentski_vibori_2019_rezultati_golosuvannya_vibori_u_verhovnu_radu_n1180469.

Allisor, Roy. 2014. Russian 'Deniable' Intervention in Ukraine: How and Why Russia Broke the Rules. *International Affairs* 90 (6): 1255–1297. https://doi.org/10.1080/15387216.2016.1183221.

Androshchuk, Oleksandr. 2010. V. Chornovil ta Ideia Federalizatsii Ukrainy: Evoliutsiia Pohliadiv [V. Chornovil and the Idea of Federalising Ukraine: An Evolution of Views]. Ukrainskyi Istorychnyi *Zhurnal* [*Ukrainian Historical Journal*] 1: 24–33. http://dspace.nbuv.gov.ua/bitstream/handle/123456789/104943/03-Androshchuk.pdf?sequence=1.

Bludsha, Maryna. 2014. Zakon pro 'Amnistiyu' dlya 'Separatystivi Terorystiv' Ne mozhlyvo Zastosuvatyna Praktytsi—Eksperty [It is Impossible to Enforce the Amnesty Law for Separatists and Terrorists in Practice—Experts]. http://justice.org.ua/politika-i-pravo-podiji-fakti-komentari/zakon-pro-amnistiyu-dlya-separatistiv-i-teroristiv-nemozhlivo-zastosuvati-na-praktitsi-eksperti.

Bond, Ian. 2014. Devolution in Ukraine: Panacea or Pandora's Box? Centre for European Reform, May 23. https://www.cer.eu/insights/devolution-ukraine-panacea-or-pandoras-box.

[43] "Fragment Seriala 'Sluganaroda'—Karta Ukrayiny Budushcheye" [Scene from TV series "Servant of the People"—Map of Future Ukraine], Youtube video, Not Na, March 31, 2019, https://www.youtube.com/watch?v=4nOBO1C0PRg.

244 J. BARBIERI

Brunson, Jonathan. 2019. Implementing the Minsk Agreements Might Drive Ukraine to Civil War. That's Been Russia's Plan All Along. *War on the Rocks*, February 1. https://warontherocks.com/2019/02/implementing-the-minsk-agreements-might-drive-ukraine-to-civil-war-thats-been-russias-plan-all-along/.

Cabinet of Ministers. 2015. Pro Zatverdzhennya Metodyky Formuvannya Spromozhnykh Terytorial'nykh Hromad [On the Approval of the Methodology on the Formation of Capable Territorial Communities], April 8. https://zakon.rada.gov.ua/laws/show/214-2015-п/ed20150408.

———. 2017. ZMINY, Shcho Vnosyatsya do Metodyky Formuvannya Spromozhnykh Terytorial'nykh Hromad [CHANGES that Are Being 2015 Added to the Methodology on the Formation of Capable Territorial Communities], August 30. https://zakon.rada.gov.ua/laws/show/662-2017-п#n10.

———. 2019. Changes to the Constitution Are an Antivirus for Decentralization, Says Hennadii Zubko, June 27. https://www.kmu.gov.ua/en/news/zmini-do-konstituciyi-ce-antivirus-dlya-decentralizaciyi-gennadij-zubko.

Censor.net. 2010. Markov Schitayet, Chto Odessa Dolzhna Stat' Tsentrom Ukrayinskogo Federalizma, Potomu Chto 'Kiyevu Eto Ne Interesno. Donetsku i Luhansku Uzhe Ne Interesno po Opredelennym Prichinam [Markov Believes that Odessa Should Become the Center of Ukrainian Federalism, Because "Kyiv Is Not Interested. Donetsk and Luhansk are No Longer Interested for Other Reasons], October 15. https://censor.net.ua/news/136355/markov_schitaet_chto_odessa_doljna_stat_tsentrom_ukrainskogo_federalizma_potomu_chto_quotkievu_eto.

———. 2016. Separatysts'kyy Proekt Medvedchuka. Rozsliduvannya Diyal'nosti 'Terytorial'nykh Hromad' (Video) [Medvedchuk's Separatist Project. Investigation on "Territorial Communities" (Video)], December 12. https://censor.net.ua/blogs/1103928/separatistskiyi_proekt_medvedchuka_rozsldu-vannya_dyalnost_teritoralnih_gromad_vdeo.

———. 2019. Pidtrymuyu Pidpysannya 'Formulu Shtaynamyera', Ale Ne Zhodeniz Tym, Yak Yiyi Traktuye Zelenskyy,—Medvedchuk [I Support Signing the "Steinmeier Formula", However I Disagree with How Zelenskyy Interprets It—Medvedchuk], October 2. https://censor.net.ua/ua/news/3151688/pidtrymuyu_pidpysannya_formuly_shtayinmayera_ale_ne_zgoden_iz_tym_yak_yiyi_traktuye_zelenskyyi_medvedchuk.

Chasopys. 2019. Khto Ye Khto v 'Terytorial'niy Hromadi Ternopolya'? Chastyna II. [Who's Who in the "Territorial Community of Ternopil'"? Part II.], September 10. http://chasopys.te.ua/polityka/2902-chastyna-2.

Council of Europe. 2014. Opinion on the Draft law Amending the Constitution of Ukraine, Submitted by the President of Ukraine on 2 July 2014, endorsed by the Venice Commission at its Plenary Session (Rome, 10–11 October). https://www.venice.coe.int/webforms/documents/?pdf=CDL-AD(2014)037-e.

Decentralization. 2019. Vykonkomy Rad ta Prefekty Zamist' ODA ta RDA—Yakymy Budut' I Koly Zapratsyuyut' Zminy do Konstytutsiyi v Chastyni Detsentralizatsiyi [Executive Committees of Councils and Prefects instead of Regional State Administrations and District State Administrations—What They Will Look Like and When to Expect Constitutional Changes on Decentralization?], August 20. https://decentralization.gov.ua/news/11452.

———. 2020. "Monitorinh Protsesu Detsentralizatsiyi Vlady ta Reformuvannya Mistsevoho Samovryaduvannya – Stanom na 10 Sichnya 2020" [Monitoring the Process of the Decentralization of Power and Reform of Local Self-Government – as of 10 January 2020]. https://decentralization.gov.ua/uploads/library/file/526/10.01.2020.pdf.

Depo.Odesa. 2015. U Vyshi Kivalova Zmushuyut' Studentiv Pidpysuvaty Petytsiyina Yoho Koryst' (FOTO) [Students from Kivalov's Alma Mater Are Being Forced to Sign Petitions in His Favor (PHOTOS)], October 1. https://odesa.depo.ua/ukr/odesa/u-pidrahuya-primushuyut-studentiv-pidpisuvati-petitsiyi-na-01102015134000.

———. 2016a. Odeski Opozytsionery 'Vparyuyut'' Mistyanam Separatyzm v Obhortsi 'Porto-Franko' [Odessa Opposition "Instils" Separatism among Townspeople under the Guise of Porto-Franco], March 21. https://odesa.depo.ua/ukr/odesa/odeski-opozitsioneri-vparyuyut-mistyanam-separatizm-v-obzorttsi-21032016142300.

———. 2016b. Dlya Choho u Putina Prosuvayut' Ideyu 'Porto-Franko' dlya Odeshchyny [Why Is Putin Promoting the Idea of "Porto-Franco" for the Odesa Region], March 31. https://odesa.depo.ua/ukr/odesa/dlya-chogo-u-putina-prosuvayut-ideyu-porto-franko-dlya-odesh-chini-30032016200000.

———. 2016c. Putin Vidkryvaye Druhyi ta Tretiy Front na Odeshchyni [Putin Is Opening a Second and Third Front in the Odesa Region], April 18. https://odesa.depo.ua/ukr/odesa/yak-truhanov-pishe-pidruchniki-pro-novorosiyu-ta-dozvolyae-shabashi-18042016170000.

Depo.ua. 2017. Za 'Zakhoplennya Derzhavnoyi Vlady' Khmelnyts'ki Orhanizatory 'Narodnykh Pidpryyemstv' Vidpovidatymut' [Khmelnytskyi-Based Organizers of "National Enterprises" Will Be Held Accountable for the "Appropriation of State Authority"], March 19. https://khm.depo.ua/ukr/khm/za-zahoplennya-derzhavnoyi-vladi-organizatori-narodnih-pidpriyemstv-vidpo-vidatimut-pered-zakonom-20170319539258.

Derevinskyy, Vasyl. 2018. Vyacheslav Chornovil ta Kryms'ke Pytannya [Vyacheslav Chornovil and the Crimean Question]. In *Viziya Maybutnyoho Ukrayiny*, ed. Vasyl Derevinskyy, 47–55. Kyiv–Ternopil': Beskydy, http://shron2.chtyvo.org.

ua/Zbirnyk_statei/Chornovolivski_chytannia_Viziia_maibutnoho_Ukrainy_ Materialy_III_i_IV_naukovykh_konferentsii_prysvia.pdf.

Dudley, William. 2019. *Ukraine's Decentralization Reform*. Berlin: German Institute for International and Security Affairs. https://www.swp-berlin.org/ fileadmin/contents/products/arbeitspapiere/Ukraine_Decentralization_ Dudley.pdf.

Durnev, Dmitriy. 2019. 'Tol'ko Pyat' Ballov!' Kak Idet Bor'ba za Shkol'nikov Samoprovozglashennykh Respublik Donbassa ["Only a Five-Point Based System!" Developments in the Fight over School Pupils in the Self-Proclaimed Donbas Republics]. Sprektr Press, September 2. https://spektr.press/ tolko-pyat-ballov-kak-idet-borba-za-shkolnikov-samoprovozglashennyh-respublik-donbassa/.

Dyachenko, Vitaliy. 2015. Medvedchuk Pochav Tvoryty Dnipropetrovs'ku Narodno-Ekonomichnu Respubliku [Medvedchuk Started Creating the Dnipropetrovsk People's Economic Republic], *Depo.ua*, November 23. https://www.depo.ua/ukr/politics/medvedchuk-pochav-tvoriti-dniprope-trovsku-narodno-ekonomichnu-23112015170000.

Electronic petitions. 2015. Zaprovadyty v Suverenniy Ukrayini v Odes'komu Mors'komu Portu Rezhym Vil'noyi Ekonomichnoy Zony 'Porto-Franko' [Introducing A Free Economic Zone "Porto-Franko" in Sovereign Ukraine at the Odessa Seaport], September 21. https://petition.president.gov.ua/ petition/9785.

Financial Times. 2015. Full Text of the Minsk Agreement, February 12. https:// www.ft.com/content/21b8f98e-b2a5-11e4-b234-00144feab7de.

Fluri, Philipp, and Valentyn Badrack. 2017. *Security Aspects of Political Decentralization in Ukraine: Visions, Realities, and Possible Implications*. Kyiv: Center for Army, Conversion and Disarmament Studies.

Golos.ua. 2015. V Kiyeve Proshel Kruglyy Stol v Podderzhku Sozdaniya Osobogo Regiona 'Slobozhanshchina' v Khar'kovskoy Oblasti [In Kyiv, A Round Table Was Held in Support of the Creation of A Special Region "Slobozhanschina" in the Kharkiv Region], December 3. https://golos.ua/i/348227.

Grigas, Agnia. 2016. *Beyond Crimea: The New Russian Empire*. New Haven and London: Yale University Press.

Grinevetsky, Sergiy. 2015. Strasti za 'Porto-Franko [Passions around "Porto-Franco"], Dt.ua, April 3. https://dt.ua/internal/strasti-za-porto-franko-_.html.

Hamilton, Robert E.W. 2019. Coal Mines, Land Mines and Nuclear Bombs: The Environmental Cost of the War in Eastern Ukraine. FPRI, September 26. https://www.fpri.org/article/2019/09/coal-mines-land-mines-and-nuclear-bombs-the-environmental-cost-of-the-war-in-eastern-ukraine/?fbclid=IwAR2 XUyHyxlWymIjhlGB93d0zZmQGulYfXZ9RcR4RXJjeqkVkww9RHbphZt4.

Handzyuk, Kataryna. 2016. Viktor Medvedchuk Kroyetsya v Detalyakh [Medvedchuk Hides in the Details], *Argument.ua*, August 6. http://argumentua.com/stati/viktor-medvedchuk-kroetsya-v-detalyakh.

Holub, Andriy. 2019. Detsentralizatsiya: Nezavershena Reforma [Decentralisation: Unfinished Reform]. *Ukrayins'kyi Tyzhden*, February 11. https://tyzhden.ua/Politics/226325.

Honchar, Mykhaylo. 2016. Vid 'Velychi Rosiyi' do 'Velykoyi Yevraziyi': Viyna Hibrydnoho Typu Yak Mekhanizm Heopolitychnoy Ekspansiyi RF [From 'Great Russia' to 'Great Eurasia': Hybrid War as a Tool for the Geopolitical Expansion of the RF]. In *Natsyonal'na Bezpeka i Oborona [National Security and Defense]*, ed. Razumkov Centre, 72–80. http://razumkov.org.ua/uploads/journal/ukr/NSD167-168_2016_ukr.pdf.

Honcharenko, Oleksiy. 2019. Yak Zakon pro Stolytsyu Ukrayiny Domomahaye Protsesu Federalizatsii Ukrayiny [How the Law on the Capital of Ukraine Contributes to the Federalization Process in Ukraine]. *Ukrayins'ka Pravda*, October 10. https://www.pravda.com.ua/columns/2019/10/10/7228728/.

Hromadske Radio. 2017. Ukraine Calling 'Russia is the Aggressor, October 13. https://hromadskeradio.org/en/programs/ukraine-calling/russia-is-the-aggressor-ukraine-creates-new-legal-framework-with-donbas-reintegration-laws.

Ihnat, Ivan. 2016. Spetsial'nyi Ekonomichnyi Status ta Vybornist' Hubernatora Dopomozhut' Podolaty Sotsial'no-Ekonomichnu Kryzu u Zakarpatti (FOTO) [Special Economic Status and Election of Governor Will Help Overcome the Socio-Economic Crisis in Zakarpattya]. *Ua-reporter*, February 12. https://ua-reporter.com/uk/news/specialnyy-ekonomichnyy-status-ta-vybornist-gubernatora-dopomozhut-podolaty-socialno.

Interfax. 2014. Amnesty International NapolyahayenaVnesenniPravok do 'Zakonu pro Amnistiyu', shchob Unyknuty Bezkarnosti Tykh, Khto Katuvav Zaruchnykiv [Amnesty International Insists on Amendments to Amnesty Law to Avoid Avoidance of Prosecution for Those Who Tortured Prisoners], September 24. https://ua.interfax.com.ua/news/political/225256.html.

Kazanskyi, Denis. 2014. Kazanskyy: Na 'Mistsevomu Referendumi' 1994 Roku 80% Zhyteliv Donbasu Holosuvaly za Federalizatsiyu [Kazanskyy: During the 1994 Local Referendum, 80% of Donbas Residents Voted in Favor of Federalization]. *Ukrayins'kyi Tyzhden'*, December 19. https://tyzhden.ua/News/126090.

———. 2019. Detsentralizatsiya: Ne Vtratyty Krayinu [Decentralization: How Not to Lose the Country]. *Ukrayins'kyi Tyzhden*, February 12. https://tyzhden.ua/Politics/226331.

Kolibelkin, Anton. 2016. Putin Vidkryvaye Druhyi ta Tretiy Front na Odeshchyni [Putin Opens A Second and Third Fronts in Odessa]. *Depo.Odesa*, April 18.

https://odesa.depo.ua/ukr/odesa/yak-truhanov-pishe-pidruchniki-pro-novorosiyu-ta-dozvolyae-shabashi-18042016170000.

Kommersant. 2019. Podpisi Vsekh Storon pod 'Formuloy Shtaynmayera' [Signatures of All Parties under the "Steinmeier Formula"], October 2. https://www.kommersant.ru/doc/4111132.

Kompaniiets, Alesia. 2018. Decentralization Projects in the Context of Resolving the Crisis in Ukraine. *Gagra Institute*, April. https://gagrainstitute.org/wp-content/uploads/2018/08/Alesia-Kompaniiets-Decentralisation-Projects-in-the-Context-of-Resolving-the-Crisis-in-Ukraine.pdf.

Korrespondent. 2015. Rada Online: Kryvavi Zavorushennya pid Budivleyu Parlamentu [Rada Online: Violent Clashes under Parliament's Building], August 31. https://ua.korrespondent.net/ukraine/3557261-rada-onlain-kryvavi-zavorushennia-pid-budivleui-parlamentu.

———. 2019a. RF Trebuet Pys'menno Zakrepit' Formulu Shtaynmayera [Russia Demands to Have Written Confirmation of Steinmeier Formula], September 13. https://korrespondent.net/ukraine/politics/4139618-rf-trebuet-pysmenno-zakrepyt-formulu-shtainmaiera.

———. 2019b. Ukrayina Nazvala Umovy za 'Formuloyu Shtaynmayera' [Ukraine Named Conditions for the "Steinmeier Formula"], September 18. https://ua.korrespondent.net/ukraine/4141268-ukraina-nazvala-umovy-za-formuloui-shtainmaiera.

Kremlin. 2013. Kontseptsiya Obshchestvennoy Bezopasnosti v Rossiyskoy Federatsii [Public Safety Concept of the Russian Federation], November 20. http://kremlin.ru/acts/news/19653.

Kuromiya, Hiroaki. 2002. *Svoboda i Teror u Donbasi. Ukrayins'ko-Rosiys'ke Prykrodonnya, 1870–1990-i Roky* [Freedom and Terror in the Donbas. A Ukrainian-Russian Borderland, 1870s–1990s]. Kyiv: Osnovy.

Leitch, Duncan. 2015. Decentralization: The Wrong Solution to the Wrong Problem? *Ukrainian Week*, June 25. https://ukrainianweek.com/Politics/139503.

Mazur, Evgeniya. 2019. Vidnovlennya Separatyzmu v Odesi: Chy Zmozhe 'Porto-Franko' Znyshchyty Ukrayins'ku Ekonomiku [Revival of Separatism in Odessa: Can Porto-Franco Destroy Ukraine's Economy]. *24 Novyny*, April 12. https://24tv.ua/vidnovlennya_separatizmu_v_odesi_chi_zmozhe_porto_franko_znishhiti_ukrayinsku_ekonomiku_n1139815.

Minakov, Oleksiy. 2019. P'yat' Nehatyvnykh Naslidkiv Cherez Ofitsiyne Uzhodzhennya 'Formuly Shtaynmayyera' [Five Negative Implications Following the Official Agreement of the Steinmeier Formula]. *Facebook*, October 3. https://www.facebook.com/olexiy.minakov/posts/2698944920139442.

Minregion. 2015. Prefekt. Khto Vin dlya Mistsevoho Samovraduvannya? [The Prefect. What Is Its Role in Local Self-Government?], December 14. http://www.minregion.gov.ua/wp-content/uploads/2015/12/perfekt.png.

Moser, Michael. 2013. *Language Policy and the Discourse of Languages in Ukraine under President Viktor Yanukovych (25 February 2019–28 October 2012)*. Stuttgart: ibidem-Verlag.

Nayem, Mustafa. 2019. Formula Shtaynmayera: Pochemu Kritichno Vazhna Pozitsiya Narodnykh Deputatov [Steinmeier's Formula: Why the Position of MPs Is Critically Important], October 2. https://24tv.ua/formula_shtaynmayera_pochemu_kritichno_vazhna_pozitsiya_narodnyih_deputatov_n1213530.

News.online.ua. 2016. V RF Obyasnili, Pochemu Putin Pokhoronil Ideyu "Novcrossii" [The Russian Federation Clarified Why Putin Buried the Idea of "Novcrossiya"], April 23. https://news.online.ua/740501/v-rf-obyasnili-pochemu-putin-pohoronil-ideyu-novorossii/.

Novosti. 2019. Velychezna Pomylka Zelenskoho [Zelenskyy's Huge Mistake], October 3. https://nv.ua/ukr/opinion/zelenskiy-ta-formula-shtaynmayyera-shcho-pridumav-kreml-novini-ukrajini-50045983.html

Peters, Tim, and Anastasiia Shapkina. 2019. The Grand Stalemate of the Minsk Agreements. Konrad Adenauer Stiftung. https://www.kas.de/documents/252038/4520172/The+Grand+Stalemate+of+the+Minsk+Agreements.pdf/fc13c8d8-d7e3-7041-b959-a94282b3f8af?version=1.0&t=1549899307207.

Polegkyi, Oleksii. 2011. Changes in Russian Foreign Policy Discourse and Concept of "Russian World". *Pecob's Papers Series*, no. 11: 1–25. https://repository.uantwerpen.be/docman/irua/a3e907/139593.pdf.

Polishchuk, Iryna. 2019. Yak Ukrayini Traktuvaty Zayavu Vatazhkiv ORDLO Shchodo Pidpysanoyi Formuly Shatynmayera [How Ukraine Should Interpret the Statement from "DPR"/"LPR" Militias on the Signed Steinmeier Formula], *24 Novyny*, October 2.

Potapchuk, N. 2016. Chy Znaye Prem'yer pro Skarhu 'Tytul'noho Suverennoho Narodu Ukrayiny'? [Does the Prime Minister Know About the Complaint from Titular Sovereign People of Ukraine?]. *Ukrinform*, April 26. https://www.ukrinform.ua/rubric-other_news/2006963-ci-znae-premer-pro-skargu-titulnogo-suverennogo-narodu-ukraini.html.

President of the Russian Federation. 1999. Federal'nyi Zakon: O Gosudarstvennoi Politike Rossiiskoi Federatsii v Otnoshenii Sootechestvennikov za Rubezhom [Federal Law: On the State Policy of the Russian Federation regarding Compatriots Abroad]. http://www.kremlin.ru/acts/bank/13875/page/1.

Prestupnosti.NET. 2016. Zaderzhannaya v Khar'kove Kommunistka Pytalas' Podkupit' Mestnykh Deputatov za Golosovaniye po Federalizatsii,—SBU [The Communist Detained in Kharkov Tried to Bribe Local Deputies Regarding the

Vote on Federalization,—SBU], June 26. https://news.pn/ru/criminal/163309.

Protsyuk, Oksana. 2016. Anatoliy Tkachuk: Stvorennya Detsentralizovanoyi Ukrayiny Vyvodyt' Yiyi z Kremlivs'koyi Matrytsi [Anatoliy Tkachuk: Creating A Decentralized Ukraine Removes It from the Kremlin Matrix]. *Decentralization*, September 19. https://decentralization.gov.ua/news/3302?page=92.

RBK. 2017. Krym Vmyesto DNR: Kak v Pravitel'stvye Obsuzhdayut Otkaz ot Pomoshchi Donbasu [Crimea Instead of DPR: How the Government Is Discussing the Rejection of Assistance to Donbas], September 15. https://www.rbc.ru/economics/15/09/2017/59b84cc99a7947ce896ad25c?utm_source=dlvr.it&utm_medium=twitter#xtor=AL-%5Binternal_traffic%5D%2D%2D%5Brss.rbc.ru%5D-%5Btop_stories_brief_news%5D.

RFE/RL. 2019. HPU Vidkryla Spravu Proty Medvedchuka za Pidozroyu v Derzhradi [GPO Opened Proceedings against Medvedchuk for Treason], February 5. https://www.radiosvoboda.org/a/news-medvedchuk-gpu-derzhrada/29752478.html.

RIA Novosti. 2019. V DNR Prinyali Zakon o Gosgranitse [The DPR Adopted A Law on State Border], November 29. https://ria.ru/20191129/1561741247.html.

Rogin, John. 2017. Trump Administration Approves Lethal Arms Sales to Ukraine. *Washington Post*, December 20. https://www.washingtonpost.com/news/josh-rogin/wp/2017/12/20/trump-administration-approves-lethal-arms-sales-to-ukraine/?utm_term=.c15f8064dbaa.

Ryzhkov, Vladimir. 2014. Putin's Federalization Card in Ukraine. *The Moscow Times*, April 7. https://www.themoscowtimes.com/2014/04/07/putins-federalization-card-in-ukraine-a33715.

Samokhvalova, Dana. 2012. Navishcho Ukrayini Federalizatsiya vid Kuma Putina [What Is Ukraine's Federalization from Putin's Crony for]. *UNIAN*, July 19. https://www.unian.ua/politics/675233-navischo-ukrajini-federalizatsiya-vid-kuma-putina.html.

Sargsyan, Anna. 2019. Unpacking Complexity in the Ukraine Peace Process. *CSS ETH Zuric*, no. 243. https://css.ethz.ch/content/dam/ethz/special-interest/gess/cis/center-for-securities-studies/pdfs/CSSAnalyse243-EN.pdf.

Sasse, Gwendolyn. 2001. The 'New' Ukraine: A State of Regions. *Regional & Federal Studies* 11 (3): 69–100.

Segodnya. 2017. V SBU Rospovily, Chym Nebezpechni 'Feykovi Hromady' i Khto Nymy Keruye [The SBU Explained Why "Fake Communities" are Dangerous and Who is Managing Them], May 23. https://ukr.segodnya.ua/politics/v-sbu-rasskazali-chem-opasny-feykovye-gromady-i-kto-imi-rukovodit-1023417.html.

Shandra, Alya, and Robert Seely. 2019. *The Surkov Leaks. The Inner Workings of Russia's Hybrid War in Ukraine.* London: RUSI. https://rusi.org/sites/default/files/201907_op_surkov_leaks_web_final.pdf.

Shevel, Oxana. 2011. Russian Nation-building from Yeltsin to Medvedev: Ethnic, Civic or Purposefully Ambiguous? *Europe-Asia Studies* 63 (2): 179–202.

Skorokhod, Olha. 2019. Vitse-Prem'yer Hennadiy Zubko: 'My Zmenshymo Kil'kist' Rayoniv, Ale Nablyzymo Posluhy do Lyudey'. KARTA [Deputy Prime Minister Gennady Zubko: 'We Will Reduce the Number of Districts but Bring Services Closer to the People'. MAP]. *Censor.net*, August 29. https://censor.net.ua/resonance/3145090/vtsepremr_gennadyi_zubko_mi_zmenshimo_klkst_rayionv_ale_nablizimo_poslugi_do_lyudeyi_karta.

Sluzhba Bezspeky. 2017. U Sumakh SBU Prypynyla Nezakonnu Diyal'nist' Feykovoyi 'Teryorial'noyi Hromady' [In Sumy the SBU Stopped Illegal Activity of the Fake "Territorial Community"], April 6. https://ssu.gov.ua/ua/news/1/category/2/view/3118#.TczI2zOz.dpbs.

Spirin, Yevhen. 2019. Usi Obhovoryuyut' 'Formulu Shtaynmayera' i Kazhut' pro 'Kapitulyatsiyu', A Ya Nichoho Ne Rozumiyu. Dopomozhit'! Shcho Tse Vse Oznachaye? [Everyone Is Discussing the Steinmeier Formula and There Is Talk about 'Capitulation,' But I Don't Understand Anything. Help! What Does This All Mean?], September 19. https://thebabel.com.ua/amp/texts/35908-usi-obgovoryuyut-formulu-shtaynmayera-i-govoryat-pro-kapitulyaciyu-a-ya-nichogo-ne-rozumiyu-dopomozhit-shcho-ce-vse-oznachaye-spoyler-nichogo.

Socor, Vladimir. 2019. Steinmeier's Formula: Its Background and Development in the Normandy and Minsk Processes (Part One). *Eurasia Daily Monitor* 16 (130). https://jamestown.org/program/steinmeiers-formula-its-background-and-development-in-the-normandy-and-minsk-processes-part-one/?mc_cid=3c4d533e1e&mc_eid=f414a65734.

Sologoub, Ilona et al. 2019. Decentralization Cannot Be Rolled Back Because The Reform Is Too Popular Among People. *Vox Ukraine*, July 1. https://voxukraine.org/en/decentralization-cannot-be-rolled-back-because-the-reform-is-too-popular-among-people/.

Sultanova, Yulia. 2015. Detsentralizatsiya yak Shcheplennya vid Separatyzmu [Decentralization as Vaccination against Separatism]. *Unian*, March 2. https://decentralization.unian.ua/1050526-detsentralizatsiya-yak-scheplennya-vid-separatizmu.html.

Swain, Adam, and Vlad Mykhnenko. 2007. The Ukrainian Donbas in 'Transition'. In *Reconstructing the Post-Soviet Industrial Region*, ed. Adam Swain, 7–46. London and New York: Routledge.

TASS. 2019. Pushilin Predlozhil Sdelat' Russkiy Yedinstvennym Gosudarstvennym Yazykom v DNR [Pushilin Proposed To Declare Russian the Only Official Language in the DPR], December 2. https://tass.ru/obschestvo/7242393.

252 J. BARBIERI

Terhromada.blogspot.com. 2016. Krayina z Oznakamy Derzhavnoho Separatyzmu [A Country with Symptoms of Separatism], December 17. http://tergromada.blogspot.com/2016/12/blog-post_17.html

Texty.org.ua. 2016a. Separatysts'kyy Proekt Medvedchuka. Pid Vyhlyadom 'Terytorial'nykh Hromad' po Vsiy Ukrayini Stvoryuyut'sya 'L-DNRy' [Medvedchuk's Separatist Project. Under the Guise of "Territorial Communities", "L-DNRs" are being created all over Ukraine], July 5. http://texty.org.ua/pg/article/txts/read/68839/Separatystskyj_projekt_Medvedchuka_Pid_vygladom_terytorialnyh_gromad.

———. 2016b. Na Chernihivshchyni Z'yavylysya Friky-Separatysty—Ale Seryozno Finansovanii Pidhotovani (FOTO) [Separatist Freaks Appear in the Chernihiv Region—But Properly Funded and Prepared (PHOTOS)], October 21. http://texty.org.ua/pg/news/textynewseditor/read/71710/Na_Chernigivshhyni_zjavylysa_frikyseparatysty__ale_serozno.

Todorov, Ihor. 2019. Uryvky z Shchodennyka (Poky Nenapysanoho) [Excerpts from A Diary (Yet To Be Written)"], Den', March 24. https://day.kyiv.ua/uk/blog/suspilstvo/uryvky-z-shchodennyka-poky-nenapysanogo.

TSN. 2015. SBU Sorvala Vozmozhnoe Sozdanie 'Zaporozhskoy Narodnoy Respubliki [The SBU Disbanded a Prospective Meeting of the "Zaporizzhyan People's Republic"], December 12. https://ru.tsn.ua/politika/sbu-sorvala-vozmozhnoe-sozdanie-zaporozhskoy-narodnoy-respubliki-543071.html.

———. 2018. Uryad Skhvalyv Zakonoproekt pro Novyi Terytorial'nyi Ustriy Ukrayiny [The Government Approved the Bill on the New Territorial Structure of Ukraine], February 21. https://tsn.ua/politika/uryad-shvaliv-zakonopro-ekt-pro-noviy-teritorialniy-ustriy-ukrayini-1113201.html.

Ukraine Crisis Media Center. 2017. Feykovi Hromady: Zahroza Natsional'niy Bezpetsi [Fake Communities: A Threat to National Security], June 29.

Ukrainian Weekly. 2019. The 'Steinmeier Formula': Possible Scenarios for the Upcoming Normandy-Format Meeting, September 20. http://www.ukrweekly.com/uwwp/the-steinmeier-formula-possible-scenarios-for-the-upcoming-normandy-format-meeting/.

Ukrayins'ka Pravda. 2016. Lutsenko Rozpoviv pro Novu Skhemu Medvedchuka—Terytorial'ni Hromady [Lutsenko Speaks About Medvedchuk's New Scheme—Territorial Communities], July 16. https://www.pravda.com.ua/news/2016/07/16/7114993/.

———. 2017. SBU: Rosiya Finansuye Deyaki Ukrayins'ki Politychni Proekty [SBU: Russia Is Bankrolling Certain Ukrainian Political Projects], February 21. https://www.pravda.com.ua/news/2017/02/21/7136042/.

Ukrayins'kyi Vybir. 2014. VHR 'Ukrayins'kyy Vybir' Proponuye Kontsept Federatyvnoyi Reformy v Ukrayini [All-Ukrainian Social Movement "Ukrainian Choice" Proposes the Concept of Federal Reform in Ukraine], March 23. http://vybor.ua/article/zayavlenie/vgr-ukrayinskiy-vibir-proponue-koncept-federativnoyi-reformi-v-ukrayini.html.

———. 2016. Zayavlenie [Statement], July 16. http://vybor.ua/article/zayavlenie/zayavlenie-1-2-3-4-5-6-7-8-9-10-11-12-13-14-15-16-17-18-19-20-21-22-23-24.html.

Ukrinform. 2019. Nova Rada Mozhe Pryinyaty Zakoni Vyrishyty 'Problemu 2020'—ekspert [The New Parliament Could Approve the Bill and Solve the "Problem of 2020"—Expert], May 27. https://www.ukrinform.ua/rubric-regions/2708934-nova-rada-moze-prijnati-zakon-i-virisiti-problemu-2020-ekspert.html.

Umland, Andreas. 2019. How Ukraine's Decentralization Makes the Country More Resilient and Helps Post-Soviet Democratization. *New Eastern Europe*, January 31. http://neweasterneurope.eu/2019/01/31/how-ukraines-decentralisation-makes-the-country-more-resilient-and-helps-post-soviet-democratisation/.

Unian. 2009. Zatulin o Khmel'nitskom, Yushchenko i Znake v Nuzhnyy Moment [Zatulin on Khmel'nytskyy, Yushchenko and Signalling at the Right Time], January 12. https://www.unian.net/world/179446-zatulin-o-hmelnitskom-yuschenko-i-znake-v-nujnyiy-moment.html.

———. 2018a. Lavrov Zayavil, Chto Zakon o Reintegratsii Donbassa 'Perecherkivaet' Minskie Dogovorennosti [Lavrov Claimed That the Law on the Reintegration of Donbass "Crosses Out" the Minsk Agreement], January 19. https://www.unian.net/politics/2356165-lavrov-zayavil-chto-zakon-o-reintegratsii-donbassa-perecherkivaet-minskie-dogovorennosti.html.

———. 2018b. V MID RF Podnyali Isteriku iz-za Zakona Ukrainy o Deokupatsii i Nazvali Yevo 'Podgatovkoi k Novoi Voyne' [The Russian Foreign Ministry Raised a Tantrum Because of the Law of Ukraine on De-occupation and Called It 'Preparation for a New War"], January 18. https://www.unian.net/politics/2353853-v-mid-rf-podnyali-isteriku-iz-za-zakona-ukrainyi-o-deoku-patsii-i-nazvali-ego-podgotovkoy-k-novoy-voyne.html.

———. 2019. Ukraine's Foreign Minister 'Already Agreed' to 'Steinmeier Formula' of Donbas Settlement, September 18. https://www.unian.info/politics/10690209-ukraine-s-foreign-minister-already-agreed-to-steinmeier-formula-of-donbas-settlement.html.

Verkhovna Rada. 2006. Pro Zahal'ni Zasady Stvorennyai Funktsionuvannya Spetsial'nykh (Vil'nykh) EkonomichnykhZon [On the General Principles of the Creation and Functioning of Special (Free) Economic Zones]. https://zakon.rada.gov.ua/laws/show/2673-12.

———. 2014a. Pro Skhvalennya Kontseptsiyi ReformuvannyaMistsevoho Samovryaduvannya ta Terytorial'noyi Orhanizatsiyi Vlady v Ukrayini [On Approval of the Concept of the Reform of Local Self-Government and Territorial Organization of Power in Ukraine]. April. https://zakon5.rada.gov.ua/laws/show/333-2014-p.

254   J. BARBIERI

————. 2014b. Pro Spivrobitnytstvo Terytorial'nykh Hromad [On Cooperation of Territorial Communities], June 17. https://zakon2.rada.gov.ua/laws/show/1508-18.

————. 2014c. Pro Osoblyvyi Poryadok Mistsevoho Samovryaduvannya v Okremykh Rayonakh Donets'koyi ta Luhans'koyi Oblastey [On the Special Order of Local Self-Government in Certain Districts of the Donetsk and Luhansk Regions], September 17. https://zakon.rada.gov.ua/laws/show/1680-18/ed20140916.

————. 2014d. Verkhovna Rada Ukrayiny Ukhvalyla Zakon 'Pro Nedopushchennya Peresliduvannya ta Pokarannya Osib-Uchasnykiv Podiyna Terytoriyi Donets'koyi ta Luhans'koyi Oblastey' [The Verkhovna Rada of Ukraine Adopted the Law "On Prevention of Persecution and Punishment of Individuals Who Participated in the events in the Donets'k and Luhans'k Regions"], September 16. https://www.rada.gov.ua/news/Novyny/Povidomlennya/97812.html.

————. 2015a. Pro Dobrovil'ne Ob'yednannya Terytorial'nykh Hromad [On Voluntary Amalgamation of Territorial Communities], February 5. https://zakon.rada.gov.ua/laws/show/157-19/ed20150205.

————. 2015b. Pro Vnesennya Zmin do Byudzhetnoho Kodeksu Ukrayiny Shchodo Osoblyvostey Formuvannya ta Vykonannya Byudzhetiv Ob'yednanykh Terytorial'nykh Hromad [On Amendments to the Budget Code of Ukraine on Features of Formation and Execution of Budgets of United Territorial Communities], November 26. https://zakon.rada.gov.ua/laws/show/837-19.

————. 2015c. Proekt Zakonu pro Vnesennya Zmin do Konstytutsiyi Ukrayiny (shchodo Detsentralizatsiyi Vlady) [Draft Law on Amendments to the Constitution of Ukraine (on Decentralization of Power)], July 1. http://w1.c1.rada.gov.ua/pls/zweb2/webproc4_1?pf3511=55812.

————. 2015d. Pro Vnesennya Zminy do Statti 10 Zakonu Ukrayiny 'Pro Osoblyvyi Poryadok Mistsevoho Samovryaduvannya v Okremykh Rayonakh Donets'koyi ta Luhans'koyi Oblastey [On Amendment to Article 10 of the Law of Ukraine "On Special Order of Local Self-Government in Separate Districts of the Donetsk and Luhansk Regions"], March 17. https://zakon.rada.gov.ua/laws/show/256-19/ed20150321#n2.

————. 2015e. Pro Skhvalennya Zvernen' vid Imeni Ukrayiny do Rady Bezpeky Orhanizatsiyi i Ob'yednanykh Natsiy ta Rady Yevropeys'koho Soyuzu Stosovno Rozhortannyana Terytoriy i Ukrayiny Mizhnarodnoyi Operatsiyi z Pidtrymannya Myrui Bezpeky [On the Approval of the Application on Behalf of Ukraine to the United Nations Security Council and the Council of the European Union Concerning the Deployment of An International Peace and Security Operation in Ukraine], March 17. https://zakon3.rada.gov.ua/laws/show/253-19/paran2#n2.

8 THE DARK SIDE OF DECENTRALIZATION REFORM IN UKRAINE... 255

———. 2015f. Pro Vnesennya Zmin do Deyakykh Zakoniv Ukrayiny shchodo Vyznachennya Daty Pochatku Tymchasovoyi Okupatsiyi [On Amendments to Some Laws of Ukraine on Establishing the Starting Date of the Temporary Occupation], September 15. https://zakon.rada.gov.ua/laws/show/685-19#n7.

———. 2017. Proekt Zakonu pro Stvorennya Neobkhidnykh Umovd dlya Myrnoho Vrehulyuvannya Sytuatsiyi v Okremykh Rayonakh Donetskoyi ta Luhanskoyi Oblastey [Draft Law on Creating the Necessary Conditions for the Peaceful Resolution of the Situation in Certain Districts of the Donetsk and Luhansk Regions], October 6. https://zakon.rada.gov.ua/laws/show/2167-viii.

———. 2018a. Proekt Zakonu pro Zasady Administratyvno-Terytorial'noho Ustroyu Ukrayiny [On the Principles of the Administrative and Territorial Structure of Ukraine], February 22. http://w1.c1.rada.gov.ua/pls/zweb2/webproc4_1?pf3511=63508.

———. 2018b. Pro Osoblyvosti Derzhavnoyi Politykyiz Zabezpechennya Derzhavnoho Suverenitetu Ukrayiny na Tymchasovo Okupovanykh Terytcriyakh u Donets'kiy ta Luhans'kiy Oblastyakh [On the Aspects of State Policy on the Restoration of the State Sovereignty of Ukraine over the Temporarily Occupied Territory of the Donetsk and Luhansk Regions], January 18 https://zakon.rada.gov.ua/laws/show/2268-viii.

———. 2019a. Proekt Zakonu pro Nedopushchennya Kryminal'noho Peresliduvannya, Prytyahnennya do Kryminal'noyi, Administratyvnoyi Vidpovidal'nosti ta Pokarannya Osib- Uchasnykiv Podiy na Terytoriyi Donetskoyi, Luhanskoyi Oblastey [Draft Law on Prevention of Persecution, Criminal Prosecution, Administrative Responsibility and Punishment of Individuals Who Participated in the Events in Donetsk, Luhansk Regions], August 29. http://w1.c1.rada.gov.ua/pls/zweb2/webproc4_1?pf3511=66338.

———. 2019b. Proekt Zakony pro Misto Kyiv—Stolytsyi Ukrayiny [Draft Law on the City of Kyiv—Capital of Ukraine], September 24. http://w1.c1.rada.gov.ua/pls/zweb2/webproc4_1?pf3511=66939.

Vynohradov, Oleksiy. 2016. Severodonetskiy S'yezd 2004 Goda Byl Repetitsiyey Pered Nastoyashchey Agressiyey Rossii—Politolog [For Russia, the 2004 Severodonetsk Congress Was A Rehearsal Before the Real Aggression—(Says) Political Scientist]. RFE/RL Radio Svoboda [Radio Freedom], November 28. https://www.radiosvoboda.org/a/28144452.html.

Wilson, Andrew. 2016. The Donbas in 2014: Explaining Civil Conflict Perhaps, But Not Civil War. *Europe-Asia Studies* 68 (4): 631–652.

Wolczuk, Kataryna. 2002. Catching Up with 'Europe'? Constitutional Debates on the Territorial-Administrative Model in Independent Ukraine. *Regional and Federal Studies* 12 (2): 65–88.

256   J. BARBIERI

Wolff, Stefan, and Marc Weller. 2005. Self-determination and Autonomy: A Conceptual Introduction. In *Autonomy, Self-Governance and Conflict Resolution. Innovative Approaches to Institutional Design in Divided Societies*, edited by Stefan Wolff and Marc Weller. London and New York: Routledge.

Youngs, Richard. 2014. Decentralization: Ukraine's Rub. *Carnegie Europe*, May 16. https://carnegieeurope.eu/strategiceurope/55612.

Zolkina, Mariia, and Sydorenko, Serhiy. 2019. Ukrayinizatsiya Shtaynmayera: Yak Zrobyty Ideyu Kremlya Bezpechnoyu dlya Ukrayiny. *Ukrayins'ka Pravda*, September 19. https://www.eurointegration.com.ua/articles/2019/09/19/7100928/.

PART IV

Decentralization, Its Perceptions and Linkage to Democratization, Modernization, and European Integration of Ukraine

CHAPTER 9

Decentralization and a Risk of Local Elite Capture in Ukraine

Max Bader

INTRODUCTION

The decentralization of government has been one of the most comprehensive and consequential of Ukraine's reforms since the Euromaidan Revolution. It is poised to stimulate economic development outside the major cities, increase the quality of governance at the subnational level, and strengthen accountability and popular participation in local and regional politics. Most existing accounts of the effects of decentralization so far describe the reform as a success, emphasizing in particular the increased budgets of local communities and their greater financial autonomy.

Less attention has been paid to other effects of the reform, including its effects on the practice of local government. In the theoretical literature on decentralization, there are several arguments for why it is related to democratization. Decentralization in particular is asserted to give a boost to popular participation in political processes, and to strengthen

---

M. Bader (✉)
Leiden University, Leiden, The Netherlands
e-mail: m.bader@hum.leidenuniv.nl

© The Author(s) 2020
H. Shelest, M. Rabinovych (eds.), *Decentralization, Regional Diversity, and Conflict*, Federalism and Internal Conflicts,
https://doi.org/10.1007/978-3-030-41765-9_9

259

accountability mechanisms by bringing government closer to people. The theoretical research on decentralization, however, also warns of certain risks, including that of local elites exploiting decentralization reform to further their personal interests at the expense of the public good.

This study considers the risk of local elite capture in the ongoing decentralization reform in Ukraine. Drawing on empirical evidence, it finds a number of reasons to assume that the implementation of the decentralization reform in a range of places has likely created opportunities for local elite capture. Data for this study have been collected through extensive fieldwork in Kharkiv Oblast and Odesa Oblast and analysis of reports in (mostly) local Ukrainian media. In Kharkiv Oblast and Odesa Oblast, 149 interviews were conducted with representatives of the newly formed amalgamated territorial communities of these regions, as well as with local civic activists, between March 2017 and April 2018. The insights gained from fieldwork in Kharkiv Oblast and Odesa Oblast serve as an illustration of broader consequences and potential consequences of decentralization in Ukraine.

Section "The Promise and Flaws of Decentralization in Ukraine" discusses elements of the decentralization reform that are relevant for the subsequent discussion. Section "Decentralization and Democracy" looks at the relationship between decentralization and democratization as described and analyzed in academic and non-academic theoretical literature, and outlines the benefits and risks for democracy and the quality of local government that are associated with decentralization. Section "The Risk of Local Elite Capture", the main section, looks at the available evidence that points to the risk of local elite capture in current decentralization reform.

I. The Promise and Flaws of Decentralization in Ukraine

Government at the sub-national level in Ukraine comprises elements of state administration in the form of governors and district (*rayon*) heads, both appointed by the central authorities, as well as elements of self-government, represented by respective councils at the regional, district, and municipal level and by elected municipality heads. In this "dual model of authority" (Aasland and Lyska 2016, 4), state administration has traditionally been much more powerful than self-government. At the municipal level, executive heads are directly elected, along with legislative councils, but appointed governors and district heads in practice wield great influence over the affairs of the municipalities. This status quo has long been viewed as one of the biggest flaws of governance in Ukraine. The dominant influence of higher-level authorities on municipalities has disempowered local communities and has violated the principle of subsidiarity (Tkachuk 2012, 7). In addition, the weakness of self-government has likely impeded economic development and negatively affected the quality of government in municipalities (Hanushchak 2013, 12).

1. Decentralization Reform in Ukraine: The Essentials

The Euromaidan Revolution of 2013–2014 provided new impetus to the objective of decentralizing government. Soon after the Revolution, on April 1, 2014, the Verkhovna Rada adopted the order "On the Approval of the Reform Concept of Local Self-Government and the Territorial Organization of Power in Ukraine," which set out the basic principles of the new government's decentralization reform.[1] This reform essentially has two tracks. The first concerns a comprehensive overhaul of subnational government, requiring a set of amendments to the Constitution.[2] As a consequence of the overhaul of subnational government, three types of sub-national administrative entities are slated to remain: regions, districts, and communities. State administrations at the regional and district levels will be abolished, and instead district legislatures and regional legislatures will form executive bodies. Centrally appointed prefects will monitor compliance with the constitution by subnational administrations and coordinate the work of state institutions at the subnational level. The constitutional amendments are highly controversial and, as of March 2020, have not been adopted.

The second track of the decentralization reform, which is more relevant to this study, concerns the merging of municipalities into so-called amalgamated territorial communities (ATCs), coupled with a devolution of powers and resources from districts to the newly formed ATCs. The creation of larger municipalities is intended to remedy two existing obstacles of local self-government in Ukraine. The first of these is the inability of

---

[1] The reform concept can be consulted here: http://zakon5.rada.gov.ua/laws/show/333-2014-%D1%80.

[2] The proposed constitutional amendments can be consulted here: http://w1.c1.rada.gov.ua/pls/zweb2/webproc4_1?pf3511=55812.

most municipalities to generate substantial revenues. Before the decentralization reform, the biggest share of municipal budgets generally consisted of transfers from higher-level state administrations (Chumak and Shevliakov 2009, 8). Municipal authorities, moreover, largely lacked the power to decide on how funds were disbursed inside the municipality (Sydorchuk 2015, 2). The shortage of self-generated resources and limited financial autonomy are seen as a reason for the low quality of service delivery in the municipalities (Chumak and Shevliakov 2009, 6). The second obstacle to effective self-government that the creation of larger municipalities addresses is the lack of qualified professional staff at municipalities' executive level (Chumak and Shevliakov 2009, 21; Tkachuk 2017). Many rural communities in Ukraine are confronted with depopulation, as young people in particular move away, and many of the over 10,000 rural municipalities, half of which had fewer than 1,000 residents, existed before the start of the reform, and suffered from a shortage of qualified professional staff.

Two pieces of legislation have been crucial for the implementation of the second track of the decentralization reform. Amendments to the tax and budget codes of Ukraine, which were adopted in December 2014, stipulate that a larger share of taxes is to be transferred to local budgets and that municipalities, including ATCs, receive greater opportunities to levy taxes locally (Sydorchuk 2015, 3). ATCs gain additional powers, responsibilities, and resources once they are recognized by the regional authorities as sufficiently capable. Altogether, the newly formed ATCs should both have larger budgets and enjoy greater financial autonomy. The Law of Ukraine "On Voluntary Amalgamation of Territorial Communities," adopted in February 2015, opened a way for the process of the ATC formation,[3] which, in its turn, follows a number of fixed steps, including public hearings in all municipalities that would unite in a prospective ATC, a vote in the relevant municipality councils, and a decision by regional authorities on whether the formation of the ATC meets legal requirements. Crucially, the amalgamation of municipalities must be voluntary, meaning that it is initiated from within the municipalities, supported by the municipal councils of all relevant municipalities, and free from coercion by external forces. At the same time, regional authorities draw up a so-called "prospective plan" outlining the borders of

---

[3] The Law of Ukraine "On Voluntary Amalgamation of Territorial Communities" can be consulted here: http://zakon5.rada.gov.ua/laws/show/15719/print1457728359241365.

prospective ATCs in the region. These "prospective plans," however, are not binding and cannot be imposed.

2. Decentralization and Its Discontents

From the moment when a substantial number of ATCs had been formed, the decentralization reform has often been hailed as a success story. President Poroshenko, for instance, in December 2017, described decentralization as one of the most successful reforms undertaken during his presidency.[4] Whenever the decentralization reform is presented as a success story, reference is typically made to the larger budgets and greater financial autonomy of ATCs.[5] According to figures mentioned by president Poroshenko, the budget of all municipalities had increased from 69 billion hryvnia to 171 billion hryvnia (approximately 6 billion euros) by 2017. There are many reports of newly formed ATCs which have constructed new public facilities, built roads, and taken on long-overdue repair works.

The decentralization reform process, however, is not without problems. ATC formation is to a great extent uneven and uncoordinated. According to the draft constitutional amendments of the first track of decentralization, all municipalities that existed before the start of the decentralization reform should join ATCs. The prospective plans envision that altogether around 1,500 ATCs will be formed. By the end of 2019, the number of ATCs stood at 662.[6] While this may suggest that a substantial share of the prospective ATCs had already been formed by the end of 2017, only 3,094 of the almost 12,000 municipalities had been amalgamated.[7] Many newly formed ATCs comprise fewer former municipalities than planned. Most ATCs, moreover, are not formed in accordance with the prospective plans that were developed by the regional authorities. It is

---

[4] See "Petro Poroshenko: Detsentralizatsiya stala odnieiu z nayuspishnishykh, nayrezultatyvnishykh reform" [Decentralization became one of most successful reforms, reforms with best results," December 4, 2017, https://prm.ua/petro-poroshenko-detsentralizatsiya-stala-odniyeyu-z-nayuspishnishih-nayrezultativnishih-reform/.

[5] E.g. Ministry of Regional Development, *Detsentralizatsiya. Vykonannya dokhodiv mistsevykh byudzhetiv za 10 mesiatsiv 2016 roku* [Decentralization. Execution of the revenue of local budgets during the first 10 months of 2016], http://old.decentralization.gov.ua/pics/attachments/MinReg_December-mini_(DRUK).pdf.

[6] By the end of 2019, the number of newly formed ATCs had increased to 995.

[7] Calculations made on the basis of data from https://gromada.info/.

not clear how the process of ATC formation will be completed. In some regions, such as the Bessarabia region of Odesa Oblast, there seems to be little appetite for ATC formation. In other regions, ATCs have formed but many municipalities have been left out. Provisions for municipalities to join already formed ATCs are in place, but there are relatively few places where this has happened. There has been widespread speculation that at some point "remaining" municipalities would be forcibly joined to already existing ATCs, but it is not clear how this would be done.

There are a number of explanations why more ATCs have not yet been formed, and why the ATCs that have been formed comprise relatively few former municipalities. The most common explanation offered is that stakeholders at different levels, from municipalities to the national legislature, resist the formation of ATCs. Municipality heads and members of the executive committees of municipalities which would be located outside the center of a prospective ATC are in many cases likely to lose their positions; hence, they are often reluctant to join an ATC. Municipality heads whose settlement is in the center of a prospective ATC face the likelihood of having to compete in and win an election to become the head of the new ATC, so they, too, have an incentive to hold back ATC formation. District authorities, in their turn, face an uncertain future because of the decentralization reform. When ATCs are formed, substantial powers and resources are devolved from the districts to the ATCs. After the first track of the reform is finally implemented, the number of districts will be reduced, and district heads, members of the executive staff in the districts, and members of district legislatures may lose their positions. Thus in many regions they seek to block ATC formation or to lobby for the formation of ATCs whose borders coincide with those of currently existing districts. Yet other actors with strong motives to resist ATC formation are lawmakers in regional legislatures and the Verkhovna Rada, because they may fear losing influence over their districts (constituencies).[8]

Another problem generated by decentralization is new tensions in local communities arising from decentralization processes (e.g. Diprose and Ukiwo 2008). There are many instances where ATC formation has sparked

---

[8] Elena Dospekhova, "Anatolyi Tkachuk: Vtoraya volna dobrovolnogo obedineniya obshchin nachnyotsya vo vtorom polugodii 2016 g., nezavisimo ot togo, khochet etogo politikum ili net." [Anatolyi Tkachuk: Second wave of communities' voluntary amalgamation will start in the second half of 2016, independent of whether politicians want it or not], June 5, 2016, http://www.dsnews.ua/temy_nomerov/anatoliy-tkachuk-vtoraya-volna-dobrovolnogo-obedineniya-05062016212800.

a conflict among residents of municipality, between residents of different municipalities, and between residents of municipalities and higher-level authorities. Such conflicts come about because the formation of an ATC can go ahead despite resistance from a significant part of the population of affected municipalities. Although there is a fixed set of procedures through which municipalities have to pass, including the conducting of public hearings, the decision to join an ATC ultimately requires a mere simple majority vote in the municipality council. Where a council is split between those for and against ATC formation, or where residents are opposed to ATC formation, conflicts may arise. ATC formation has proved especially difficult in areas with an ethnically diverse population, such as Bessarabia and parts of Zakarpattya. It is likely that in the coming years regional authorities will increasingly push municipalities to undertake ATC formation, meaning that the decentralization reform could upset the delicate balance of peaceful relations in some areas, instigating conflicts in the local population or between citizens and local authorities.

II. Decentralization and Democracy

On the face of it, decentralization reform in Ukraine should strengthen local democracy. Before decentralization reform, unelected politicians, especially governors and district heads, had great influence over municipalities. As a result of the decentralization reform, directly elected ATC heads and ATC councils gain power and influence, and can be held more directly accountable by ATC residents. This is one of a number of reasons why decentralization, on average, is conducive to democratization. Most of the positive arguments revolve around participation (Blair 1998; Crook and Manor 1998). Decentralization creates incentives to run for public office because elected officials and politicians now have greater powers. Decentralization stimulates voting because voters now have the opportunity to interact more directly with elected representatives about issues that are familiar to them and, moreover, address a level of government that is physically and mentally closer to them (Azfar et al. 2001; Seddon 2002, 15–18). Participation in democracy is often viewed as intrinsically desirable and is associated with desirable outcomes (Meinzen-Dick and Knox 1999, 5). Increased participation includes that of minority groups who previously may have been under-represented or disenfranchised. The increased participation of minorities may help repair historical injustices, improve democratic representation, and decrease the potential for local conflict (Diamond and Tsalik 1999).

Increased participation also strengthens elements of a civic culture, including social capital and interpersonal trust, which are beneficial to the quality of democracy (De Mello 2004). A further benefit of increased participation lies in its contribution to political education and leadership recruitment. Through participation in local politics, citizens gain a greater understanding of democratic processes and are prepared to participate in these processes at higher levels of government. Local politics in that sense is a training ground for potential future leaders. Local politicians, who prove especially adept, can, for instance, be recruited by central government or political parties to work in the central state administration or compete in national elections (Blair 1998; Brinkerhoff and Azfar 2006).

In addition to increasing political participation, decentralization is widely considered to make local government more accountable and responsive (Conyers 2000; Webster 1993, 129). To understand why local government becomes more accountable as a result of decentralization, it is useful to invoke the image of a free market, in which citizens purchase good governance and local administrations sell good governance. At the local level, administrations are better able to signal to voters what they have to offer, and citizens are better able to signal what they want. Citizens who are unhappy with their purchase can choose to switch to different service-providers by voting local politicians out of office (Blair 1998, 7). In order to avoid being voted out of office, local politicians have to be responsive to voters' preferences. Thus, they should become more responsive to the needs of citizens because they will tend to have better insight into those needs than politicians with less proximity to their constituents (Seddon 2002). When local government is more responsive to the needs and preferences of citizens, the quality and efficiency of services it provides tend to improve. Decentralization, therefore, is also associated with higher-quality governance (Ostrom et al. 1993).

While decentralization may be a boon to participation, accountability, and responsiveness, this is far from certain to occur in practice. The main risk of decentralization undermining rather than strengthening democracy is local elites exploiting decentralization reform to further their personal interests at the expense of the public good (Bardhan 1997; Brinkerhoff and Azfar 2006; Crook and Manor 1998; Migdal 1998). When local governments in places with a weak democratic culture acquire more power as a result of decentralization, the reform may result in the entrenchment of existing networks of vested interests. The corruption and patronage held in place by those networks inhibits responsive, accountable government, thereby decreasing the quality of governance (Brinkerhoff and Goldsmith 2004; Migdal 1998). In addition, minorities may be poorly protected against the powerful if the latter are not monitored by higher-level authorities (Bardhan and Mookherjee 2000, 135).

There is substantial empirical evidence supporting this more somber view of decentralization. A study of fiscal federalism in Uganda, for instance, finds that optimistic expectations of the benefits of decentralization were dashed, and that local governments were instead captured by elites (Azfar and Livingston 2002). Other studies on decentralization in Africa similarly conclude that decentralization did not break the power of local elites who were unresponsive to the general interest (Crook 2003), and that local leaders turned out to be no more accountable to the local population than representatives of higher-level authorities (Ribot 2002). The main explanation offered in the academic literature as to why decentralization often leads to local elite capture rather than increased participation and accountability points to specific features of local government. Local levels of government in democratic countries tend to lack many of the institutional checks and balances that operate at the national level. Elites at the local level, consequently, have greater opportunities to abuse power (Bardhan 2002). In large part, this is a matter of economy of scale. While in democratic states there is often a diverse landscape of media reporting on national affairs, there are, typically, fewer media outlets engaged in critical reporting at the local level. Similarly, local politics is often less pluralist than national politics because there are fewer political forces present at the local level. In the absence of political pluralism and press scrutiny, abuse of power is more likely to go unchecked, and long-standing practices of elite collusion are more likely to persist (Cammack et al. 2007). In local communities, people are also more often connected through kinship and other personal relations, or are employed in one or only a small number of enterprises. Where this is the case, there is a bigger chance that elections are characterized by clientelism and intimidation, and that patronage becomes a stable feature of government (Brinkerhoff and Goldsmith 2004). To the extent that there is greater participation in local politics when government is decentralized, this can be a result of clientelist mobilization rather than vigorous political pluralism (Hetland 2008).

Even in cases where decentralization generally contributes to a greater accountability and citizen participation, authoritarian enclaves may still exist in some areas. Conversely, even in the most inhospitable

268   M. BADER

environments for democracy, it is not inevitable that elites will capture local government. It is, in other words, unlikely that decentralization will have similar political consequences across all local communities: political practices and governance practices vary widely both in most democracies and in most autocracies (Hutchcroft 2001). Whether decentralization leads to greater participation and accountability or to local elite capture depends on a range of factors, including levels of inequality within communities, local state capacity, and political traditions (Bardhan 2002).

III. The Risk of Local Elite Capture

During the years since the Euromaidan Revolution, Ukraine has been a flawed democracy in which neo-patrimonialism has remained an organizing principle in politics and public administration (Fisun 2015). In Ukraine, politics at the local level is in some ways a microcosm of national politics. As in national politics, wealthy individuals at the local level attempt to influence political processes by capturing elements of the state. Aided by the small size of many communities, informal and corrupt practices in local government are common. And in the absence of national political forces, alliances in local politics tend to change quickly and often. There is great diversity in local government. Many municipalities feature a healthy degree of political pluralism, citizen participation, and accountability through elections and functioning checks and balances. There are also municipalities, however, that can fairly be described as fiefdoms because the municipality head, or a "clan," rules without much opposition or accountability.[9] In practice most municipalities in Ukraine represent neither model democracies nor outright fiefdoms, but are in a grey zone where pluralism and accountability are lacking to various degrees.

A structural problem of local government in Ukraine is the lack of an effective separation of powers.[10] Municipality heads and members of the municipality council are elected in simultaneous elections. Following the election, the municipality head issues proposals regarding a composition

[9] An example is the Zarichansk village in the Zakarpattya Oblast, which, according to one account, "reminds one of a separate principality which exists outside the democratic state and acts according to its own laws" under its autocratic village head. See Mila Serheeva, "Silrada chi udilne kniazivstvo" [Council of the village or the local principality], August 5, 2010, http://archive.mistovechirne.in.ua/content/archive/989-2010-08-05-08-04-19.

[10] Executive–legislative relations on self-government are determined through the 1997 Law of Ukraine "On Local Self-Government in Ukraine."

of the municipality's executive committee, which are approved or rejected by the municipality council. The municipality head personally chairs the executive committee and in addition organizes the work of the municipality council and presides over its meetings. These executive–legislative relations, which are still largely based on the Soviet model of local government, remain unchanged as a result of current decentralization reform. Translated into national politics, executive–legislative relations in local government would be characterized as resembling those of presidential rule, with concomitant perils of personalization of politics and a winner-take-all mentality. The problem of a true lack of separation of powers in local government in Ukraine is compounded by shortcomings typical of government at a small scale, such as a lack of press scrutiny and the prevalence of patron–client relations and clientelism.

In addition to the provisions of the 1997 Law on Local Self-Government, there are other explanations for the lack of separation of powers in Ukraine's local government. One explanation that is relevant here is the use of the majoritarian principle in most elections for municipal councils. Of the 662 ATCs that formed by the end of 2017, 583 are comprised of villages (*sela*) or centered on a town (*selishche*). While elections to municipal councils in cities use a proportional formula, council members in other municipalities are elected from single-member districts with often just a few hundred registered voters. A great majority of council members in villages and towns do not represent political parties but instead run as self-nominated candidates.[11] Council members without a political party affiliation are likely to be more susceptible to manipulation or control by powerful individuals.

A related explanation for the poor quality of democracy at the local level is the existence of often sharp horizontal inequalities in local communities Comparatively wealthy entrepreneurs, or local "oligarchs," often seek to control local politics by running for public office themselves or through controlling those already in office. Members of a municipal council who are controlled by outsiders are commonly referred to as "pocket deputies." Through their control of members of the executive committee, including the municipality head or members of the municipal council, powerful local "oligarchs" can succeed in capturing elements of local government, and in extreme cases turn a municipality into a personal fiefdom.

---

[11] The affiliation of candidates in the local legislative council elections of 2015 and 2016 can be consulted on the website of the Central Election Commission: http://www.cvk.gov.ua/pls/vn-2015/wm001.

Altogether, a substantial share of municipalities across Ukraine do not have a political culture in which representative institutions are commonly held accountable. These municipalities also lack an organized civil society with the capacity to influence a decision-making and hold local government to account. As one analyst has noted, "[a]n active, responsible, critically thinking community, which truly holds the authorities accountable, has yet to be formed" (Avksent'ev 2017c). Granting a greater degree of self-government to municipalities with serious flaws in their exercise of democracy may exacerbate the existing problems of local government in Ukraine, with negative consequences for its citizens. In the remainder of this section we outline why it is likely that some degree of local elite capture is common in many newly formed ATCs.

1. Elite-driven Amalgamation

The formation of an ATC is supposed to follow a number of fixed, mandatory steps, including the organization of public hearings in all municipalities that will unite in the prospective ATC, a vote in the relevant municipality councils, an elaboration of plans by a working group for the formation of the ATC, and a decision by regional authorities on whether the formation of an ATC meets legal requirements. A crucial element in ATC formation is that the process must be voluntary: the municipality councils of all involved municipalities must agree to the amalgamation, which, moreover, should take place free of coercion by external forces. The initiative for the formation of an ATC, according to the law, must come from within one of the municipalities of the future ATC. Four different entities can act as an initiator of the process: a municipality head, at least one-third of members of the municipality council, a group of citizens through the launch of a "local initiative," and existing bodies of self-organization.[12] According to one study, an initiative for ATC formation was taken in three out of four cases by the head of the municipality which sought to become the center of the newly formed ATC (Krupnik et al. 2016). This finding has been corroborated by our interviews in twenty ATCs in Odesa and Kharkiv regions.

ATC formation, consequently, often does not so much result from communities coming together and agreeing through a deliberative

---

[12] See article 5 of the Law of Ukraine "On Voluntary Amalgamation of Territorial Communities," *Vidomosti Verkhovnoi Rady*, 2015, no. 13

process that they need to join forces, but from the considerations of elite actors.[13] These can be local elite actors, such as a municipality head and colleagues in the executive committee of the municipality, or local "oligarchs" or politicians and officials from higher-level authorities. Municipality heads in numerous cases have been accused of pushing through ATC formation to advance their personal ambition. The mayor of Irpin in Kyiv Oblast, for instance, has been criticized for aiming to "expand his dominion" to a range of surrounding villages.[14] The head of Polyana municipality in Zakarpattya Oblast, similarly, has been accused of seeking, through the formation of a large ATC, to "realize his life-long dream of being a high-ranking official with unlimited powers."[15] There are also allegations that some ATCs have been formed in the interests of large landowners or agricultural enterprises. One analyst, for example, claims that "in the meantime the ATCs transform into organized crime groups, headed by some type of a large landowner of agricultural magnate with a deputy's mandate in his pocket or with an affiliation to the executive authorities" (Pozhyvanov 2017). An alleged example of such a "feudal estate" controlled by the owners of an agricultural enterprise is Khrestovska ATC in Kherson Oblast, where the ATC head and 15 out of 22 members of the ATC council are affiliated with the biggest agricultural enterprise of the ATC (Kopyt'ko 2017). Another type of actor involved in ATC formation is a member of a regional council and of the national parliament. Examples of Verkhovna Rada members who allegedly have a defining vote over ATC formation in their respective districts are Bohdan Dubnevych, the "unofficial ruler" of Pustomytsivskiy district in Lviv oblast, and his brother Yaroslav Dubnevych, whose district, Sambir, is also in Lviv oblast.[16]

[13] E.g. "Dve storony detsentralizatsii v Ukraine" [Two sides of decentralization in Ukraine], June 30, 2017, http://hvylya.net/analytics/politics/dve-storonyi-detsentralizatsii-v-ukraine.html.

[14] "Stalo vidomo, yak mer Irpenia Karpliuk khoche rozshyryty svoi volodinnia do Zhytomyrskoi trasy" [It becomes known how the mayor of Irpin Karpliuk wants to broaden his land up to Zhytomyr road"], February 26, 2017, http://mykyivregion.com.ua/2017/02/26/stali-vidomo-yak-mer-irpenya-karplyuk-hoche-rozshiriti-svoyi-volodinnya-do-zhitomirskoyi-trasi/.

[15] "Ob ednana terirotorialna hromada chy Polianćka huberniia (Lyst u redaktsiiu)" [Amalgamated territorial community or Polianćka province, Letter to the editorial office], September 13, 2016, from: https://zakarpattya.net/Обєднана-територіальна-громада-чи-П/.

[16] "Lialkovodstvo Dubnevychiv ta parad samovysuvantsiv: vybory u 8 OTG Lvivshchyny 29 zhovnia" [Puppeteer Dubnevychiv and the parade of self-nominated: elections in eight

Regional councils have the authority to ratify ATC formation, and they are expected to use this authority to prevent the formation of ATCs which are clearly unviable, or in cases where procedures for ATC formation have not been followed. Yuriy Hanushchak, one of the country's main experts on decentralization, argues that members of regional parliaments often abuse this authority by increasing their control over prospective ATCs in their own electoral district.[17]

As noted, ATCs are supposed to be formed according to a "prospective plan" that is developed by the regional authorities. When they take into account the interests of powerful stakeholders at the regional level, the prospective plans themselves may turn out to be an outcome of "elite games." Otherwise, and preferably, the prospective plans can play an important role in preventing the formation of ATCs that are guided by the interests of municipality heads or other powerful local actors. In fact, however, most ATCs are not formed in accordance with prospective plans. Of the 25 ATCs that were formed in Odesa Oblast up to the end of 2017, only six followed the region's prospective plan (Zatishanska, Tsebrivska, Znamenska, Novokalchevska, Rozkvitinska, and Tairovska ATCs).[18] Of the twelve ATCs that had formed in Kharkiv Oblast by the end of 2017, only two were in accordance with the region's prospective plan. The first of these is Rohanska ATC, in which a small rural municipality has been amalgamated with the city of Rohan, just outside Kharkiv. In the case of Kolomatska ATC, the second ATC in Kharkiv Oblast to follow the prospective plan, the ATC comprised all of Kolomatsksa district.[19]

Considering that for many newly formed ATCs the process of ATC formation has been driven by elite interests, and has proceeded without the explicit consent of local residents, it is clear that the process risks being tainted by conflict. This is even more visible in cases where newly formed ATCs display a clear asymmetry between settlements in the ATC in terms

ATCs of Lviv region on October 29], October 8, 2017, http://varta.com.ua/news/ukraine/1143485.

[17] "Formirovanie territoryy gromad: nelzya daf oblsovetam sozdavaf votchiny—ekspert" [The formation of communities' territory: oblast councils shall not be allowed to create principalities," February 9, 2018, https://www.ukrinform.ru/rubric-regions/2400149-formirovanie-territorij-gromad-nelza-dat-oblsovetam-sozdavat-votciny-ekspert.html.

[18] The prospective plan of Odesa Oblast can be consulted at: http://ofis.odessa.gov.ua/wp-content/uploads/2016/04/protokol-10.pdf.

[19] The prospective plan of Kharkiv Oblast can be consulted at: http://old.kharkivoda.gov.ua/uk/article/static/id/802.

of size or resources (Asotsiatsiya Spriyannya Samoorhanizatsii Naselennya 2016). Villages that previously were the central settlement of a municipality had a municipality head, executive committee, and village council. In the new situation, where they are now on the periphery of a newly formed ATC, the residents of such villages elect a number of representatives to the ATC council and a chief (*starosta*), who is supposed to represent the village's interests in the ATC executive committee. While this may not be a nationwide phenomenon, there are many reports of residents of settlements that find themselves outside the center of a newly formed ATC claiming that their interests are being ignored to the benefit of the central settlement.[20]

2. Entrenched Leaders

Municipality heads from settlements which are unlikely to become a center of an ATC often resist the amalgamation of their settlement. By contrast, ATC formation is generally seen as attractive by municipality heads from settlements which, according to the ATC formation plan, are to become centrally positioned. These municipality heads, however, still have to compete in the first ATC election in order to retain (and expand) their power. We should expect, therefore, that primarily municipality heads who are confident of electoral victory, take the initiative or support the initiative for ATC formation. Indeed, the overwhelming majority of heads of newly formed ATCs are former heads of the central municipality of the new ATC: this is the case in 71 out of 89 city ATCs (80 percent), 148 out of 195 town ATCs (76 percent), and 292 out of 377 village ATCs (77 percent).[21] These high percentages are remarkable: after all, the ATCs are new administrative entities, and anyone, including the former heads of the municipalities outside the center of the ATC, can compete in the ATC elections. Altogether 511 ATC heads out of 662 (77 percent) are the former heads of the central municipality of the ATC. Of the remaining 151

[20] E.g. "Detsentralizatsiia na Kharkovshchine: tsel opravdyvaet sredstva?" [Decentralization at Kharkiv region: End justifies the means], July 14, 2017, http://insidernews.info/decentralizaciya-na-xarkovshhine-cel-opravdyvaet-sredstva/; "U Holobśkiy OTG—Skandal cherez lyst z pidroblenymy pidpysamy" [In Holobśkiy ATC there is a scandal due to a letter with fake signatures], November 29, 2016, Retrieved from https://www.volynnews.com/news/authority/u-holobskiy-oth-skandal-cherez-lyst-z-pidroblenymy-pidpysamy.

[21] Information about the candidates in the ATC elections can be found on the website of Ukraine's Central Election Commission, http://www.cvk.gov.ua.

ATC heads, 20 were previously heads of the district council in which the ATC is located. Most of these are from districts where the borders of the ATC coincide with that of the district, i.e. where all municipalities of the district have been amalgamated.

In Kharkiv Oblast, ten out of the twelve heads of ATCs that had been formed by the end of 2017 were formerly head of the central settlement of the ATC. In Zolochivska ATC, the head of the central settlement of the ATC (Zolochiv) lost the election to the head of the district council, Leonid Kanivets, who was helped by the fact that only one-third of voters in Zolochivska ATC live in Zolochiv (Avksent'ev 2017a). In Starosaltivska ATC, the head of the central settlement of the ATC had been in his position only since 2015, and lost to Eduard Konovalov, who was supported by the regional administration and a powerful local figure and member of the regional council (Zelenina 2017). Many of the ATC heads have served as head of the central settlement of the ATC for a long time. Extreme examples include Fedir Shevchenko, mayor of Rohan (now part of Rohanska ATC) who has served since 1980, and Mykola Maydebura, village head of Krasnosilka (now part of Krasnosilska ATC) who has served since 1986.

A long tenure for municipality heads is common in Ukraine. Unlike the president, who can serve only two consecutive terms, there are no term limits for municipality heads in Ukraine. The lack of term limits allows municipality heads to cement their position in power, thereby increasing the likelihood of reelection. Many municipality heads in Ukraine are entrenched: benefitting from the lack of effective separation of powers in many municipalities, they have built patronage networks over time and now face minimal opposition. Reflecting this lack of political competition, elections for the head of the ATC in many new amalgamations have featured only the minimum number of candidates (two), with the second candidate fulfilling merely a nominal role. In Zachepylivska ATC in Kharkiv Oblast, for instance, the former municipality head of Zachepylivka, Yuri Kryvenko, won the elections against his single opponent with a 54 percent margin of victory. Hennadyy Zahoruyko, head of Oskilska ATC, also in Kharkiv oblast, was re-elected municipality head of Chervonyy Oskil in 2015 in an elections in which he was the sole candidate. In the 2017 ATC head elections, he faced off against one candidate, winning 81 percent of the vote, according to official results.

In part because of the lack of serious competition in many ATC elections, turnout tends to be low. In Novovodolazska ATC (Kharkiv Oblast), for instance, the current ATC head Oleksandr Esin won 81 percent of the vote, but on a turnout of only 27 percent. The 2016 elections in Merefyanska ATC (Kharkiv Oblast) featured eleven candidates, but the incumbent mayor of Merefa won with a 48 percent margin on a turnout of 30 percent. Elections in a minority of newly formed ATCs have, on the other hand, been highly competitive. Some particularly competitive ATC elections have been marred by allegations of fraud. In Shabska ATC in Odesa Oblast, the elections, won (by a 4 percent margin) by the former head of a municipality that became part of the ATC, was surrounded by allegations of vote-buying.[22] In the highly competitive and contentious elections in Tairovska ATC (Odesa Oblast), people were allegedly brought in from outside the ATC to vote for one of the candidates.[23]

In sum, the formation of ATCs, rather than bringing change to the personnel composition of local government in Ukraine, has in most cases entrenched incumbent authorities, and in particular the former municipality heads, who have repositioned themselves as ATC heads. These ATC heads have often built up patronage networks and so face little opposition. In many cases they are themselves part of patronage networks headed by politicians and officials at higher levels of government. The previously mentioned Dubnevych brothers, who had been members of the Petro Poroshenko Bloc (BPP) faction in the Verkhovna Rada until 2019, for instance, wield control over two districts in Lviv Oblast through their ties with local politicians. Patronage networks are also fostered by political parties. The political force affiliated with President Poroshenko in some regions in particular, including Kharkiv Oblast, has co-opted municipality heads into the party. Through these forms of patronage, the heads of the newly formed ATCs further strengthen their position, and political pluralism at the local level is further undermined.

---

[22] "Na Odeshchinyni holosami vybortsiv torhuyut u mahazinakh" [In Odesa region people's votes are traded in shops], October 27, 2017, http://podrobnosti.ua/2207161-na-odeschin-golosami-vibortsv-torgujut-u-magazinah-vdeo.html.

[23] "Vyboroy v Tairovskiy OTG: psevdovybortsi ta vydalennia z ditnytsi kandidata i sposterihacha" [Elections in Tairovskiy ATC: Fake voters and the removal of a candidate and observer from the polling station], December 24, 2017, https://izbirkom.org.ua/news/vybory-2016-26/2017/vibori-v-tayirovskii-otg-psevdovibortsi-ta-vidalennia-z-dilnitsi-kandidata-i-sposterigacha.

3. Lacking Pluralism

There is a limited degree of pluralism in the politics of most ATCs, especially in those that are centered on a town or a village (as opposed to ATCs in cities). This has in part to do with the type of people who participate in the ATC council elections as candidates. Candidates in local elections in Ukraine are often recruited from among those whose salaries are paid by the local government, such as schoolteachers, doctors, and communal service workers. Considering that the local authorities manage the finances of local state institutions, ATC council members tend to be loyal to the municipal authorities. They also disproportionately often represent the same political force as the ATC head. In Kharkiv Oblast, for example, in eight of the twelve ATCs that had formed by the end of 2017, a majority of council members represented the same political party as the ATC head. In ten ATCs in Kharkiv Oblast, the ATC head had been co-opted by President Poroshenko's political force, BPP (Avksent'ev 2017b). While it is extremely common in Ukraine for local council members not to be a member of a political party and run on a non-partisan ticket, in eight of the ten ATCs with an ATC head co-opted by BPP (Kolomatska, Malodanylivska, Oskilska, Natalinska, Novovodolazska, Malynivska, Zachepilovska, Zolochivska ATCs), the majority of, and in some cases almost all council members represent BPP. In the two remaining ATCs (Rohanska and Starosaltivska ATCs), BPP representatives constitute a plurality of council members. There are two ATCs in the region whose heads have not been co-opted by BPP: in Merefyanska ATC, the ATC head represents the Vidrodzhennia party, as do a plurality of council members; in Chkalovska ATC, the ATC head ran as an independent candidate, and all but four of the council members were elected on a non-partisan ticket.

The fact that the political affiliation of council members so often parallels that of the ATC head cannot be explained by historical trajectories, as both BPP and Vidrodzhennia are recent creations. It is more likely that candidates for ATC councils follow the example of the prospective ATC head. The consequence of this, of course, is that, at least formally, there is little political opposition within the ATC council to act as a counterweight to the ATC head and the executive committee. In interviews with council members in a range of ATCs in Kharkiv Oblast and Odesa Oblast, they confirmed that there was no sustained opposition faction within the council. The consequent collegial mode of operation of their ATC council was generally assessed by them as a positive.[24]

A factor which contributes to the lack of political pluralism in many ATCs is their small size. As noted in section "Decentralization and Democracy", in small communities people are often connected through kinship and other personal relations or employed in one or only a small number of enterprises. Where this is the case, candidates for council elections are more likely to be recruited through patron–client relations, and national political parties may find it hard to gain a foothold in local communities. Together, these circumstances work against pluralism.

Early prognoses of decentralization reform envisioned that, upon its completion, there would be around 1,500 ATCs.[25] As there were close to 12,000 municipalities before the start of decentralization reform, this means that the average ATC should comprise some eight former municipalities. Of the 662 ATCS that had formed by the end of 2017, most were significantly smaller. Table 9.1 shows, for the three types of ATCs (city, town, and village), the number of former municipalities per ATC.

The average number of former municipalities per ATC, at 4.7, is well below the expected figure of eight. The median value of number of former municipalities per ATC is five for city ATCs, four for town ATCs, and three for village ATCs. Moreover, Table 9.1 shows that there are many

Table 9.1 The number of former municipalities in newly formed ATCs[a]

	Number of municipalities per ATC								
	2 (%)	3 (%)	4 (%)	5 (%)	6 (%)	7 (%)	8 (%)	9 (%)	10 or more (%)
City (*misto*) (N = 89)	19	17	4	12	6	7	4	3	27
Town (*selishche*) (N = 195)	23	22	10	10	8	7	4	3	14
Village (*selo*) (N = 376)	36	23	18	11	6	2	1	1	2

[a]Quantitative data on all ATCs were retrieved from https://gromada.info/

[24] Interviews with ATC heads, other executive committee members, and council members in Konoplyane ATC, Krasnosilska ATC, Marazliivka ATC, Rozkvit ATC, Velyka Mykhaylivka ATC, Rohan ATC, Nova Vodolaha ATC, and Staryi Saltiv ATC.

[25] Yurii Hanushchak, one of the main experts on decentralization in Ukraine, for instance, drafted a model of ATC creation according to which 1,408 ATCs would be formed. See http://despro.org.ua/media/articles/dodatok1.pdf.

ATCs comprising only two former municipalities, giving the impression that in many cases only the minimum requirement was fulfilled for ATC formation. The 662 ATCs that had been formed by the end of 2017 had a total number of some 6.3 million residents, or 9,366 on average. The average number of residents was 19,894 residents for city ATCs, 10,892 for town ATCs, and 6,233 for village ATCs. There are many town and village ATCs that are so small that they are unlikely to form a pluralistic political community.

CONCLUSION

Since the start of decentralization reform, the Ukrainian media have featured many positive reports on its effects, highlighting in most cases the increased budgets of local communities and their greater financial autonomy. While these are real and important accomplishments, decentralization reform has also been accompanied by its fair share of failures and drawbacks. The adoption of constitutional amendments which would provide a comprehensive overhaul of subnational government has been delayed. ATC formation has been slower in many regions than anticipated, and the ATCs that have formed generally incorporate fewer municipalities than envisioned. In a significant number of places, conflicts have arisen among municipality residents and between municipality residents and authorities at different levels. The implementation of ATC creation, finally, has provided opportunities for local elite capture.

In a romantic view of ATC creation, citizens come together to decide, through a deliberative process, for or against the amalgamation of their municipality with others. In reality, the formation of ATCs has predominantly been driven by elites. In most cases, these have been incumbent municipality heads who have either acted autonomously and repositioned themselves as a head of a newly formed ATC, or acted in tandem with other powerful actors such as wealthy businesspeople or politicians at higher levels of government. Rather than bringing change to the personnel composition of local government in Ukraine, ATC formation has in most cases entrenched those already in positions of authority. The old–new ATC heads and their clients have often built up patronage networks over time, as a result of which they now face little opposition. This is apparent in the lack of competition in many of the elections for ATC head, and in the lack of political pluralism among ATC council members.

Local elite capture often undermines the legitimacy of local government and reduces the quality of governance at the local level in Ukraine. Now that entrenched and often unaccountable municipal authorities control bigger budgets and have greater powers, the problems related to local elite capture in Ukraine may grow. Experts on decentralization in Ukraine agree that some degree of oversight over the process is necessary. As one analyst has hyperbolically stated, "without control by the state, decentralization may transform into feudalization" (Levchenko 2017). Another analyst has argued that one ministry should have monitored and guided the implementation of the reform, as has been the case in other countries (Tkachuk 2017). One measure which may yet mitigate the problem of local elite capture is the appointment of prefects as foreseen by the package of constitutional amendments of the first track of decentralization. Prefects, once operational, may execute state oversight over local self-government bodies and, where the constitution or other laws are violated, suspend the decisions of local councils. For the prefects or a similar institution to start becoming operational, however, the parliament of Ukraine has to finally move ahead with adopting the necessary constitutional amendments.

REFERENCES

Aasland, Aadne, and Oleksii Lyska. 2016. Local Democracy in Ukrainian Cities: Civic Participation and Responsiveness of Local Authorities. *Post-Soviet Affairs* 32 (2): 152–175.

Asotsiatsiya Spriyannya Samoorhanizatsii Naselennya [Association for Promoting Population Self-Organization]. 2016. *Periferiyni Terytoriyi Ob'ednanykh Hromad: Mekhanizm Zakhistu Prav ta Realizatsiyi Interesiv (na Prykladi Pivdnya Ukrayiny)*. Samoorg. [The Peripheral Territories of the United Communities: A Mechanism for the Protection of Rights and the Realization of Interests], July 7.

Avksent'ev, Anton. 2017a. Elektoral'nyi Rakurs Detsentralizatsii na Kharkovshchine: Vybory v Zolochevskoi OTG. Analitychnyi Tsentr «Observatoriia Demokratii» [Democracy Observatory Think Tank], November 26, 2019. http://od.org.ua/en/.

———. 2017b. Khroniki detsentralizatsii v Kharkovskoi oblasti: sentyabr'-noyabr' 2017 goda [Chronicles of Decentralization in the Kharkiv Region: September-November 2017], December 1. Newsroom. http://newsroom.kh.ua/blog/hroniki-decentralizacii-v-harkovskoy-oblasti-sentyabr-noyabr-2017-goda.

280 M. BADER

———. 2017c. Sami sebe khoziaeva: kak prokhodit detsentralizatsiia v Kharkovskoi oblast, 12 June 2017. Accessed May 3, 2018. http://newsroom.kh.ua/blog/sami-sebe-hozyaeva-kak-prohodit-decentralizaciya-v-harkovskoy-oblasti.

Azfar, Omar, and Jeffrey Livingston. 2002. *Federalist Disciplines or Local Capture? An Empirical Analysis of Decentralization in Uganda*. University of Maryland, Center for Institutional Reform and the Informal Center.

Azfar, Omar, Satu Kähkönen, and Patrick Meagher. 2001. *Conditions for Effective Decentralized Governance: A Synthesis of Research Findings*. University of Maryland, Center for Institutional Reform and the Informal Sector.

Bardhan, Pranab. 1997. Corruption and Development: A Review of Issues. *Journal of Economic Literature* 35 (3): 1320–1346.

———. 2002. Decentralization of Governance and Development. *The Journal of Economic Perspectives* 16 (4): 185–205.

Bardhan, Pranab, and Dilip Mookherjee. 2000. Capture and Governance at Local and National Levels. *The American Economic Review* 90 (2): 135–139.

Blair, Harry. 1998. *Spreading Power to the Periphery: An Assessment of Democratic Local Governance*. Washington, DC: U.S. Agency for International Development.

Brinkerhoff, Derick W., and Omar Azfar. 2006. *Decentralization and Community Empowerment: Does Community Empowerment Deepen Democracy and Improve Service Delivery*. Washington, DC: USAID.

Brinkerhoff, Derick W., and Arthur A. Goldsmith. 2004. Good Governance, Clientelism, and Patrimonialism: New Perspectives on Old Problems. *International Public Management Journal* 7: 163–186.

Cammack, Diana, Fred Golooba-Mutebi, Fidelis Kanyongolo, and Tam O'Neil. 2007. *Neopatrimonial Politics, Decentralisation and Local Government: Uganda and Malawi in 2006*. London: Overseas Development Institute.

Chumak, Viktor, and Ihor Shevliakov. 2009. *Local Government Functioning and Reform in Ukraine*. In *An Overview of Analytical Studies of Local Government System and Local Services Provision in Ukraine*. Oslo: Norwegian Institute for Urban and Regional Research.

Conyers, Diana. 2000. Decentralisation: A Conceptual Analysis (Parts 1 and 2). *Local Government Perspectives: News and Views on Local Government in Sub-Saharan Africa* 7 (3): 1–13.

Crook, Richard C. 2003. Decentralisation and Poverty Reduction in Africa: the Politics of Local–Central Relations. *Public Administration and Development* 23 (1): 77–88.

Crook, Richard C., and James Manor. 1998. *Democracy and Decentralisation in South Asia and West Africa: Participation, Accountability and Performance*. Cambridge: Cambridge University Press.

De Mello, Luiz R., Jr. 2004. Can Fiscal Decentralization Strengthen Social Capital? *Public Finance Review* 32 (1): 4–35.

Diamond, Larry, and Svetlana Tsalik. 1999. Size and Democracy. The Case for Decentralization. In *Developing Democracy. Toward Consolidation*, ed. Larry Diamond, 117–160. Baltimore and London: The Johns Hopkins University Press.

Diprose, Rachael, and Ukoha Ukiwo. 2008. *Decentralisation and Conflict Management in Indonesia and Nigeri*. Oxford: University of Oxford Centre for Research on Inequality, Human Security and Ethnicity.

Fisun, Oleksandr. 2015. The Future of Ukraine's Neopatrimonial Democracy. *PONARS Eurasia Policy Memo* No. 394. http://www.ponarseurasia.org/memo/future-ukraine-neopatrimonial-democracy.

Hanushchak, Yurii. 2013. *Reforma Teritorialnoi Orhanizatsii Vladi*. Kyiv: DESPRO.

Hetland, Øivind. 2008. Decentralisation and Territorial Reorganisation in Mali: Power and the Institutionalisation of Local Politics. *Norsk Geografisk Tidsskrift-Norwegian Journal of Geography* 62 (1): 23–35.

Hutchcroft, Paul D. 2001. Centralization and Decentralization in Administration and Politics: Assessing Territorial Dimensions of Authority and Power. *Governance* 14 (1): 23–53.

Kopyt'ko, Aleksey. 2017. *Knyazhestvo svoimi rukami: budni detsentralizatsii*, 17 March. Accessed May 5, 2018. http://sprotyv.info/ru/news/kiev/knyazhestvo-svoimi-rukami-budni-decentralizacii.

Krupnik, A. S. et al. 2016. *Uchasti hromads'kosti v ob"ednanni ta rozvitku teritorial'nykh hromad* [Public Participation in Integration and Development of Territorial Communities] Analtical Note on the Results of the Interregional Research. Odesa: Renaissance. http://www.irf.ua/content/files/draft_doslidzhennya.pdf.

Levchenko, Ihor. 2017. *Tretiy Rik Detsentralizatsii: Prohres, Feodalizatsiia Chi Destabilizatsiia?* [The Third Year of Decentralization: Progress, Feudalisation or Destabilization?], May 31. Glavkom. https://glavcom.ua/publications/tretiy-rik-decentralizaciji-progres-feodalizaciya-chi-destabilizaciya-17860.html.

Meinzen-Dick, Ruth, and Anna Knox. 1999. Collective Action, Property Rights, and Devolution of Natural Resource Management: A Conceptual Framework. Draft Paper for Workshop, July 15.

Migdal, Joel. 1998. *Strong Societies and Weak States: State-Society Relations and Capabilities in the Third World*. Princeton: Princeton University Press.

Ostrom, Elinor, Larry Schroeder, and Susan Wynne. 1993. *Institutional Incentives and Sustainable Development: Infrastructure Policies in Perspective*. Boulder, CO: Westview.

Pozhyvanov, Mikhaylo. 2017. Unified Territorial Communities: There Is Currently More Harm Than Good. *Radiosvoboda*, September 26. https://www.radiosvoboda.org/a/28757609.html.

282 M. BADER

Ribot, Jesse C. 2002. African Decentralization: Local Actors, Powers and Accountability. *UNRISD Programme on Democracy, Governance and Human Rights, Paper no. 8.*

Seddon, Jessica. 2002. Participation, Civil Society, and Decentralization. In *Decentralization Briefing Notes*, ed. Jennie Litvack and Jessica Seddon. Washington, DC: World Bank Institute.

Sydorchuk, Oleksii. 2015. *Decentralization Reform in Ukraine: Prospects and Challenges.* Kyiv: Ilko Kucheriv Democratic Initiatives Charitable Foundation.

Tkachuk, Anatolii. 2012. *Mistseve Samovryaduvannya ta Destsentralizatsiya* [Local Self-Government and Destentralization]. Kyiv: DESPRO.

———. 2017. Pro Detsentralizatsiyu, Uspikhy, Ryzyky I rol' Parlamentu [On Decentralization, Success, Risks and the Role of Parliament]. Dzerkalo Tizhnya, January 13.

Webster, Neil. 1993. Panchayati Raj in West Bengal: Popular Participation for the People or the Party? *Development and Change* 23 (4): 129–163.

Zelenina, Elena. 2017. Detsentralizatsiia kak Vektor Publichnoi Politiki [Decentralization as a Vector of Public Policy]. *Timeua*, May 26. Accessed May 5, 2018. http://timeua.info/post/oborona-i-bezopasnost/decentralizaciya-kak-vektor-publichnoj-politiki-07754.html.

CHAPTER 10

Signs of Progress: Local Democracy Developments in Ukrainian Cities

Aadne Aasland and Oleksii Lyska

INTRODUCTION

The effective functioning of local self-government is considered a key factor of democracy (Melo and Baiocchi 2006). From the breakup of the Soviet Union in 1991 and until the so-called Euromaidan revolution in 2013–2014, when the infamous Yanukovych regime fell, Ukrainian authorities were not eager to do away with the centralized governance structure inherited from the Soviet period. The political color of the government or the president was hardly significant: Those in power did nothing or very little to decentralize. Power was further recentralized when

---

This chapter has benefited from financial support from the Ministry of Foreign Affairs of Norway and the Research Council of Norway (NORRUSS Plus program, project no. 287620).

A. Aasland (✉)
OsloMet – Oslo Metropolitan University, Oslo, Norway
e-mail: aadnea@oslomet.no

O. Lyska
Independent Researcher, Kharkiv, Ukraine

© The Author(s) 2020
H. Shelest, M. Rabinovych (Eds.), *Decentralization, Regional Diversity, and Conflict*, Federalism and Internal Conflicts,
https://doi.org/10.1007/978-3-030-41765-9_10

283

Yanukovych took office in 2010, when important responsibilities were transferred back from regions (*oblasti*) and districts (*rayony*) to central ministries (Jarábik and Yesmukhanova 2017).

However, after the Maidan popular uprising and demands for democratization, the new authorities responded by introducing more fundamental decentralization reforms (Chaisty and Whitefield 2017). The reform was also meant to be a tool to mitigate the conflict in Donbas and restrict the expressions of separatism. Instead of a federal model, which, it was feared, could lead to demands for enhanced regional autonomy and possibly further disintegration, the authorities instead have chosen a model where power and resources are being transferred to the local, municipal level. Simultaneously, in the new set-up the relative influence of oblasti and rayony is being reduced (Levitas and Djikic 2017).

For proper local democracy to develop, however, it is not enough that meaningful authority is devolved to local units of governance. A condition for a good local democracy is that the local authorities[1] (hereafter LAs) are accessible and accountable to the local citizenry (Blair 2000). This requires active citizens who make their voices heard, as well as LAs that are responsive to citizens' concerns. Such interaction between citizen participation in political processes at the local level, and the perceived responsiveness of LAs toward their concerns, is the topic of this chapter.

A nationwide local democracy survey carried out in 20 Ukrainian cities in the summer of 2014 found that people in general had a rather negative perception of the responsiveness of their local authorities. Also, the survey showed relatively low levels of activity among ordinary Ukrainian citizens, in terms of their political involvement, participation in civil society organizations, or perceived influence on local politics. Differences between individual cities, however, were striking: some cities displayed much better quality of interaction between citizens and local authorities than others (Aasland and Lyska 2016).

Since that survey was conducted, a long awaited decentralization reform was initiated. Its implementation has not been straightforward, however. So far, the reform has been deprived of a proper legal foundation, since the inclusion of controversial provisions from the Minsk

---

[1] Since members of the public are not always able to distinguish between appointed officials of local self-government bodies and elected council members at the local level, in this chapter (and in the two surveys that the chapter builds on) we do not make a strict distinction between them. We use the concept of Local Authorities (LA) to combine the two.

Agreements about the special status of Donetsk and Luhansk has resulted in a failure to pass the necessary amendments to the Constitution. Thus, the reform is still precarious and can be changed or revoked by a simple majority in parliament. Strong regional elites are fighting to preserve their power status and trying to influence reform outcomes. In addition, more poorly developed areas with low levels of income from taxes have so far seen few benefits from the reform (Aasland and Larsen 2018).

On the other hand, municipalities can now keep much more of the tax income generated in their territory and are also in a position where they have much more autonomy over their budgets. Thus, a preliminary verdict by both national and international experts is that decentralization is among the more successful reforms undertaken in Ukraine since the Maidan revolution (Makarenko 2017). Ukrainian cities of oblast significance are said to be the greatest beneficiaries of the reform process (Levitas and Djikic 2017, 3).

It is probably too early to assess the effects of the ongoing decentralization reform on the quality of local democracy. In addition, citizens' perception of local democracy is also influenced by several other factors, such as developments in living conditions, the fight against corruption, the rule of law, and the interaction with national politics. Still, we believe it is worthwhile to examine how people perceive whether and how local democracy has developed in the period from the turbulent time just after the Maidan revolution to the present. Do people recognize progress compared to the rather bleak picture revealed by the 2014 survey? Or have unfulfilled expectations and, for many, no improvement in economic well-being resulted in a further negative trend? To provide an answer, a new survey was conducted at the end of 2017 in the same cities as the 2014 survey.

I. Data and Methods

This chapter builds on results of two nation-wide opinion surveys on local democracy carried out in July 2014 and November–December 2017 respectively.[2] Professional pollsters conducted the interviews, with local

---

[2] The surveys were initiated by the Association of Ukrainian Cities (AUC) and organized in collaboration with the Norwegian Association of Local and Regional Authorities (KS) and the Norwegian Institute for Urban and Regional Research at Oslo Metropolitan University within the framework of the project "Evidence-Based Local Government Policy Development in Ukraine," financed by the Ministry of Foreign Affairs of Norway. The project home page with more details on the project and links to its publication is http://

interview corps throughout Ukraine.[3] The data were collected in the form of personal interviews in the respondents' homes, using questionnaires that could be answered in Ukrainian or in Russian. On average, an interview took about 30 minutes. The data were transformed into computer-readable form using advanced statistical software (SPSS).

The two-stage samples were based, first, on purposeful selection of 20 Ukrainian cities, chosen to provide variation in terms of geographic location, population size, and administrative status. The sample included the capital, ten cities of oblast significance, and nine cities of rayon significance. Of the latter nine cities, seven have more than 100,000 inhabitants. Second, a total of at least 100 respondents were then interviewed in each city. The respondents were randomly selected, but to ensure representative data we applied quotas for age and gender groups, as well as geographical distribution in the city. In total, 2,000 (in 2014) and 2,120 (in 2017) respondents were interviewed. Though not fully representative of Ukraine as a whole, due to the large number and variation of cities as well as the large number of respondents included, we feel confident that much of the variation among the Ukrainian urban population has been covered. Several identical questions were asked in a national telephone survey among 1,074 respondents conducted by the same pollster in parallel with the city surveys in 2017; the survey results can thus be compared to the national average.

As in any survey, data reliability is also affected by the response rate. For this survey, the response rate was 37 percent in 2014 and 38 percent in 2017. Overall, there is good reason to assume that the survey provides a fairly reliable picture of how urban residents in Ukraine perceived local governance at two different points in time. However, we cannot rule out a certain bias for univariate distributions on key dependent variables, although such bias is much less of an issue when examining relationships in multivariate analyses where, as in this chapter, a variety of background variables is controlled for (Rindfuss et al. 2015).

The collection, storage, and analysis of the survey data are based on compliance with ethical standards and protection of the rights of the survey participants regarding voluntary participation, anonymity, and confidentiality.

---

www.ks.no/fagomrader/samfunn-og-demokrati/internasjonalt-samarbeid/prosjekter/cooperation-project-in-ukraine/.

[3] In 2014 the survey was carried out by Socio Consulting (based in Kyiv), while in 2017 OperativnaSotsiologia (Dnipro) conducted the survey.

II. Perceptions of Local Authority Responsiveness: Trust Is the Key Factor

Responsiveness presupposes that elected representatives are accountable to the local population (Smith 2007, 105). The survey respondents were presented a series of statements about the responsiveness of the LAs to citizens and asked to what extent they agree with each of the statements according to a four-point scale ranging from "Fully disagree" to "Fully agree." Figure 10.1 shows the average responses in the 20 surveyed cities in respectively 2014 and 2017.

Taking into account that a neutral average for each item would have been 2.5, the level of responsiveness of Ukrainian local authorities in 2017 as assessed by urban citizens can still be considered to be rather toward the negative side of the scale. The most positive assessments are given for general satisfaction with the performance of LA and for LAs' ability to inform citizens about relevant questions. The most negative response is given for people's assessment of their own ability to influence LA decisions.

Despite the rather negative picture, there are also some promising signs. For most items we can observe slow progress over the 2014–2017 period. This is particularly the case when it comes to LAs' ability to inform citizens about relevant questions and especially about the use of taxpayers' money. There is also increased positivity in citizens' assessment of LAs'

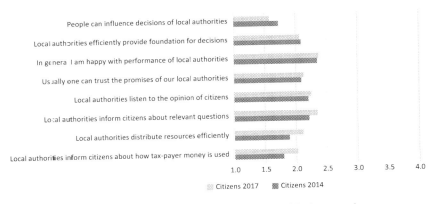

Fig. 10.1 Responses to statements about local authorities' responsiveness among citizens of 20 Ukrainian cities in 2014 and 2017. Average level of agreement on a scale from 1 (Fully disagree) to 4 (Fully agree). Responses "Do not know" and "Refuse to answer" (between 7 percent and 25 percent for individual items) have been removed. (Source: AUC Local Democracy Surveys 2014 and 2017.)

efficiency in the distribution of resources.[4] One item stands out as having significantly worse results in 2017 than in 2014—citizens' assessment of the possibility of influencing LA decisions.

When comparing results in the surveyed cities in 2017 with results from the telephone survey at the national level that took place in parallel, we find that results are quite similar. However, there is a tendency fort respondents nationally to be somewhat more satisfied with their local authorities than respondents in the surveyed cities when it comes to distribution of funds and listening to the opinion of citizens. Mean responses for the statements for which there were identical questions are presented in Table 10.1.

Further analysis (reliability analysis) confirmed a very high correlation between the eight items,[5] making it reasonable to assume that the battery of questions provides a robust and reliable measurement of respondents' perceptions of the responsiveness of LAs. An index was made, the "LA Responsiveness Index," ranging from 1 (respondent fully disagrees with all eight statements) to 4 (full agreement with all items).[6] The mean index score was respectively 2.06 (2014) and 2.11 (2017), which is a statistically significant difference ($p < 0.05$). For both years we observe the average tendency of partial disagreement with the listed items in both surveys.

Table 10.1 Responses to statements about local authorities' responsiveness among citizens of 20 Ukrainian cities and the national average in 2017

	20 cities	National survey
People can influence decisions of LA	1.58	1.57
LA listen to the opinion of citizens	2.25	2.53
LA inform citizens about relevant questions	2.34	2.43
LA distribute funds effectively	2.11	2.30
Information about tax money	2.02	2.00

Average level of agreement on a scale from 1 (Fully disagree) to 4 (Fully agree)

---

[4] Another sign of progress is an answer to the question whether people need to pay under the table for services locally: while 53 percent acknowledged this to be the case in 2014, in 2017 this had fallen to 46 percent.

[5] Chronbach's Alpha of respectively 0.90 (2014) and 0.87 (2017).

[6] Only those with at least four valid responses (excluding "Do not know" and "Refuse to answer") were included in the index.

Table 10.2 Local Authority Responsiveness Index in 20 Ukrainian Cities, 2014 and 2017, and difference between the two years. (Mean index score.)

	2014	2017	Difference
Kharkiv	1.79	2.23	0.44
Mykolaiv	1.65	2.04	0.40
Ivano-Frankivsk	1.86	2.24	0.38
Chuhuiv	2.08	2.42	0.34
KryvyiRih	1.89	2.19	0.30
Chernigiv	1.85	2.12	0.27
Korosten	2.08	2.33	0.25
Pavlograd	1.95	2.18	0.23
Kyiv	1.84	2.02	0.18
Cherkasy	1.83	1.97	0.14
Lutsk	2.10	2.11	0.00
Lviv	2.14	2.10	−0.04
Dnipro	2.05	1.95	−0.10
Kamianets-Podilski	2.37	2.26	−0.11
Vinnytsya	2.28	2.17	−0.12
Rivne	2.08	1.87	−0.21
Kremenchug	2.22	1.89	−0.33
Berdiansk	2.75	2.41	−0.34
Boryspil	2.29	1.87	−0.42
Pervomaisk	2.13	1.69	−0.44

Source: AUC Local Democracy Surveys 2014 and 2017

Notes: Responses "Do not know" and "Refuse to answer" (between 7 percent and 25 percent for individual items) have been removed

Moving from overall results to results in individual cities, we see some interesting developments. Table 10.2 shows the results in 20 cities in respectively 2014 and 2017, sorted by the difference between the two years. Kharkiv, Mykolaiv, and Ivano-Frankivsk are the cities that have had most progress in the period between the two surveys, while the largest regress has been observed in Pervomaisk, Borispyl, and Berdiansk. Berdiansk, which had an extraordinarily high score in 2014, is still among the cities that stand out with high scores in 2017, together with Chuhuiv and Korosten. At the other end of the scale we find Boryspil, Rivne, and Pervomaisk. Again we stress that the results can only be considered as indicative since the number of respondents in each city is relatively small and margins of error therefore considerable. Nevertheless, differences between cities with a high and a low score are more than large enough to be statistically significant.

As can be seen from the table, a high score in 2014 is no guarantee of a corresponding high score in 2017, and vice versa. Thus, LA responsiveness, as perceived by citizens, is not something that is achieved once and forever, but a quality that needs to be subject to continuous attention from local authorities.

What factors can explain the individual scores on the index? Regression analysis provides some hints. We performed a multiple linear regression with the index score as the dependent variable, and the following independent variables that one would expect might have an effect on the outcome of the dependent variable:

- Year of survey (2014 or 2017)
- Size of city (small; ordinary city; city of regional significance, capital city)
- East or west Ukraine[7]
- Gender
- Age (in years)
- Household standard of living, subjective (four-point scale)
- Political activity (index)
- Level of education (four-point scale)
- Interest in local politics (four-point scale)
- Trust in societal institutions (index)

Table 10.3 presents the results of the linear regression analysis. The explanatory power of the model is rather strong, indicated by an adjusted R squared of 0.31. This means that close to one-third of the variation on the index score can be ascribed to the responses to the independent variables in the model. Several of the independent variables have a statistically significant correlation with the dependent variable (Responsiveness Index) when controlling for the other variables in the model.

The level of trust in a variety of societal institutions is clearly the independent variable in the model with the strongest correlation with people's perception of LAs' responsiveness, as seen by the value of the standardized coefficients. The more people express trust in these institutions, the more are they inclined to report that the LAs are responsive to the needs

---

[7] In line with the division made in the survey 2014, which was an operational definition based on election preferences, i.e. whether majority voted for Yanukovych or Tymoshenko in the 2010 presidential elections.

10 SIGNS OF PROGRESS: LOCAL DEMOCRACY DEVELOPMENTS... 291

Table 10.3 Multiple linear regression—perceived LA responsiveness

	Unstandardized coefficient	Standard error	Standardized coefficient	Significance
Constant	0.73	0.09		0.000**
Survey year (low = 2014)	0.15	0.02	0.12	0.000**
Small city (vs. city of regional significance)	0.13	0.03	0.06	0.000**
Medium city (vs. city of regional significance)	0.16	0.02	0.12	0.000**
Capital city (vs. city of regional significance)	−0.08	0.05	−0.03	0.062
Eastern or western location (low = east)	−0.03	0.02	−0.02	0.157
Gender (low = women)	0.00	0.02	0.00	0.846
Age (in years)	0.00	0.00	0.01	0.466
Educational level (4-point scale)	0.04	0.01	0.06	0.000**
Living standard (4-point scale)	0.03	0.01	0.03	0.025*
Participation in political activities (index)	0.02	0.00	0.06	0.000**
Interest in local politics (4-point scale)	0.01	0.01	0.02	0.261
Institutional trust (index)	0.40	0.01	0.53	0.000**

Dependent variable: Responsiveness index. High value = perceived high responsiveness

Individuals with responses to less than four of the responsiveness items were not included in the regression

Source: AUC Local Democracy Surveys 2014 and 2017

*Significant at 0.05 level

**Significant at 0.01 level

of citizens. The link between degree of social trust and evaluation of LAs is hardly a surprising finding, but it is worth noting that Ukraine is among the European countries with the lowest levels of trust in institutions and the government (Zmerli 2012, 120). According to our survey, trust in institutions has been reduced from an already low level over the 2014–2017 period.

The low level of trust may be one of the explanations of the rather poor evaluation of LA responsiveness in the survey. What is the cause and what is the effect may be debated, however, since poor responsiveness on the part of government institutions may correspondingly explain the low level of trust expressed by Ukrainians. Of the eleven institutions listed in our survey, highest trust levels were expressed in 2017 toward the city mayor, followed by civil society organizations, local councils, and deputies from own constituency. At the other end of the scale, we find that lowest trust is expressed towards the national parliament, to the government, to judges, and to the president. It is worth noting that the latter enjoyed the highest level of trust in the post-Maidan 2014 era. In 2017, LAs on average enjoy considerably higher trust levels than other listed government institutions.

Participation in local political activities increases the likelihood of expressing a positive opinion on LA responsiveness. Such civic participation can, in addition to trust, be considered a dimension of social capital (Bjørnskov 2006), which appears to have a positive effect on perceptions of LA responsiveness. However, personal political interest, as expressed subjectively by survey respondents, does not have a statistically significant effect on the Responsiveness Index score, as shown in Table 10.3.

The alleged east–west divide in Ukraine has been a recurrent theme in analyses of Ukrainian politics (Barrington and Herron 2004; Holdar 1995; Kubicek 2000). It is therefore worth noting that our survey results indicate that residence in the western or eastern part of the country has no statistically significant effect on the LA responsiveness score. The great variation among individual cities was shown in Table 10.2, and it is important to stress that these differences do not have a systematic east–west pattern.[8] The size of the city, however, appears to matter: inhabitants of cities of regional significance perceive LA performance to be better than those without this status. Whether or not this has to do with selection of cities rather than size is, however, hard to say due to the limited number of cities in the sample. The finding is, however, in line with the claim that it is exactly these cities that have benefited most from the decentralization reform (Levitas and Djikic 2017, 3)

While education and a higher living standard have a positive effect on the score on the dependent variable (people with more education and better living standard give a more positive evaluation of LA performance), demographic variables such as gender and age do not have statistically significant effects on the Responsiveness Index score, after controlling for all the other variables in the model.

---

[8] The east–west division is a simplification of a more complex regional division which our survey data do not allow us to control for, a consequence of the limited number of cities in different regions of the country.

III. Citizens' Participation Builds on Political Interest But Not Trust

A good-quality local democracy requires active citizens who make their voices heard. Citizens' participation at the local level may take many different forms. It is common to operationalize the concept by differentiating between community or social participation, usually in the civil society sphere, on the one hand, and political participation in the form of voting, political party, and other political activities on the other. Full citizenship can be realized only if people have opportunities for actual influence on political processes.

We have chosen to concentrate on two aspects of civic participation that are relevant for local democracy. First, we look at different forms of political participation. Second, we examine membership and involvement in different types of civil society organizations and political parties.

Figure 10.2 shows the percentage of respondents that participated in various forms of political activity locally during the previous 12 months in respectively 2014 and 2017. As the figure demonstrates, some types of activity have become more widespread, particularly various forms of appeals, proposals, and complaints to local authorities; participation in

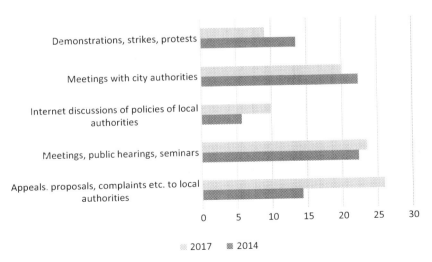

Fig. 10.2 Reported participation in different forms of public activities at local Level in 2014 and 2017

such activities has almost doubled from 14 to 26 percent of the respondents. Though at a lower level, internet communication has also become much more widespread (from 6 to 10 percent participation). That different types of protest activities have become more rare (from 14 to 9 percent) can probably be explained by the special situation in the months preceding the survey in 2014 when many people were engaged in Maidan and post-Maidan demonstrations.

The biggest obstacles that people reported as preventing them from having an impact on decision making are the belief that their efforts would anyway be useless (37 percent), lack of time (17 percent), an alleged poor legislative base (15 percent) and lack of knowledge of the relevant legislation (12 percent). In addition, 10 percent of the respondents said they were simply not interested in these types of activity. There were no big differences in the frequencies of reasons given in 2014 and 2017.

An index was computed based on a more detailed question about participation in different types of activity as reported by the respondents.[9] We included only participation items with a high internal correlation to ensure that we had a robust one-dimensional measurement.[10] The index ranges from 0 (participated in none of the listed activity types) to 16 (participated in all). While in 2014 66 percent of the respondents had not participated in any of the activities, this was the case with 58 percent of the respondents in 2017. Similarly, while the mean number of activity types in 2014 was 0.9, by 2017 it had increased to 1.5. At the same time the variation (as measured by the standard deviation) between respondents was higher in 2017 than in 2014.

When comparing participation levels in the 20 surveyed cities in the autumn of 2017 with the results from national survey that was conducted in parallel, we find that the proportion having participated in demonstrations was very similar (9.1 percent in the surveyed cities and on average 9.3 at national level). Participation in internet discussions was more common at the national level (20.3 percent vs. 9.9 percent in the surveyed cities), and so was participation in meetings, public hearings, and seminars (33.8 percent vs. 23.5 percent respectively). This could have to do with

---

[9] Examples: appeals, inquiries, petitions, public hearings, political speech, local initiatives, public discussions, seminars, internet discussions, meetings with mayor or local deputies.

[10] This means that protest activities, which are not correlated with the other items, were not included in the index. Such activities are, however, included in the correspondence analysis presented below. We were left with an index with a Chronbach's Alpha of 0.85.

the great activity surrounding discussions on amalgamation of territories that at the time affected smaller municipalities to a much larger degree than cities. On the other hand, participation in meetings with city authorities were more common in the 20 surveyed cities (19.9 percent) than the national average (12.3 percent).

Table 10.4 gives an overview of activity levels in individual cities for the two survey years, and again we have sorted it according to the difference between the two years. As was the case with responsiveness, there is considerable variation between the cities when it comes to citizen participation. The overwhelming majority of cities have seen a positive development, in the sense that participation has increased considerably in the 2014–2017 period. Only five of the cities have seen a negative development, and most of them show only a moderate decline. Only Berdiansk has seen a very

Table 10.4 Citizen Participation Index in 20 Ukrainian Cities, 2014 and 2017, and difference between the two years. (Mean Index Score.)

	2014	2017	Difference
Chernigiv	0.51	2.65	2.14
Pervomaisk	0.34	1.95	1.61
Boryspil	0.74	2.27	1.53
Mykolaiv	0.50	1.88	1.38
Kyiv	1.89	2.73	0.84
Vinnytsya	0.58	1.29	0.71
Pavlograd	0.78	1.48	0.70
Chuhuiv	0.77	1.38	0.61
Kamianets-Podilski	0.69	1.28	0.59
KryvyiRih	0.48	1.01	0.53
Dnipro	0.78	1.28	0.50
Korosten	0.83	1.31	0.48
Rivne	1.61	2.08	0.47
Kremenchug	0.62	1.00	0.38
Kharkiv	0.08	0.42	0.34
Cherkasy	0.93	0.91	−0.02
Lviv	1.18	1.12	−0.06
Ivano-Frankivsk	2.01	1.90	−0.11
Lutsk	1.45	1.21	−0.24
Berdiansk	2.03	0.66	−1.37

Source: AUC Local Democracy Surveys 2014 and 2017

Notes: Responses "Do not know" and "Refuse to answer" (between 7 percent and 25 percent for individual items) have been removed large reduction in citizen participation, and it is noteworthy that this city was at the top of the list in 2014 but was lowest by 2017. Chernigiv, Pervomaisk, Boryspil, and Mykolaiv are cities with the largest positive improvements. It is, however, Kyiv that ranks highest on the Participation Index in 2017, followed by Chernigiv, while Kharkiv and Berdiansk stand out at the other end of the scale.

Another observation is that cities that have a high participation score do not necessarily have a high score on the Responsiveness Index (Table 10.2). In fact there is a negative correlation between the two (Pearson's $R = -0.16$) which is not, however, large enough to be statistically significant given the small number of cities included in the study.

Again we are interested in the factors that can help to explain individual scores on the Participation Index. To help us with providing an answer, we performed another multiple linear regression, this time with the Participation Index as dependent variable and the same independent variables as in the previous regression (exchanging the responsiveness and participation indices as respectively dependent and independent variables). Results are shown in Table 10.5.

This regression gives a rather different picture from the one derived on LA responsiveness (Table 9.3). Initially it should be mentioned that the strength of this model is considerably lower; with an adjusted R squared of 0.11, only 11 percent of the variation on participation among respondents can be ascribed to the score on the independent variables. Still, there are many statistically significant effects. Again, we find that the difference between the survey years is robust, confirmed in the multivariate analysis: people participate more in 2017 than in 2014 after controlling for the other independent variables in the model.

The largest effect (as shown by the unstandardized coefficients) is in the level of interest in local politics. This is reasonable, given that people who are interested tend to engage more also in political activities.

A perhaps surprising finding, however, is that institutional trust, which had a strong and positive effect on LA responsiveness, has a minor *negative* effect on participation levels. It seems people participate locally regardless of their trust in authorities and public institutions. One possible explanation could be that people seeking to ensure that their voices are heard see a need to participate more when they do not find public institutions trustworthy. Education as well as subjective living conditions are both positively associated with participation, though for living conditions the effects are quite small. The effects of other demographic characteristics

Table 10.5 Multiple linear regression—participation

	Unstandardized coefficient	Standard error	Standardized coefficient	Significance
Constant	−2.25	0.34		0.000**
Survey year (low = 2014)	0.58	0.07	0.13	0.000**
Small city (vs. city of regional significance)	0.03	0.12	0.00	0.779
Medium city (vs. city of regional significance)	−0.04	0.09	−0.01	0.669
Capital city (vs. city of regional significance)	0.93	0.17	0.09	0.000**
Eastern or western location (low = east)	0.36	0.08	0.08	0.000**
Gender (low = women)	−0.02	0.07	0.00	0.798
Age (in years)	0.00	0.00	0.00	0.928
Educational level (4-point scale)	0.31	0.05	0.11	0.000**
Living standard (4-point scale)	0.11	0.05	0.04	0.021*
Perceived LA responsiveness (index)	0.27	0.06	0.08	0.000**
Interest in local politics (4-point scale)	0.55	0.04	0.23	0.000*
Institutional trust (index)	−0.10	0.05	−0.04	0.045*

Dependent variable: Participation Index. High value = perceived high participation

Individuals with responses to less than four of the responsiveness items were not included in the regression

Source: AUC Local Democracy Surveys 2014 and 2017

* Significant at 0.05 level

** Significant at 0.01 level

(age and gender) are negligible. There is little difference between cities of different sizes, though people in the capital, Kyiv, participate considerably more than the average of other city types, also after controlling for the independent variables. While location in the east or west of the country was not decisive for a score on the Responsiveness Index, it does count for participation: respondents living in the west of Ukraine tend to demonstrate higher levels of political participation than respondents from cities in the east. Differences in social capital and civic culture between the west and the southeast of Ukraine could be a likely explanation of this finding, analogous to what Putnam (1993) found in southern and northern Italy. Finally it is no surprise that there is an association between the Responsiveness Index and the Participation Index, as was pointed out in the first regression.

The 2014 survey confirmed a low level of organizational membership in Ukrainian cities, though this is perceived important for development of local democracy (Putnam 1993). In 2017, we observe positive changes among all institutions mentioned in the questionnaire (NGO, political party, condominium, street committee, neighborhood committee, and public council). The most dramatic changes can be observed for membership in condominiums (increased more than fourfold[11]), political parties and NGOs (Fig. 10.3). Moreover, in all categories of organization, the survey demonstrates an increase not only in the percentage of respondents who participate in the institutions in a formal way, but also of those who are actively involved in these organizations. The number of actively

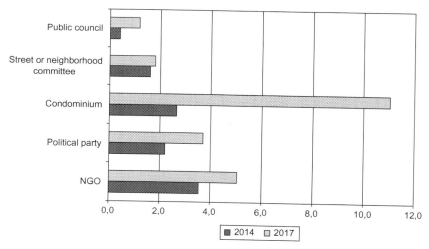

Fig. 10.3 Percentage of respondents reporting membership in organizations. Responses "Do not know" and "Refuse to answer" (less than 1 percent for individual items) have been removed. (Source: AUC Local Democracy Surveys 2014 and 2017)

---

[11] During the same period (2014–2017) the number of condominiums in Ukraine increased 1.7 times—from 16,200 to 27,400.

involved persons in 2017 doubled with regard to membership in political parties (up to 1.5 percent of the respondents) and tripled as regards condominiums (up to 3.1 percent). The percentage of active members of NGOs increased 1.5 times—up to 3.2 percent of the respondents.

For each city, we calculated the mean scores[12] of membership in each institution, and then calculated differences between 2017 and 2014. It turned out that the difference between the two years of the citizen Participation Index has a rather strong and statistically significant positive correlation with the difference of the mean scores of memberships in political parties (Pearson's $R = 0.67$), street committees ($R = 0.67$), and public councils ($R = 0.46$). This means that the changes in respective memberships are associated with the changes in the Participation Index. On the other hand, the correlations between the difference in the Participation Index and changes in the membership in NGOs, condominiums, and neighborhood committees are much smaller and not statistically significant.

Finally, it should be noted that even with rather strong signs of progress during the 2014–2017 period, the current level of organizational membership in Ukrainian cities remains quite low.

IV. Correspondence Analysis

A complex picture emerges from regression analysis on citizens' perception of local authorities' responsiveness and their own participation in political activities at local level. While these are internally correlated, the predictors of the two phenomena are not the same, and sometimes even contradictory. To obtain a better grasp of the association between the different variables, and some other variables that we believed could further expand the picture, we conducted an exploratory correspondence analysis. In order not to mix the two survey years, we restricted the analysis to the 2017 data.

Correspondence analysis is a data analysis tool that enables underlying structures in a dataset to be revealed. It summarizes the relationship among categorical variables in a large table, and provides a visual presentation that facilitates a holistic interpretation of trends in the data. Categories with similar distributions are represented as points that are close in space, whereas categories with very dissimilar distributions are positioned far apart (Clausen 1998).

---

[12] The three-point scale ranges from 0 (no membership) to 2 (active membership).

In addition to the variables included in the regression analysis we included protest activity to see if protest activity and other types of political activities are part of the same dimension or not. We also included organizational memberships to see how it relates to local political activities. The results of the correspondence analysis are illustrated in the Correspondence Analysis Plot (Fig. 10.4). As the plot is at first sight rather complex, we will go through it step by step.

The correspondence analysis generates two dimensions. The horizontal dimension we interpret as largely reflecting political engagement and

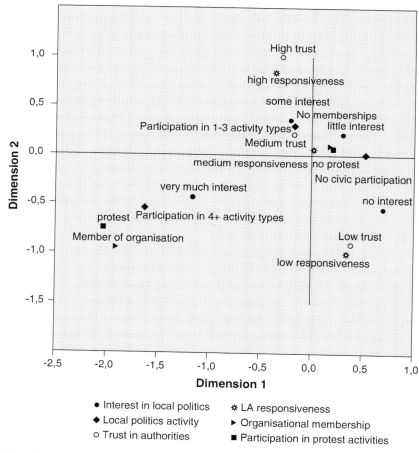

Fig. 10.4 Correspondence analysis plot

activity levels of the individual. On the right-hand side (the counterintuitive direction of the dimension, with low level of engagement associated with positive values, was produced by our statistical software) are people who lack interest in local politics, who report no organizational membership, and who have participated in few political activities. On the left-hand side are politically active (relatively speaking) citizens, with an interest in local politics, and higher-than-average participation levels. We term this dimension "Civic participation" (Fig. 10.5). Interestingly, participation in

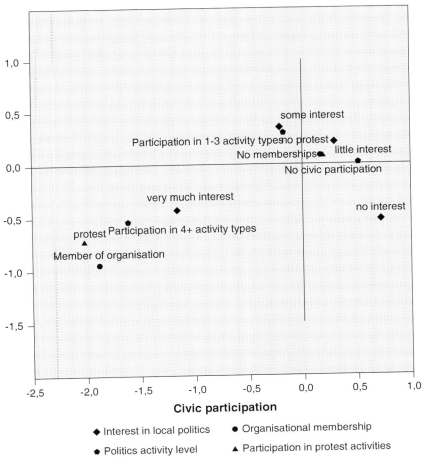

Fig. 10.5 Correspondence analysis plot: civic participation dimension

protest activities is associated with the same dimension, so that people who have participated in such activities are located towards the left end of the plot.

The vertical dimension (Fig. 10.6) can be read as a reflection of the perception of LA responsiveness. In the lower part, we find respondents who perceive the LAs to be unresponsive to citizens ("do not take ordinary people's opinions into account, misuse their powers for personal gains," etc.). Those who tend to consider the LAs as being responsive to the needs the citizenry are located at the top end of the plot. This dimension is also closely associated with the level of institutional trust—as could have

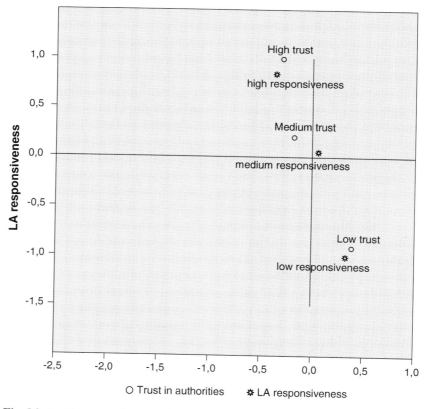

Fig. 10.6 Correspondence analysis plot: local authority responsiveness dimension

been expected, given the strong association between these variables shown in the previous regression analysis. This dimension is called "LA responsiveness". The two dimensions look like the dimensions identified in an analysis of the 2014 results (Aasland and Lyska 2016), confirming the robustness of the results.

It should be noted that location in the plot gives average positions of the different groups and categories, and may hide considerable internal variation among different categories of respondents. Moreover, an apparently high score on one dimension does not necessarily represent a high score in absolute terms, as both responsiveness and engagement levels are low in Ukraine, and the plot reflects relative levels. Furthermore, since, as we showed in the regression analyses, participation and responsiveness are statistically associated, the categories do not completely match the x- and y-axes of the two dimensions in the plot.

Based on the score on the two dimensions we can identify four "ideal types" of citizen, taken from Aasland and Lyska (2016) (see Fig. 10.7):

In the lower right part of the plot, we find "alienated" citizens. These are people who are dissatisfied with local authorities and have low trust in institutions. Even so, they do not engage in political or civil society activities and do not follow politics.

In the lower left part of the plot, we find "protesters"—people with a high level of political and civil society activity (including protests), but who tend not to trust the authorities and give a weak assessment of LA responsiveness.

At top left, we find "interactive" citizens—engaged individuals who interact with LAs and tend to respond positively to inquiries about their attitude to LAs.

At top right we find people who we could call "compliant." They are not overly unhappy about the performance of local government, but they are passive and are neither interested nor involved in political or civil society activities themselves.

Based on mean scores of inhabitants of individual cities, we have positioned the cities into a correspondence analysis plot (Fig. 10.8). Five cities are located in the "alienated" part of the plot: Pervomaisk, Dnipro, Kremenchug, Cherkasy, and Lviv. Five are "compliant": Lutsk, Chuhuiv, KryvyiRih, Berdiansk, and Kharkiv. Then we have five cities of the "protester" type: Chernihiv, Boryspil, Kyiv, Rivne, and Mykolaiv. The final five cities fall into the "interactive" category: Vinnytsya, Korosten, Pavlohrad, Ivano-Frankivsk, and Kamianets-Podilski.

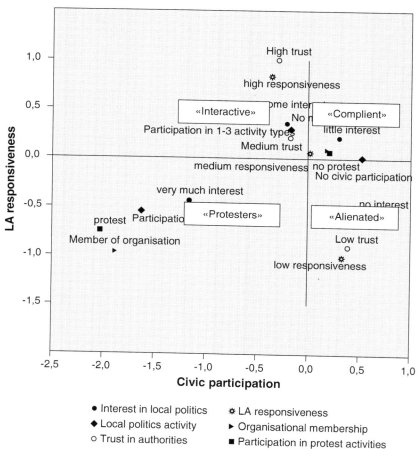

Fig. 10.7 Correspondence analysis plot: typology of cities

It should be stressed that these results are indicative and should be read with some caution, and we again emphasize the exploratory nature of the analysis. As shown by the plot, many of the cities have results for one or both dimensions close to the mean (0), and the relatively low number of respondents in each city makes our estimates somewhat uncertain. Cities that are near each other in the plot may be classified in different categories, often with cities that are positioned further from them in the plot.

10 SIGNS OF PROGRESS: LOCAL DEMOCRACY DEVELOPMENTS...   305

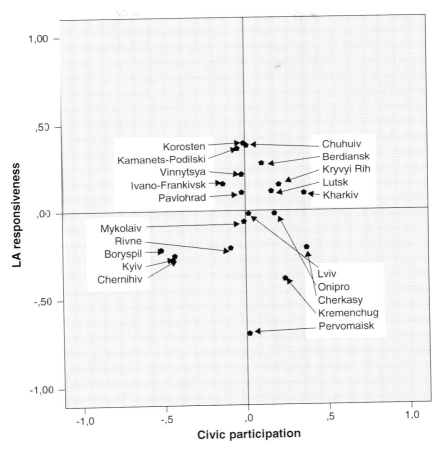

Fig. 10.8 Correspondence analysis plot: city location in the plot

However, the findings are likely to be robust for the most distinctive cities within each of the categories, as differences between cities on both dimensions are more than large enough to be statistically significant.

This should also be kept in mind when comparing the results of 2014 with those of 2017. Table 10.6 shows the distribution of cities in the two survey years. We see that the majority of cities have changed position, only seven of the 20 surveyed cities have remained in the same position over the two surveys. None of the "interactive" cities from 2014 has moved

306 A. AASLAND AND O. LYSKA

Table 10.6 Patterns of "citizen types" in 20 Ukrainian cities in 2014 and 2017 surveys, based on correspondence analysis results

		2017			
		Alienated	Compliant	Protesters	Interactive
2014	Alienated	*Cherkasy*	Chuhuiv, KryvyiRih	Chernihiv, Mykolaiv	Pavlohrad
	Compliant	Pervomaisk, Dnipro, Kremenchug	*Kharkiv*		
	Protesters	Lviv		*Kyiv, Rivne*	Ivano-Frankivsk
	Interactive		Lutsk, Berdiansk	Boryspil	*Vinnytsya, Korosten, Kamianets-Podilski*

into the "alienated" position, and three of them have remained "interactive": Vinnytsya, Korosten, and Kamianets-Podilski. Pavlohrad has seemingly had the most dramatic, and arguably positive, move from being "alienated" to becoming "interactive". However, when looking at the plot, this city is close to the mean on both dimensions. Cherkasy is the only city that has remained "alienated" in the two surveys. However, it should be noted that the results are relative and that the plots give average scores in 2014 and 2017, where the mean in both years is 0 on both dimensions. Thus, the improvement on the two dimensions that has been recorded in the period between the two survey years is not reflected in the correspondence plot.

There could be many reasons for the change of position from 2014 to 2017. Cities that have seen an improvement may have targeted the interaction between citizens and local authorities as one of the priorities in LA work and introduced qualitatively new measures to this end. However, cities where we observe a relative deterioration may have done many of the right things, but people's expectations may have risen, resulting in a more critical assessment. Furthermore, some objective conditions may have changed, e.g. labor market or economic issues, with an impact on the public mood. Thus, one should be careful about making a direct link between LA performance and citizens' assessments and political involvement. While explanations for the results of individual cities vary, this is outside of the scope of this chapter.[13]

V. Better or Worse?

What do the results from the local democracy surveys of 2014 and 2017 tell us about local democracy developments during the post-Euromaidan period? As shown in previous sections, both in terms of citizens' perceived responsiveness of local authorities as well as, and in particular, citizen political participation at local level we have seen signs of progress in most cities. A caution is that we see improvement mostly in inhabitants' assessment of the way local authorities distribute resources and information, but a negative tendency when they evaluate their own possibilities for influencing politics locally. Still, people *do* participate more actively in politics according to our survey data. The question then is what they get in return for their participation.

While differences in citizens' responses between 2014 and 2017 for the most part appear as relatively modest, a clear sign of progress is also reflected in respondents' answers when they are asked in a direct question whether the performance of local government has improved or deteriorated since the start of decentralization reform in April 2014. Only 11 percent say that LA performance is worse, 39 percent say that it is as before, and 41 percent assert that it has improved; the remaining 9 percent are undecided. Again it is trust in authorities that is the strongest predictor of respondents' assessments. Whether or not people themselves participate actively has no statistically measurable effect on the response to this question. It is noteworthy that neither eastern or western location is relevant for citizens' opinion on progress. However, in line with the argument that cities of oblast significance have benefited the most from the decentralization reforms (Levitas and Djikic 2017), it is exactly in these cities where people are most satisfied with the LA post-Euromaidan performance. Older people are more negative than the younger generation, but gender, educational level, and living conditions are of little relevance.

Another promising sign, at least from the authorities' perspective, is that people are positively inclined towards the ongoing Ukrainian

---

[13] As part of the project, dissemination researchers visited ten of the cities participating in the survey.

decentralization reform: 39 percent support it, 30 percent are neutral, and only 18 percent express opposition; the remaining 13 percent are undecided or did not want to answer. Again we performed a regression analysis (not shown here), and the results demonstrate that improvement experienced at local level is the most decisive item for predicting support for the reform. This is a clear indication that the reform needs to have a positive impact on people's local lives to be supported. The size of the city does not affect the results, perhaps surprisingly given the claim that the larger cities of regional significance have benefited more than smaller cities and towns. However, it may be explained by the fact that the territorial aspects of the reform have until now for the most part affected smaller geographical units. Neither is east–west location relevant; people all over the country are equally supportive. Trust in authorities, not unexpectedly given the previous results, is positively associated with support to the reform. Women are more positively inclined towards the decentralization reform than men are, but we do not observe any strong generational differences. The well-educated and those with a higher living standard are the most supportive, perhaps because they have reaped more benefits of the reform.

Our analysis has shown that even if there have been clear signs of progress, people at the end of 2017 were still in general more negative than positive towards LA performance. One should not underestimate the importance of the fact that decentralization reforms have been introduced under very difficult circumstances, with an ongoing violent conflict in the eastern part of the country and with economic setbacks and turbulence for many. The mass acceptance of and even support for decentralization reform as indicated in the survey is therefore highly desirable, and possibly necessary to secure stability. At the same time, our survey results indicate that the extremely low level of trust expressed in public institutions, especially at national level, is likely to be a hindrance to faster improvement. Ukrainian authorities have the daunting task of handling the conflict in the east while at the same time proceeding with pressing domestic reforms, including meaningful decentralization. To enhance public trust the battle against corruption and arbitrary exercise of power seems particularly important, as the goals of territorial and fiscal decentralization are unlikely to be reached unless fundamental anti-corruption measures are undertaken.

References

Aasland, Aadne, and Christian Larsen. 2018. En vei å gå for ukrainsk lokaldemokrati. *Kommunal Rapport*, 01.02.2018, 1. https://kommunal-rapport.no/meninger/kronikk/2018/02/en-vei-ga-ukrainsk-lokaldemokrati.

Aasland, Aadne, and Oleksii Lyska. 2016. Local Democracy in Ukrainian Cities: Civic Participation and Responsiveness of Local Authorities. *Post-Soviet Affairs* 32 (2): 152–175.

Barrington, Lowell W., and Erik S. Herron. 2004. One Ukraine or Many? Regionalism in Ukraine and Its Political Consequences. *Nationalities Papers* 32 (1): 53–86.

Bjørnskov, Christian. 2006. The Multiple Facets of Social Capital. *European Journal of Political Economy* 22 (1): 22–40.

Blair, Harry. 2000. Participation and Accountability at the Periphery: Democratic Local Governance in Six Countries. *World development* 28 (1): 21–39.

Chaisty, Paul, and Stephen Whitefield. 2017. Citizens' Attitudes Towards Institutional Change in Contexts of Political Turbulence: Support for Regional Decentralisation in Ukraine. *Political Studies* 65 (4): 824–843.

Clausen, Sten-Erik. 1998. *Applied Correspondence Analysis: An Introduction*. Vol. 121. *Quantitative Applications in the Social Sciences*. Thousand Oaks, CA: Sage.

Holdar, Sven. 1995. Torn Between East and West: The Regional Factor in Ukrainian Politics. *Post-Soviet Geography* 36 (2): 112–132.

Jarábik, Balázs, and Yulia Yesmukhanova. 2017. Ukraine's Slow Struggle for Decentralization. Carnegie Endowment for International Peace. https://carnegieendowment.org/2017/03/08/ukraine-s-slow-struggle-for-decentralization-pub-68219.

Kubicek, Paul. 2000. Regional Polarisation in Ukraine: Public Opinion, Voting and Legislative Behaviour. *Europe-Asia Studies* 52 (2): 273–294.

Levitas, Tony, and Jasmina Djikic. 2017. *Caught Mid-Stream: "Decentralization," Local Government Finance Reform, and the Restructuring of Ukraine's Public Sector 2014 to 2016.* Swedish Association of Local and Regional Authorities (SKL) and Swedish International Development Agency (Sida). http://sklinternational.org.ua/wp-content/uploads/2017/10/UkraineCaughtMidStream-ENG-FINAL-06.10.2017.pdf.

Makarenko, Olga. 2017. *Decentralisation: The Mortal Threat to Ukraine's Entrenched Elites.* Euromaidan Press. http://euromaidanpress.com/2017/11/07/decentralization-the-mortal-threat-to-ukraines-entrenched-elites/.

Melo, Marcus Andre, and Gianpaolo Baiocchi. 2006. Deliberative Democracy and Local Governance: Towards a New Agenda. *International Journal of Urban and Regional Research* 30 (3): 587–600.

Putnam, Robert. 1993. *Making Democracy Work: Civic Tradition in Modern Italy.* Princeton: Princeton University Press.

Rindfuss, Ronald R., Minja K. Choe, Noriko O. Tsuya, Larry L. Bumpass, and Emi Tamaki. 2015. Do Low Survey Response Rates Bias Results? Evidence from Japan. *Demographic Research* 32: 797.

Smith, B.C. 2007. *Good Governance and Development.* Houndmills: Palgrave Macmillan.

Zmerli, Sonja. 2012. Social Structure and Political Trust in Europe. *Society and Democracy in Europe* 89: 111.

CHAPTER 11

Decentralization Reform: An Effective Vehicle for Modernization and Democratization in Ukraine?

Olga Oleinikova

INTRODUCTION

The link between decentralization and modernization in the post-communist transitional societies is "one of the most important theoretical problems that directly affect practical politics" (Inozemtsev 2010, 7) and democratic development. The transition process of the last three decades in Ukraine has refuted the simplified understanding that democratization inevitably leads to deep social and technological modernization. A number of issues are delaying visible results of modernization and decentralization in Ukraine, a process that has been noticeably hampered since its start in 2014. These are the conflict in and around Ukraine, centralization of administrative tasks, an absence of well-defined responsibilities, local authorities' lack of organizational, technical and financial resources,

O. Oleinikova (✉)
University of Technology Sydney, Sydney, NSW, Australia
e-mail: Olga.Oleinikova@uts.edu.au

© The Author(s) 2020
H. Shelest, M. Rabinovych (eds.), *Decentralization, Regional Diversity, and Conflict*, Federalism and Internal Conflicts,
https://doi.org/10.1007/978-3-030-41765-9_11

311

312   O. OLEINIKOVA

duplication of structures and, in some cases, a resultant weakness and incompetence of local authorities.

A range of theoretical and empirical scholarship has acknowledged decentralization is strongly associated with democracy (Panizza 1999; Arzaghi and Henderson 2005; Letelier 2005; Treisman 2006; Canavire-Bacarreza et al. 2017). In similar fashion, modernization is argued to have strong links to democracy (Lerner, 1958; Lipset 1959; Rostow 1960; Moore 1966; Huntington 1991; Andorka and Spéder 1994; Machonin 1997; Adamski 1998; Zapf 1998; Domański 1999; Zaslavskaia 1999; Keller and Westerholm 2007; Zapf et al. 2002). The central element of the process of creating prerequisites for the development of democracy is modernization.

By "modernization" this chapter means changing social, economic, and political conditions that foster technological advance, urbanization, changes in the economy (particularly regional, and moving from rural to industry-based) and nurture a democratic culture. It is no exaggeration to say that "modernization and democratization at this stage of history are almost identical" (Inozemtsev and Dutkiewicz 2013, 9). Success in modernization inevitably becomes a basis for democratization, failure in it becomes a basis for the failure of democratic projects. Furthermore, the history of the twenty-first century has shown how precarious democracy can be if voters who are dissatisfied and in disbelief when they cast their votes. The most widely studied theme within the social sciences—the relation between socioeconomic development and political democracy—has also been a subject of an immense critique and consideration. Modernization does not produce democracy, but creates the necessary prerequisites for it, and it indicates which countries are capable of creating stable democratic institutions and which are not.

The history of the last 60 years shows that almost all successfully modernized states either switched from an authoritarian regime to a democratic one, or significantly expanded the degree of freedom of citizens and strengthened mechanisms for protecting their rights, that is, they created the necessary conditions for the development of democracy (Oleinikova 2019; Oleinikova and Bayeh 2019). And, on the contrary, countries that have come to a halt in their development and were unable to implement a modernization program and reform ultimately came to experience strengthened authoritarian tendencies or took the path of building "imitation democracy" (Furman 2008). Nowadays, it is hard to be a democrat without being a supporter of modernization, as nothing contributes to the spread and consolidation of democratic norms as strongly as successful economic reforms and economic progress as a whole. These are also confirmed by global development trends and Ukraine's accelerated efforts to democratize and to reform since 2014 Euromaidan protests.

Decentralization, being a significant dimension of political and administrative reform in many developing countries, rests on the idea that local self-government promotes democracy, individual liberties, and the right of citizens to participate in decision-making on a local level. There is a plethora of definitions surrounding the concept of "decentralization." This chapter uses the following working definition of decentralization: the process through which central government transfers its powers, functions, responsibilities, and finances, or a decision-making power, to other entities away from the center, either to lower levels of government, or dispersed central state agencies, or the private sector (Olum 2010). Its main assumption is that the assignment of political, fiscal, and administrative responsibilities to actors and institutions at regional and local levels (Litvack et al. 1998, 4) will help achieve balanced economic development and accelerate modernization across regions.

In Ukraine, decentralization has become a strategic policy for governmental restructuring, and emerged as one of the key priorities in 2014. After Ukraine's independence in 1991, discussions and initiatives for structural transformation of the country's government have been pursued at various points in history. However, it was only in 2014 that a reform plan was considered important, deemed essential for achieving the levels of balanced and sustainable economic regional development and administrative capacities that would enable Ukraine to successfully synchronize its internal market and legislation with that of the European Union (EU) and further its efforts on the path to eventual eligibility for EU membership.

Surprisingly, given the much-discussed links between democracy and modernization on the one hand, and democracy and decentralization on the other, not much exploration has taken place in the theoretical and empirical field around the direct link between modernization and decentralization. This chapter offers insights from current modernization efforts in Ukraine as part of its decentralization reform that help to understand whether decentralization is an effective strategy to promote and achieve modernization and advance Ukraine's troubled democracy on its path to European integration. In particular, it focuses on obstacles facing decentralization from a modernization perspective. It examines how decentralization reform in Ukraine so far has been effective in promoting

314   O. OLEINIKOVA

modernization in the regions. One of the key findings discussed is that the new attempts at devolving power and responsibilities to the local structures/ governments should be more flexible, to adapt to local conditions, rather than being directed by national reform policy and guided in the traditional central administration manner. The discussion offered in this chapter suggests that a "middle way" in managing local government and governance changes should be adopted in order to develop a more pragmatic localism that will accelerate modernization. This strategy is held to benefit Ukraine's democratization.

The chapter is organized as follows: Section "Democracy, Modernization, and Decentralization: Theorizing Democratic Transition" explores the conceptualization of the link between modernization, democracy, and decentralization from the view of transition scholarship, and establishes working definitions for these concepts. Section "Decentralization Reform in Ukraine: An Effective Way to Promote Modernization?", relying on this conceptualization, discusses decentralization reform as a priority of post-Maidan Ukraine with a focus on the modernization dimension, before examining the obstacles to modernization and discussing whether decentralization reform is an effective way to promote modernization in Ukraine. In conclusion, there is a discussion around necessary conditions for successful modernization of post-Euromaidan Ukraine, within the decentralization reform framework.

I. Democracy, Modernization, and Decentralization: Theorizing Democratic Transition

The present era of democratization as the new social reality, which is believed to be the dominant trend in current social and political processes in the advanced and democratically developed West, has advanced differently in post-Soviet Eastern Europe (Toffler 1981; Bauman 2001; Sztompka 2001). The fact that the former Soviet states have shifted to democratic political regimes, and correspondingly to their capitalist economic systems, has often been overshadowed by other domestic factors and is still waiting to receive proper attention in the mainstream literature and transition scholarship. By the same token, most attempts by the post-Soviet Eastern European countries (including Ukraine) to create market economies, to modernize, and to decentralize have proved problematic. Thirty years of steady promotion of democratic reforms and efforts to repudiate the structural legacies of the communist past have not produced significant and stable levels of democracy. This is apparent in the merely semi-democratic forms of decision-making at the state level in Ukraine, Russia, Belarus, and Moldova, along with a sharp socioeconomic differentiation among regions within the countries and between their social groups. By "democratization," I mean not only political transition and introduction of the democratic system and principles in post-authoritarian states, but a way of life committed to greater equality and public accountability of power that rests on history, civil society, economic development, and associated individual agency and structural shifts.

Indeed, various studies have questioned whether structural changes have had any positive outcomes in post-communist eastern European states (Carothers 2002; Knack 2004; Burnell 2007; Merkel 2010). Given the limits of current transition research and the lack of a clear paradigm for understanding what is happening politically, economically, and socially in these societies, there is a need for a different approach (Oleinikova 2017)—one which would widen our understanding of the current modernization efforts and decentralization reforms in societies still undergoing transition (Oleinikova 2013). Currently, an approach that would consider the interplay and the combination between democracy, modernization, and decentralization is rarely applied to understand the empirical reality of modern post-communist states.

1. Modernization, Democracy, and Decentralization: From Western to East European Perspective

Over the past two centuries, the theory of modernization has repeatedly appeared in the center of political, social, and economic discussions. In the nineteenth and twentieth centuries, the Marxist concept of modernization inspired the most powerful political parties and movements. In the 1970s, critics claimed that the theory of modernization had died—but after the end of the Cold War, modernization theory experienced a revival, as it became clear that it could be used to understand the processes of democratization. The concept of modernization is based on the assumption that economic and technological progress is generated by predictable social and political changes. Modernization theory has experienced its revival in the1990s, but remains a controversial model. To understand modernization efforts in Ukraine, let us first conceptualize and define the connection between modernization and democracy.

Transition research starts in the early 1950s up to the 1960s in the West, at a time "when democratic forms of government were the exception rather than the rule" (Wucherpfennig and Deutsh 2009). Lipset (1959), an early theorist in the field, introduced what he called the "requisites of democracy." By doing so, he contributed the first formative input and laid out the transition research agenda for generations to come. He established the first theoretical link between the level of development of a given country and its probability of being democratic. Under "requisites of democracy," Lipset (1959) described the foundations for successful democratic consolidation, which he saw as variables that create conditions favorable for democratization and economic development (modernization)—such as urbanization, wealth, and education.

Concerned with structural and societal conditions conducive to democracy, especially in socioeconomic terms, Lipset (1959) outlined a structure-centered framework that analyzed transitions in terms of economic development and legitimacy. He argued that these two key structural characteristics were necessary to sustain democratic political systems (he used examples of European and English-speaking nations, and Latin American nations). Lipset's (1994) idea that economic modernization leads to democracy was further developed by Rostow (1960) and Deutsch (1961), who theorized that the path from economic modernization to democracy is linear and inevitable. Rostow (1960) was later criticized by Moore (1966), who formulated a historical analysis and critique, in which structural transformations caused by socioeconomic development (industrialization) were not necessarily conducive to democracy.

Contrary to the modernization approaches of the 1950s and 1960s that were concerned with structural transitions, at the beginning of the 1980s Western research on transition was driven by the agency-centered perspective propagated specifically in the writings of O'Donnell and Schmitter (1986). The retrospective analysis of transition research undertaken by O'Donnell and Schmitter (1986) helped scholars to understand that the incorporation of concepts such as human agency—in addition to structural factors—bore more fruit. O'Donnell and Schmitter (1986), identified factors influencing the success or failure of transitions that revolved around the ruling elite as a driving force in initiating shifts at all levels. They believed that any type of transition was possible if the relevant elite groups (ruling and opposition) could agree on common ways of implementing democracy (O'Donnell and Schmitter 1986). Socioeconomic conditions, as stressed by the pioneers (Lerner 1958; Lipset 1959; Rostow

1960; Moore 1966), were now understood to be irrelevant for transition research (Merkel 2004a, b).

In Eastern Europe in the1980s no similar research was being done, as few scholars could even conceive of a possible future shift from communism to democracy that would actually necessitate research on transition. Any work on Eastern Europe was done in the West. Interestingly though, around the same time as the end of the USSR, the Western agency perspective faced challenges in the form of a wave of "structuralism and the wave of pessimism" towards democracy (Merkel 2010, 19). The main focus of Western theoretical explanations of transition shifted from agency back to structure-centered transition theories, and Eastern European scholars were part of this rethink. Merkel argued that scholars such as O'Donnell and Schmitter (1986) overestimated the power of political elites. The belief that democracy can be promoted, supported or even imposed from the outside began to dominate (Merkel 2004a). Agency perspectives in the form of action theory were claimed to have shown themselves to be deficient in the analysis of the political and socioeconomic system transformations that overwhelmed post-communist Eastern Europe. The works of Levitsky and Way (2002), Merkel (2004b, 2010), Nathan (2003), Ottaway (2003) and Carothers (2007) highlight the shift in the ordinary citizens' perception of the democratic changes in new post-Soviet democracies from the optimistic attitudes of the early 1990s to the more pessimistic attitudes that have been increasingly common since the 2000s.

Therefore, in the first years after the dissolution of the Soviet Union and communism's collapse, most studies of a state transition to market economy and democracy, which tended to emerge from the West, were rather formal and structural, as more and more Western scholars, lacking contextual expertise, identified post-communist Eastern Europe as a natural laboratory for testing their generalizing transition theories. The authors of the new wave of Western theories explaining transition (Mansfield and Snyder 2002; Zakaria 2003; McFaul et al. 2004; Acemoglu and Robinson 2012) tried to take into account some of the features of the post-Soviet countries. For example, they sought explanations for the development of modernity in the history of particular countries. These scholars emphasized the negative role of the Soviet legacy as a factor that not only inhibited processes of liberal democratization but made it impossible to even apply general theoretical concepts of democratization to the post-communist region. Their assessment of the prevailing state of affairs in the

318   O. OLEINIKOVA

post-Soviet countries was pessimistic, although they did not discount the possibility of a gradual change towards democratization.

This led to significant debate, especially in the political and social sciences, about the relative value of these Western studies for providing an explanation of the post-Soviet transition towards democracy. Much of the contestation hinged upon how much one needed to know about national and local culture and history to produce a good explanatory framework that went beyond modernization and economic development dimensions.

The first scholarly works on transition in post-Soviet eastern European scholarship appeared relatively recently, after 1990, by which time it had finally become apparent that there was a real need to understand the consequences of reforms and transitions from the inside. The first research on transition in post-communist countries was determined by the dominant structural paradigm, which was drawn from existing research in the Western tradition. Post-Soviet social science in the late 1980s and early 1990s favored the authority of Western theories, and applied them, almost without adaptation, to explanations of the post-Soviet social reality. These theories included path dependence theory[1] (Collier and Collier 1991; Mahoney 2000; Pierson 2000), the third wave of democratization theory[2] (Huntington 1991), and political mobilization theory.[3]

---

[1] "Path dependence" is an important concept for social scientists engaged in studying processes of change. Being based on models of technological development used in economics, the first wave of scholarship in political science and sociology applied the concept of path dependence to political institutions, emphasizing lock-in and increasing returns (Pierson 2000), self-reinforcing sequences (Mahoney 2000), and the "mechanisms of reproduction" (Collier and Collier 1991) of particular historical legacies. These works played an important role in developing arguments about historical causation and interdependency of global development, when less-developed countries follow the development logic of more advanced states with successful democracies. Referring to the social developmental sequences, it was later labeled "path dependent social dynamics" (Durlauf and Young 2004, 21; Blume and Durlauf 2006, 15). The path-dependence theory of democracy underwent a harsh critique for overstating the degree of institutional stability of the exemplar democratic states (Thelen 1999; Alexander 2003; Crouch and Farrell 2004; Hacker 2011).

[2] Huntington (1991) argued that international structural factors during the 1970s were the causal sources for initiating Third-Wave democracy. Under structural factors he understood the "regional contingency factor" or the Soviet equivalent of the "domino theory," where the success of democracy in one country causes other countries to democratize. He suggested that post-Soviet states are being influenced by democratization effects, most notably by the efforts to spread democracy by the European Union and the United States.

[3] Political mobilization is a framework utilized to understand political participation in a transition period.

Furthermore, theories of modernization were revived to explain democratic transition in post-Soviet countries, particularly in Ukraine. This involved dominant discourses such as "catching up" with processes of modernization and westernization, the need for development, overcoming dependency, and reforming the state. In a search for their own approach, post-Soviet scholars started to apply and develop early ideas about the path from economic modernization to democracy and empirically test the relation between democracy and economic development. As in the early 1950s to mid-1960s (Lipset 1959; Rostow 1960; Moore 1966), structural factors such as the degree of development of national economies, the power of social classes, the autonomy of the state, and the efficiency of its bureaucracy, once again became central to research on system transformations (Merkel 2010). Despite the fact that the critique of modernization theory from the Third World was severe (Frank 1969; Roxborough 1988)—in terms of promoting the paternalism of developed states over underdeveloped states—Pye (1990) and Lipset (1959) proclaimed the renaissance of a series of modernization theories by, Lipset (1959), Moore (1966), and Roxborough (1979) in the post-Soviet democratization and transition theoretical discourse. In 1999, Zaslavskaia, a Russian scholar, under the influence of Roxborough (1979), described "modernization in post-Soviet countries as contributing to a growing capacity for social transformations" (Zaslavskaia 1999). In this approach, the argument was that underdeveloped post-Soviet states, in terms of democracy and market economy, are subject to social transitions only through structural modernization effects.

East European scholars argued that a positive feature of modernization theory was the emphasis on, and concrete analysis of, a wide range of modernization processes that took place immediately after the collapse of Soviet rule: urbanization, industrialization, rationalization, secularization, marketization of the economy, democratization policy, the progress of education, and other cultural processes. In other words, it suggested a framework for the interconnected study of all major aspects of social development that took place in the post-Soviet countries. An important step in the development and application of modernization theory in the post-socialist countries was undertaken by well-known scientists and sociologists in Hungary (Andorka and Spéder 1994), Poland (Adamski 1998; Domański 1999), the Czech Republic (Keller and Westerholm 2007; Machonin 1997), and Germany (Zapf et al. 2002; Zapf 1998). These scholars, applying modernization theory to the post-Soviet context, ended up criticizing it for its failure to reflect the multidimensionality of the transition process and for its limited explanation of structural and cultural factors in the development of the post-socialist countries of central and eastern Europe. Their criticism even extended to the updated and renewed versions of the "catching-up" and "reflexive" modernization theories proposed by Beck and colleagues (Beck et al. 1994; Keller 2002).

Therefore, the more research was done using modernization theories to understand social change in the post-Soviet countries, the more challenges were encountered and the more concerns eastern European scholars had. These critiques of modernization theories and their applicability to post-Soviet transition context were based on the argument that they did not sufficiently explain the nature of the structural shifts that were taking place in the post-Soviet space "simply because the historical vector of these changes was not objectively set up, not preconditioned" (Yadov 1999, 14).

This growing critique of modernization theory was further escalated after the release of a provocative series of publications by Przeworski et al. (2000) in the West, questioning the relationship between development and the transition to democracy. It was argued that economic factors alone are not sufficient to account for the fates of democratic and authoritarian regimes. The theories emphasizing the role of economic growth (Lipset 1994; Przeworski et al. 2000) were replaced in the West as well as in post-Soviet scholarship by more moderate concepts. These concepts include the concept of "gradual transition" (O'Donnell and Schmitter 1986; Carothers 2007), where transition is understood to gradually develop from a time of "liberalization" to "democratization," followed by the deepening of democracy and its adoption by all social groups at the stage of socialization. This latter stage provides a transition to a more "stable democracy" which is the ultimate goal of transition. As Carothers (2002) suggests, "gradual transition" is based on a recognition of the possibility and inevitability of constant evolutionary change towards democracy, even in those countries with strong authoritarian regimes.

In one form or another, Western theories of transition have long been among the decisive explanations and conceptualizations influencing the writing of theoreticians and sociologists, economists, and social reformers in post-Soviet Eastern Europe (Kutsenko 2001; Babenko 2004). Given the rapidly changing preferences of post-Soviet scholars following Western research trends in analyzing changes in and prospects for political development, it can be argued that the primary post-Soviet research on transition was not conducive to a deep understanding and explanation of post-Soviet development of democracy.

Ukrainian and Russian scholars (Naumova 1995; Zlobina 2003) argue that, given the limits of the structural transition paradigm of the 1990s for understanding what is happening in post-Soviet societies, and in Ukraine in particular, there is a need for a different approach with more of a focus on an agency that would explain the structural shifts related to changes on the level of agency (micro-level). Naumova explains that a new theory should be able to widen our understanding of societies in transition to include deeper, spontaneous shifts in social and individual consciousness that find expression primarily in the transformation of a value system and in the formation of new, individual life strategies (Naumova 1995, 7).

Consequently, by the beginning of the new century, scholars in the post-Soviet countries had begun to create theories related to the cultural and historical originality of post-Soviet people to explain the unique historical development of their political tradition, national mentality, and cultural heritage (Kohn et al. 2008, 141; Titarenko 2008, 23). At the start of the 2000s, post-Soviet scholars made significant advances in empirical descriptions and conceptualizations of post-communist transitions. These scholars suggest that the most theoretically pertinent way to approach the inter-relation between the components of transformation processes in the post-Soviet space is to focus on: (1) targeted reforms of basic institutions; (2) decentralization; and (3) semi-natural changes in the social structure and change in agency (Panina 2002; Kutsenko 2004; Golovakha and Panina 2006; Kohn et al. 2008; Zaslavskaia and Iadov 2008).

This is when the topic of decentralization enters discussions about the transition to democracy and modernization in post-Soviet countries, including Ukraine, on both theoretical and empirical levels. In most democracies there is "often a close connection between decentralization and democracy, though not necessarily a causal one" (Pandey 2005, 2). Decentralization can be conceptualized as a multidimensional process, composed of political, fiscal, and policy reforms. Decentralization strengthens private autonomy and political self-government and permits a market-like process in political decision-making. Political decisions become more democratic, processes become more open, and civic freedom expands. When we refer to processes of decentralization in any democratic political economy, one question strikes our mind: Does decentralization facilitate

322   O. OLEINIKOVA

modernization and democracy? Analyzing Ukraine's decentralization reform, the discussion in section "Decentralization Reform in Ukraine: An Effective Way to Promote Modernization?" leads to the conclusion that decentralization does facilitate modernization and democracy.

II. Decentralization Reform in Ukraine: An Effective Way to Promote Modernization?

There is a widely held assumption that the administrative decentralization is a precondition for, or connected to, economic growth and social modernization (Rondinelli 1981). The modernization potential of a country is determined by the presence of a strong industrial sector. In 2015, countries adopted the UN 2030 Agenda for Sustainable Development and its 17 Sustainable Development Goals (SDGs) that offered a new road map for humanity's development. It serves as evidence that the world is experiencing a renewed interest in the problems of the industrial sector of the economy.[4] The new goals have been developed to replace the Millennium Development Goals, which had been in place for the last fifteen years. SDG Goal #9—"to build resilient infrastructure, promote inclusive and sustainable industrialization and foster innovation" (UNGA 2015)—refers to an active increase in the share of industrial production in the total employment index and GDP by 2030. This is envisioned to be achievable through integration between small industrial enterprises and enterprises from other sectors, modernization of infrastructure and industries to increase the efficiency of the use of resources, the use of clean and environmentally safe technologies and industrial processes, expansion of scientific development, modernization of technological opportunities, and support for innovation.

In the context of industrial development and modernization, decentralization is seen as a reform that has the potential to address a number of social and economic development problems facing both developed and less developed economies. Today, Ukraine is a country of paramount interest for decentralization scholars globally, given its deep process of devolution granting greater autonomy to regional governments that has emerged with decentralization reform since 2014. This process dates back to a strategy of democratization of the centrist post-communist Ukrainian state as well as a modernization to improve efficiency in delivering public services and give more power to local authorities and elites.

---

[4] https://sustainabledevelopment.un.org/post2015/transformingourworld.

The irrelevance of the previous economic development model (before 2014) in Ukraine, which was mainly focused on the export of raw materials, as well as the lack of consensus among political and economic elites around the new priorities to meet EU conditions for development and innovation, indicated the need for a new modernization framework. The regional and local government architecture of post-Maidan Ukraine contained some of the formal elements of a decentralized and balanced system, but in practice functioned in a similar manner to the highly centralized, top-down structures that characterized the Soviet model of local governance.

The idea of decentralization in Ukraine emerged in early 2000s. By 2014 the country had accumulated enough theoretical expertise on the subject of decentralization among civil society and political elites, and sufficient familiarity with challenges of translating European norms of local self-government into Ukrainian law, to adopt decentralization reform and draw up an obligatory plan of action. The goal of modernization in modern Ukraine is to build an economic system that meets the requirements of today's democratic society. This system is based on the intensification of production, promoting the development of innovative and competitive industries, creating new jobs, significantly increasing the share of high-tech products in the national export structure, and working well with EU legal frameworks.

The rationale for the government's decentralization strategy was set out in two central documents, the "Concept of Reforming Local Self-Government and Territorial Structure of Power," approved by the Cabinet of Ministers in April 2014, and the "State Strategy for Regional Development 2015—2020," approved in August 2014. The "Concept of Reforming Local Self-Government" identified the fragile financial and material position of Ukraine's territorial communities (approximately 12,000) as a serious hindrance to economic growth and living standards in the regions. The reform documents emphasize the need for structural reforms, which would produce "economic stability" by establishing different levels of local self-governance with clear mandates and the financial and administrative resources to provide quality public services. It is evident from the foregoing analysis that the amalgamation of territorial communities and their ongoing development into the first port of call for public services, together with technological innovation, will have profound implications for the economic development and modernization of the local government system and regions.

A number of issues are delaying visible results of decentralization reform, and as a result modernization has been noticeably hampered since its start in 2014. The key issues are: the conflict in and around Ukraine, centralization of administrative tasks, an absence of well-defined responsibilities, local authorities' lack of organizational, technical, and financial resources, duplication of structures, and, in some cases a resultant weakness and incompetence in local authorities. Among the numerous obstacles facing decentralization reform, the following have had a significant slowing effect on modernization processes in Ukraine: (1) de-industrialization; (2) lack of a clearly identified national modernization strategy; (3) absence of necessary constitutional amendments; (4) under-resourced local governments and centralization of administrative tasks; (5) incomplete division of roles and functions between local and central government. Let us explore these five key challenges in more detail below.

1. De-industrialization of Ukraine

The world's most advanced economies have for some time been characterized by a long-term trend of de-industrialization (a long-term decrease in the importance of manufacturing) (Rodrik 2016; Hamnett 2018). The steady decline in production is most noticeable in terms of employment. For this reason, debates about de-industrialization often focus on job losses. The share of manufacturing in national employment is steadily declining in many parts of the world. Even in countries such as Republic of Korea, Turkey, Mexico, and eastern European states, which saw a rise in industrial production and employment in the 1970s and 1980s, manufacturing's share of total employment is now in decline.

In recent years, de-industrialization processes have been recorded in Ukraine, showing not only quantitative but also qualitative deterioration of industrial output. The number of employees in the manufacturing sector decreased from 2,917,000 in 2000 to 1,511,000 in 2014, that is by 48 percent (State Statistics Service of Ukraine 2014, 131). The proportion of the labor force in processing industries decreased from 21.3 percent in 2000 (State Statistics Service of Ukraine 2009, 189) to 16.9 percent in 2014. Manufacturing's share of GDP decreased almost by three times. Such trends have negative implications on the productivity of the working age population. The generally declining demographic and employment trends in the last five years are also consequences of conflict in and around

Ukraine which has contributed to a growth in death rates, massive emigration, and a wave of internal and external displacement.

The level of depreciation of fixed assets of processing enterprises is increasing (67.5 percent in 2010 versus 60.2 percent in 2007). Among the largest industries the highest depreciation levels are recorded in mechanical engineering (84.3 percent in 2010 versus 68.9 percent in 2007; State Statistics Service of Ukraine 2010, 75), very bad figures for an industry that is, worldwide, a driver of innovative economic development.

Labor productivity in manufacturing is declining sharply. Measured by a labor productivity indicator, Ukraine lags far behind the other former Soviet republics. Expert opinion attributes this phenomenon to a weakening of motivation to increase productivity, low education and skills, wage strain, an increase in recent years in social transfers in the structure of the population's incomes compared to wages. Among the important actions necessary to increase labor productivity are the restructuring of employment in the direction of increasing the share of innovative positions, which implies the need for a systematic increase of labor productivity, as opposed to employment in low-productive forms of economic activity (Lisogor 2010). However, it is impossible to ensure sustained economic growth without solving the problem of profit sources and the formation of effective institutional models of profit maximization (Lisogor 2010).

2. No Clearly Outlined National Modernization Strategy

The need for modernization in contemporary Ukraine was first identified in Heyets (2010). More comprehensive ideas of modernization were further developed in the National Aid document prepared by the social sciences and humanities section of the National Academy of Science of Ukraine. After being scientifically tested, the idea of modernization formed the basis of the President of Ukraine's 2014 address to the Verkhovna Rada "Modernization of Ukraine is Our Strategic Choice." Various aspects of modernization are also defined in the State Regional Development Strategy for the period up to 2020. However, in Ukraine there is still no clearly outlined national project of modernization, although the decentralization of governance is seen as a reform that addresses a number of social and economic development and modernization problems.

National industrial policy is the fundamental base in shaping a modernization framework which will enable the transition of the economy to an innovative model of development. In order to modernize the economy, the priorities for industrial development must be clearly defined and set out in the laws of Ukraine and in the strategic documents of the Cabinet of Ministers relating to the development of ministries and departments and the strategies for socioeconomic development of the regions. In Ukraine, the process of industrial policy making in previous years was unsatisfactory. The last State Industrial Development Program was in place from 2003 to 2011. It was not until 2013 that the concept of a national targeted economic program for industrial development for the period up to 2020 was approved. Restoration of the processes of state regulation of economic development requires the development and adoption of a priority action plan for the development of industrial sector. Its main directions of reform should be the elimination of resistance to innovative technological modernization of the industrial sector; an adoption of new technological structures to bring about advanced processing and manufacturing of final-consumption products; and introduction of energy-saving technologies, particularly expansion in the use of non-traditional and renewable energy sources (Kindzerskyi 2013).

3. Absence of Necessary Constitutional Amendments

The process of local government reform and decentralization often depends on changes to the Constitution. In Poland, for example, the decentralization of power began with an introduction of amendments to the country's Constitution. The Constitution of the Republic of Poland was first amended immediately after the election of a Senate (the upper house of parliament) in June 1989. Further, over the next nine years, a number of normative acts were adopted aimed at implementing the process of decentralization of power in Poland.

Unlike the Polish experience of local self-government reforms, in Ukraine the draft law on amendments to the Constitution of Ukraine has not been adopted. As of 2014, the government started the reform within the framework of the effective Constitution. The major package of new legislation has been developed and became effective, the priority legislative initiatives of which legislation are currently being implemented. However, as of March 2020 Verkhovna Rada (the parliament of Ukraine) has not introduced the necessary amendments on decentralization to the Constitution. In the first instance, such amendments had to resolve the issue of establishment of executive bodies within oblast (regional) and rayon (district) councils, the re-organization of local state administrations into controlling and supervisory bodies, and provide a clear definition of the united territorial community as a political-administrative subdivision. Despite the necessary constitutional amendments not having been adopted, the proposals for such amendments stipulate that the powers of local self-government bodies should be financed. Local governments receive a share of national taxes (not just subsidies). Thus, local governments actually have their own financial resources and will not have a rigid dependence on the national government apparatus.

Therefore, the process of decentralization requires legislative implementation in a logical and consistent manner, according to which changes are first made to the basic law (e.g. Constitution) followed by other normative acts being adopted accordingly. Only then can local government reform increase the efficiency of the use of budget funds, improve the quality and accessibility of public services to the population, create the basis of regional development, solve a number of infrastructure problems (transport, garbage and waste disposal, water supply, maintenance and repair of roads), act to reverse the emergence of depressed territories, and provide stability, transparency, and other conditions for conducting business, improving the inflow of investments, and develop the economy.

4. Under-Resourced Local Governments and Centralization of Administrative Tasks

As mentioned above, modernization in Ukraine requires there to be conditions under which industrial problems can be solved. One such condition is the participation of regions and territorial communities in ensuring the industrial development of their territories. Effective modernization of industry is not possible without modernization of the state economic policy associated with the redistribution of powers between national and local levels of authorities. Such changes occur through decentralization.

The most important principle of the decentralization reform adopted in 2014 is subsidiarity, which implies the transfer of decision-making powers from central to local organizational levels, with appropriate financial security. This principle is applied as a political and an organizational norm of the European Union, according to which political decisions must be taken at the level closer to citizens, but with sufficient authority for their effective implementation. In practice, finding the optimal setting of the decision-making center may be the result of arrangements made between the center and the local government.

The principle of subsidiarity is reflected in the Budget Code of Ukraine: distribution of expenditures between the state budget and local budgets is based on the need to maximize the provision of guaranteed services to their direct recipients (Budget Code of Ukraine 2015). At the same time, however, the principle of subsidiarity is absent from the current Law of Ukraine "On Local Self-Government in Ukraine."

The transfer of powers from the state bodies to a lower level of administrative and territorial structures is ensured by the transfer of necessary resources for this purpose and by giving the local government authority the right to decide on delegated powers based on local peculiarities. Therefore, decentralization is accompanied by increased capacity and power for local self-government bodies through the consolidation of administrative-territorial units or through the creation of inter-municipal unions.

In 2015, the Law of Ukraine "On Voluntary Amalgamation of Territorial Communities" (ATCs) was adopted, which aims to unite neighboring local communities to form and secure their economic, social and cultural capacity; to establish the order of association of communities of villages, settlements, and cities; to provide state support to the united territorial communities.

This law is aimed at supporting the will of ATC residents and giving them an opportunity to form an economic, social, and cultural environment of villages, towns and cities on their own. It is believed that the integration of territorial communities will contribute not only to cultural and social improvement, but also to economic development, of communities through integration, as the integration of territorial communities' budgets will provide an opportunity for the implementation of larger, innovative projects. To implement this law, a special procedure for forming wealthy territorial communities was developed and approved, containing practical provisions detailing the process of uniting territorial communities. The amalgamation process got into full swing in 2016, and by the beginning of February 2019, 878 ATCs had been established. These communities were composed of about 4,018 former local councils, with a population of 9 million (Decentralization Report 2019).

Another Law of Ukraine "On Cooperation of Territorial Communities" provides an opportunity to address the issues of socioeconomic and cultural development of territories, improving the quality of services provided to the population based on common interests and goals of communities. By 2019, the register of co-operation agreements for territorial communities contained 325 co-operation agreements (Decentralization Report 2019), which mainly related to the implementation of joint projects on environmental protection and the, maintenance and repair of social and transport infrastructure. In total, 925 communities had taken advantage of the mechanism (Decentralization Report 2019).

At present, in Ukraine, the state level of economic and administrative management is still too concentrated in the center; the local level is not provided with sufficient resources and accordingly the functioning of the local executive system is not sufficiently dynamic. There are contradictions in the system of local authorities. Without having to deal with their citizens and failing to address their needs, the authorities are able to launch only one style of modernization—mobilization, imposed from above and restricted, eliminating the possibility of citizens making choices and exercising freedom, which means that authorities are unlikely to meet public needs (Kindzerkyi 2013). Successful modernization of industry within the ongoing decentralization reform requires a clear definition and distribution of powers, resources, and responsibilities for conducting the industrial policies assigned to each entity in government. At the same time, local government must serve to solve the problems of industrial development in their territories, and not create new administrative and bureaucratic mechanisms that will stand in the way of local initiatives. It is recommended that local authorities draw on the experience of countries which have had positive industrial policy outcomes in the context of decentralization of public administration, adapting these experiences to Ukrainian national and regional characteristics.

5. Incomplete Division of Roles and Functions Between Local and Central Government

The division and optimization of local government functions has not been completed yet. The system of distribution of state functions and the competence of each level of government have not been fully established in the relevant legislative acts. As a result, uncontrolled expansion of the central state bodies' functions seems to be the order of the day.

- The roles, functions, and powers of the central and local governments has not been separated and allocated; a duplication of functions still remains. In certain sectors of government, there is a noticeable hierarchical pyramid of competence, where functions and responsibilities between local and central management clash. Such overlap of functions leads to ineffective management and chaos in terms of responsibility and accountability, wasteful spending of budget funds, and a decrease in the quality of services provided by the state. As a result, distribution of powers at "oblast–rayon" level has no uniform, stable character, which results in a failure to change and modernize in regional territories.

- The current system of central–local budget relations is characterized by a lack of stability in the medium term, lacking clear and understandable principles for the distribution of income. Expenses and budget transfers between levels are not clearly defined. Uneven distribution of income between the regions due to the huge variation in the economic development of territories determines the need for an active policy of equalizing budgetary provision of the regions and territorial communities in order to achieve equal access to public services and modernization.

This list of obstacles facing decentralization and effective modernization in Ukraine makes it clear that all further developments in the ongoing reform of governance and public administration system must be aimed at optimizing functions and ensuring their effective distribution and performance across all levels of government. The essence of decentralization should not be the presence of formal legal features, but rather its practical implementation.

It seems evident that a more decentralized governance system is likely to be a more democratic and modernized system. As noted, decentralization provides more opportunities for civic space and citizen participation and, consequently, for independent groups to emerge, for new economic models to appear, for modernization of the old regional systems, for political opposition to develop and for individuals to practice and experience the exercise of free choice in democratic governance. For all those reasons, decentralization is a significant strategy in the efforts to modernize and democratize Ukrainian society. However, decentralization reform in Ukraine needs several more years to bring about visible regional modernization.

Conclusion

Decentralization and regionalization have become the guiding principles in world politics since 1960s, in line with accelerated modernization evidenced by foreign experience in managing the development of regions (Arghiros 2016). While most developing national economies have intellectually accepted the notion of decentralization as an essential condition for political, economic, and social development, some have not been prepared to take on the costly burden of long-neglected institutional development at the local–regional level. Moreover, in some developing countries political elites at the center have fought to retain their power, while the elite at the local level, who are generally well-networked with central government authorities and may even have been paid to remain loyal to the center, have been reluctant to disturb the status quo for fear of losing the influence and benefits of their position. Despite resistance, policies of decentralization have appeared in the planning documents and presidential speeches of developing countries around the world, and some significant experiments with decentralization theory have been undertaken (Crook and Manor 2018).

Ukraine is a good example here. Decentralization reform is one of the few reforms in Ukraine that has a solid plan, strategy, and a clear concept. An important feature of this transformation is the implementation of several reforms in public administration in the context of decentralization: reform of the territorial organization of power; reform of local government; reform of regional policy. Despite the failure of the government to introduce the required constitutional amendments in 2014, decentralization has arguably been the subject of one of Ukraine's most successful reforms since the Maidan Revolution. The government has demonstrated a genuine commitment to transferring responsibilities and resources to local government authorities on an unprecedented scale, as reflected in the extent of fiscal decentralization that has taken place for towns of oblast significance and the new ATCs. Like Poland, where decentralization played a significant role in the processes of economic development and industrial restructuring, in the early 1990s Ukraine faced challenges after the breakup of the USSR due to the imperative to reorient its exports from the Soviet market to the European market. According to experts, the restoration of the old industrial regions in Poland was a success due to the cooperation of state authorities and local governments. The restructuring of the economy was the task of the state government, the development of small and medium-sized businesses was the responsibility of local authorities. To attract investment local government provided the necessary infrastructure, had the authority to offer tax incentives and privileges for utility bills, had the right to communalize businesses and so on. As a result of effective local development, Poland has increased its share of high-tech exports. Ukraine in some ways is following the Polish scenario.

Can we conclude by saying that there is a positive linkage between decentralization and modernization in Ukraine? How can the goal of empowering local governments to act as efficient modernizers of the social, economic, and political environment in their local territories be achieved? Practical experience indicates several conditions necessary for successful modernization as a result of decentralization. There is the condition of secure existence and financing. This is a first necessary condition for strong local government, without which they cannot perform properly because their existence is in perpetual jeopardy vulnerable to authorities at higher levels of government having the power to dissolve them easily or to change their territories. The "middle way" in managing local government and governance changes to develop a more pragmatic localism will help accelerate modernization. Then, citizens are more likely to participate because their participation has greater meaning and practical impact.

The second necessary condition is that the priorities of industrial development in Ukraine must be clearly defined and set out in law. Adoption of a clear modernization strategy for the country at national and regional levels, which will enable the effective transition of the economy to an innovative model of development, is crucial. The process of industrial policy-making has to be upgraded from the unsatisfactory level of previous years.

The success of modernization efforts depends largely on the availability of sufficient resources and the possibility of using these resources autonomously for the development of economic and social initiatives in regions. Autonomy refers here to democratic accountability and accelerated implementation of local modernization initiatives. It is apparent that although there might not be a straightforward causal relation between modernization and decentralization, the process of decentralization furthers modernization and democratization. The results of modernization of Ukraine are not yet visible, as there are still issues, outlined in section "Decentralization Reform in Ukraine: An Effective Way to Promote Modernization?", that are delaying the satisfactory completion of decentralization reform in Ukraine.

References

Acemoglu, Daron, and James A. Robinson. 2012. *Why Nations Fail: The Origins of Power, Prosperity, and Poverty.* Crown Books.

Adamski, Wladyslav. 1998. *The Legacy of State Socialism as a Challenge to System Transformation.* Berlin: Wissenschaftszentrum Berlin für Sozialforschung (WZB).

Alexander, Neville. 2003. *An Ordinary Country: Issues in the Transition from Apartheid to Democracy in South Africa.* Berghahn Books.

Andorka, Rudolf, and Zsolt Spéder. 1994. A magyartársadalomszerkezete, 1994 [The Structure of Hungarian Society, 1994]. In *Magyarországpolitikai Évkönyve (1995),* ed. S. Kurtan, P. Sándor, and L. Vass. Budapest: DKMPA.

Arghiros, Daniel. 2016. *Democracy, Development and Decentralization in Provincial Thailand.* Routledge.

Arzaghi, M., and J.V. Henderson. 2005. Why Countries Are Fiscally Decentralizing. *Journal of Public Economics* 89 (7): 1157–1189.

Babenko, Svetlana. 2004. Sotsyalnyi mechanism post-sovetskoytransformatsyi: deyatelnostno-strukturnyipodhod [Social Mechanism of Post-Soviet Transformation: Agency-Structure Approach]. In *Postkomunystycheskye Ttransformatsiyi: Vektori, Napravleniya, Soderzhaniye* [Postcommunist Transformations: Vectors, Dimensions, Content], ed. Olga D. Kutsenko and S.S. Babenko, 251–274. Kharkiv: V.N. Karazin Kharkiv National University Publisher.

Bauman, Zygmunt. 2001. *The Individualised Society.* Cambridge: Polity.

Beck, Ulrich, Antony Giddens, and Scott Lash. 1994. *Reflexive Modernization. Politics. Tradition and Aesthetics in the Modern Social Order.* Stanford, CA: Stanford University Press.

Blume. Lawrence E., and Steven N. Durlauf, eds. 2006. *The Economy as an Evolving Complex System, III: Current Perspectives and Future Directions.* Oxford University Press.

Burnel , Peter. 2007. Does International Democracy Promotion Work? Discussion Paper. Bonn: Dt. Inst. Für Entwicklungspolitik. http://www.uwe-holtz.uni-bonn.de/lehrmaterial/begleit_burnell.pdf.

Canavi e-Bacarreza, Gustavo, Jorge Martinez-Vazquez, and Bauyrzhan Yedgenov. 2017. Re-examining the Determinants of Fiscal Decentralization: What Is the Role of Geography? *Journal of Economic Geography* 17 (6): 1209–1249.

Carothers, Thomas. 2002. The End of the Transition Paradigm. *Journal of Democracy* 13 (1): 5–21.

———. 2007. How Democracies Emerge: The Sequencing Fallacy. *Journal of Democracy* 18 (1): 12–27.

Collier. Ruth Berins, and David Collier. 1991. *Shaping the Political Arena: Critical Junctures, the Labor Movement, and Regime Dynamics in Latin America.* Princeton, NJ: Princeton University Press.

Crook, Richard, and James Manor. 2018. Democratic Decentralization. In *Making Development Work. Development Learning in a World of Poverty and Wealth*, ed. Robert Picciotto, 83–104. Routledge.

Crouch, Colin, and Henry Farrell. 2004. Breaking the Path of Institutional Development? Alternatives to the New Determinism. *Rationality and Society* 16 (1): 5–43.

Decentralisation. 2019. Monitorinh—Stanom na 10 Zhovtnya 2019 [Monitoring—As of 10 October 2019]. https://decentralization.gov.ua/uploads/library/file/477/10.10.2019.pdf.

Deutsch, Karl W. 1961. Social Mobilization and Political Development. *American Political Science Review* 55 (3): 493–514.

Domański, Henryk. 1999. Major Social Transformations and Social Mobility: The Case of the Transition to and from Communism in Eastern Europe. *Social Science Information* 38 (3): 463–491.

Durlauf, Steven N., and H. Peyton Young, eds. 2004. *Social Dynamics: Economic Learning and Social Evolution 4*. MIT Press.

Frank, Andre Gunder. 1969. *Latin America: Underdevelopment or Revolution*. Monthly Review Press.

Furman, Dmitri. 2008. Imitation Democracies: The Post-Soviet Penumbra. *New Left Review 54*: 28–47.

Golovakha, Evgeniy I., and Nataliya V. Panina. 2006. Osnovnye Etapy i Tendencyi Transformacii Ukrainskogo Obschestva: ot Perestroiki do Orangevoi Revolutsii [Main Stages and Trends in the Transformation of Ukrainian Society: from *Perestroika* to the Orange Revolution]. *Sociology: Theory, Methods, Marketing* 3: 32–51.

Hacker, Jacob. 2011. The Institutional Foundations of Middle-Class Democracy. *Policy Network* 6: 33–37.

Hamnett, Chris. 2018. A World Turned Upside Down: the Rise of China and the Relative Economic Decline of the West. *Area Development and Policy 3* (2): 223–240.

Heyets, Valerii M. 2010. Liberal-Democratic Foundations: A Course Towards the Modernization of Ukraine. *Ukrainian Economy* 3: 4–20.

Huntington, Samuel P. 1991. *The Third Wave: Democratization in the Late 20th Century*. University of Oklahoma.

Inozemtsev, Vladislav L. 2010. On the Edge of the Centuries. Economic Tendencies and Their Noneconomic Consequences. *Halchynskyi AS Economic Methodology. Innovation Logic, K.:"ADEF–Ukraine*.

Inozemtsev, Vladislav L., and Piotr Dutkiewicz, eds. 2013. *Democracy Versus Modernization: A Dilemma for Russia and for the World*. Routledge.

Keller, K.L. 2002. Modernizacia—Gumanizacia Obshchestva ili Korozia Bytia? Kriticheskie Zametki o Teorii Modernizacii [Modernization—Humanization of Society or Corrosion of Existence? Critical Notes on the Theory of Modernization]. *Sociological Researches* 7 (219, Jan.): 48–53.

Keller, Alister, and P. Joakim Westerholm. 2007. Benchmarking a Transition Economy Capital Market, Australasian Accounting. *Business and Finance Journal* 1 (3): 49–60.

Kindzerskyi, Yurii V. 2013. *Industry of Ukraine: Strategy and Policy of Structural and Technological Modernization: Monograph*. Kyiv: NAS of Ukraine.

Knack, Stephen. 2004. Does Foreign Aid Promote Democracy? *International Studies Quarterly* 48 (1): 251–266.

Kohn, Melvin L., Valeriy Khmelko, Vladimir I. Paniotto, and Ho-fung Hung. 2008. Social Structure and Personality during the Process of Radical Social Change: A Study of Ukraine in Transition. In *New Frontiers in Comparative Sociology*, ed. Masamichi Sasaki. Vol. 109 of International Studies in Sociology and Social Anthropology, 119–170. Brill.

Kutsenko, Olga D. 2001. Deyatelnastnaia perspectiva v ponimanii obschestva: popytka deiatelnostno-structurnogo sinteza [Agency Perspective in Understanding Society: An Attempt of Structure-Agency Synthesis]. *Sociology: Theory, Methods, and Marketing* 1: 27–41.

———. 2004. Fazy i Puti Sistemnyh Transformacii: Podobia i Razlichia v Byvshyh Stranah Gosudarstvennogo Socializma [Phases and Ways of Systemic Transformations: Similarities and Differences in the Former Countries of State Socialism]. In *Postkomunystycheskye Transformatsiyi: Vektori, Napravleniya, Soderzhaniye* [Post-Communists Transformation: Vectors, Directions, Content], 251–274. Kharkiv: V.N. Karazin Kharkiv National University Publisher.

Lerner, D. 1958. *The Passing of Traditional Society*. New York: Free Press.

Letelier, L. 2005. Explaining Fiscal Decentralization. *Public Finance Review* 33 (2): 155–183.

Levitsky, Steve, and Lucan A. Way. 2002. The Rise of Competitive Authoritarianism. *Journal of Democracy* 13 (2): 51–65.

Lipset, Seymour Martin. 1959. Some Social Requisites of Democracy: Economic Development and Political Legitimacy. *The American Political Science Review* 53 (1): 69–105.

———. 1994. The Social Requisites of Democracy Revisited: 1993 Presidential Address. *American Sociological Review* 59: 1–22.

Lisogor, L.S. 2010. Labor Productivity in Ukraine: Problems and Prospects for Improvement. *Instytut Demohrafii ta Sotsialnykh Doslidzhen* [Institute of Demography and Social Research.] http://dse.org.ua/arhcive/14/14.pdf.

Litvack, Jennie, Junaid Kamal Ahmad, J., and Bird, Richard M. 1998. Rethinking Decentralization in Developing Countries. *World Bank Sector Studies Series*. http://documents.worldbank.org/curated/en/938101468764361146/Rethinking-decentralization-in-developing-countries

336   O. OLEINIKOVA

Machonin, Pavel. 1997. *Social Transformation and Modernization: On Building Theory of Societal Changes in the Post-communist European Countries*. Vol. 3. Praha: Sociologickén akladatelství.

Mahoney, James. 2000. Path Dependence in Historical Sociology. *Theory and Society* 29: 507–548.

Mansfield, Edward D., and Jack Snyder. 2002. Democratic Transitions, Institutional Strength, and War. *International Organization* 56 (2): 297–337.

McFaul, Michael, Nicolai Petrov, and Andrei Ryabov. 2004. *Between Dictatorship and Democracy. Russian Post-communist Political Reform*. Washington, DC: Carnegie Endowment for International Peace.

Merkel, W., ed. 2004a. *Consolidated or Defective Democracy? Problems of Regime Change*. London: Taylor & Francis.

Merkel, Wolfgang. 2004b. Embedded and Defective Democracies. In *Consolidated or Defective Democracy? Problems of Regime Change*, ed. Ariel Croissant and Wolfgang Merkel. London: Taylor & Francis.

———. 2010. *System Transformation. Eine Einfuhrung in die Theorie und Empirie der Transformationsforschung*. Wiesbaden: VS Verlag für Sozialwissenschaften.

Moore, Barrington, Jr. 1966. *Social Origins of Dictatorship and Democracy*. New York: Beacon Press.

Nathan, Andrew J. 2003. Authoritarian Resilience. *Journal of Democracy* 14 (1): 6–17.

Naumova, Nina Fedorovna. 1995. Zhyznennaya Strategya Cheloveka v Perehodnom Obschestve [Individual Life Strategy in a Transitional Society]. *Journal of Sociology* 1: 2–12.

O'Donnell, Guillermo, and Philippe C. Schmitter. 1986. *Transitions from Authoritarian Rule: Prospects for Democracy*. Baltimore: Johns Hopkins University Press.

Oleinikova, Olga. 2013. Beyond Two Decades of Social Transition in Ukraine: The Underestimated Power of Agency in Transition Research. *Australian and New Zealand Journal of European Studies* 5 (2): 45–60.

———. 2017. Foreign Funded NGOs in Russia, Belarus and Ukraine: Recent Restrictions and Implications. *Cosmopolitan Civil Societies: An Interdisciplinary Journal* 9 (3): 85–94.

———. 2019. Democratic Transition Research: From Western to Post-soviet East European Scholarship. *East/West: Journal of Ukrainian Studies* 6 (1): 147–167.

Oleinikova, Olga, and Jumana Bayeh. 2019. *Democracy, Diaspora, Territory: Europe and Cross-Border Politics*. London: Routledge.

Olum, Yasin. 2010. Participatory Budgeting in Decentralized Local Governments in Uganda. *The Uganda Journal of Management and Public Policy Studies* 1 (1): 98–119.

Ottaway, Marina. 2003. Promoting Democracy After Conflict: The Difficult Choices. *International Studies Perspectives* 4 (3): 314–322.

Pandey, Sanjay. 2005. Democracy and Decentralisation. 10.2139/ssrn.878432. https://ssrn.com/abstract=878432.

Panina, N.V. 2002. Ukrainske Suspilstvo 1992–2002. Sociologichnyi Monitoring [Ukrainian Society 1992–2002. Opinion Poll]. Kyiv: Institute of Sociology UNAS.

Panizza, Ugo. 1999. On the Determinants of Fiscal Centralization: Theory and Evidence. *Journal of Public Economics* 74 (1): 97–139.

Pierson, Paul. 2000. Increasing Returns, Path Dependence, and the Study of Politics *American Political Science Review* 94 (2): 251–267.

Przeworski, Adam, Jose Antonio Cheibub, Michael E. Alvarez, and Fernando Limongi. 2000. *Democracy and Development: Political Institutions and Material Well-Being in the World, 1950–1990*. Cambridge: Cambridge University Press.

Pye, Lucian W. 1990. Political Science and the Crisis of Authoritarianism. *American Political Science Review* 84 (1): 3–19.

Rodrik, Dani. 2016. Premature Deindustrialization. *Journal of Economic Growth* 21 (1): 1–33.

Rondinelli, Dennis A. 1981. Administrative Decentralisation and Economic Development: The Sudan's Experiment with Devolution. *The Journal of Modern African Studies* 19 (4): 595–624.

Rostow, W.W. 1960. *The Stages of Economic Growth: A Non-communist Manifesto.* Cambridge: Cambridge University Press.

Roxborough, Ian. 1979. *Theories of Underdevelopment.* London: Macmillan.

———. 1988. Modernization Theory Revisited. A Review Article. *Comparative Studies in Society and History* 30 (4): 753–761.

State Statistics Service of Ukraine. 2009. Statistical Collection "Labor of Ukraine in 2009", LLC "Consultant". Kyiv. http://www.ukrstat.gov.ua.

———. 2010. Statistical Collection "Industry of Ukraine 2007—2010, LLC "Consultant". Kyiv. http://www.ukrstat.gov.ua.

———. 2014. Statistical Collection "Labor of Ukraine in 2014" LLC "Consultant". Kyiv. http://www.ukrstat.gov.ua.

Sztompka, Piotr. 2001. Cultural Trauma in Post-communist Society. *Sociological Research* 2: 3–12.

Thelen. David. 1999. Rethinking History and the Nation-State: Mexico and the United States. *The Journal of American History* 86 (2): 438–455.

Titarenko, Larissa. 2008. Post-Soviet Transformation of Democracy: Western and Domestic Interpretations. *Philosophy and Social Science: Scientific Journal* 1: 21–27.

Toffler, Alvin. 1981. *The Third Wave.* Bantam Books.

Treisman, Daniel M. 2006. Explaining Fiscal Decentralisation: Geography, Colonial History, Economic Development and Political Institutions. *Commonwealth & Comparative Politics* 44 (3): 289–325.

338 O. OLEINIKOVA

UNGA (United Nations General Assembly). 2015. Transforming Our World: The 2030 Agenda for Sustainable Development, A/RES/70/1, September 25. https://www.un.org/ga/search/view_doc.asp?symbol=A/RES/70/1&Lang=E.

Verkhovna Rada. 2015. Budget Code of Ukraine. http://zakon0.rada.gov.ua/laws/show/2456-17.

Wucherpfennig, Julian, and Franzisca Deutsh. 2009. Modernization and Democracy: Theory and Evidence Revisited. *Living Reviews in Democracy* 1: 1–9.

Yadov, V.A. 1999. Rosia Kak Transformirushcheesia Obschestvo (Rezume Mnogoletnei Diskusii Sociologov) [Russia as a Society in Transition (Summary of Sociological Discussions)]. *Society and Economy* 10 (11): 65–72.

Zakaria, Fareed. 2003. *The Future of Freedom: Illiberal Democracy at Home and Abroad*. W.W. Norton.

Zaslavskaia, Tatyana I. 1999. Transformation Process in Russia: Socio-Structural Aspect. In *Social Trajectory of the Reforming Russia: Research of Novosibirsk School of Economics and Sociology*, ed. T.I. Zaslavskaia and Z.I. Kalugina. Novosibirsk: Siberian Enterprise.

Zaslavskaia, Tatiana I., and Vladimir A. Iadov. 2008. Sotsial'nye Transformaztsii v Rossii v Epokhu Global'nykh Izmenenii [Social Transformations in Russia in the Epoch of Global Changes]. *Sotsiologicheskii zhurnal* 4: 8–22.

Zlobina, O. 2003. Osobystisna skladova suspilnyh zmin: sociologichnyi kontekst [Agency component of the societal changes: sociological context]. *Sociology: Theory, Methods, Marketing* 3: 32–45.

CHAPTER 12

Decentralization in Ukraine and Bottom-Up European Integration

Anne Pintsch

INTRODUCTION

The ongoing decentralization process in Ukraine is considered one of the most successful reforms in the country so far. It started in 2014 with the Concept of the Reform of Local Self-Government and Territorial Organization of Power in Ukraine (Government of Ukraine 2014), adopted by the government in the wake of the Euromaidan protests. One of its main elements is the merging of smaller communities into so-called Amalgamated Territorial Communities (abbreviated as ATCs in the following) or *Ob'yednani Terytorial'ni Hromady*. With their voluntary unification, these newly established communities obtain more authority and financial means (Rabinovych et al. 2018).

Political scientists ascribe many positive aspects to decentralization, including the high responsiveness of public services to people's needs, higher levels of citizen participation, and lower levels of corruption (Saito 2011, 486–487). Despite the short lifetime so far of decentralization

---

A. Pintsch (✉)
University of Agder, Kristiansand, Norway
e-mail: anne.pintsch@uia.no

© The Author(s) 2020
H. Shelest, M. Rabinovych (eds.), *Decentralization, Regional Diversity, and Conflict*, Federalism and Internal Conflicts,
https://doi.org/10.1007/978-3-030-41765-9_12

339

340 A. PINTSCH

reform in Ukraine, scholars and experts have thoroughly examined the process, with mixed conclusions (e.g. International Alert and UCIPR 2017; Aasland 2018; OECD 2018; Dudley 2019). In all cases, the authors report positive developments, but they voice concerns, too. Overall, however, decentralization reform seems to assist Ukraine's movement towards its official goals of good governance, democratization, and overcoming corruption. The same is reflected in European statements. The EU–Ukraine Parliamentary Association Committee "[c]onsiders that the decentralization process has been and continues to be highly beneficial for Ukrainian citizens, in particular regarding improved quality of services, the reduction of corruption at local level and the increased ownership of local decision-making by citizens" (EU–Ukraine Parliamentary Association Committee 2019, 8).

Given this positive relationship between decentralization and other domestic reforms, the question arises whether and how the delegation of power contributes to Ukraine's strategic foreign policy goal of European integration. This question can be approached from different perspectives. Most generally, one can ask whether the successful implementation of reform would bring the country closer to EU membership, as recently codified in Ukraine's Constitution. The answer, however, is clearly negative: membership is currently not offered by the EU. While there may be some form of future "procedural entrapment" for the EU should Ukraine comply with all reform requirements (Sasse 2008), this corresponds more to a hypothetical than a real scenario. There is currently no EU membership conditionality towards Ukraine. Alternatively, one can also approach the question by asking whether the successful implementation of the decentralization agenda could be seen as a sign of Ukraine's compliance with the EU–Ukrainian Association Agreement (EU–Ukraine 2014). However, decentralization reform is not directly related to this agreement (Hanushchak et al. 2017), and progress will not directly contribute to Ukraine's further inclusion into the EU market or agencies.

Against this background, this chapter follows a sociological approach and takes a different perspective on the question whether decentralization fosters Ukraine's European integration. In doing so, the European integration of Ukraine is not primarily understood in a formal–institutional way, i.e. as the country's inclusion into the EU system of institutions or regulations. Instead, it draws on the conceptualization of integration in terms of transnational social relationships. As Langenohl (2019) summarizes: "European integration can thus be understood as a political project with a sociological imagination that puts the broadening and deepening of 'sociation' (*Vergesellschaftung*, Georg Simmel) at center stage" (78).

More specifically, the chapter looks at the transnational relations of the newly established ATCs, in particular at the existence of community twinning partnerships with counterparts abroad and membership in transnational European networks. In doing so, it builds on a literature that stresses the significance for European integration of transnational cooperation at local level. Section "Ukraine's Decentralization Reform" presents some basic points about Ukraine's decentralization reform. Section "Decentralization Reform and Ukraine's European Integration" reviews the literature on the relationship of decentralization reform with Ukraine's European integration. Section "Sociological Perspective on European Integration" introduces a sociological perspective on European integration, and section "Community Twinning, Networks and European Integration" takes a closer look at the role of community twinning and networks. Section "The External Relations of Ukrainian ATCs" presents empirical findings from a survey conducted among the authorities of the 159 ATCs founded in 2015 and analyzes ATCs' participation in municipal networks. The chapter closes with some conclusions and prospects.

I. Ukraine's Decentralization Reform

According to Saito (2011), decentralization "is a process through which subnational governments increasingly partake in deciding on and administering essential public policies" (484). Despite previous attempts to devolve power to local communities in Ukraine, serious and successful steps were taken by the post-Maidan government only in 2014. On April 1, 2014, it adopted the Concept of the Reform of Local Self-Government and Territorial Organization of Power in Ukraine and kicked off one of the most successful reforms (Sologoub et al. 2019). Since then, power has been transferred from the central authorities to the ATCs, in the fields, among others, of urban planning, education, and public health (Rabinovych et al. 2018; Government of Ukraine 2019). However, decentralization in Ukraine involves more than reallocating competences between different levels of governance. On the one hand, political decentralization is matched by fiscal decentralization (Betliy 2018), the second pillar of the reform; on the other hand, it is interwoven with a seemingly contradictory process of power concentration. Amalgamation, i.e. the merging of small communities into ATCs, is the third pillar of the reform. The amalgamation process started in 2015 on a voluntary basis. By 2019, there were 882 ATCs uniting 4,043 communities (villages, towns, etc.), which corresponds to 36.7 percent of the total number of local councils that existed at the beginning of 2015. ATCs accounted for 38 percent of Ukraine's territory and about 69 percent of the country's population in 2019 (Government of Ukraine 2019). The rationale of this process is to create larger units that are more capable than their smaller predecessors of policy making and service provision.

The Ukrainian Constitution is the fundamental legal basis of decentralization. Local self-government is guaranteed by Chap. 11. Moreover, in 1997, the country signed the European Charter of Local Self-Government, which came into force in Ukraine on January 1, 1998. This document is remarkable because it states the right of local authorities to "external relations": according to Article 10 of the Charter, local authorities shall be entitled to co-operate, to belong to national or international associations, and "to co-operate with their counterparts in other States" (Council of Europe 1985). As will become evident in more detail below, this right to independent transnational relations is at the basis of the relationship between decentralization and Ukraine's European integration.

II. Decentralization Reform and Ukraine's European Integration

Decentralization reform has a firm place in EU–Ukrainian relations. In Article 446, the Association Agreement provides that Ukraine and the EU "shall promote mutual understanding and bilateral cooperation in the field of regional policy, on methods of formulation and implementation of regional policies, including multi-level governance and partnership" (EU–Ukraine 2014).

The 2015 Association Agenda, devised to prepare and facilitate the implementation of the EU–Ukraine Association Agreement, states that dialogue and cooperation should cover, among other matters (EU–Ukraine 2015, 8), "strengthening of the functioning of local and regional self-government, and legal status of the service in local self-government bodies, including through a decentralization reform devolving substantial competences and related financial allocations to them, in line with the relevant standards contained in the European Charter on Local Self-Government".

In order to substantiate its support of Ukraine's decentralization reform, the EU has contributed to it both financially and with the expertise of its Support Group for Ukraine (European Commission 2014, 2019). Still, decentralization and Ukraine's European integration are related in an indirect rather than straightforward way. Although the EU supports and monitors the progress of decentralization in Ukraine (European Commission and High Representative of the Union for Foreign Affairs and Security Policy 2018), it does not make its relationship to Ukraine conditional on it. In contrast to many other reforms in Ukraine, decentralization "plays a negligible role in the 'conditionalities' that govern Ukraine's Association Agreement with the EU and the strengthening of relations between them" (Dudley 2019, 5). The Association Agreement does not include an obligation for Ukraine to take steps towards decentralization. Consequently, even though it may be successful, decentralization in Ukraine cannot be expected to be directly rewarded with a closer relationship to the EU, let alone a membership perspective.[1]

Against this background, scholars have outlined some potential indirect effects that decentralization may have on Ukraine's European integration. Andreas Umland (2019) describes two of them. He stresses that a successful reform enhances the compatibility of Ukraine's internal organization with existing forms of decentralization in EU member states. In particular, he points to the principle of subsidiarity as one of the EU's fundamental principles, based on Article 5(3) of the Treaty on European Union (TEU) and a principle implemented in the EU's member states. Shifting power from Ukraine's central government to local communities could therefore be seen as a precursor to future steps of further integration, up to EU membership: "The more deconcentrated and subsidiary Ukraine becomes, the more similar it will thus look to other European nations, and the better she will later be prepared for full accession to the EU" (Umland 2019). This argument can be taken even further. In its present form, it presupposes an external integration impetus: while decentralization is valuable as and when Ukraine takes steps towards integrating into the EU, it does not influence the probability that such steps would happen in the

[1] While the EU has no common institutional model regarding the public administration of its member states, in 1995 it added an administrative criterion to the Copenhagen Criteria setting forth the conditions for accession. Furthermore, a regionalized system of administration is part of the EU's *Acquis Communautaire* on regional and cohesion policy, which had and still has to be adopted and implemented by candidate countries. The EU, however, does not prescribe a particular model of regional governance (LePlant et al. 2004).

first place. One could, however, endogenize European integration in a rationalist argument stating that the progress of decentralization reform will have a positive effect on the cost–benefit analyses of EU member states with regard to closer EU–Ukrainian relations. While the state of decentralization would most likely be only one factor among many, the prospect of well-designed and well-implemented intra-Ukrainian governance arrangements between the central authorities and local communities could lower the expected future costs of integration and might even be considered a benefit. Thus, by influencing EU member states' cost–benefit calculations, decentralization reform could contribute to Ukraine's European integration, even if not decisively.

Apart from the practical benefits stemming from the compatibility of decentralized systems, Umland identifies a second, ideational contribution decentralization could make towards Ukraine's European integration. By decentralizing decision-making in Ukraine, the country does away with centralist traditions originating in the Tsarist and Soviet past, and underlines its European character. In doing so, Ukraine "demonstrates her belonging to the Western normative and cultural hemisphere. That in turn makes Ukraine's ambition to enter the EU and NATO a more natural affair than it may have otherwise been" (Umland 2019).

This is an implicitly constructivist argument, according to which a country strives for membership in organizations that represent the international community it predominantly identifies with. From this constructivist perspective, it could be added to Umland's argument that decentralization reform influences not only Ukraine's ambitions for EU membership, but also the perceptions of the recipients of a potential membership application and, consequently, willingness to accept Ukraine as an EU member. The more Ukraine is perceived to share the EU's fundamental norms, the more closely it will be integrated into the EU's structures.

A third potential effect decentralization has on Ukraine's European integration is mentioned by Dudley (2019), who points to the developmental agenda behind the policy (5–6). Faced with various socioeconomic problems throughout the country, the government perceives local self-government as a tool to address these challenges. If successful, this would put Ukraine in a position to fulfil the obligations resulting from the Association Agreement. As Dudley (2019) reports, "decentralization from the Ukrainian government's perspective is associated primarily with attaining the level of regional economic development and competitiveness required for alignment with European standards" (6). As discussed above, successful decentralization and, subsequently, successful implementation of the Association Agreement may have a positive impact on the EU member states' cost–benefit calculations with regard to the further integration of Ukraine.

What unites the three presented ideas—underlining anticipatory rule adoption and resulting rule compatibility, ideational similarity, and enhanced compliance capability—is their focus on formal institutions. Umland explicitly speaks of Ukraine's "accession to" or "entering" the EU, whereas Dudley refers to the terms of the EU–Ukraine Association Agreement. This has two drawbacks: the EU currently has fundamental reservations about further enlargement (e.g. Marciacq 2019), so the mechanisms may be (partly) obsolete in practice. Furthermore, they neglect the societal basis of European integration, highlighted by sociological approaches. In a country in which 55 percent of the population has never been abroad and another 16 percent goes abroad every ten years or less (Interfax-Ukraine 2016), the fundament for European integration might be rather thin when attention is paid to formal institutions only.

III. Sociological Perspective on European Integration

Sociological approaches to European integration have long led a shadowy existence. Recently, however, they have come to the fore again (e.g. the contributions in Saurugger and Mérand 2010b). In contrast to focusing on formal political institutions, they turn their attention to European integration as a societal process. Beyond this fundamental consensus, however, sociological perspectives on European integration are rather heterogeneous. While some studies attend to a "European society" more broadly, others concentrate on individual EU officials and the decisions they take in Brussels, with particular attention to the decision makers' social context (Saurugger and Mérand 2010a).

Sociological approaches, furthermore, differ with regard to epistemology and the use of qualitative vs. quantitative data. Favell and Guiraudon (2009) distinguish between research that enquires the "social bases" of European integration following a bottom-up perspective and research that identifies the effects of European integration on European society through a top-down approach. With regard to the latter, they present examples of studies on social stratification, social class, and identity. With regard to the former, they list studies on regional ties and social networks created through student exchanges, projects, and town twinning.

It is argued here that such bottom-up sociological approaches are worth extending to both Ukraine's relationship with the EU in general and to the specific question of the relationship between the country's decentralization and European integration. As pointed out above, political science approaches focusing on formal institutions are likely to face limitations when applied in the decentralization–integration case. Furthermore, a sociological perspective would more closely reflect the opinion of Ukrainian citizens. For them, successful European integration is not primarily a matter of improved formal relations between the EU and Ukraine.

According to polls, it is mainly connected with "improved service at social infrastructure facilities (hospitals, kindergartens, or schools)" (38.72 percent), improving "transport infrastructure [...] (e.g. rebuilt roads or comfortable and safe public transportation)" (33.36 percent), and "new jobs and foreign investors in my city or village" (33.14 percent) (New Europe Center 2018). All these demands are closely related to decentralization reform, which aims to shift decision-making powers in the fields of healthcare and education to the community level (Rabinovych et al. 2018). If decentralization entails significant socioeconomic improvements for the inhabitants of the ATCs, we can expect an increase in positive domestic attitudes towards Ukraine's formal European integration. This in turn would give more legitimacy to Ukraine's European agenda.

IV. Community Twinning, Networks and European Integration

1. History of Community Twinning

According to sociological approaches, there are various ways to advance European integration "from below." This section presents two mechanisms that help extend and strengthen regional ties as fundaments of integration: community twinning and transnational municipal networks. The former refers to cross-border partnerships between communities, which rely on formal agreements. These relationships are meant to last for an unlimited period of time and do not focus on a single, specific objective (cf. Tausendpfund and Schäfer 2018, 1–2).[2] The link between

---

[2] In order to get a more comprehensive picture, the chapter will deal with informal twinning, too. In this case, cross-border cooperation between communities takes place in the absence of a formal agreement.

cross-border community or town twinning and European unification was established in the 1950s (Bock 1994, 13) and has been confirmed ever since. When asked about the value and benefit of community twinning with a French or German counterpart, French and German respondents most often refer to its contribution to a united Europe (Keller 2018, 35).

While the integration potential of twinning was initially seen in the framework of German–French reconciliation, it was later related to functional cooperation, too. Bernhard Köhle detects a shift in Europe from "partnerships of reconciliation" to "partnerships of integration" (cited in Joennemi and Jańczak 2017, 424). This could be observed when ties between the EU and Central and Eastern Europe mushroomed and a good deal of administrative know-how was transferred from the West to the East, not least with a view to EU enlargement (Köhn 2006, 467–469; Woesler 2006, 423–425). As Richter summarizes, such a functionalist approach is no less conducive to European integration: "Problem-oriented cooperation is the impulse that sets processes of integration into motion" (Richter 1994, 49; own translation). This optimistic view, however, stands in contrast to more skeptical attitudes to such instrumentalist developments. As critics warn, there is a danger that this new direction replaces the intrinsic value of community twinning and squeezes laypersons out of the twinning exchange (Langenohl 2019, 94). The active involvement of citizens, however, is essential for the affective identification of Europeans with Europe and the EU's cohesion. Twinning has been found to contribute to pro-European attitudes (Fiedler 2006, 398). In a recent empirical study, Tausendpfund and Schäfer (2018) found that town twinning promotes citizens' specific and diffuse support of the EU. More specifically, they maintain that an individual's engagement in town twinning activities correlates with a positive attitude towards the EU.

The EU itself has financially supported town twinning since 1989 (European Commission 1997). This move was justified with a reference to European integration: "The Community action in favour of town-twinning aims to encourage the involvement of ordinary people and their elected representatives in European integration and to promote their sense of belonging to the European Union" (European Commission 1997, 12). Without explicitly referring to sociological approaches to European integration, the EU seems to expect the same dynamics: "The events organized by towns and their inhabitants through twinning schemes are a reproduction in miniature of the process of integration pursued by the Member States. Each twinning is a mini-Europe in itself .... Our towns

348 A. PINTSCH

really are building an integrated Europe" (European Commission 1997, 11). Interestingly, from the outset, the program was not only open to towns located in EU member states but deliberately included town-twinning schemes with partner communities in "other European countries" (European Commission 1997, 13).

Around the mid-1980s, an additional process connecting municipalities in Europe started. In the wake of the Single European Act, Transnational Municipal Networks (TMN) began to emerge (Kern and Bulkeley 2009, 312). The EU has actively initiated or supported these networks with a view to transnational knowledge transfer in many cases, among others on environmental issues (Giest and Howlett 2013, 341). The EU's system of "de-centralization and de-concentration of powers" (Giest and Howlett 2013, 342) has been particularly conducive to the growth of TMNs, even beyond the EU's borders. As Kern and Bulkeley outline, these networks foster communication and cooperation among municipalities. Among other activities, they facilitate exchange on best practices, organize study tours, provide funding for joint projects, and encourage joint bids. Thus, beyond working towards their particular policy goal, the internal governing of those networks "serves to tie member municipalities more closely together through day-to-day dealings on projects and to enhance these cities' connection to the network" (Kern and Bulkeley 2009, 321).

2. Community Twinning in Ukraine

Even though the city of Odesa was the first in Europe to be paired with a transatlantic partner, namely with Vancouver in Canada in 1944 (Brkusanin and Ellwood 2011, 12), there is no deeply rooted tradition of town twinning in Ukraine. Reflecting the generally weak role local communities have long had in the division of powers between the territorial levels of government, twinning was described as "a vodka drinking occasion for respective mayors" (Bartlett and Popovski 2013, 13). In 2010, Ukraine counted 799 town twinnings, more than half of which were with communities in Poland. Poland in turn—although comparable in size of population and composed of significantly fewer local municipalities—counted 3,508 town twinnings. Slovakia—with a population of about 5.4

million—counted a comparable number of 801 twinnings (CEMR 2010).[3] The reasons for the comparatively low number of Ukrainian communities involved in town twinning are certainly manifold, but decentralization reform, and in particular the amalgamation process, may contribute to increasing the ties between Ukrainian and non-Ukrainian communities. A too-small size of communities has long been known to be an obstacle to twinning (European Commission 1997, 12). In the past, many Ukrainian communities were too small to provide adequate public services to the residents (Romanova and Umland 2019, 6). In 2014, Ukraine was ranked 32nd among 40 European countries in mean population size of its municipalities (Swianiewicz et al. 2017, 10). It can thus be expected that the creation of larger ATCs through amalgamation enhances the capacities of Ukrainian communities and, in combination with fiscal decentralization, gives them sufficient resources to participate in community twinning.

V. The External Relations of Ukrainian ATCs

1. The Survey

In order to study municipal external relations, and in particular the twinning of ATCs with counterparts outside Ukraine, a survey among all ATCs founded in 2015 was conducted in spring 2019. The decision to restrict the study to ATCs amalgamated during the first year of the reform was made under the assumption that it would take some time to establish contacts abroad and set up partnerships. ATCs founded in 2015 are most likely to have developed a working routine and built relationships with communities outside Ukraine. This restriction could lead to slightly biased findings. Given that the process of amalgamation is voluntary, it may be the case that communities created early on in the reform process are generally more open to reforms (e.g. by having more reform-minded leaders), external cooperation, and innovation. Consequently, the findings may be more optimistic for these communities than for latecomers. On the other hand, ATCs founded after 2015 may find it easier to set up international contacts because they can draw on the experiences of older ATCs. As elaborated in more detail below, the membership data of thirty-eight ATCs in

---

[3] Number of local municipalities in 2012: Ukraine: 11,517; Poland 2012: 2,479; Slovakia: 2,930. Council of European Municipalities and Regions (CEMR), Members map, https://www.ccre.org/pays/map/id:16, 8 November 2019.

350 A. PINTSCH

the transnational Covenant of Mayors network show that age of an ATC is not correlated with its network activity.[4] Thus, no excessive bias is expected.

Based on recommendations in the methodological literature (Kirchhoff et al. 2010; Porst 2014), the questionnaire and the letter of invitation were developed by the author in German and translated into both Ukrainian and Russian by a student assistant originally from Ukraine enrolled in political science studies at the University of Mannheim.[5] While the German version of both documents was checked and commented on by a survey specialist,[6] the Russian version was pre-tested by a Russian native speaker with a political science background.[7] Starting on March 19, 2019, the survey was sent to the e-mail addresses given on the ATC's websites. It was addressed to the heads of the respective ATCs (*golova hromady*), indicated on their websites.[8] The e-mail contained two versions of the questionnaire. First, as Word documents in both Ukrainian and Russian. These could either be downloaded, filled in and returned by e-mail or printed, filled in, scanned and returned as an e-mail attachment. The second option was to follow a link to an online survey set up under Unipark.[9] Users could choose between a Ukrainian and a Russian version at the start of the survey.

After a couple of days, reminders were sent to the ATCs that had not responded (or preferred not to indicate their name). In addition, the author called the ATCs that had not responded after the reminder in order to ask whether the e-mail was received.[10]

By May 31, 2019, sixty-six ATC representatives had completed the survey and returned the questionnaire. Ten ATCs returned the files by e-mail (two of them in a scanned version, one was a duplicate of the online survey), whereas fifty-seven ATCs used the online version. In fifty cases, the survey was started but abandoned before the end. Since many of these

---

[4] Among the 38 ATCs that are members of the network, ten were founded in 2015, 13 in 2016, 14 in 2017, and one in 2018 (Covenant of Mayors 2019).

[5] I thank Nataliia Larina for her help with the translations.

[6] I thank Christiane Grill for many helpful recommendations with regard to this project.

[7] I thank Timur Koroliuk for his help with the pre-test.

[8] However, it is not possible to ascertain that it was the heads of the ATCs who filled in the questionnaires. Given the rather hierarchical administrative culture in Ukraine, it can yet be assumed that the heads were at least informed about the survey.

[9] https://www.unipark.com/.

[10] It turned out, however, that calls were often not answered or only busy signals were reached.

12 DECENTRALIZATION IN UKRAINE AND BOTTOM-UP EUROPEAN... 351

dropouts happened early on in the survey, too many answers were missing and the data could not be used. Still, the overall response rate can be considered satisfactory. Table 12.1 summarizes the number of ATCs per region (oblast)[11]—thus, the maximum number of questionnaires that

Table 12.1 Number and origin of replies (by May 31, 2019)

Name of oblast	Number of ATCs founded in the oblast(s) in 2015	Completed questionnaires from ATCs located in the oblast(s)
Vinnytsia	2	2
Volyn	5	3
Dnipropetrovsk	15	5
Donetsk	3	1
Zhytomyr	9	2
Zakarpattya	2	1
Zaporizhzhya	6	3
Ivano-Frankivsk	3	2
Kirovohrad	2	1
Luhansk	2	1
Lviv	15	2
Odesa	8	3
Poltava	12	5
Rivne	5	0
Ternopil	26	6
Kharkiv	0	–
Khmelnytsk	22	9
Cherkasy	3	1
Chernivtsi	10	6
Chernihiv	5	0
Oblasts with only one ATC founded in 2015:	4	1
• Kyiv		
• Mykolaiv		
• Sumy		
• Kherson		
Anonymous	–	12
Total	*159*	*66*

[11] Since the survey participants were assured of the anonymous presentation of results, only the *oblasts* in which the respective ATCs are located are mentioned here. To guarantee the anonymity of respondents in oblasts where only one ATC was founded in 2015, the results were aggregated.

could be returned from there, and the number of actually completed surveys. Returned questionnaires came from almost all relevant oblasts. Twelve respondents decided to reveal neither the name of their ATC nor the oblast in which their ATC was located.

2. *Community Twinning*

When asked how they generally assess the value of international cooperation for the work of the newly founded ATCs, a large majority of fifty-three respondents replied with "very important," and six more found it "important." Figure 12.1 shows all replies.

Experience with international cooperation is spread widely among the ATCs: fifty-one out of sixty-six replied that they had taken part in some kind of internationally funded program or project. Many referred to the EU's U-LEAD program.[12] Eleven ATCs, however, did not report any involvement in such activities. Four did not reply to the question. Given the high level of ATCs' participation in international programs and

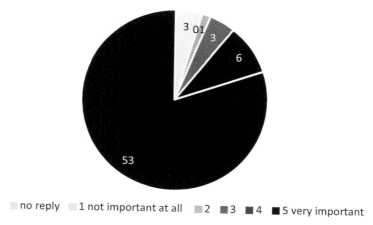

Fig. 12.1 General value of international cooperation for ATCs

---

[12] U-LEAD with Europe: Ukraine Local Empowerment, Accountability and Development Programme, https://eeas.europa.eu/headquarters/headQuarters-homepage/27392/u-lead-europe-ukraine-local-empowerment-accountability-and-development-programme_en.

projects, it is surprising to see a general lack of staff responsible for EU or foreign affairs. Only a few ATCs reported having such specialists. Of sixty-six ATCs, fifty-one have neither an EU nor a foreign relations-responsible employee. Eleven ATCs have at least one of the two, four did not reply. Staff responsible for general foreign relations are slightly more widespread, with ten positions. Five ATCs employ personnel who deal with EU affairs, but only four ATCs have both an EU and a foreign relations officer.

Whereas ATCs' participation in externally funded assistance programs is quite high, the same cannot be said for ATCs' involvement in formal or informal twinning of cities/ communities beyond Ukraine.[13] Only a few reported such partnerships. Seventeen ATCs have established at least one formal partnership with a community located outside Ukraine, but forty-five ATCs, however, do not have formally established partnerships with communities abroad, and four did not reply. Thirteen ATCs have partnerships not formalized by a written document and forty-nine do not; four did not reply. Eight communities turned out to be very active networkers with both formal and informal partnerships abroad. Twenty-two ATCs have at least one formal or informal external twinning partnership. The flipside of this number is represented by those thirty-nine communities that are involved in neither formal nor informal twinning exchange. For five communities the result cannot be established due to missing data.

Further analysis demonstrates that eleven of the seventeen communities with formal ties have a twinning relationship with just one foreign community. Three ATCs have two partner communities each. Finally, there is one community each with three, five and nine formal partnerships. Thus, overall, thirty-four formal partnerships were reported. One community mentioned a formal trilateral twinning relationship, which was counted as two formal partnerships. The oldest of these partnerships was established in 2006, the most recent in 2019. Twenty-four of these twinning partnerships were concluded after the start of the decentralization reform and three before. For seven, the founding date was not mentioned. The first group includes at least three communities that mentioned a recent founding date of their twinning partnerships but, in fact, look back on a previous partnership that was confirmed and extended to the newly founded ATC. Within the second group, all previously existing twinning partnerships have been extended to the whole ATC. There is one case in

---

[13] Please note that this is not identical with the EU's technical assistance twinning program: https://ec.europa.eu/neighbourhood-enlargement/tenders/twinning_en.

which a previously established twinning relation of one of the entities that united to form the ATC remained intact after the amalgamation and was not extended to the ATC. Four communities mentioned previous partnerships that do not exist anymore. These partnerships concern counterparts in Germany, Poland, Romania, and the Russian Federation.

By far the most twinning relationships were established with communities in Poland: the country was named twenty times. Other formal partnerships exist with communities in Belarus (2), Georgia (2), Romania (2), Slovakia (2), Czech Republic, Hungary, Latvia, Moldova and Slovenia, with one reply missing. Given the chapter's focus on Ukraine's European integration, it should be noted that the large majority of partnerships involves communities in EU member states, with the exception of Belarus, Georgia and Moldova.

Regarding informal twinning partnerships of thirteen ATCs, seven ATCs have just one partner community, one has two, two have three, one has at least two, and two did not reply. Overall, there are at least seventeen informal partnerships in place. Given the informal nature of the relationships, only four communities indicated a date when the partnership started. All of these four partnerships commenced after the launch of the decentralization reform. As with the formal community twinning, Poland emerged as the country with most mentions; at least ten partner communities are located there. The other informal partnerships include communities in Belarus, Bulgaria, Czech Republic, Estonia, Germany, Hungary and Romania, with one partnership each. Again, the majority of partners are located in EU member states. However, as in the case of the formal partnerships, there is a very strong orientation towards the Central and Eastern European countries that acceded to the EU in 2004 and 2007. The only partnership with a community in an EU founding member state is the one with a German town.

Given the relatively low number of partnerships in general, it is not surprising that only thirteen ATCs have designated an official for the relationships with foreign communities. Forty-eight ATCs do not have such a contact person, and five did not reply. This may be connected to the lack of specialists some ATCs mentioned when asked about problems in establishing twinning partnerships. Of the thirty-nine ATCs without any formal or informal partner communities abroad, eighteen replied to the question why they have not established any such ties (yet). In addition to the lack of specialized personnel, several ATCs referred to a lack of experience with such partnerships and general problems in finding a partner community.

There may be a variety of reasons for the difficulty in finding a partner community, including scarcity of information, a lack of responsiveness from potential partner communities, or long preparatory phases. Several answers created the impression that the lack of an existing twinning partnership represents rather a high hurdle for establishing (further) partnerships. Other ATCs asked us to bear in mind that the administrative reform in the ATCs was still going on. One respondent pointed to unresolved issues of competences in this regard, and another one stated that there were (more) urgent problem to solve in the communities at this stage. In one community, establishing links with neighboring ATCs was given priority over external partnerships. One respondent traced the lack of partnerships back to a limited knowledge of foreign languages, while another one referred to the geographical distance between the respective community and Ukraine's western border. In one ATC, a lack of awareness of the opportunity to twin was seen as the main factor impeding such partnerships. Another respondent saw missing support as a barrier to new partnerships. All these reasons might be seen to be at the root of ATCs' inactivity in setting up twinning relationships.

3. Transnational Municipal Networks

Exchange between European communities is possible through not only twinning but also by participating in international associations and transnational municipal networks. However, only three instances were mentioned in the survey: the Council of European Municipalities and Regions (CEMR, indirect membership through national association), the Mayors for Economic Growth (M4EG) Initiative, and the EU Covenant of Mayors for Climate and Energy. The analysis of the three membership lists revealed that more ATCs are involved in the networks than had stated in the responses to our questionnaire.

As the oldest and broadest European association of local and regional governments, the Council of European Municipalities and Regions (CEMR) brings together national associations from forty-one countries. Founded in 1951, CEMR "promotes the construction of a united, peaceful and democratic Europe founded on local self-government, respect for the principle of subsidiarity and the participation of citizens" (CEMR 2019). It is currently active in five issue areas, among them "Governance, democracy and citizenship," "Environment, climate and energy," and "International engagement and cooperation." Ukrainian communities are

356   A. PINTSCH

represented through two different associations: the Association of Ukrainian Cities (*Asociaciya Mist Ukrayiny; AUC*) and the Ukrainian Association of District and Regional Councils (*Ukrayinska Asociaciya Rayonnykh ta Oblasnykh Rad*), both based in Kyiv. The latter is not of direct relevance to ATCs, because it represents councils at higher (rayon and oblast) levels. The former has 339 ATCs among its 781 members (AUC 2019). Of the 159 ATCs formed in 2015, sixty-seven are organized in the AUC (September 2019), which corresponds to 42 percent. Of the fifty-four ATCs that completed the survey in a non-anonymous way, twenty-eight are members, i.e. approximately 52 percent. Interestingly, however, when asked about relationships with international associations, only one of them referred to the AUC.

One ATC mentioned the Mayors for Economic Growth (M4EG) Initiative when asked about participation in international networks. This EU initiative was launched in 2016 and is targeted specifically at local authorities in Eastern Partnership (EaP) countries. Once communities have become members of the "M4EG Club," they receive support for improving the local business environment in a sustainable and social way. While much of the support comes from the initiative's secretariat, the network also aims at "cross-country cooperation between local authorities in the EaP region" (Mayors for Economic Growth 2017, 9). According to the initiative's website, 108 ATCs have become members by September 2019 (Mayors for Economic Growth 2019). Among them, at least ten were founded in 2015. When considering only the communities that returned the survey questionnaire, the number shrinks to five.

Finally, another ATC mentioned its accession to the EU Covenant of Mayors for Climate & Energy. This initiative was launched by the European Commission in 2008. It aims at local communities that voluntarily agree to implement EU climate and energy objectives. With the "Covenant of Mayors East" initiative, the EU has particularly supported the participation of Eastern Partnership countries from 2011 onwards. After the merger with the "Compact of Mayors" in 2016, the original initiative became part of the "Global Covenant of Mayors for Climate and Energy." Until September 2019, 270 Ukrainian municipalities joined the "Covenant community" (Covenant of Mayors 2019). There are 38 ATCs among the signatories, including ten founded in 2015. Of these, five returned the survey questionnaire.

4. Future Prospects

Five years into decentralization reform, the newly founded ATCs have developed manifold ties to international projects, transnational municipal networks, and communities beyond Ukraine. A vast majority of ATCs acknowledge the value these forms of cooperation have for their work. However, the chapter also reveals some contradictions. The bulk of exchange takes place in technical assistance projects, involving partners from the EU, EU member states, the United States or Switzerland. Yet, only few ATCs have officials who are explicitly responsible for relations with the EU or other international actors.

Sixty-one of sixty-six ATCs agree that twinning partnerships could make an important or very important contribution to Ukraine's European integration. However, only twenty-two ATCs have at least one formal or informal twinning partner abroad. At the moment, it is difficult to assess whether bottom-up European integration through ATCs' twinning partnerships will gain momentum in the future. On the one hand, forty-four ATCs reported that a new partnership with a foreign community was planned. Eighteen ATCs do not have plans to establish new partnerships (four did not reply). Of the twenty-two ATCs that already have at least one formal or informal partnership, twenty aim to initiate at least one more, which corresponds to 91 percent. In contrast, only twenty-three out of thirty-nine ATCs without any twinning partnerships have plans to become the twinning partner of a foreign community, which corresponds to 59 percent (one of those communities did not reply). These numbers reflect one of the problems that respondents mentioned above. Having no twinning partner yet represents a major obstacle to establishing new partnerships. Among ATCs striving for new partnerships, there is a clear trend towards a twinning community in the EU: forty-three ATCs affirmed this aim. Ten ATCs replied that they plan to find twinning partners in Europe beyond the EU (multiple replies were possible). The same number of ATCs is open towards twinning partnerships throughout the world. Five ATCs are planning to establish twinning relations with communities in the EU, within Europe more broadly, and across the world.

When it comes to concrete steps for initiating a new partnership, the number of ATCs replying positively drops to less than half. Only nineteen ATCs reported that they have already taken action to set up a new partnership. In accordance with the above-mentioned trend towards partnerships with communities located in the EU, sixteen ATCs mentioned such communities as addressees of their activities. Two ATCs have taken steps towards establishing partnerships with European communities beyond the EU, and three others have started preparations for worldwide twinning partnerships (multiple replies were possible).

Thus, whereas many ATCs have plans and are optimistic with regard to the conclusion of new twinning partnership agreements, these plans and hopes are not necessarily matched by concrete activities. Despite the relatively limited number of concrete activities to create new partnerships, the majority of ATCs is (very) optimistic that they will found at least one (more) twinning relation with a community outside Ukraine within the next five years (Fig. 12.2).

In addition to the somewhat contradictory findings, some methodological shortcomings make it difficult to assess the prospects of Ukraine's European integration "from below." For instance, we do not know much yet about the depth of ATC's twinning relationships or the strength of their ties to networks. The fact that some ATCs did not mention their membership in the Mayors for Economic Growth Initiative or the Covenant of Mayors could be a sign that these relationships are not relevant in their day-to-day business. This can only be confirmed by further research. Further studies would be necessary to find out to what degree citizens take an active part in community twinning. Still, by mapping

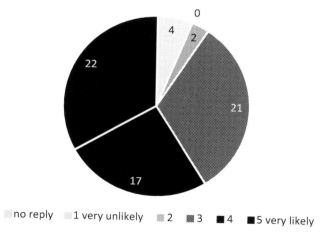

Fig. 12.2 Likelihood of establishing a new partnership within the next five years

ATCs' societal links to European communities and networks, the chapter substantiates the relevance of a sociological perspective on Ukraine's European integration and the role played by decentralization.

CONCLUSIONS

The survey revealed that a large majority of respondents see municipal twinning partnerships as conducive to Ukraine's European integration. This opinion coincides with a sociological perspective on European integration and with empirical studies. Twinning, however, has not yet unfolded its full potential in Ukraine. On the one hand, the number of existing twinning relationships is still comparatively low. On the other, ATCs' plans to establish new twinning partnerships are often not matched by concrete steps towards this goal. In order to close this gap, national and transnational associations such as the AUC and the CEMR could promote new twinning among their members even more actively.[14] Existing partnerships could be strengthened by including Ukraine in the EU's Citizens for Europe Programme. So far, EU member states, Albania, North Macedonia, Montenegro, Serbia, Bosnia Herzegovina, and Kosovo participate in the program.[15] Public bodies and non-profit organizations from these countries are eligible to apply for funding related to town twinning and networks of towns. Neither the European Neighbourhood Instrument Cross-border Cooperation Programme nor the Eastern Partnership Territorial Cooperation Support Programme represent equivalents because they are restricted to neighboring regions and fixed-term project cycles. What is more, the latter program only includes Eastern Partnership countries and is thus of limited relevance for ATCs planning to establish new twinning partnerships with communities located in the EU. Community twinning and community networks could also be included as focus areas in programs supporting decentralization in Ukraine, such as U-LEAD with Europe

---

[14] Both the AUC and the CEMR already support communities in finding twinning partners, among others by collecting and publishing requests for partnerships under http://2. auc.org.ua/page/partnerstvo-mist-tvining and http://www.twinning.org/en/request/ ContactDeta ls#.XdHc8NUxmUk.

[15] Iceland, Liechtenstein, and Norway are potentially participating countries.

REFERENCES

Aasland, Aadne. 2018. *Mot økt folkelig innflytelse? Desentralisering og lokaldemokrati i Ukraina* (Towards Greater Popular Participation? Decentralization and Local Democracy in Ukraine). Nordisk Østforum. vo. 32: 174–194, (in Norwegian).

AUC. 2019. Mista-Chleny AMU. [Cities-Members of the Association of Ukrainian Cities] Association of Ukrainian Cities. http://2.auc.org.ua/members.

Bartlett, Will, and Vesna Popovski. 2013. *Local Governance and Social Cohesion in Ukraine*. Barcelona: SEARCH Working Paper WP5/22.

Betliy, Oleksandra. 2018. Fiscal Decentralization in Ukraine: Is It Run Smoothly? *4liberty.eu Review* 9: 124–137.

Bock, Hans Manfred. 1994. Europa von Unten. Zu den Ursprüngen und Anfängen der Deutsch-Französischen Gemeindepartnerschaften. In *Gemeindepartnerschaften im Umbruch Europas*, ed. Annette Jünemann, 13–35. Frankfurt am Main: Lang.

Brkusanin, Maja, and Sophie Ellwood. 2011. *New Twin Manual. Innovation and Practical Ideas for Town Twinning.* Rome: CESIE—Centro Studi ed Iniziative Europeo.

CEMR. 2010. Table Showing the Number of Twinnings in the Wider Europe in 2010. Council of European Municipalities and Regions. http://www.twinning.org/uploads/assets/news/Number%20of%20twinnings%20in%20Europe%20in%202010.pdf.

———. 2019. Introducing CEMR. Council of European Municipalities and Regions. https://www.ccre.org/en/article/introducing_cemr.

Council of Europe. 1985. European Charter of Local Self-Government Strasbourg, 15.X.1985. European Treaty Series-No. 122. https://localgovernment.gov.mt/en/DLG/Legislation/Documents/Legislation/122.pdf.

Covenant of Mayors. 2019. Covenant Community. Signatories. https://www.covenantofmayors.eu/about/covenant-community/signatories.html.

Dudley, William. 2019. *Ukraine's Decentralization Reform.* Berlin: Stiftung Wissenschaft und Politik: Working Paper, Research Division Eastern Europe and Eurasia, 1/2019.

EU–Ukraine. 2014. Association Agreement between the European Union and Its Member States, of the One Part, and Ukraine, of the Other Part. *Official Journal of the European Union* L161 (29.5.2014): 3-2137.

———. 2015. EU–Ukraine Association Agenda to Prepare and Facilitate the Implementation of the Association Agreement. As endorsed by the EU–Ukraine Association Council on 16 March 2015. http://eeas.europa.eu/archives/docs/ukraine/docs/st06678_15_en.pdf.

European Commission. 1997. *A Europe of Towns and Cities. A Practical Guide to Town Twinning*. Luxembourg: Office for Official Publications of the European Communities.

———. 2014. EU Supports Decentralisation and Regional Policy Reforms in Ukraine With €55 Millions. IP/14/2221. https://europa.eu/rapid/press-release_IP-14-2221_en.htm.

———. 2019. EU–Ukraine Summit: EU Provides Additional Support to Decentralisation, Fight Against Corruption, Empowerment of Civil Society and Accountable and Efficient Governance in Ukraine. IP/19/3811. https://europa.eu/rapid/press-release_IP-19-3811_en.htm.

European Commission, and High Representative of the Union for Foreign Affairs and Security Policy. 2018. *Association Implementation Report on Ukraine*. Brussels, 7.11.2018: SWD(2018) 462 final.

EU–Ukraine Parliamentary Association Committee. 2019. *Final Statement and Recommendations*. Strasbourg: Ninth Meeting, March 13–14.

Favell, Adrian, and Virginie Guiraudon. 2009. The Sociology of the European Union: An Agenda. *European Union Politics* 10 (4): 550–576.

Fiedler, Thomas. 2006. Regionale Vernetzung—Innovative Städtekooperationen. In *Europafähigkeit der Kommunen. Die lokale Ebene in der Europäischen Union*, ed. Ulrich von Alemann and Claudia Münch, 395–411. Wiesbaden: VS Verlag für Sozialwissenschaften.

Giest, Sarah, and Michael Howlett. 2013. Comparative Climate Change Governance: Lessons from European Transnational Municipal Network Management Efforts. *Environmental Policy and Governance* 23 (6): 341–353.

Government of Ukraine. 2014. "Розпорядження від 1 квітня 2014 р. № 333-р, Київ, "Про схвалення Концепції реформування місцевого самоврядування татериторіальної організації влади в Україні"." https://zakon2.rada.gov.ua/laws/show/333-2014-%D1%80#n8.

———. 2019. "Decentralization reform." accessed 20 September 2019. https://www.kmu.gov.ua/en/reformi/efektivne-vryaduvannya/reformadecentralizaciyi.

Hanushchak, Yuri, Oleksii Sydorchuk, and Andreas Umland. 2017. Ukraine's Most Underreported Reform. *New Eastern Europe*, April 4. http://neweasterneurope.eu/2017/04/13/ukraine-s-most-underreported-reform-decentralisation-after-the-euromaidan-revolution/.

Interfax-Ukraine. 2016. Over Half of Ukrainians Never Make Trips Abroad. *Kyivpost*, December 16. https://www.kyivpost.com/ukraine-politics/half-ukrainians-never-make-trips-abroad.html.

International Alert, and UCIPR. 2017. Decentralisation in Ukraine. Achievements, Expectations and Concerns. https://www.international-alert.org/sites/default/files/Ukraine_Decentralisation_EN_2017.pdf.

362   A. PINTSCH

Joenniemi, Pertti, and Jarosław Jańczak. 2017. Theorizing Town Twinning—Towards a Global Perspective. *Journal of Borderlands Studies* 32 (4): 423–428. https://doi.org/10.1080/08865655.2016.1267583.

Keller, Eileen. 2018. *Städtepartnerschaften—den Europäischen Bürgersinn Stärken. Eine Empirische Studie.* Gütersloh: Bertelsmann Stiftung.

Kern, Kristine, and Harriet Bulkeley. 2009. Cities, Europeanization and Multi-level Governance: Governing Climate Change Through Transnational Municipal Networks. *Journal of Common Market Studies* 47 (2): 309–332.

Kirchhoff, Sabine, Sonja Kuhnt, Peter Lipp, and Siegfried Schlawin. 2010. *Der Fragebogen. Datenbasis, Konstruktion und Auswertung.* 5th ed. Wiesbaden: VS Verlag.

Köhn, Klaudia. 2006. Von Reformen und Begriffsverwirrungen—Tschechiens Lokale und Regionale Ebene auf dem Weg in die Europäische Mitbestimmung. In *Europafähigkeit der Kommunen. Die lokale Ebene in der Europäischen Union,* ed. Ulrich von Alemann and Claudia Münch, 458–476. Wiesbaden: VS Verlag für Sozialwissenschaften.

Langenohl, Andreas. 2019. European Integration, Valuation, and Exchange: Toward a Value Theoretic Understanding of Transnational Sociality in the European Union. *Przegląd Socjologiczny* LXVIII (68) (1): 77–98.

LePlant, James T., Michael Baun, Jiri Lach, and Dan Marek. 2004. Decentralization in the Czech Republic: The European Union, Political Parties, and the Creation of Regional Assemblies. *Publius* 34 (1): 35–51.

Marciacq, Florent. 2019. Where to Now for Enlargement. Key Challenges to Western Balkans' Accession into a Brexiting European Union Nice Centre International de Formation *Européenne CIFE.* Policy Paper No 82.

Mayors for Economic Growth. 2017. Introduction to Mayors for Economic Growth (M4EG). General Principles and Approaches. https://www.m4eg.eu/media/1787/m4eg-concept-eng.pdf.

———. 2019. Pidpysanty. [Signatories]. https://www.m4eg.eu/uk/signatories/.

New Europe Center. 2018. New Europe: What Do Ukrainians Think?, July 10. http://neweurope.org.ua/en/analytics/nova-yevropa-yak-yiyi-bachat-ukray-intsi/ and http://neweurope.org.ua/wp-content/uploads/2018/07/NEC.xlsx.

OECD. 2018. *Maintaining the Momentum of Decentralisation in Ukraine.* Paris: OECD Publishing.

Porst, Rolf. 2014. *Fragebogen. Ein Arbeitsbuch.* 4th ed. Wiesbaden: Springer VS.

Rabinovych, Maryna, Anthony Levitas, and Andreas Umland. 2018. *Revisiting Decentralization After Maidan: Achievements and Challenges of Ukraine's Local Governance Reform.* Washington, DC: Kennan Cable 34.

Richter, Emanuel. 1994. Die Gemeinde als Basis Europäischer Integration—Subsidiarität und Bürgernähe. In *Gemeindepartnerschaften im Umbruch Europas,* ed. Annette Jünemann, 37–55. Frankfurt am Main: Lang.

Romanova, Valentyna, and Andreas Umland. 2019. *Ukraine's Decentralization Reforms Since 2014. Initial Achievements and Future Challenges, Ukraine Forum*. London: Chatham House.

Saito, Fumihiko. 2011. Decentralization. In *The SAGE Handbook of Governance*, ed. Mark Bevir, 484–500. Los Angeles: Sage.

Sasse, Gwendolyn. 2008. The European Neighbourhood Policy: Conditionality Revisited for the EU's Eastern Neighbours. *Europe-Asia Studies* 60 (2): 295–316.

Saurugger, Sabine, and Frédéric Mérand. 2010a. Does European Integration Theory Need Sociology? *Comparative European Politics* 8 (1): 1–18.

———, eds. 2010b. Mainstreaming Sociology in EU Studies. *Comparative European Politics* 8 (1).

Sologoub, Ilona, Olena Shkarpova, and Yar Batoh. 2019. "Decentralization cannot be rolled back because the reform is too popular among people. Interview with Georg Milbradt." VOX Ukraine 1 July 2019. https://voxukraine.org/en/decentralization-cannot-be-rolled-back-because-the-reform-is-too-popular-among-people/.

Swianiewicz, Paweł, Adam Gendźwiłł, and Alfonso Zardi. 2017. *Territorial Reforms in Europe: Does Size Matter?* Council of Europe: Centre of Expertise for Local Government Reform.

Tausendpfund, Markus, and Lisa Schäfer. 2018. Town Twinning and Political Support. *Local Government Studies* 44 (4): 552–576. https://doi.org/10.1080/03003930.2018.1465934.

Umland, Andreas. 2019. International Implications of Ukraine's Decentralization. *VOX Ukraine*, January 30. https://voxukraine.org/en/international-implications-of-ukraine-s-decentralization/.

Woesler, Dietmar M. 2006. Städtepartnerschaften in Neuem Licht. In *Europafähigkeit der Kommunen. Die lokale Ebene in der Europäischen Union*, ed. Ulrich von Alemann and Claudia Münch, 412–433. Wiesbaden: VS Verlag für Sozialwissenschaften.

CHAPTER 13

Conclusions and Directions for Further Research

Maryna Rabinovych and Hanna Shelest

Ukraine

In this volume, we have sought to contribute to the debate on territorial self-governance (TSG) arrangements as a conflict-resolution tool by highlighting the complexity of the crisis in and around Ukraine. To demonstrate this complexity authors have analyzed both historical and contemporary aspects, legal and political backgrounds that led to the regional diversity and self-identification of the regions of Ukraine. This particular case was chosen not only because it is in progress, but also, as chapters of this book demonstrate, because it gives a good basis for checking positive as well as negative correlations between a decentralization and conflict resolution.

Myshlovska's chapter illustrates that the case of Ukraine is characterized by its vulnerability to the securitization and politicization of regional diversity issues, rooted in the history of contemporary Ukraine, as well as

---

M. Rabinovych (✉)
University of Hamburg, Hamburg, Germany

H. Shelest
Security Studies Programme, Foreign Policy Council "Ukrainian Prism",
Odesa/Kyiv, Ukraine

© The Author(s) 2020
H. Shelest, M. Rabinovych (eds.), *Decentralization, Regional Diversity, and Conflict*, Federalism and Internal Conflicts,
https://doi.org/10.1007/978-3-030-41765-9_13

an insufficient attention to diversity in pre-Euromaidan policies. Moreover, as underlined by Lachowski, Barbieri, and Rabinovych in their respective chapters, the conflict in eastern Ukraine should not in any case be regarded as an internal conflict, determined by ethnic, linguistic, or history-related cleavages. It is instead marked by an intense yet "hybrid" foreign support of separatists, promoting narratives based on the securitization of diversity. Last but not least, such foreign intervention creates multiple pressures for the settlement process, in general, and on an application of the TSG arrangements in particular. An insight into the debate surrounding the implementation of the Minsk Agreements (as a debate, preceding the recent Normandy Four Summit in December 2019 in Paris, and the summit communiqué itself) shows that the decentralization of Ukraine is not only an internal affair of Ukraine, but creates much room for manipulation by the parties to the conflict and even mediators. Against this background, the case of regional diversity and decentralization in Ukraine, and the Russian–Ukrainian conflict, can offer a number of lessons for both policy makers, engaged in the "making" of regional policy, designing and implementing TSG arrangements, and scholars studying conflicts and TSGs.

The main conclusions of this volume can be grouped as follows. Firstly, the legacies of complex and overlapping history should not be ignored in policy making, even if it may seem that ethnic, linguistic, religious, or cultural differences do not develop a conflict potential. An example of the long-lasting prevalence of the "Two Ukraines" concept in explaining diversity in Ukraine also testifies to the fact that catchy, yet simplified models of diversity bring at least two crucial risks. Foremost, the prevalence of such models prevents policy makers and wider society developing a nuanced understanding of the substance of regional differences, and the dynamics of diversity and identities, including the impact that policies and laws have on them. Even more evidently, a general adoption of simplified constructs and the lack of strategy for accommodating diversity and passing appropriate legislation creates fertile ground for outsiders to cultivate a conflict. As perfectly proved by Myshlovska, conflicts emerge not because of regional differences *per se*, but because of their interpretations by internal and external actors, as well as because of their (non)-reflection in center–periphery relations and state policies. In this light, the "ringing phrase" for us has been "the sense of abandonment from Kyiv," articulated by a well-known researcher of Ukraine in Berlin, as a decisive factor, underlying Donbas residents' support for separatism. Such a sense of abandonment by central government in its executive actions, its policies, and its legislation seems to generate significant conflict potential.

Secondly, as illustrated by Part I of the volume, there are at least three "perfect means" for governments to create such a "sense of abandonment." As mentioned above, the simplest one is to take part in little or no discourse on regional diversity. The second one is through political manipulations pertaining to regional differences, as demonstrated by Nekoliak and Pettai, who researched a strategic use of the Constitutional Court of Ukraine by members of the parliament in language-related issues. Finally, a crucial source of citizens' sentiments of abandonment is rooted in the country's neo-patrimonial legacy. Excessive centralization, non-transparent budget relations, and a lack of funding for socioeconomic development and infrastructure initiatives hamper regional development and promote dissatisfaction with a central government that can be manipulatively exploited by foreign actors seeking to destabilize the state. Therefore, an important lesson all regionally diverse states with pronounced neo-patrimonial legacies can learn from the Ukrainian case is that a preventive "fixing" of center–periphery relations is better for the state's and regions' development than implementation of TSG arrangements in post-conflict settings.

Thirdly, foreign support tends to play a decisive role in activities of the secessionist movements, with autocracies being significantly more prone than democracies to support such movements. Hence, Russia's support for so-called "DPR" and "LPR", and its initial and continuing misleading appeal to ethnic, linguistic, and memory-related cleavages in Ukraine, constitute essential factors to be taken into account, when proposing decentralization rights as (part of) the conflict solution. As Ukrainian case demonstrates, it is necessary to keep in mind that foreign support for secessionism encompasses the active spread of disinformation on regional diversity issues, sometimes reaching extremes (e.g. President Putin's December 2019 allegations that Donbas can become Srebrenica in case the control over the Russian-Ukraine border be given back to Ukraine before separate districts of Donetsk and Luhansk regions get their special status fully operational). Even if structural reasons for the intrastate dimension of the conflict are being addressed in terms of the TSG arrangements, misleading discourses can be used to re-ignite mistrust and serve the interests of a foreign state.

Next, as it can be substantiated by the case of "fake" territorial communities, investigated by Barbieri in her analysis, foreign "support" is difficult to identify and counter, given the extensive networks that a third state can establish at the regional and local level throughout a "maternal" state. Furthermore, foreign support for separatism is difficult to qualify under international law and virtually impossible to address outside the diplomatic realm. In sum, these findings once again demonstrate the value of preventive monitoring of regional diversity dynamics, regional policy, and potential foreign support for separatism in heterogeneous societies.

Fourthly, the Russian Federation's discourse on Ukraine's federalization, discussed by Koval, testifies to the fact that states that give support to separatists may manipulate not only through diversity issues, but with TSG solutions as well. Subsequently, different objectives behind TSG solutions, as interpreted and advocated by both non-democratic and democratic actors engaged in conflict resolution, immensely politicize issues of federalization, decentralization, or other TSG arrangements. In other words, in conflict or post-conflict societies, changes to the administrative-territorial structure of the state and a status of government's sub-national levels become a matter of international politics, even though they belong to domestic affairs in societies not affected by the conflict. Such a situation entails numerous threats to a "maternal" state, such as it being forced to accept a controversial externally promoted TSG solution in an exchange for progress on security matters, a lack of local ownership of the new self-government design, and, in an extreme cases, a relapse into secessionism. Thus, while there is no consensus in the literature regarding favorable circumstances for TSG arrangements' effectiveness as a means of conflict resolution, foreign support to one of the conflict sides and related politicization of the choice of the TSG solution is a hindrance to conflict resolution. Consequently, a "maternal" state needs to exercise extreme caution when agreeing to the TSG in the framework of the international settlement talks, including TSG-related obligations to change domestic legislation.

In sum, the case of Ukraine is illustrative of the complex and overlapping nature of themes that arise in relation to conflicts that involve foreign manipulation over diversity issues and are characterized by both intra- and interstate contradictions. Such themes include *inter alia* a historical constitution of diversity and its interpretations, center–periphery relations in states with neo-patrimonial legacies, a fuel power of foreign support, a legal qualification of the separatists status, a politicization of the TSG arrangements as a form of influence-seeking, trust-building, and preventing the relapses of secessionism. Securitization of diversity issues and regional particularities during international peace talks is dangerous if looked at from the "do no harm" perspective, as provoking construction of division lines, rather than leading to the reintegration of the conflict-affected states. Notwithstanding the prominence and frequency of cases of the TSG application as a conflict-resolution/ management tool in different parts of the world, often proposed by mediators or other third parties involved, an impact, both positive and negative of such arrangements, remains under-researched, and deserves further empirical investigation.

INDEX[1]

A

Amalgamated Territorial Communities (ATCs), 12, 222, 223, 260–265, 269–278, 272n16, 273n21, 275n23, 277n24, 277n25, 328, 331, 339, 341, 342, 346, 349–352

C

Conflict in and around Ukraine, 1–12, 154, 174, 204, 220, 311, 324
Conflict resolution, 2, 5–11, 19–41, 120, 188–191, 193–198, 200, 201, 203, 204, 241, 365, 368, 369
Conflict transformation, 9, 107–136
Crimea, 3–6, 8, 20, 21, 26–30, 33, 35–38, 41, 65, 72, 81–84, 86, 88, 89, 91–102, 95n12, 100n13, 131, 145, 147, 149n3, 150, 152, 152n6, 152n7, 153, 155–158, 162, 164, 169, 172, 173, 193–195, 197, 203–205, 217, 218, 235
Crimean Tatars, 8, 27, 28, 36, 37, 81–102, 153, 217
Crisis in and around Ukraine, 4, 6, 8–10, 108, 145, 365

D

Decentralization, 1–12, 33, 111, 171, 188, 211–243, 259, 260, 311–332, 339–359, 365
Democracy, 5, 11, 113, 120, 168, 190, 191, 204, 222, 227, 259, 260, 265–270, 312–322

---

[1] Note: Page numbers followed by 'n' refer to notes.

© The Author(s) 2020
H. Shelest, M. Rabinovych (eds.), *Decentralization, Regional Diversity, and Conflict*, Federalism and Internal Conflicts,
https://doi.org/10.1007/978-3-030-41765-9

372 INDEX

Democratization, 6, 11–12, 19, 114,
   188, 191, 198, 259, 260,
   265, 311–332
Donetsk People's Republic (DPR), 4,
   9, 9n3, 107–109, 108n1,
   124–126, 145–154, 147n1, 159,
   162, 164, 165, 169, 171–174,
   224, 228–230, 233, 235,
   237–240, 240n41, 367

E
Ethnopolitics, 50–52, 60, 68, 69, 72

F
Federalism, 10, 187–205, 216,
   217, 267
Federalization, 2, 9–11, 30, 31, 40,
   113, 125, 126, 165, 171, 174,
   188, 189, 191, 193–198, 193n1,
   200–202, 204, 205, 213, 213n4,
   214, 216, 217n9, 218, 226,
   229–242, 368

H
Hybrid war, 8, 188, 192

I
Identity, 1, 7, 8, 19, 25, 28, 29, 32,
   37, 50, 61, 62, 72, 82–102, 121,
   165n11, 168, 172, 190,
   241, 345
Internally Displaced Persons (IDPs),
   86, 91, 100, 154
International law, 4, 9, 50, 59, 108,
   108n1, 124, 131, 133, 135, 136,
   145–174, 202, 368

L
Language, 3, 7, 8, 19, 20, 22, 23, 25,
   26, 28, 35–37, 39, 41, 49–73,
   85–87, 91, 92n9, 93–96, 101,
   102, 110, 112, 114, 116, 121,
   125, 128, 134, 168, 170, 194,
   195, 198, 214, 238, 240, 355
Local self-government, 3, 5, 70, 127,
   197, 201, 222, 223, 226n15,
   234, 259, 261, 268n10, 269,
   279, 313, 323, 326, 328, 339,
   341, 342, 344, 355
Luhansk People's Republic (LPR), 4,
   9, 9n3, 107–109, 108n1,
   124–126, 145–154, 158, 159,
   162, 164, 165, 169, 171–174,
   224, 229, 230, 233, 235,
   237–239, 240n41

M
Minsk II Agreement, 5, 127–129
Modernization, 6, 11–12, 20, 23,
   203, 311–332

P
Power-sharing, 2, 3, 34, 38, 39, 41,
   114, 214n5, 221
Putin, 125, 150, 167, 214, 214n5,
   218, 229, 367

R
Region, 19, 19n2, 20, 25–29, 31–33,
   36–38, 41, 52, 65, 72, 84, 109,
   111, 135, 146, 148, 151, 194,
   198, 211, 218, 230–232,
   240n41, 263, 264, 272n16,
   273n20, 275n22, 317, 351, 356

Regional diversity, 1–12, 19, 34, 36, 50, 83–84, 87, 164, 168, 169, 171, 365–368
Reintegration, 8–9, 114, 118, 127, 129–132, 136, 145–174, 234, 235, 239, 241, 369
Russian Federation, the, 3–6, 8, 10, 38, 81, 83, 86, 88, 92, 99, 102, 108, 109, 112, 113, 118, 119, 121, 125–126, 129–131, 135, 145–150, 151n5, 152, 153, 155–165, 167, 169–171, 173, 174, 197, 212n1, 218, 235, 240, 368

S

Separatism, 10, 36, 38, 94, 102, 149, 211–243, 260, 366, 368

Special status, 10, 52, 111, 114, 115, 127–130, 132–134, 136, 151, 165, 171, 197, 198, 201, 213, 214, 219, 220, 232–242, 261, 367
Steinmeier Formula, 9, 9n3, 109, 129, 129n6, 132, 135, 136, 151, 152, 165, 171, 201, 236–238, 241

T

Territorial self-governance (TSG), 2, 10, 365–369
Transitional justice, 9, 145, 164–165, 174

Z

Zelenskyy, Volodymyr, 10, 133, 134, 151, 151n5, 173, 214, 240–243

Printed in the United States
by Baker & Taylor Publisher Services